On the Theory of Socialist Market Economy

Liu Guoguang

Translated by Sun Weiwei

Paths International Ltd

中国社会科学出版社
CHINA SOCIAL SCIENCES PRESS

Preface: market economy and socialism

I came across an article titled "Abandoning 'the Worship of Market Economy'" after I finished this collection of my papers. This article pointed out that those who sold the idea of full realization of market economy based themselves on the pseudo-market-economy theory falsely attributed to Deng Xiaoping, and pushed for a market economy that is meant to cripple public ownership and thus fully realize privatization. This paper cited, according to the author, two "most concentrated and clarified" statements made by Deng Xiaoping concerning market economy. They are as follows: "Why can't we develop a market economy under socialism? We can also introduce market economy under socialism." "A planned economy is not equivalent to socialism, because there is planning under capitalism too; a market economy is not capitalism, because there are markets under socialism too. Planning and market forces are both means of controlling economic activity." The author argued that neither statement by Deng Xiaoping can prove that "market economy must be practiced under socialism". He also added, "Since planning and market are both economic means, and 'means' do not equate to the 'system', the so-called 'establishment of the system of market economy' is against Deng Xiaoping's will."

At the start, his argument that neither statement can prove "market economy must be practiced under socialism" seems quite logical and makes sense. However, when the paper concludes that "the establishment of the system of market economy is against Deng's will", it has already been far away from facts. According to *"Chronology of Deng Xiaoping's Career: 1975-1997*, on June 12th, 1992, four months before the opening of the 14th Congress of the Communist Party of China, Mr. Deng Xiaoping held a talk with Jiang Zemin, then Chairman of the Central Military Commission, Mr. Deng approved of the term of "socialist market economy" and said, "if everybody agrees with it, we will set this as the theme of the 14th National Congress of the CPC"[1]. Having watched reportage of the conclusion of the 14th National Congress on the 19th of October, Deng Xiaoping exclaimed, "It is so exhilarating that the whole nation is in jubilation!". In that afternoon, when he was meeting all the deputies, he said to Jiang Zemin, "this conference is a great success." [2]All these indicated that the establishment of the system of market economy did not go against the will of Deng Xiaoping, but instead, it was approved by him and adopted in the 14th National Congress of the CPC.

One thing worth mentioning here is that there is an extremely important modifier, i.e., "socialist" before "market economy" in the version that the 14th National Congress came up with. Even the aforementioned author also admitted in his article that, on the basis of Deng Xiaoping's statement that China can develop a market economy under socialism, "socialism" should be put in the first place with "market economy" coming next to it, so as to develop and improve socialism rather than undermine it. His interpretation is right and I agree with him in this respect.

As for the issue of whether to add a modifier, i.e., "socialist" before "market economy" while setting the goal for China's economic restructuring, it is not a matter of minor importance, because it concerns the nature of the market economy China aims to establish and the direction of economic restructuring. "After the goal of establishing a system of socialist market economy was set forth, some

1 *Chronology of Deng Xiaoping's Career: 1975-1997* II , pp.1347-1348.
2 ibid, p.1355.

people kept asking the same question, 'it is good for China to introduce market economy, but why should there be a modifier *socialist* before it?' they thought this modifier was redundant and thus an eyesore," a Central Committee leader said during his inspection in Tianjin in December 1992. However, almost two decades later such doubt still lingers on. Some people still believe that market economy fits all countries and recognizes no boundaries between socialism and capitalism. They oppose the socialist direction of the reform; rather, in their eyes, China simply needs to carry out the "marketization reform". However, just as what that leader put it in Tianjin inspection, "As we are practicing a socialist market economy, the modifier *socialist* is not superfluous and thus cannot be omitted, because it is the final touch that states clearly what China's market economy actually is." [1]

Besides, some people who opposed making a distinction between socialism and capitalism disguised themselves as advocates of Deng Xiaoping's idea of "emancipating the mind", distorting the real meaning of Deng Xiaoping by saying that "emancipation of the mind" means to free our mind from any distinctions between capitalism and socialism. However, Deng Xiaoping just meant it when it comes to the issue of planning and market forces as both means of regulating economic activities. He said, "there is planning under capitalism and there are markets under socialism, too. But planning and market are both economic means." Therefore, Deng Xiaoping has never opposed making distinctions between socialism and capitalism in general terms. On the contrary, Deng Xiaoping ever said "the crux matter is whether the road is capitalist or socialist" while mentioning that some people dare not break the new ground during the process of reform and opening-up. He explained further that the chief criterion for making that judgment should be whether it promotes the growth of the productive forces in a socialist society and increases the overall strength of the socialist state etc. Besides, he also repeatedly stressed that China should adhere to two basic

1 Jiang Zemin, *On Socialist Market Economy*, pp.202-203.

principles of socialism, i.e., public ownership as the mainstay and common prosperity without polarization. All these prove that Deng Xiaoping did care whether the road is socialist or capitalist when it concerns the matter of principle. So, how could it be possible that Deng Xiaoping indiscriminately opposed differentiating socialism from capitalism in general terms?

Besides, Deng Xiaoping also pointed out sharply, "Some people intended to steer China into capitalism, while holding high banners of reform and opening-up. They aimed to change the nature of our society." Those who are opposed to adding modifier "socialist" before "market economy" and making distinctions between capitalism and socialism are exactly whom Deng Xiaoping referred to!

The Outline of the Book

One important thing I'd like to point out here is that, this preface is not irrelevant to the theme of this book. Instead, all articles in the book are centered on one theme, i.e., the relations between "socialism" and "market economy" in the process of economic restructuring. That is to say, they all focused on one issue as to how to improve and develop China's socialist economic system through means of market economy.

In this collected works, three articles in Part 1 were written in the 1990s and the rest after 2000.

In part 1, the first two articles were written in 1991 and 1992 respectively (before the 14th National Congress), when the term "socialist market economy" hadn't been officially put forward yet. These two articles, titled as "On the Theory of Socialist Commodity Economy" and "On Several Issues Concerning the Theory of Socialist Market Economy", serve as kind of introductory chapters. The third article concerns the historical transition from planned economy to socialist market economy.

The articles in the second part were written at the time when China needed to make a preliminary summary after many years' practice in socialist market economy. During this period of time, China has made huge progress and piled up many problems as well.

After a review of how the theory concerning socialist commodity/market economy and the system of socialist market economy were established in the previous two parts; in the issue of socialist which part 3 market economy as an organic unity between "socialism" and "market economy" is elaborated. It is made very clear that China's market-oriented reform aims to achieve the self-improvement of socialist economic system rather than evolve into capitalism.

The rest sections are devoted to analyzing the basic characteristics of socialist market economy (which set it apart from capitalist market economy) respectively. These characteristics are:

First, as far as ownership structure is concerned, socialist market economy is based on the basic socialist economic system in which public ownership is the mainstay and other kinds of ownership develop side by side.

Second, as far as economic mechanism is concerned, socialist market economy also has planning, that is to say, we should let market forces, subject to state macroeconomic regulation by planning, serve as the basic means of regulating resource allocation.

Third, as far as its goal is concerned, socialist market economy strives to pay attention to both efficiency and equity with more emphasis on social equity and thus to achieve common prosperity.

Very obviously, the debates over these issues are as heated as the one concerning whether to combine "socialism" with "market economy". Those who opposed socialist market economy also argued from the same perspectives but held ideas just to the opposite. They are as follows:

First, they advocated privatization, opposing public ownership as the mainstay of the economy.

Second, they advocated pure liberalization, opposing state macroeconomic regulation by planning and government intervention in economic management.

Third, they advocated polarization, opposing common prosperity.

Quite obviously nobody has ever issued any statements so overtly like that, but these three aspects are the real nature hidden beneath some people's propaganda. Though nobody dared to openly advertise polarization in opposition to common prosperity, some vested interest groups and their spokespersons in the government or academia did sell these ideas under the disguise of some "theories" or "policies".

We surely need tell right from wrong in theoretical debates, but it is more of a battle between different interest groups in current China. Though extremely wealthy and have strong influence, those who advocate privatization, liberalization and polarization and opposed combination between socialism and market economy just stand for the interests of very few people. In contrast, those who advocate that "socialism" must be combined with "market economy", public ownership must keep the mainstay of the economy, market economy must be subject to macroeconomic regulation by planning and that the ultimate goal of common prosperity must be achieved represent the wishes and aspirations of the great masses of workers, peasants and intellectuals.

The prospect of China's economic reform is not determined by the outcome of debate, but by the will of the great masses of people instead.

The appendix containing nine articles. The first five articles are concerned with the author's interpretations of the relations between planning and market in the initial period of China's reform and opening-up. The rest articles written in recent years cover a lot of issues closely related to the topic in main chapters, but do not fall right into the category of their subdivisions. That's why I chose to put them in the appendix for readers' reference.

Contents

Part III China's Socialist Market Economy: an Organic Unity between "Socialism" and "Market Economy" / 99

Part IV Socialist Market Economy does Have Planning / 155

Part I

Establishment of the Theory of Socialist Commodity/Market Economy in China

On the Theory of Socialist Commodity Economy

1. Interpretations of "planned commodity economy"

According to the theory of socialist commodity economy, socialist economy is a planned commodity economy, which is the greatest breakthrough we've ever made in economic theories as well as one of the most important theoretical bases for our economic reform. However, Karl Marx and Friedrich Engels used to envisage that commodity economy would disappear in the future socialist society; besides, commodity economy has been repelled for rather long in China's concrete practice of socialism over the past several decades. Against this backdrop, the Third Plenary Session of the 12th Central Committee of the CPC adopted "the Decision on Economic Restructuring", proposing that socialist market economy is a planned commodity economy, which is of epoch-making significance in China's modern history. This is the result of Chinese people's painstaking efforts in their long-term exploration in both theory and practice, which is very crucial to people's universal understanding of the nature of socialism and the direction of economic restructuring.

After the Third Plenary Session of the 12th Central Committee of the CPC, people including economic theorists are rather divided on what planned commodity economy is. Some focused on "commodity economy" whilst some "planning". For instance, several years ago, a professor from Beijing University said in his article, "socialist reform aims to establish a commodity economy in the first place, and what comes next to it is a planned economy." Obviously, he placed more emphasis on commodity economy than planning, but the latter was not thereby denied.

A professor from Renmin University of China, who held opposite ideas, said in his article, "Planned economy or regulation by planning should always play a dominant role in the socialist economy." Just the other way around, he focused on planned economy rather than commodity economy, which suggests that different focuses would lead to different understandings of the essential characteristics of socialist economy. Aside from public ownership and distribution according to work, which are universally acknowledged to be the two essential characteristics of socialist economy, does the socialist economy have a third essential characteristic? If it does have one, what is it? Is it planned economy or commodity economy? There are several opinions.

Such debate is still going on in recent two or three years. In 1989, there used to be a period of time when the academia was in favor of socialist commodity economy. However, it did not last long. Afterwards, the pendulum ever swung back to planned economy again. For example, an article said that socialist economy is a planned economy in nature, just with some commodity properties in the current stage. Another article made a similar point by saying that socialist economy is a planned economy as far as its nature is concerned. These views are very typical ones in recent two or three years. In contrast, some people still then viewed commodity economy as a nature of socialist economy. For instance, an article said that socialist commodity economy, along with public ownership and distribution according to work, is another essential characteristic of socialism. However, neither side has so far gained any new grounds. They still clang to their old ideas.

After the Seventh Plenary Session of the 13th Central Committee of the CPC, more and more economic theorists came to realize that "planned economy" versus "commodity economy" or "planning" versus "market" is not the essential characteristic of capitalism or socialism at all. Socialism also needs market and capitalism requires state planning or government intervention as well. Therefore, many economists tended not to associate planned economy or commodity economy with the nature of socialist economy or capitalist economy any longer. Rather, they believed that what really sets socialism apart from capitalism should be ownership and distribution system, just as classic writers said. Under socialism, public ownership is the mainstay of the economy and distribution according to work is the dominant mode of distribution. As for planning and market, they are both economic operating mechanisms as well as means of regulating resource allocation, rather than the nature of socialism.

As we all know, *the Decision on Economic Restructuring* (which would later be called *the Decision* in short), adopted in the Third Plenary Session of the 12th Central Committee of the CPC, has made very clear the definition of commodity economy and its significance as well. The *Decision* says, "Commodity economy, an important condition for modernization, can therefore not be skipped in the development of socialism." Xue Muqiao (25 October 1904—22 July 2005), a Chinese economist, elaborated on it in the postscript to the Japanese translation of *A Study on China's Socialist Economy (revised edition)*. "Without the development of commodity economy, there would be no socialized mass production and thus no birth of socialism," he said.

In discussions about the role of commodity economy, some people proposed to "criticize the myth of commodity economy" to confront Xue Muqiao's such idea. An article titled "Breaking the Myth of Commodity Economy" published in 1989 says, "Commodity economy was once overstated as the decisive force in human development, which thereby gave rise to the myth of commodity economy." This author had probably intended to give a fair and objective evaluation of the role of commodity economy, but he appeared to impress the readers with his depreciation of such matter. In his another article published this year, he said that exchange of equal values goes against the essential interests of socialism, which are characterized by equal exchange of labor. He also said that the current wage is de facto the "labor ticket" rather than the real wage. As we all know, the notion of "labor ticket", which was put forward by Karl Marx in *Critique of Gotha Programme*, applies to a non-commodity economy or product economy for the future. Though the idea of non-commodity economy has been out of date, some economic theorists still firmly believe it. Therefore, such issue deserves our attention.

2. The relationship between public ownership and commodity economy

These years have seen wider discussions about whether public ownership is compatible with commodity economy, which appears to be an old problem, too. Generally speaking, it seems to have been solved because *the Decision* adopted in the Third Plenary Session of the 12th Central Committee of the CPC has confirmed that socialist economy is a planned commodity economy based on private ownership. In this logic, public ownership is surely compatible with commodity economy, and moreover, it has already been universally acknowledged by the people. However, in the past few years, some people argued repeatedly from different perspectives that public ownership is contradictory to commodity economy and came to different conclusions. The following three views are very typical ones.

The first view is quite conventional, which holds that commodity economy is the product of private ownership. Since socialism is based on public ownership, commodity economy shouldn't and couldn't be practiced under socialism at all. This view opposes socialist economy to commodity economy, which is still being spread by word of mouth.

The second view leads to an opposite position, though it still holds that public ownership is incompatible with commodity economy and that the latter can only be based on private ownership. They believe that public ownership has to be replaced by private ownership for the sake of the development of commodity economy. As a matter of fact, they are trying to sell the idea of privatization by using the contradiction between public ownership and commodity economy. The first view opposes commodity economy in the name of public ownership; in sharp contrast, the second opposes public ownership in the name of commodity economy. In spite of different perspectives, they both agreed that commodity economy is incompatible with public ownership. Both of them are definitely unacceptable to the overwhelming majority in the academic world.

However, some scholars warned that we cannot thereby deny the fact that commodity economy does somewhat contradict with public ownership. Some scholars also said that there has been some progress with our theoretical studies since the reform and opening-up, that is, we have come to realize that public ownership does contradict somewhat with commodity economy currently. They believe that not only the very public ownership, under which purchase and distribution of all commodities are controlled by the state, does not suite commodity economy, but even the collective ownership under which government administration isn't separated from enterprise management should also be reformed. Therefore, the reform should build a market mechanism and enterprise management model to suite the needs of commodity economy.

One thing in the third view must be pointed out, that is, they believe that the very public ownership contradictory to commodity economy just refers to the one at the current stage or the conventional one, rather than public ownership in general. There do exist some aspects contradictory to commodity economy within the current public ownership. For example, non-separation of government administration from enterprise management; that of ownership from management; and enterprises just as the auxiliary body of the administrative organ, etc. All these defects are surely incompatible with commodity economy and therefore should be reformed. Rather than reform the public ownership in general or totally deny it, we just need reform the current form of public ownership to keep up with the development of commodity economy. To sum up, such view holds that the current form of public ownership, somewhat contradictory to commodity economy, needs to be reformed, which is radically different from the one embracing privatization, as the former upholds public ownership and requires improvements.

However, the third view gives rise to another problem. Since we should reform the current form of public ownership to suite the needs of commodity economy, such a question was raised by some people: does ownership determine commodity economy or the other way round? These people argued that such view goes against the principle of Marxism that ownership is the very basis. A scholar argued back in his article that in principle ownership does determine commodity economy, but the latter also affects the former. Why can't socialist ownership relations be adjusted to suite the needs of commodity economy, since the reform is the self-improvement of socialism? I personally believe that the latter explanation makes more sense.

I also analyzed the relationship between economic restructuring and the development of commodity economy in a broader sense in a report in 1986, in which I made two points regarding this. First, in order to develop commodity economy, we have to reform the economic structure that hinders its development; Second, how should we carry out economic restructuring? the key is to meet the requirements of commodity economy, i.e., the socialist planed commodity economy, including the reform of ownership structure, enterprise management, economic operational mechanism, market system and macroeconomic management system. Therefore, the reform of ownership must be carried out to suite the needs of a planned commodity economy.

3. Can socialist economy be called "socialist market economy"?

Recently, the issue as to whether "socialist commodity economy" can be called "socialist market economy" or whether "a planned commodity economy" can be called "a planned market economy" has been widely discussed. Some economists believed that socialist economy has de facto been considered as a planned market economy because socialist economy is a planned commodity economy, and commodity economy is also inseparable from market. Though these scholars came up with different versions, they all agreed to use the term of "socialist market economy".

Besides, another group of people associated market economy or planned economy with social system. For example, they believed that market economy is capitalism and planned economy socialism; they also held that "market economy" is not equal to "commodity economy", and the existence of "market" or the use of "regulation by market forces" is not equivalent to market economy, because they had ever referred to some encyclopedia and found some supporting evidence from them. *The Encyclopedia of Japanese Economy* had a similar way of classifying countries as UN. They both considered centrally planned economies as socialist countries and market economies capitalist states. Therefore, those who opposed using the term of "socialist market economy" maintained that this term is not scientific because market economy is based on private ownership. It was also said that only under capitalist mode of production would commodity economy be market economy. They concluded that any confusion of regulation by market forces with market economy would inevitably lead to the wrong denial of planned economy.

Many economists represented by Xue Muqiao disapproved of such opinion. In an interview of Xue Muqiao made by a journalist from *Special Economic Zone Times*, Xue said, "Whether we should draw a distinct line between regulation by market forces and market economy still remains to be discussed. It seems to me that they are the same in nature, as neither of them is equivalent to capitalism. As long as public ownership of the means of production plays the dominant role, neither of them would be called a capitalist market economy. Therefore, ownership, rather than planning or market, is the very criterion to tell capitalism from socialism." "The time hasn't been ripe yet for the solution of such issue, as it is sill regarded as a taboo in theoretical studies. But it shouldn't be. Instead, for the sake of scientific research, people should discuss the issue freely and conscientiously, rather than evade them," he also added.

This debate reminded me of another question put forward by the late Chinese economist, Sun Yefang, in 1950s: "Can we say 'socialist profit'?" At that time, such question caused quite a stir. Is "profit" associated with social system or not? Is it peculiar to capitalism? Or is it shared by socialized production and commodity production? Many people bore witness to its twists and turns before it was eventually recognized.

It also brought back my memories of the initial period of the reform and opening-up and even the days of the Sixth Plenary Session of the 11th Central Committee of the CPC, when the party was summing up experience since the founding of the PRC. At that time, it can only be said that there exist commodity production and commodity exchanges in the socialist society; however, socialist economy must not be simply called commodity economy; otherwise, the boundaries between planned commodity economy and anarchic capitalist economy would be blurred, and essential differences between socialist economy and capitalist economy would thus disappear. This view actually still equated commodity economy with capitalist economy. At last, *The Decision on Economic Restructuring* adopted in the Third Plenary Session of the 12th Central Committee of the CPC ended the protracted controversy.

History tends to repeat itself. Now let's look at the recent development. Since the Seventh Plenary Session of the 13th Central Committee of the CPC, people were more and more inclined to consider planning and market as both means of regulating resource allocation and economic operational mechanisms rather than associate them with socialism or capitalism. Therefore, it would not be so hard to predict or tell whether "socialist market economy" or "planned market economy" would gain a footing in socialist economics. But it is natural that new ideas would not be immediately and widely accepted by the people. The term of "socialist commodity economy" is a very good example. So, the new idea of "socialist market economy" will not be an exception, either.

In spite of that, we kept renewing our theoretical knowledge and enriching socialist economics in the reform; we have come to realize that socialist economy is a planned commodity economy based on public ownership, which cannot do without market and regulation by market forces. So we should combine planning with market. Under the circumstances, many people began to study the relations between planning and market and came up with a lot of opinions and suggestions; besides, it also gave rise to the debate as to whether the term of "socialist market economy" can be used or not. All these discussions are crucial to our correct understanding of the nature of socialist economy and the right orientation of our reform, and thereby they must go on, and even more deeply.

4. How to interpret "the market-oriented reform"

There used to be many proposals on the relations between planning and market. Now, the official version is that planned economy is to combine with regulation by market forces, which was however rather objected in the economics circle. In spite of that, many scholars supported such policy with forcible argument in published articles. Especially those who emphasized that planned economy is the essential characteristic of the socialist economy worked even more dedicatedly to prove the scientific soundness of the official version. For example, some article argued forcibly that this policy is the continuation and development of the previous policy of "planned economy in the main and regulation by market forces as the supplement", which suggests that China's reform is not to weaken or abandon planned economy, but to implement a certain degree of regulation by market forces while adhering to the system of planned economy.

Since the adoption of *The Decision on Economic Restructuring* in the Third Plenary Session of the 12th Central Committee of the CPC in 1984, the previous slogan of "planned economy in the main and regulation by market forces as the supplement", which opposed the equal status of planning and market, hasn't been mentioned for a period of time. However, the recent two or three years has witnessed its revival. Besides, some people also opposed the equal status of planning and market from other perspectives. For example, several years ago, a scholar proposed a model of "double regulation". According to this model, we should carry out regulation by market forces in the first place; only if market doesn't work, planning should be used; state planning makes up for the deficiency of market in economic regulation.

With planning being secondary to market, this idea is an upside-down version of "planned economy in the main and regulation by market forces as the supplement". It was then met with a lot of criticism and doubts. Besides, some scholars also suggested in recent years that market be the major means of regulating resource allocation. For example, a very famous scholar said in his article, "Economic restructuring is in essence transformation of the means of regulating resource allocation, that is to say, market is to replace administrative orders and become the major means of regulating resource allocation." Those who held such ideas did not deny the guiding role of planning and the necessity of state administrative management; rather, they put it secondary to market and regarded market as the major means of regulating resource allocation.

For instance, a journal ever published a scholar's opinions on this issue. The scholar said, "Planning refers to conscious efforts to maintain economic equilibrium in terms of economic operation, which can be achieved by the reinforcement of state macroeconomic management and administrative guidance with market forces as the basic means of regulating resource allocation." Here, market serves as the major means of regulating resource allocation, and at the same time it is also very necessary to enhance state macroeconomic management and administrative guidance.

Those who advocated market as the major means of regulating resource allocation tended to define such change as a "market-oriented" reform, and are also joined by many economists who interpreted it differently though. In sharp contrast, those who associated planning and market with social system disapproved of the term of "market-oriented reform". Some scholars even claimed that market-orientation is to uphold capitalism and non-market orientation socialism.

So how should we interpret the market orientation? An economist proposed that there are three types of orientation of China's economic restructuring: orientation of planning, orientation of market, and a combination between planning and market. Such way of categorization does impress people with brevity but not with preciseness, which fails to reflect the real division in academia. Currently, it has been acknowledged in theoretical circles that planning can and should be combined with market. But this tripartite classification seems to tell us that only the third category approves of such combination, which however goes against the facts.

Besides, the term of "market-oriented reform" was indeed put forward by economic theorists in black and white, whereas "the orientation of planning" was never stated explicitly despite some emphasis on the role of planning. The scholar who made such tripartite classification seemed to understand the orientation of reform differently, believing that it is determined by the focus of combination in the reform target. That is to say, if emphasis is laid on planning during combination, it is called a planning-oriented reform; if more importance is attached to market, it is called a market-oriented reform; if equal emphasis is placed on planning and market, it is classified as the combination of planning with market forces.

However, in my point of view, the orientation of reform is not determined by the focus of combination in the target structure, but by the tendency of reform, i.e., the direction in which the economic structure should be transformed. In essence, our reform aims to change the economic structure. Previously, we excluded market and practiced a centrally planned economy, which was mainly based on natural economy and product economy. Now, we are required to introduce the market mechanism and adjust the planned economy to the needs of commodity economy market laws.

On the one hand, we should introduce commodity economy and expand the scope of regulation by market forces; on the other, in order to achieve a successful transition to planned commodity economy or market economy characterized by combination between planning and market, we should consider more the needs of commodity economy and market laws while reforming the traditional planned economy.

To put it simply, this reform aims to achieve a successful transition from the previous policy of rejecting and restricting the market mechanism to the current one of introducing it and bringing its role into full play. In this sense, it can be called a "market-oriented" reform. The first achievement of reform would be the market orientation of planned economy.

As we all know, we just had a unitary public sector before the reform, and it was believed that sufficiently large communes under exclusive public ownership should be the best form of socialism. Economic management through mandatory planning and direct administrative control was quite necessary in the early days of New China and did play a positive role. However, such planned economy is in nature antagonistic to market and the market mechanism. Since the reform, many kinds of ownership began to develop side by side while public ownership plays the dominant role. Besides, decision-making powers of enterprises within the public sector were also expanded, which thus made it possible that these enterprises might act according to the rule of market.

In the meanwhile, market and the market mechanism kept growing steadily, and the focus of macro-economic management has been gradually shifted to indirect management, which is no more than a type of management through the market mechanism and economic levers. These changes have reflected the ongoing expansion and deepening of marketization in the process of economic restructuring. Undoubtedly, market orientation is based on public ownership rather than private ownership; it aims to establish a market mechanism subject to macroeconomic regulation and planned management, rather than a market economy characterized by anarchy and spontaneity. Therefore, in the aforementioned tripartite classification, it is at least very imprecise for the scholar to oppose market orientation to planning, or refer to it as "anti-planning". So, why must market orientation be guided by planning and subject to macroeconomic control in the socialist economic reform? How to explain it in theory? I will answer them later.

In the past decade or so, our reform has made remarkable achievements. Are they the result of intensified efforts to implement administrative orders or that of the reform of traditional planned economy by expanding the role of market in accordance with the law of value? The latter makes more sense. Why did China succeed in the reform whilst the Soviet Union decay and fail? First of all, Soviet Union's introduction of "glasnost" and "pluralism" has led to ideological confusion and the weakening of leadership of the party; but what is more to blame is its economic policy. Despite many setbacks, China has made a lot of substantial progress in the reform, but the Soviet Union hasn't. Since the reform, Chinese people have benefited a lot from a vibrant economy and an abundance of commodities. In sharp contrast, since the reform, Soviet Union's economic conditions got even worse than the period of "shortage economy", suffering from a severe shortage of commodities. It had never carried out the market-oriented reform very conscientiously, though they had come up with many economic proposals such as economic acceleration in the past few years.

Now, let's take a look at our own economic map. We can see that the more oriented a region, sector or enterprise is towards market, the greater vigor its economy will enjoy. Thanks to the economic rectification campaign, our economy has recovered since March 1990. The sector or region whose economy picked up very soon proved to be closely linked with market, whereas the sector or region having little to do with or failing to make good use of market tended to recover very slowly. They are all indisputable facts, which cannot be evaded. Therefore, in the next decade, we should advance our reform in the same direction, that is to say, we should carry on the market-oriented reform under the guidance of planning and subject to macro-economic regulation. After pretty much progress is made, we should expand the role of market and reform planning to suite the needs of commodity economy and market laws in an effort to establish a planned commodity economy or market economy characterized by combination between planning and market.

It follows that the theories concerning the orientation of reform fall into two camps: support for market orientation and opposition to market orientation. When it comes to the practical sense, quite many people elected to embrace market orientation. However, in theoretical terms, quite many scholars opposed it based on the following two reasons: First, they held that market orientation is to practice market economy and capitalism. Second, they believed that the loss of macroeconomic control several years ago and current economic problems had something to do with more emphasis on market directly or indirectly. The first reason falls into the ideological category. However, Deng Xiaoping said in his recent speech that planning/market should not be associated with socialism/capitalism. In this sense, the first reason can be ignored. As for the second reason, i.e., the loss of macroeconomic control, some people argued that it is not the result of introduction of too much market economy; rather, imperfect market (directly or indirectly caused by the inadequate reform of traditional planned economy) as well as the unsystematic and incomplete market-oriented reform are to blame. Therefore, we still need further develop the market mechanism and reform planned economy in order to establish a new socialist economy with a combination between planning and market.

5. Banishing blind faith & Overcoming shortcomings

In order to establish an economic system characterized by combination between planning and market, we aim to bring all merits of market and planning into full play. The advantages of planning lie in its capacity of gathering necessary financial, human and material resources together in the whole society to accomplish some great things, adjusting incomes and ensuring social equity. The strengths of market lie in its capacity of promoting technical and management progress through competition and the law of "survival of the fittest" so as to link production with demand. However, in practice, we often fail to combine planning with market in an effective way. For instance, rather than combine their merits, we tended to bring their defects together, throwing our economy into a vicious cycle, that is, once control is tightened, the economy would be stagnant; once loosened, the economy would be thrown into a chaos. So, it is very hard to achieve the combination. We do desire for a better combination between planning and market, however, in reality, we ended up having neither planning (or failure to carry out the plans) nor market so that the law of "the survival of the fittest" is not fit at all. Therefore, some economists especially those from abroad jumped to the conclusion that it is unlikely to achieve a combination between planning and market. However, we believe that we can do it, so long as we know perfectly well their merits and demerits and handle them properly. While discussing the relations between planned economy and regulation by market forces, I ever made two points. First, we should adhere to "regulation by planning" but avoid any blind faith in planning; second, we should further advance the "market-oriented" reform but avoid any blind faith in market. To put it simply, we should banish blind faith in both planning and market! First of all, I would like to talk about "no blind faith in market".

The so-called regulation by market forces refers to the spontaneous regulation by the "invisible hand" put forward by Adam Smith, i.e., the law of value. We should attach importance to the law of value, but it does not mean that they are capable of doing everything so that we would leave all matters to it. In my point of view, at least the following things cannot be left to the law of value alone. The first thing is the economic equilibrium—regulation of aggregate supply and aggregate demand. If we just count on the law of value to do this job, we will surely end up with cyclical fluctuations and frequent crises.

The second thing concerns the major structural change in terms of agriculture, industry, heavy industry, light industry, primary, secondary and tertiary industry, consumption and accumulation, processing industry and basic industry, etc. The industrial structure needs to achieve rationalization, modernization and supererogation in a short period of time, say, ten, twenty, thirty years, at lower costs. It is not unlikely to achieve major restructuring spontaneously through market alone in regulating allocation of human and material resources, but it would probably take rather long at a higher price with many repeated crises before it is accomplished. we cannot afford it at all.

The third thing concerns fair competition. The belief that market forces guarantee fair competition is a sheer myth. Even in the period of laissez-faire capitalism, fair competition cannot be ensured, because the market rule of "big fish swallowing little fish" (the strong bullying the weak) will definitely result in monopoly, i.e., unfair competition. That's why some capitalist nations are also making the anti-trust law or competition law.

The fourth major task concerns ecological balance, environmental protection and "external dis-economy". "External dis-economy" is a phenomenon in which enterprises might benefit from certain development pattern, which, however, might cause damages to natural resources and ecological environment, such as air and water pollution. These short-term benefits are detrimental to social interests and even the survival of mankind in the long run. So, the market is not capable of solving these problems.

The fifth one is the relationship between equity and efficiency. The market alone cannot guarantee social equity in a real sense, but just exchange of equal values instead, which only ensures that people get equal compensations. In this sense, it does promote efficiency and social progress, however, spontaneous regulation by the market alone would inevitably lead to social polarization and a dramatic gap between the rich and the poor. While we were introducing the market mechanism, some symptoms had already developed, causing anxiety among people and dampening their enthusiasm. In response to this, the government should take some measures to prevent this from deteriorating.

As we can see, at least the five aforementioned tasks cannot be assigned to the invisible hand alone, in the meanwhile, the visible hand, namely, state planning and government management, must be also used. The so-called complete and pure market economy is not what our market-oriented reform is driving at. Even in western capitalist countries, market economy has become less pure and typical due to government interventions through policies or planning. Any proposal on pure marketization in China is just wishful thinking, not to mention ideological factors. As we are practicing a socialist planned commodity economy, we have better reason to emphasize the guiding role of state planning and macroeconomic regulation and avoid any bind faith in the market while carrying out the market-oriented reform, that is to say, we should value the important role of "cage".

The size of this cage can be either large or small, varying from sector to sector, and from product to product. As we all know, the cage can be made of different materials, such as steel, plastic or rubber etc., and the same is true with the "cage" of planned management, which therefore has distinctive characteristics. For instance, mandatory planning is as rigid as steel, and guidance planning as elastic as rubber. In short, to carry out the market-oriented reform, we should not have blind faith in market or neglect the necessary role of "cage", namely, government management and planning. Actually, the reform of planned economy is automatically included in the market-oriented reform, and therefore, we should adjust planning to the development of commodity economy and strengthen planned management.

On the other hand, we shouldn't have blind faith in planning while implementing "regulation by planning", because it would also lead to mistakes and thus bad consequences. Socialist economy based on public ownership just makes proportional economic development possible, but it is not sure to happen. If planning fails to consider market supply and demand and the law of value, the economy will also be out of control or end up with major mistakes. We've already made a lot of mistakes of such kind.

In the past, our traditional planned economy has witnessed many major imbalances and undergone many ups and downs, such as the "Great Leap forward" in late 1950s, several breakthroughs in late 1960s, another great leap forward in late 1970s characterized by the irrational and excessive introduction of advanced technologies and equipment, overheated economy in late 1980s, etc. In recent years, planning commissions of all local governments above the county level have the final say on the approval of fixed assets investment projects. Now we have already had over 160 color TV production lines, over 90 refrigerator production lines and many latex gloves or beer production lines etc. However, the utilization ratio of production line in some enterprises are even lower than 50% to 60%. Many of them are homogeneous and redundant. It shows that even the planning body still failed to put the situation under control. Humans do err, so planning will inevitably have limitations and thus lead to many contradictions hard to overcome, such as the contradiction between subjectivity and objectivity, one of the major problems in planning.

First, man have limitations in knowing and understanding the world, including real situations and objective laws. We ever made many mistakes in planning such as rush for quick results disregarding the real national conditions. Second, man have limitations in collecting and transmitting information. Planning needs information, but collection and transmission of information will never end and thus will never be complete. No matter how many times computers are updated, how advanced technology is, how widely it is used, it will still be impossible for man to collect and process all the economic data in time. By the time we have finished processing the information, it will probably not be needed any longer.

Third, men are also bounded by their interest relations, positions and perspectives. Each planning commission or macroeconomic management organ is affiliated to a certain department, falls to a certain region, has a certain position or perspective, stands for different interests, and is thus bounded by certain interest relations. Besides, government leaders and planning personnel are all humans: man is not the almighty God, and humans do err. All these limitations might lead to deviations of their work from real situations and objective laws, and thus result in major mistakes in planning and macroeconomic management. In the past several decades we have experienced it more than once.

Therefore, in order to carry out regulation by planning, we should keep increasing our knowledge, and improving our planning so as to adjust our work to the requirement of objective laws and real situations, especially market supply and demand and the law of value as well.

All in all, we must implement regulation by planning but avoid any blind faith in planning; we should carry out the market-oriented reform but avoid any blind faith in market. We should not only bring their merits into full play, but overcome their demerits and flaws while combining planning with market. This complicated task needs to be carefully studied, requiring joint efforts from many sectors such as the planning body, financial sector, banks, marketing departments, commercial sector, and material supply departments etc. and even cooperation between both central and local governments at all levels for gradual solution.

6. A new understanding of the formula of "the market being regulated by the state; the enterprise being guided by market forces"

After 12 years' explorations of reform both in theory and practice, our understanding of both planning and market has been deepened profoundly. Nowadays, what concerns people the most is how to integrate planning with market more practically. We should steer our discussion onto this topic!

There used to be many proposals as to how to combine planning with market. Some focused on theoretical models, and some management of the national economy. After several years' discussion, some progress has been made in this regard. Here I would like to give some examples.

In the past, the method of horizontal classification was applied to studying combination between planning and market. For instance, management of the national economy falls into three types, namely, mandatory planning, guidance planning and regulation by market forces; besides, the national economy is subdivided into macro-economy and micro-economy. Considering some overlaps in the logical sense, an expert re-synthesized the two classifications into a new model called "a two-level combination/division". The national economy is still subdivided into macroeconomic level and micro-economic level. That is to say, macroeconomic activities are still mainly regulated by the government through state planning, whereas micro-economic activities market forces. What is rather new is that the past tripartite classification concerning the management of the national economy, which used to apply to the national economy as a whole, is now confined to micro-economic level. Here, mandatory planning still plays a small but necessary part whereas guidance planning needs to play a larger part. Besides, regulation by market forces also needs to be expanded. So the tripartite classification does apply to micro-economic level. But why do we have to keep mandatory planning? Why do planning and market have to be combined like two plates joining together?

In theory, we still have an imbalanced market with a severe shortage of resources, which cannot be solved immediately through regulation by market forces. Therefore, it's still necessary to keep mandatory planning. Besides, we also have two systems at work in terms of economic management: On the one hand, we use price to regulate economy; on the other, we also use quantity to control economy. Price alone cannot solve some issues like imbalances in the market, and therefore it should also be joined by direct control on quantity. And this is the so-called mandatory management. In my opinion, the synthesis of these horizontal classifications can deepen our understanding of this issue.

Next comes the vertical analysis. With the passage of time, the relationship between planning and market has evolved during the reform. It used to be believed by some people that models of combination between planning and market (plate-joining model, inter-penetrating model, and the model of organic whole) should be considered as joined phases rather than mutually exclusive targets. In this logic, the reform should undergo the following phases.

In the first phase, i.e., before the reform, a centrally planned economy was practiced, and there was just a unitary public sector. In the second phase, i.e., the initial period of reform, the market was introduced as a supplement and then joined with the "plate" of planning. In the third stage, i.e., the period of deepening the reform, planning and market began to permeate into each other and overlap somewhat. In the last phase, planning and market are to form an organic whole and cease to exist side by side. This is the very source of the so-called "ubiquitous influence of both planning and market" and the formula of "the market being regulated by the state; the enterprise being guided by market forces" proposed in the 13th National Congress report.

It was ever said that we would rather not consider them as isolated ones, but as phases of a whole connecting with each other. It sounds pretty good in general, however, the process of reform cannot be taken too mechanically like that. In other words, we should not divide them strictly into several distinct phases. For example, we should not wishfully think that by the time we establish a new economic system, there would be just one model of combination between planning and market, i.e., planning and market being formed into an organic whole, whose influence will be ubiquitous in the whole society, and that the "plate-joining" and "inter-penetrating" combination would not exist any more; besides, it is also impossible to have the market exclusively regulated by the state and enterprises guided by the market.

It has turned out that the latter two models of combination will not disappear in the short run but be prolonged in certain fields instead, such as natural monopoly, products with lower elasticity in supply and demand, and public service, which should be directly controlled by the state.

However, we should also follow the law of value while implementing direct planned management. In this sense, the plate-joining combination and inter-penetrating combination are inextricably intertwined. We used to have a pure "plate-joining" combination while practicing planned economy, but it will never happen again after the reform. Besides, it should be noted that we cannot let the law of value dictate everything as what had been envisaged while exercising direct management. Otherwise, direct planning will be replaced by indirect regulation. It is still necessary to impose administrative intervention or direct mandatory planning because market is not all-powerful due to many defects in the market mechanism just as I mentioned earlier.

Some matters concerning the overall situation in the long run must be put under direct state control instead of being totally subject to the law of value, or else social interests would be in jeopardy. In terms of direct management, the state should take market factors into consideration rather than manage the economy directly through market. That is to say, the state can order the administrative organ to manage the economy.

In this sense, the formula of "the market being regulated by the state; the enterprise being guided by market forces" fails to apply to the whole society. However, since indirect regulation is going to become the major means of macroeconomic management, we still need to manage the economy through market and to guide the development of enterprises by regulating the market.

In this way, this formula cannot be bypassed, which is indispensable to the combination between planned economy and regulation by market forces.

(This article is an excerpt from the author's academic report in the Party School of the Central Committee of the CPC on Oct. 15, 1991.)

On Several Issues Concerning the Theory of Socialist Market Economy

The recent months have seen an upsurge in the study of Deng Xiaoping's South China Tour Talks, among which socialist market economy is one of the hottest topics as well a big concern of the people. However, it is not a brand new problem. On November 26th, 1979, Deng Xiaoping spoke of it while meeting the vice-chairman of the Compilation Committee of Encyclopedia Britannica, Inc. of the United States. "It is wrong to maintain that market economy is exclusive to capitalist society. Why can't we develop a market economy under socialism? Market economy was in its embryonic stages as early as feudal society. So we can surely develop it under socialism," he said. Again, in an interview by a delegation of senior American entrepreneurs in 1985 he mentioned it a second time. In his south China tour talks earlier this year, he elaborated on the issue of planning and market more comprehensively, having provoked further thoughts on socialist economy. His exposition of planning and market, an integral part of the theory of socialism with Chinese characteristics, must be thoroughly understood and carried though in the process of China's socialist economic reform and development.

My report includes two parts. The first section recounts the development of discussions about theoretical issues concerning socialist market economy, i.e. the evolution of people's perceptions of planning and market (such as planned economy, commodity economy, and market economy etc.) The second part is my own understanding of several key issues concerning the theory of socialist market economy after the study of Deng Xiaoping's South China Tour Talks.

1. Conceptions of planning and market: in evolution

It has been 13 years since we carried out economic restructuring. For years, the academic world of economics has been discussing the issue as to what structure our reform aims to establish. The core of such issue is how to understand and deal with the relationship between planning and market correctly, which is also related to conceptions of planned economy, commodity economy and market economy. After many twists and turns in explorations, our understanding of these issues has been deepened a lot.

However, it has been found out that Karl Marx or Friedrich Engels has never touched upon any concepts like commodity economy or market economy despite the fact that they did ever elaborate on commodity production, commodity exchange and monetary economy. They have never mentioned the concept of planned economy, either, although they did mention that in the future "the apportionment (of labor-time) in accordance with a definite social plan maintains the proper proportion between the different kinds of work to be done and the various wants of the community".

As a matter of fact, It was Vladimir Lenin that firstly used the concepts of "commodity economy", "market economy" and "planned economy". In the wake of revolutionary victory, Lenin pointed out repeatedly that commodity economy should be wiped out, capitalism would inevitably be replaced by socialism and that planned economy would eventually be practiced in a new society. But he also opposed coverall planning by depicting it as a sheer fantasy. In the era of "New

Economic Policy", aside from the fact that free trade was permitted in the abstract, business rules (i.e., market rules) also somewhat applied to state-run enterprises, that is to say, state-run enterprises can also gain access to market for free trade.

Unfortunately, Joseph Stalin put an end to it in the early 1930s by developing a planned economy which was antagonistic to commodity economy. For long, commodity economy had been considered as an antithesis of planned economy. Stalin ever mentioned commodity production and the law of value very narrowly, if at all, but he still firmly believed that planned economy is incompatible with commodity economy, not to mention market economy.

In the era of planned economy, market did exist but just marginally as a supplement to planning in socialist countries. The same is true with Pre-reform China, for example, the policy of "planning on major products; free market in minor ones", permission of markets, and trade of three categories of supplies on the market, etc. Notwithstanding this, market was still restricted, and commodity economy and market economy were still repelled.

After the Third Plenary Session of the 11th Central Committee of the CPC, the state began to loosen its grip on market and to acknowledge the necessity of the combination between planning and market. The *"Resolution on Historical Lessons Learned since the Founding of PRC"* adopted at the Sixth Plenary Session of the 11th CPC Central Committee confirmed that there do exist commodity production and exchanges under socialism and therefore the law of value should be consulted. However, "commodity economy" was not mentioned because it was then still held that commodity economy was exclusive to the capitalist society based on private ownership.

Even after the 12th National Congress of the CPC had already come up with the policy of "planned economy in the main and regulation by market forces as the supplement", the concept of "commodity economy" still failed to see daylight. However, before the congress, discussions over socialist commodity economy had already been held in theoretical circles, and some people even came up with the concept of "socialist market economy".

Besides, the people were also kept in the dark, when Deng Xiaoping met the vice-chairman of the Compilation Committee of Encyclopedia Britannica, Inc. of the United States on December 26th, 1979. Therefore, concepts like "commodity economy" and "market economy" still remained as taboo subjects in our society in that period of time. It was not until the Third Plenary Session of the 12th CPC Central Committee that the proposition that "socialist economy is a planned commodity economy based on public ownership" was firstly and officially written into the "*Decisions*", which marks a great breakthrough in the theory of socialist market economy. Deng Xiaoping sang highly of it, remarking in the congress that the "*Decisions*" had broken a new ground in Marxist political economics. It is definitely true that China had gone through a lot before such progress was achieved.

Despite the fact that classic writers like Karl Marx and Friedrich Engels ever envisaged commodity economy would disappear in the future socialist society and another fact that the role of market has been repelled in China for long during its socialist explorations, the Third Plenary Session of the 12th CPC Central Committee still proposed that "socialist economy is a planned commodity economy (based on public ownership)", which is of extreme epoch-making significance. In other words, such proposition has no doubt contributed a lot to the great advancement of the market-oriented reform as well as many remarkable achievements in this regard.

However, people, including economic theorists, were still divided on the conception of "planned commodity economy" after this new idea was put forward. Some people focused on "planning" while some "commodity economy". Different emphases will inevitably lead to different understandings of the essence of socialist economy and the orientation of the reform. Always, socialism is held to be distinguished from capitalism by the two following features—public ownership and distribution according to work. Aside from these two, is there a third essential feature? If yes, what is it? Is it planned economy or commodity economy? The debate is still going on.

Those who emphasized planning maintained that planned economy should be an essential characteristic of the socialist economy whilst those who emphasized commodity economy advocated that commodity should. Besides, another group of people who attached equal importance to planning and market suggested a combination between them. As to the range, way and degree of the combination, it should vary in product, sector, ownership and region. Therefore, in this case we can have more planning and in that case less. The 13th National Congress of the CPC defined the "socialist planned commodity economy" as "a system that integrates planning with the market", and also came up with the formula of "the market being regulated by the state; the enterprise being guided by market forces". Though it did not state clearly which one is in the main and which one is the supplement, we can still infer that the emphasis is indeed laid on market.

In 1989, the academia was in more and more favor of commodity economy and market while weighing them against planned economy and planning. However, after the policy of "combining planned economy with regulation by market forces", the pendulum swung back to planned economy again, because it was then necessary to have more centralization and planning for the sake of rectification and social stability. For instance, a then published article said, "socialist economy is a planned economy in nature, just with some commodity properties in the current stage." Such idea is very prevalent in recent two or three years. But still a group of scholars insisted that commodity economy be the core of socialist economy. For example, it was maintained in an article that along with public ownership and distribution according to work, socialist commodity economy is another essential characteristic of socialism.

As for the official policy of "combining planned economy with regulation by market forces", it was also met with some doubts and criticism, which however was just kept within the theoretical circles. For example, some people argued that planned economy as an economic system and regulation by market forces as a means of regulation or mechanism are not at the same levels, and therefore it is far-fetched to combine them. Notwithstanding such private disagreement, this wording has been widely used in the published articles. For example, an economist said while trying to prove the scientific soundness of this official version, "this policy is the continuation and development of the previous one of 'planned economy in the main and regulation by market forces as the supplement'. It suggested that China's reform is not to weaken or abandon planned economy, but to implement a certain degree of regulation by market forces while adhering to the system of planned economy." But those who disapproved of it criticized privately that this proposition indicated a retrogression to the policy before the 13th National Congress of the CPC. All in all, the debate on the relationship between planning and market has never ended.

Next I'd like to introduce briefly the development of discussions about several issues concerning socialist market economy.

Since the reform, people have already begun to discuss this issue and it hasn't come to an end yet. But the recent period has seen a dramatic increase in articles regarding this issue. However, these articles all sing the praises of the socialist market economy; by way of contrast, in the past, people were rather divided and kept arguing with each other on the same issue. In the initial period of reform, the concept of "socialist market economy" was already put forward in a symposium on the law of value under socialist economy held in Wuxi (a city in Jiangsu province in China) in April 1979, which was then met with both approval and criticism. Besides, it was also suggested that planned economy be combined with market economy.

After the Third Plenary Session of the 12th CPC Central Committee, in which socialist economy was defined as a planned commodity economy, a senior economist from Guangdong province said radicalness or thoroughness was much needed for theoretical concepts, suggesting that "socialist commodity economy" can also be called "socialist market economy" in the campaign of studying the *Decisions* adopted in the Third Plenary Session of the 12th CPC Central Committee. Besides, some people also proposed that there was no need to differentiate commodity economy from market economy, but the line must be drawn between socialist market economy and capitalist market economy.

In the meanwhile, such view also met up with some opposition and criticism. For instance, a professor then refuted such idea by citing the definition of "market economy" made by a Japanese economist in the western literature. The Japanese economist stated explicitly the three-doctrine of market economy, namely, no offences against property under private ownership, freedom of contract and self-accountability, which proves that a typical market economy is a capitalist economy by nature. And this Chinese professor thereby came to such a conclusion, "socialist planned commodity economy is not market economy".

Such debate has been prolonged till 1988 when the issue of market economy in the primary stage of socialism was clearly presented in a symposium held among economists from Guangdong province, which aimed to make theoretical explorations ahead of time, after Guangdong province was officially designated as the national comprehensive reform pilot area. These scholars reached a consensus that since there is already a capitalist market economy based on private ownership in the world, it is also necessary to establish a socialist market economy based on public ownership; given that there used to be a free market economy free from regulation by planning, there should be a planned market economy subject to macroeconomic regulation. Consequently, the symposium came to the conclusion that socialist market economy should be studied and put into practice.

In the second half of 1988, two important national academic symposiums were held, namely, the national symposium on the theory of economic restructuring at the end of October and the symposium on theoretical issues marking the 10th anniversary of the Third Plenary Session of the 11th CPC Central Committee in December. It was suggested in both symposiums that the concept of commodity economy should be further developed into market economy and that it is urgent we establish the theory of socialist market economy. What had happened so far is basically identical with the tendency of views by theoretical circles on the issue concerning planning versus market. Even though there still existed two opposing ideas at that time, more and more people tended to view commodity economy as a more important aspect as opposed to planning. Moreover, more people began to use the term of market economy, too.

In 1989, justified criticism has been leveled against capitalist liberalism embracing privatization in the field of economics, concurring with some criticism of socialist market economy in materials for internal circulation. The latter criticism is grounded on their beliefs as follows: given that market economy is linked with private ownership and capitalism in many western countries, many politicians and scientists from the socialist countries should be very cautious about defining socialist commodity economy, that is to say, commodity economy can be practiced under socialism, but market economy can't. Therefore, they concluded that those who coined the term of socialist market economy just schemed to establish a capitalist market economy as the reform target.

To sum up, these people associated market economy and planned economy with social systems, claiming that market economy is exclusive to capitalism and that to develop a market economy under socialism is equivalent to practice of capitalism. Surely some people disagreed with them, arguing that market economy should not be associated with social systems. Rather, they believed that market economy is just a synonym of "modern commodity economy" or "modern monetary economy". Some economists also said that our economic restructuring aims in essence to make market forces serve as the basic means of regulating resource allocation as opposed to administrative orders in the past, and therefore, socialist commodity economy can also be called socialist market economy in this sense. It follows that two opposing ideas regarding this issue still remained.

Next, let's see how Xue Muqiao, a veteran Chinese economist, viewed it. In an interview of Xue Muqiao made by a journalist from *Special Economic Zone Times* (a local paper in Shenzhen) on January 11th, 1991, Xue suggested that we should probe into the relationship between planned economy and market economy. He said, "the former used to be considered exclusive to socialism and the latter capitalism, which will do great harm to the deepening of the reform."

"Whether we should draw a distinct line between regulation by market forces and market economy still remains to be discussed. It seems to me that they are the same in nature, as neither of them is equivalent to capitalism. As long as public ownership of the means of production plays the dominant role, neither of them would be called a capitalist market economy. Therefore, ownership, rather than planning or market, is the very criterion to tell capitalism from socialism." "The time hasn't been ripe yet for the solution of such issue, as it is sill regarded as a taboo in theoretical studies. But it shouldn't be. Instead, for the sake of scientific research, people should discuss the issue freely and conscientiously, rather than evade them," he also added.

It is very necessary and natural to have encounters between different opinions, which are beneficial to the deepening of our understanding. At the beginning of this year, the debate on the socialist market economy finally came to an end after Deng Xiaoping elaborated on this issue in his South China Tour talks. He said, "A planned economy is not equivalent to socialism, because there is planning under capitalism too; a market economy is not capitalism, because there are markets under socialism too." From then on, people did not associate planning/market and planned/market economy with social system any longer. However, it will take time before the concept of socialist market economy is readily and completely accepted. When the concept of commodity economy was firstly put forward, it also took a while for the people to readily accept it. Not to mention socialist market economy!

In the initial period of reform, people already began to recognize the necessity of commodity production and commodity exchanges under socialism but still refused to accept the concept of commodity economy, because they still held that commodity economy is based on private ownership and therefore exclusive to capitalism. It took people several years, from the Third Plenary Session of the 11th CPC Central Committee to the Third Plenary Session of the 12th CPC Central Committee, to readily accept such concept. It is very hard to convince people into accepting a new theoretical concept. Sun Yefang also ever ran into the same difficulty after he put forward the concept of "socialist profit".

In the 1980s, the theory of "socialist economy as a planned commodity economy" has greatly boosted our economic reform and development. In the 1990s, we need to come up with some new theories as our reform especially the market-oriented reform deepens. Therefore, we need to establish the theory of socialist market economy, which will surely further the deepening of our reform and development.

2. Several focal issues

Next, I'd like to talk about my personal views on some focal issues concerning the theory of socialist market economy.

(1) Why is the term of "socialist commodity economy" reworded as "socialist market economy"? During the discussions, some people were rather confused and can't help asking, "since we've already had the concept of 'socialist commodity economy', why has it to be changed into 'market economy'?" "What sets 'market economy' apart from 'commodity economy'?" Some economists also spelled out their doubts in their published articles, "since we recognize no difference between socialist commodity economy and socialist market economy, why should we bother to change the wording officially rather than add a bracket for further explanation?"

However, it seems to me that it is not a simple change of word but has profound meanings. At first, we should figure out the meanings of commodity economy and market economy separately. Despite close connections, these two terms still bear different meanings. To put it simply, commodity economy, in contrast to natural economy and product economy, refers to an economic system in which products with equal values could be exchanged or compensated in social and economic activates and thus are endowed with commodity properties. To put it simple, after I give you one thing, you need to give me back another thing with equal values, be it goods or currency.

By way of comparison, natural economy does not involve any exchange of commodities with equal values. Product economy is a modern concept. It was ever envisaged that the future socialist or communist society would be just like a huge factory, and different production units or enterprises would be compared to workshops churning out different products. There will be neither circulation of currency nor commodity exchanges; rather, manufactured products will be distributed and allocated by the society among production units or social members according to their assigned quotas. In this sense, product economy involves no exchange of commodities with equal values, either. Therefore, commodity economy is a comparative term as opposed to natural economy and product economy.

Market economy is a term as opposed to planned economy in terms of resource allocation. So I'd like to talk about resource allocation at first, which was actually seldom used in China in the past. However, it has now been brought into frequent use, because it has been the core of economic life. Resources here refer to human, material, financial and land resources at human's disposal instead of untapped natural resources. Social economic resources are always limited whereas social demand for resources is huge and unlimited. The so-called resource allocation refers to the way that the society allocates limited resources among many fields, sectors, productions of goods and labor in a most or fairly effective way so as to yield maximum benefits and satisfy social needs to the largest extent.

In the modern socialized production, there are usually two means of regulating resource allocation: regulation by market forces and regulation by planning. Resource allocation regulated by planning refers to the disintegration and allocation of quotas by the government according to administrative orders. Resource allocation regulated by market forces refers to the flow of resources in and out of commodities whose prices fluctuate according to supply and demand changes. The higher the price of a certain commodity, the more profits sellers would gain and the more resources will flow in. By the time when demand falls short of supply, the price will fall and resources will flow elsewhere. This is the so-called regulation by market forces. If resources are allocated mainly by planning, it is called planned economy; if mainly by market forces, it is called market economy. Therefore, in terms of resource allocation, market economy is a concept as opposed to planned economy.

By comparison, we find out that in logical sense, commodity economy is an abstract term defined by its content; whereas market economy is a concrete term defined by its form. So, it can be said that market economy is a more developed form of commodity economy. We will get the same conclusion if it is viewed from the perspective of historical development. Commodity economy has a long history, which can be traced back to the end of primitive society when it was at its embryotic stage. After many social forms in evolution, commodity economy has now developed into an advanced form. However, market economy did not co-exist with commodity economy at every stage. Surely, goods should be exchanged in a market, but such exchange of goods is not necessarily equivalent to market economy.

For example, neither considerably prosperous Mediterranean coastal cities in the classical and medieval periods nor financial hubs like Chang'an, Luoyang, Linzi and the famous Silk Road connecting Europe and Asia in Qin and Han dynasties of ancient China can do without the market, but none of them had developed a market economy at that time. Besides, till now, small local markets still exist nearby ancient castles in foreign countries and open markets in remote backward areas of China. Though these regular markets are also a type of market, they are just a gathering place for dwellers in the vicinity to regulate their supply and demand of necessities.

To establish a market economy, a society needs to meet some requirements, i.e. the nationwide free flow of commodities and factors of production and the capacity of allocating resources to the places so as to achieve optimal benefits with minimal expenses. Therefore, domestic feudal separationist rule and man-made barriers to the flow of resources must be abolished. Whenever commodity economy develops to a certain degree, a unified domestic market should be established and even extended further to the world.

With the formation of modern nation-states and the concurrent major geographical discoveries, this unified market was gradually brought into being. So was the market economy. Therefore, the idea of "market economy as a highly developed form of commodity economy" was inspired by resource allocation, a basic concept in economics. We hadn't realized its great significance in our economic life until the reform was carried out. But we only had a very limited knowledge of it in 1984 when the concept of planned commodity economy was put forward. As the reform advanced, our understanding of its significance was gradually improved. Now, we've replaced "planned commodity economy" with the concept of market economy so as to emphasize the necessity of developing commodity economy. In terms of resource allocation, we must make market forces take the place of administrative planning and serve as the basic means of regulating resource allocation, which is also the essence of our economic restructuring. However, the concept of "planned commodity economy" would be inadequate to reflect such essence.

From the perspective of the development of knowledge, the new conception of "planned commodity economy" put forward in the Third Plenary Session of the 12th CPC Central Committee is no doubt a great breakthrough in socialist economic theories and has great significance in promoting the historical development. But inevitably, it also has its own historical limitations. Like what was analyzed before, it failed to point out which one, planning or market, should be the basic means of regulating resource allocation. As a result, people kept vacillating between different understandings of the relationship between planning and market and arguing with each other. At that time, people still regarded planned economy or market economy as a criterion for differentiating socialism from capitalism, and hence failed to realize the irreplaceable role that market mechanism is supposed to play in optimizing resource allocation and promoting the development of the productive forces.

In the beginning of 1992, Deng Xiaoping pointed out in his famous South China Tour talks, "The proportion of planning to market forces is not the essential difference between socialism and capitalism. A planned economy is not equivalent to socialism, because there is planning under capitalism too; a market economy is not capitalism, because there are markets under socialism too. Planning and market forces are both means of controlling economic activity." This scientific thesis has broken with the tradition of associating planned economy and market economy with basic social systems, overcome the "capitalism-phobia" we used to suffer from when it comes to market and market economy, and inspired people with the idea of "resource allocation", a basic concept of economics, to look into the possibility of establishing a socialist market economy as the reform target. Undoubtedly, it is another big breakthrough in socialist economic theories in the early 1990s after the concept of socialist commodity economy was put forward in the early 1980s; it will have profound implications for our reform and opening up and economic development in the future.

(2) Since planning and market forces are both means of controlling economic activities, why should we change or develop the term of "socialist planned economy" into "socialist market economy"? It has been explained earlier why should "socialist commodity economy" be developed into "socialist market economy". To spell it out, our economic restructuring aims in essence to make market forces take the place of planning and serve as the basic means of regulating resource allocation.

But here comes a problem, that is, since planning and market forces are both means of regulating economic activities and that the proportion of planning to market has nothing to do with social system, why must we achieve a combination between planning and market in the new system of market economy? Why can't we achieve the combination under the system of planned economy? In other words, why must we replace planning with market and make the latter serve as the basic means of regulating resource allocation? To answer this question, we need to make a comparison between the two means of regulating resource allocation in terms of merits, demerits and meaning. Given that we have gained wider experience from many years' practice and observation, the answer has become more and more self-evident.

Both resource allocation regulated by planning and that by market forces have distinctive advantages and disadvantages. As for resource allocation regulated by planning, the government allocates resources mainly by issuing administrative orders according to plans made beforehand. Its strength lies in its capacity of concentrating power (i.e., resources) on accomplishing several major tasks and of coordinating economic development of the society as a whole. Meantime, it also has some defects due to man's limitations. Planners and decision-makers have limitations in information collection and cognition; besides, they are placed in different positions and stand for different interests. As a result, resource allocation regulated by planning will inevitably lead to biased and rigid thinking and thus affect economic vitality and the optimization of resource allocation.

In contrast, resource allocation regulated by market forces is mainly dictated by the law of value on the basis of market supply and demand changes so that the mechanism of competition is brought into play. Its strength lies in its capacity of using price signals and regular competition to promote the survival of the fittest, to coordinate supply and demand relations and to optimize the allocation of limited resources. However, due to its spontaneity, blindness and ex-post regulation, it can barely or cannot maintain a balance between aggregate supply and aggregate demand, guard against severe economic fluctuations, readjust major economic structures properly, prevent the gap between the rich and the poor from widening drastically, avoid polarization, or protect the ecological environment or conserve natural resources etc.

Therefore, we have to foster their strengths, circumvent their weaknesses and combine them to complement each other. But so far, the question hasn't been answered yet. In my point of view, it is rather than an issue of faith or preference, but an empirical one. That is to say, we should stop obsessing about the issue in the abstract as to whether planned/market economy is associated with social system or not, but study the outcome of their competitions in the world economic arena instead. We need to figure out under what conditions they are more effective in regulating resource allocation and which one is better in general.

A broad overview of the modern world history reveals that market economy has given rise to an economic boom in the capitalist society, but at the same time it also resulted in the worsening of its internal contradictions. In the early 19th century, the fundamental contradiction in the capitalist society began to manifest itself in the form of cyclical economic crises, which got from bad to worse and thus led to social disasters such as bankruptcy of factories and unemployment.

Since the mid 19th century, socialist thought has evolved from fantasy to a science. In order to overcome these limitations, it came up with the idea of "planned distribution of labor time" and planned economy, which was later adopted in Russia after the success of October Revolution in 1917.

After world War II , some countries including China began to follow suit and developed a planned economy too, from which they all learned invaluable lessons, including both success and failures. Thanks to planned economy, the Soviet Union grew from a backward nation to a then second largest world industrial power, won a victory in the anti-fascist war, and gained a quick economic recovery after the ravages of the defensive war. However, with the expansion of economy, diversification of economic structures, the quickening of technological advances and the increasing needs of people's life since the 1960s, flaws inherent in planned economy such as rigid control and lack of incentives began to manifest themselves, resulting in the decline in economic benefits and economic slowdown. Despite its leading roles in frontier sciences and some fields in defense industries, the traditional planned economy practiced by the Soviet Union appeared to be at its end of tether when it comes to overcoming the shortage of commodities and meeting people's basic needs etc.

In comparison, western capitalist countries had been searching for cures to ills of market economy since the mid 19th century given the worsening of social contradictions. The introduction of joint stock system and trust (i.e., monopoly over the whole industry) has to some extent overcome the "planlessness" in production. In 1891, Friedrich Engels pointed out, "Capitalist production by joint-stock companies is no longer private production but production on behalf of many associated people. And when we pass on from joint-stock companies to trusts, which dominate and monopolize the whole branches of industry, this will put an end not only to private production but also to planlessness." During the second World War, governments were all forced to develop a "controlled economy", exerting strict control on manpower, materials and foreign currency etc., in order to gather resources to meet the needs of war.

Definitely, these local and temporary measures failed to prevent capitalist contradictions from worsening. With the full exposure of capitalist contradictions, the outbreak of the Great Depression from 1929 to the 1930s has led to unprecedented catastrophes in capitalist societies during peacetime. Against the background, Franklin Roosevelt, then U.S. president, came up with "Roosevelt's New Deal" and suggested that the government step in; besides, John M. Keynes put forward the theory of macroeconomic regulation in his book entitled *the General Theory of Employment, Interest and Money* as well.

Since the Second World War, this theory has been widely accepted by the western countries, and their governments began to implement macroeconomic regulation through fiscal and monetary policies. Besides, some countries like France and Japan also practiced guidance planning and countries like Swede and Germany began to use social welfare policies, too. These measures have indeed mitigated cyclical economic crises and reduced antagonism between social classes, but they would never overcome the fundamental capitalist contradiction completely as they are still predicated on private ownership of the means of production. However, after several scientific and technological revolutions, these capitalist countries not only survived from these crises but even managed to thrive with more vigor and vitality, which suggests that the 19th Century model is already inadequate and outdated.

It can be seen from this brief review that market economy and planned economy have both merits and demerits and ever underwent both success and failures. However, on the whole, modern market economy has proved to be more effective and efficient than traditional planned economy, which is also one of the most important causes for the Revolutions of 1989 (in east Europe) and the Dissolution of the Soviet Union. In China, problems like short supply of materials and low efficiency also arose afterwards in spite of its initial success in the First Five-Year Plan.

In order to solve these problems, we carried out a market-oriented reform rightly after the Third Plenary Session of the 11th CPC Central Committee. It turned out that regions, sectors and enterprises with higher level of marketization tended to enjoy more vitality and higher economic growth. For more than a decade, China has witnessed great improvements in the overall economic strength, the variety of market commodities and living standards of the people. Wholehearted support for the communist party and desire for stability by the masses of workers and peasants is a key factor that prevented China from repeating the mistakes of Soviet Union and eastern European countries, which also proves in a sense that it is very wise of china to carry out the market-oriented reform.

Besides, we also came to another conclusion, that is, planned economy cannot be thereby wrote off at one stroke because it applies to a certain range and is even more workable in particular historical conditions. So, what are these "particular historical conditions"? First, planned economy is more workable when a country is less developed with less constructions (e.g., in the period of the First Five-year Plan, China only had 156 construction projects in total); second, planned economy is more workable when economic and industrial structures are quite simple (e.g., after the elimination of the non-public sector, China focused on the heavy industry); Third, it is more effective when the motivation behind the development was very simple and focused (e.g., during wartime or war preparation period, adequate food and clothing is the first priority); fourthly, when big events other than wars take place, such as huge disasters and economic crises. Lastly, when a nation adopts a close-door and self-sufficient policy. Under these conditions, it is easier to develop a planned economy and it does work very well.

However, once the economy is more developed, construction is expanded, economic, industrial and product structures are diversified, development goals are multiplied or back to the normal (i.e. targets include meeting people's diversified needs and enhancing the national strength, especially in terms of science, technology and economy), the economy has been globalized thanks to the policy of opening-up etc., planned economy with administrative planning as the major means of regulating resource allocation will be more and more ill-suited to the trend. And then, it will be high time for us to practice a market economy with market forces as the major means of regulating resource allocation, which is the very task that our economy is currently faced with.

In the 1980s, our economy has made a rather big step forward. In the 1990s, we should seize favorable opportunities and speed up our development on the basis of optimized industrial structure and improved quality and efficiency; at the same time, we also need open up our market further to the world and compete globally. Therefore, we need establish a new economic system, i.e., socialist market economy, attaching more importance to market and making it serve as the basic means of regulating resource allocation.

On the basis of this, we should combine planning with market, both as means of regulating economic activities, in a better way. In terms of resource allocation, wherever market is capable enough to solve the problem, it should be given a free rein; in contrast, whenever the problem is beyond the reach of market, we should count on the government to solve it through policies and planning. To sum up, modern market economy shouldn't oppose any economic interventions by the government or guidance from planning; rather, it must rely on them to make up for its own deficiency; and we should always keep this in mind during the transition of planned economy to market economy.

3. Since "market economy" is not a concept associated with social system, why should the modifier "socialist" be added in front of "market economy"? What sets apart socialist market economy from capitalist one? People from

overseas also asked, "Since China is to practice 'market economy', which is pretty good, why does it bother to add a modifier 'socialist'?" They did it either on purpose or being ignorant of the real meaning of China's market-oriented reform. Actually, China's market-oriented reform aims to achieve the self-improvement of socialist system, rather than copy blindly the western-style market economy.

Some Chinese scholars also held similar doubts, but from the perspective of operational mechanism. They argued that market economies, though under different social systems, are almost the same, and that their differences, if at all, should be attributed to the basic characteristic of each social system instead of market economy itself. Therefore, some people proposed that, rather than "socialist market economy", socialist economy should be termed as "market economy under the socialist system or under socialist conditions". In my point of view, it does make some sense, but for the sake of brevity, it should be replaced by "socialist market economy" with the same meaning, which would be gradually accepted after common practice.

Besides, generality tends to manifest itself in the form of particularity in specific circumstances, so a modifier signifying particularity is usually added in front of a general term. Some frequently used terms such as "socialist modernization" and "socialist enterprises" etc. are good examples of such kind. It is advisable to term the market economy under socialist conditions "socialist market economy", because "socialist market economy" or "capitalist market economy" has both generality and individuality, and the same is true with capitalist market economy. For instance, German's market economy is not identical with that of France, and Japan's market economy is not totally the same as that of the United States, either. Not to mention socialist market economy, which surely has individuality distinct from capitalist market economy.

As for the generality shared by socialist market economy and capitalist market economy, we've mentioned many times earlier, such as the law of value, the supply and demand relations, price signals, and the role that the mechanism of competition plays in regulating resource allocation etc. As for their individuality, it is mainly stemmed from the fact that market economy is inseparable from the social system in which it is rooted. The individuality of socialist market economy is mainly determined by the essence of the socialist system, and especially by the fact that it is closely linked to the basic economic system of socialism.

In terms of the political system, the basic characteristic of our socialist system is the leadership of communist party and people's political power, which in general does not mean to benefit exclusively the interests of some groups or individuals, but serve the interests of all people instead. As far as the basic economic system is concerned, public ownership (including state ownership and collective ownership) plays the dominant role with the private sector and foreign sector serving as a supplement. Different types of ownership can be mixed together in different ways. Enterprises in different economic sectors or in different operational forms are all allowed to enter the market, developing side by side through fair competition.

The leading role of the state sector of the economy is to be realized through market competition. To correspond with the ownership structure, we establish the socialist distribution system in which distribution according to work plays the dominant role, with distribution according to other factors of production serving as a supplement. Besides, we should give due consideration to both efficiency and equity, widen the income gap properly through the mechanism of market to promote efficiency, and try to overcome inequitable distribution through many regulatory means so as to achieve common prosperity.

These basic characteristics of the socialist system have important implications for the market economy, enabling the economy to be regulated with more consciousness (rather than spontaneity) and to work for the common good. Thanks to the leadership of the CPC, public ownership as the mainstay of the economy, and the ultimate goal to realize prosperity for all, we are more likely to and even more capable of outdoing capitalist market economy in the following aspects by taking both overall interests of the society and local interests into consideration. That is, we can handle the relationship between planning and market correctly, strike a balance between the policy of invigorating the economy at micro-economic level and that of macroeconomic coordination, and deal with the relations between efficiency and social equity more properly. We are confident that we can achieve all through a comprehensive reform.

The establishment of socialist market economy is a complicated process, in which many major aspects linked with each other are to be reformed. First, we should reform the operational mechanism of enterprises, especially that of medium-sized and large state-owned enterprises (SOEs). By straightening out relationships between ownership and management of enterprises and separating government administration from enterprise management, we urge enterprises to enter the market, forging them into main market players and legal entities responsible for their own decisions concerning their operation and development and accountable for their own profits and losses.

Second, we must cultivate and improve the mechanism of market. We are required not only to develop commodity economy, but also to cultivate production factor markets so as to speed up the establishment of price mechanism in which prices of goods or services are mainly determined by their market supply and demand and to establish a set of scientific and standard market rules and management system. Third, we should establish a mechanism of social income distribution and social security system to suite the needs of market economy and conform with socialist principles. Fourthly, we should establish a mechanism of macroeconomic regulation on the basis of regulation by market forces.

That is to say, we should reduce government interventions in the management of enterprises, shifting its focus from micro-economic management in terms of money, materials and personnel to macroeconomic management in terms of planning, coordination, supervision and services through fiscal and financial policies. In one nutshell, such transformation of government functions is extremely crucial to all aspects of the reform mentioned above. Every aspect of the reform is a very complex task, and therefore I would not talk about them one by one.

All in all, socialist market economy cannot be established overnight, which involves more painstaking and conscientious efforts in the long run. It requires the whole party, all the people and all aspects concerned in the society to make joint efforts to improve on what the market-oriented reform has already achieved over the past decade, make explorations and experiments more boldly, and draw lessons in a timely manner so as to achieve a smooth transition to the new economic system. In this way, the establishment of socialism with Chinese characteristics would be much accelerated, and thus the second and third strategic goals for economic development could be possibly achieved ahead of time.

(This is the transcript of the opening speech made by Liu Guoguang in a series of lectures on "the reform and opening up and economic development in the 1990s" co-sponsored by the Organization Department of the Central Committee of the CPC, the Publicity Department of the Central Committee of the CPC, Chinese Association for Science and Technology, the Work Committee Departments under the Central Committee of the CPC and the Work Committee of the Central Government Departments under the Central Committee of the CPC on September 19, 1992. The article was published in *Economic Research Journal*, 1992, No.10)

Historical Transition from Planned Economy to Socialist Market Economy

—marking the 20th anniversary of the Third Plenary Session of the 11th Central Committee of the Chinese Communist Party

1. Evolution from the market-oriented reform to the establishment of market economy

Since 1978, the well known heated debate on the criterion of truth and the reestablishment of "seeking truth from facts" as the party's ideological line have freed economic theorists from dogmatic chains. How to draw lessons from the history, how to follow objective economic laws under socialist conditions and how to manage economic activities through economic means, in a nutshell, how to understand and use correctly the law of value, has become the highlight of the debate in the academic world of economics.

Afterwards, discussions on the relationship between the law of value and economic reforms in the academic world of economics were held even more widely and more heatedly, especially since the Third Plenary Session of the 11th Central Committee of the CPC established that the party should shift its focus to the socialist modernization drive and reform our economic management approach and system. However, these concepts such as regulation by market forces, commodity economy and even market economy were not established and widely accepted overnight, but instead, the ideological debate concerning them have long since been very heated over the two decades.

Since the Third Plenary Session of the 11th Central Committee of the CPC, people were allowed to mention the combination of regulation by planning with regulation by market forces. Concepts like commodity economy and market economy, though still considered as taboo subjects at the policy level, were widely and heatedly discussed in Wuxi Conference in 1979. Some people even boldly suggested that planned economy be combined with market economy, but for most people the combination of regulation by planning with regulation by market forces seemed to be more acceptable at that time. After all, most people at that time still considered that market economy was exclusive to capitalism.

As a matter of fact, on November 26th, 1979, while meeting Frank, B. Gibney, the vice-chairman of the Compilation Committee of Encyclopedia Britannica, Inc. of the United States, Deng Xiaoping already stated very clearly, "It is wrong to maintain that market economy is exclusive to capitalist society. Why can't we develop a market economy under socialism? Developing a market economy does not mean practicing capitalism. While maintaining a planned economy as the mainstay of our economic system, we are also introducing a market economy, but it is a socialist market economy." But his words were not made public at that time, and therefore "market economy" remained a taboo subject for some time.

Besides, the concept of "commodity economy" also underwent many twists and turns before it was established. *The Resolution Clarifying Certain Questions in the History of the Party since the Foundation of the People's Republic of China* adopted at the Six Plenary Session of the 11th Central Committee of the CPC in 1981 confirmed that there do exist commodity production and exchanges under socialism and therefore the law of value should be consulted. However, it hadn't come up with the term "commodity economy" yet because it was then still held that commodity economy was exclusive to the capitalist society based on private ownership. Although the 12th National Congress of the CPC came up with the policy of "planned economy in the main and market regulation as the supplement" in 1982 and made a big step forward, the concept of "market economy" was still not legitimized.

Later, in the Third Plenary Session of the 12th CPC Central Committee, our party for the first time defined "socialist economy" as "a planned commodity economy based on public ownership", which was then written into the *Decisions on Economic Restructuring*. This marks a great breakthrough in the theory of socialist market economy. Deng Xiaoping sang highly of it, remarking in the congress that the *Decisions* had broken a new ground in Marxist political economics. It is definitely true that China had gone through a lot before such progress was made.

Given that classic writers like Karl Marx and Friedrich Engels used to predict that commodity economy would disappear in the future socialist society and the fact that the role of market in economic regulation has been denied for decades in our socialist practice, this proposition is of epoch-making significance; besides, it has no doubt contributed a lot to the great advancement of our market-oriented reform, too.

Before that, we narrowly restricted socialist economy to a planned economy, and copied the Soviet-style economic management, i.e., mandatory planning. In September, 1982, I published an article entitled "Orientation of the Economic Restructuring" in *People's Daily*, in which I proposed that we should adopt three different ways of economic management while dealing with the relationship between planning and market in socialist economy. We should apply mandatory planning to production and allocation of major products concerning the overall economic situation; we should apply guidance planning to production and sale of general products; we must guarantee free production and sale of various daily-use goods, small wares and other subsidiary agricultural products while carrying out regulation by market forces.

Besides, I also suggested for the first time that we should gradually narrow the scope of mandatory planning and expand the role of guidance planning, since the buyer's market has been gradually formed, the price has been rationalized and some progress has been made with economic adjustment. I even proposed that guidance planning is in essence a means of economic regulation, in which regulation by planning is achieved through regulation by market forces. However, I was criticized for these ideas and had to make self-criticism. I then acknowledged that I failed to maintain unity with the Central Committee, but I've never ever admitted that my view was wrong.

Two years later, I was proved to be right by the Party's decisions at the Third Plenary Session of the 12th CPC Central Committee, and then those who used to criticize me began to accept my ideas, too. It also proved that it would take some time before any ideas were widely accepted. Everybody must have ever had the similar experience before, as nobody can be "always right". I am no exception to it. I used to maintain that we should focus on planned economy and reserve my views on the term of "commodity economy" before socialist economy was defined as the "planned commodity economy" at the Third Plenary Session of the 12th Central Committee of the CPC. Besides, I even proposed that it might be better to term socialist economy "a planned economy with properties of commodity economy".

The party came up with the policy of "planned economy in the main and regulation by market forces as the supplement" in the 12th National Congress of the CPC; at its Third Plenary Session, the 12th Central Committee defined socialist economy as "a planned commodity economy". As to which one we should lay more emphasis on, planning or commodity economy, people disagreed with one another. Varied emphases led to different understandings of the nature of the socialist economy and even the orientation of reform. Essential features of socialist economy invariably include "public ownership" and "distribution according to work". Besides, is there a third one? If so, would it be "planned economy" or "commodity economy"? People still disagree and the debate is still going on.

During his talk with other leaders of the Central Committee on February 6th, 1987, Deng Xiaoping spoke of the relationship between planning and market again. He asked, "Why do some people always insist that market is capitalist and only planning is socialist? Actually they are both means of regulating economic activities. So long as they benefit the productive forces, we should use them." "At one time we copied the Soviet model of economic development and had a planned economy; later we said that in a socialist economy planning was primary. We should not say that any longer," added he. As a result, "planned economy" was nowhere to be seen in the report of the 13th National Congress of the CPC in 1987. Besides, the report broke with the conventional idea that planning and market merely exist side by side, coming up with a new notion that "the socialist planned commodity economy should be a system that integrates planning with market". Even though it did not state clearly which is primary and which is secondary, the formula of "the market being regulated by the state; the enterprise being guided by market forces" proposed in the 13th National Congress has actually indicated that the emphasis is already laid on market.

In 1989, the academia was more and more in favor of commodity economy and market, as opposed to planned economy and planning. As a result, the government tended to loosen its control even in terms of macroeconomic regulation, resulting in an overheated economy in 1988. In response to this, the Central Committee came up with the policy of "creating a favorable economic environment, straightening out the economy, and deepening reforms in an all-round way" in September 1988. From then on, the Central Committee began to straighten out the economy and strengthen macroeconomic regulation by the government. In this way, the proportion of planning to market was raised and the economy more centrally planned.

Actually, for the sake of economic management, the government is free to choose whatever means or measures, be it market or planning, tightening or loosening control over the economy; it is also quite natural to have some missteps in the course of reform. However, some theorists and politicians who opposed the market-oriented reform rekindled a debate on the relationship between planning and market, claiming that the market orientation and the weakening of the planned economy were to blame for all economic problems and that the only way out is to restore the traditional planned economy.

Especially in 1989, "marketization" was dismissed as a major tool of "peaceful evolution", and the issue of planning and market was associated with socialism and capitalism again. At the policy level, the previous slogan of "combining planned economy with regulation by market forces" was chanted again due to some historical reasons, which was obviously a retreat from the policy of the Third Plenary Session of the 12th Central Committee of the CPC or the 13th National Congress.

The Key factor pulling our economic restructuring back to the market orientation is Deng Xiaoping's South China Tour Talks in 1992. Those thought-provoking words, almost known to every household, put an end to the long-standing hot debate concerning planning vs market in its own way. "The proportion of planning to market is not the essential difference between socialism and capitalism. A planned economy is not equivalent to socialism, because there is planning under capitalism too; a market economy is not capitalism, because there are markets under socialism, too," said he. Later Jiang Zemin also clarified it in his speech in the Party School of the Central Committee of the CPC.

As we all know, it usually takes time before one's understanding is improved. In the 14th National Congress of the CPC, it was stated officially that our economic restructuring aims to establish a socialist market economy. In comparison, this policy was indeed more precise and clarified than that of the Third Plenary Session of the 12th Central Committee of the CPC. Till Now, we have already come up with a more precise and complete policy as to how to handle the relationship between planning and market, that is, "to let market forces, subject to macroeconomic regulation, serve as the basic means of regulating resource allocation". We are now working hard to achieve this in both ideology and practice. Since 1993, we have successfully controlled inflation and achieved a "soft landing". Currently faced up with minor deflation, we began to take positive expansionary fiscal and monetary policies to stimulate domestic demand with a view to achieving a "soft start-up". Our party's capacity of managing the economy has now been greatly improved, which is no doubt closely related to the establishment of correct theories.

2. Liberation of the productive forces owing to socialist market economy (*Outlook Weekly*, 1989, Vol. 48)

The Third Plenary Session of the 11th Central Committee of the CPC reestablished "seeking truth from facts" as the party's ideological line, having freed people from "leftist" thoughts. In the two decades, China's policy in terms of reform has evolved from carrying out a market-oriented reform to establishing a socialist market economy. The reform of resource allocation, ownership, distribution system and government functions etc., has massively liberated and developed the productive forces, which is the main thread running through our economic reform over the two decades. Regardless of disagreement, complication and confusion during the reform, China has witnessed a dramatic increase in its national strength and the improvement of people's living standards, which is the hard evidence of the liberation of the productive forces.

Proper resource allocation and mobilization of peoples' enthusiasm is one of the key factors for the liberation and development of the productive forces. We've done a good job in this aspect in both theory and practice over more than two decades.

With regard to the relationship between planning and market, people have been taking planned economy as an essential feature of socialism, opposing planning to commodity economy or market economy. Still imprisoned by "leftist" thoughts, economic theoreticians dare not spell out their doubts over planned economy publicly. Sun Yefang, who boldly proposed to base planning on the law of value in the 1950s, was thrown into Qincheng Prison soon after the onset of Cultural Revolution and wasn't set free until 7 years later in 1975.

Thanks to the well known hot debate about the criterion of truth and the Third Plenary Session of the 11th Central Committee of the CPC in 1978, these ideological shackles and chains were finally broken. In April 1979, a national symposium on the role of the law of value in the socialist economy was held among economic theoreticians in Wuxi, which sparked heated discussions, but commodity economy and market economy still remained as taboo subjects at that time.

With the advancement of reforms and emancipation of our thoughts, taboos were gradually lifted and people's understanding of the relationship between planning and market was improved as well. The Sixth Plenary Session of the 11th Central Committee of the CPC confirmed that there were also commodity production and exchanges in the socialist society. The 12th National Congress in 1982 came up with the policy of "planned economy in the main and regulation by market forces as the supplement". In its Third Plenary Session in 1984, the 12th Central Committee proposed, "socialist economy is a planned commodity economy based on public ownership". In 1987, the 13th National Congress proposed that "planned commodity economy is the economic system in which planning should be integrated with market forces" and also came up with the formula of "the market being regulated by the state; the enterprise being guided by market forces". In spite of that, arguments were still very intense during that period of time.

Eventually, this problem was solved in the Third Plenary Session of the 14th Central Committee of the CPC in 1992, when the Central Committee stated clearly that we establish socialist market economy and let market forces, subject to macroeconomic regulation by the state, serve as the basic means of regulating resource allocation. Afterwards, China's economic reform and development did follow this course. The Central Committee has used different means to carry out macroeconomic regulation in different economic situations. For example, in 1993 the government successfully cooled down an overheated economy by putting inflation under control and achieved the "soft landing". Recently, the economy has lost a lot of steam, resulting in slight deflation. In response to this, the government has tried to gain a "soft startup" through fiscal and monetary policies. Economic fluctuations are inevitable, which is part of the economic law: sometimes the economy is hot and sometimes cool. In the past, we usually used planning and administrative means to regulate a highly volatile economy that tended to cause high inflation or a sharp increase in the unemployment rate, resulting in drastic economic fluctuations repeatedly. Such measure has proved to be unfavorable for the liberation and development of the productive forces.

Over the two decades since we carried out economic restructuring, not only the reform of resource allocation has promoted the liberation and development of the productive forces, but the reforms of ownership, distribution system and government functions have contributed a lot, too. Take the reform of ownership as an example: if we had just used market in lieu of planning as the means of regulating economic activities and still made the state sector play the leading role, our economy would definitely not achieve as good results as today. Having drawn valuable lessons from the past in terms of ownership since the Third Plenary Session of the 11th Central Committee of the CPC, we stepped up the development of the non-state sector while keeping public ownership as the mainstay. As a result, collective, private, foreign-owned and mixed-ownership enterprises increased rapidly; the national economy was invigorated; and the productive forces was developed, too.

However, there were still some problems with public ownership after the urban reform, among which the SOE reform still remains a big headache. Till now we haven't found good solutions, such as how to separate government administration from enterprise management, how to make SOEs responsible for their profits and losses and operate independently, how to forge them into self-disciplined major market players responsible for their capital accumulation and self-improvement. On the one hand, some government organizations still have too strict control over SOEs and are not ready to loosen their grip; on the other hand, though power has been delegated to SOEs, there are still many flaws in the state-owned asset management system, and the mechanism of supervision and restraint over operators hasn't been set up yet.

For instance, "insider control" and "drain of state-owned assets" stand out as major problems; the accredited inspector system only works for a few large SOEs whereas in many other enterprises managers tended to fill their own pockets and jeopardize the interests of enterprises. In response to these problems, the 15th National Congress of the CPC came up with more clarified policies on the issue of public ownership, such as, "we should uphold and improve the system in which public ownership is the mainstay of the economy and other kinds of ownership develop side by side", "public ownership can and should diversify". However, as to how to implement these policies, it still awaits further exploration.

Take the reform of distribution system as another example. The indiscriminate egalitarianism previously held proved to have dampened workers' enthusiasm, which has been improved a lot through many reform measures during these two decades. Our policy is to make some people in some regions prosper before others so that they can bring along backward regions to achieve common prosperity, which has indeed greatly motivated people's initiatives. However, there still exist unfairness and irregularities in distribution system. Some people who prospered before others achieved their ends through power, the back door and other unscrupulous means rather than through honest work and lawful operation, leading to an even larger gap between the poor and the rich. However, income gap does not necessarily mean unfairness. If people adhere to the principle of distribution according to work, or prosper through management expertise or contribution by other factors of production or chances, these efforts would all be appreciated. As a matter of fact, it is not usually so, which will often lead to psychological imbalances and thus do great harm to the liberation and development of the productive forces.

(The article was published in *Finance and Trade Economics*, 1998, Vol. 12.)

Part II

Origins and Development of China's Socialist Market Economy

A Retrospect of China's Explorations from the Third Plenary Session of the 11th Central Committee of the CPC to the Establishment of Socialist Market Economy

1. On the Party's explorations of the relationship between planning and market since the Third Plenary Session of the 11th Central Committee of the CPC

Since the Third Plenary Session of the 11th Central Committee of the CPC, our party has begun to touch upon the system of socialist market economy during its explorations of the relationship between planning and market. On November 26th, 1979, Deng Xiaoping ever talked about the relationship between planning and market while meeting Frank, B. Gibney, the vice-chairman of the Compilation Committee of Encyclopedia Britannica, Inc. of the United States. "While maintaining a planned economy as the mainstay of our economic system, we are also introducing a market economy, but it is a socialist market economy." "We cannot say that market economy exists only under capitalism. Market economy was in its embryonic stages as early as feudal society. We can surely develop it under socialism," he remarked. He has spoken of it many times during that period of time, but these words were not made public until later on.

It was not until the 12th National Congress in 1982 that the relationship between planning and market was stated explicitly, "planned economy is in the main and regulation by market forces as the supplement". By then we still considered planned economy as the major feature of socialism, but we've already started to use market forces as a means of regulation. At its third Plenary Session, the 12th Central Committee defined socialist economy as "a planned commodity economy based on public ownership", which is a very important step forward. Previously, we only accepted the existence of commodity production and exchanges but opposed commodity economy. "Socialist economy" being defined as "a planned commodity economy" by the the 12th Central Committee in its Third Plenary Session, just as what Deng Xiaoping put it, constitutes the political economics characterized by the integration of the basic tenets of Marxism with China's concrete practice of socialism, which has shed great light on what socialism is; besides, we've got answers to some new problems in new circumstances while exploring ways to build socialism. However, since then, the academic world of economics kept arguing over the issue for years as to which one should be attached more importance, planning or commodity economy.

On February 6th, 1987, Deng Xiaoping said that planned economy should not be put in the first place any more while talking with Wan Li and other Central Committee members. About eight months later, the Party declared at its 13th National Congress that socialist planned commodity economy should be an economic system that integrates planning with the market. Besides, it also came up with the formula of "the market being regulated by the state; the enterprise being guided by market forces", clarifying the relationship between the state, market and enterprises with its emphasis on market. At the same time, we should also expand the role of guidance planning and narrow the scope of mandatory planning, shifting the focus from direct regulation to an indirect one. Direct regulation is regulation by planning, whereas indirect regulation refers to regulation by market forces. Therefore, changes in the role of planning and market can be seen very clearly from the evolution of our policy: the 12th National Congress came up with the policy of "planned economy in the main and regulation by market forces as the supplement"; the 13th National Congress of the CPC proposed that regulation by market forces should be on an equal footing with planned economy; afterwards, the party attached more and more importance to market economy/commodity economy.

Our policy was slightly changed in 1989. On June 9th, 1989, when Deng Xiaoping met cadres of Capital forces enforcing martial law at and above the level of army commander, he said, "we will continue to combine planned economy with market economy." Though open-minded, Deng XIaoping still held reservations about market issues given the domestic situation then. Therefore, when the talk was made public, it was reworded into "we will continue to combine planned economy with regulation by market forces", which was basically a retrogression to the previous policy of the 12th National Congress. And then, we continued to use it for several years. Though this version does not state explicitly which one is in the main and which one serves as the supplement, we can infer very easily that the focus has been shifted back to planned economy since it was defined as a socialist economic system whilst market was just said to be a means of regulating economic activities.

As this policy failed to point out which one is primary and which one is secondary, the academic world of economics kept arguing over it even in 1990 and 1991. Due to differences in theoretical backgrounds, they held different views in the orientation of economic restructuring: some insisted on the orientation of planning while some advocated market-oriented reform.

With regard to the work of Central Committee, there was once a time when the government was too decentralized. Therefore, in its third meeting, the 7th Central Committee proposed to retake some power, expand the role of guidance planning, narrow the scope of mandatory planning and to reduce the role of market in economic regulation. Actually, by then we had already begun to use administrative orders as the major means of economic management, with market just playing a minor role. At the second half of 1990, things changed again. From then on, we began to intensify the reform and increase the weight of market in regulating economic activities in order to straighten out the economy.

In December 1990, Jiang Zemin, then General Secretary of the CPC Central Committee, delivered Deng Xiaoping's message in the Seventh Plenary Session of the 13th Central Committee of the CPC, that is, we should neither associate the issue of planning and market with social system nor believe that planning is exclusive to socialism nor that market is the monopoly of capitalism. Yang Shangkun, then Chinese President (1988-1993), reiterated it at an enlarged meeting of the Military Commission of the Central Committee of the CPC. When the Eighth Five-Year Plan was discussed at the Fourth Meeting of the 7th Central Committee of the CPC in 1991, the central committee clarified the policy concerning the three means of economic management. It reiterated that we should narrow the scope of mandatory planning, expand guidance planning and increase the role of market forces in economic regulation, which marks a significant change in policy. Afterwards, economic theoreticians tended not to associate planning and market with social system, and thus abandoned the previous belief that planning was exclusive to socialism and market was the monopoly of capitalism. Rather, planning and market were viewed as different means of regulating resource allocation.

In early 1992, Mr. Deng Xiaoping pointed out in his South China Tour talks that neither planning nor market is the criterion of telling one social system from another. "A planned economy is not equivalent to socialism, because there is planning under capitalism too; a market economy is not capitalism, because there are markets under socialism too," he remarked. Until then, people have reached somewhat consensus and brought the debate on the relationship between planning and market to an end after several rounds of discussions and arguments.

2. How was "the establishment of a socialist market economy" proposed?

It was my great honor that I ever participated in the drafting of the 14th National Congress report. After Deng Xiaoping made his South China Tour talks, the drafting panel collected various opinions on the target for economic restructuring. On June 9th, 1992, Jiang Zemin talked about three types of target for economic restructuring while delivering a speech in the Party School of the Central Committee of the CPC. The first one is to "establish a socialist commodity economy characterized by combination between planning and market"; the second one is to "establish a socialist planned market economy"; the third target is that we should "establish a socialist market economy".

Jiang Zemin made it very clear in and even before the speech that he preferred to the third one. We agreed on this version but also warned that in that case, "planning", which is equally important, tended to be neglected. In response to this, Jiang Zemin explained explicitly, "A planned commodity economy is equivalent to a planned market economy. Socialist economy had planning since its establishment, and everybody knows it perfectly well. Therefore, one should not infer from the missing of the word 'planned' that planning would be aborted." He made the same remark in the speech delivered in the Party School of the Central Committee of the CPC. I believe that he is very correct in saying that.

And for decades, people did think that "planning" is an intrinsic nature of socialism, just like what Jiang said. It is problematic to use the term "marketization" to define the orientation of our reform, as the socialist market economy we are to establish is not a general one, but a socialist one very rich in meaning, including the meaning of "planning" that Jiang Zemin explained earlier. But later some people, including some economists, theoreticians and even those from financial circles reduced "planning" to a taboo subject, insisting that it should be barred from talking.

I always hold that we should adhere to the market-oriented reform and avoid any blind faith in market, which has both positive and negative effects; in the meantime, we should also bring the role of planning into full play and avoid any blind faith in planning, which has a lot of flaws, too.

The 14th National Congress report stated officially that our economic restructuring aimed to establish a socialist market economy and that state planning is one of the important means of macroeconomic regulation, and therefore we must reinforce and improve macroeconomic regulation by the state. Since the reform and opening-up, we have achieved a gradual transition from planned economy to market economy, which has boosted China's economic growth vigorously. Several years ago, it was estimated that 70% of China's economy has been marketized, which means that socialist market economy had been initially established till then.

However, three decades later, inherent flaws of market economy have gradually come to the surface despite its strength in stimulating competition and optimizing resource allocation. For example, something has gone wrong with the balance between aggregate demand and aggregate supply, conservation of resources, environmental protection, and social equity. All these problems have something to do with the failure of macroeconomic regulation keeping up with the process of marketization, which surely cannot be solved by market economy alone.

We had planned to establish a socialist market economy subject to state macroeconomic regulation. All these years, China has kept improving state macroeconomic regulation. We have managed to control inflation and deflation successively while striving to mitigate short-term economic fluctuations. However, the guidance of state planning for short-term and long–term macroeconomic development has drastically declined, which has affected the effectiveness of macroeconomic management and thus led to many imbalances in the national development.

In response to that, the party proposed in the 17th National Congress of the CPC that we should "give play to the guiding role of national development plans, programs and industrial policies in macroeconomic regulation", which has great significance for straightening out the relationship between market and planning. It is very necessary for China, a great socialist power, to use planning as a means of macroeconomic regulation. Planning is the core of macroeconomic regulation; programs and industrial policies are also another form of planning.

By putting emphasis on the guiding role of state planning, we do not mean to resume the traditional planned economy, but to combine planning with market on a higher level instead, which can be manifested in the following aspects. First, the current state planning is not inclusive, but instead it only attends to the macroeconomic activities, whereas the micro-economic activities are assigned to the market. Second, market is the current basic means of regulating resource allocation, whilst planning is the necessary means to remedy the defects of the market. Third, the current plans do not mainly refer to administrative orders any more, but include guiding, strategic and predictive plans instead. And at the same time, these plans must serve as a guide and commit entities to complete tasks and take responsibility when necessary.

3. On the establishment of the basic economic system of socialism in the 15th National Congress

The 15th National Congress of the CPC was held in 1997 at the critical turn of the century, when the country was aiming to achieve the objective for the third step of its strategic plan. During this period, we were required to complete two tasks set for the first decade of the 21st century, namely, to establish a relatively complete socialist market economy and to maintain sustained, rapid and sound development of the national economy. In order to establish a relatively complete socialist market economy, we need establish the basic economic system of socialism at first.

When the 15th National Congress of the CPC officially proposed that we should uphold the basic socialist economic system in which public ownership is the mainstay and other kinds of ownership develop side by side, some people worried that the decline in the proportion of the state sector of the economy would threaten the status of public ownership as the mainstay of the economy and the leading role of the state sector. Given these circumstances, Jiang Zemin suggested that we have a thorough understanding of the significance of the public sector of the economy. He said that the public sector of the economy includes not only the state sector and the collective sector, but also state- and collectively-owned portions of mixed-ownership enterprises.

He also added that public ownership as the mainstay of the economy manifests itself as follows: First, it is reflected in the predominance of public assets; second, the state sector controls the lifeblood of the national economy and plays a leading role in the economic development. So long as we maintain the dominant role of public ownership, ensure state control on the lifeline of the national economy, and manage to enhance the predominance and competitiveness of the state sector, the nature of socialism would remain unchanged regardless of the decline in the proportion of the state sector. Jiang Zemin's words did remove people's doubts, because the state sector was then rather strong and extensive, which wouldn't be affected by some slight economic contraction. Besides, given the fact that we are still in the primary stage of socialism, we need also make room for the development of the non-public sector.

Besides, people were also very concerned about the forms of public ownership. At that time, joint stock system and joint stock cooperative system had already begun to gain momentum. It was widely feared by the people including theoreticians that the introduction of joint stock system and joint stock cooperative system might lead to privatization and even capitalism. In response to that, the 15th National Congress report elaborated on the forms of public ownership to clarify joint stock system and joint stock cooperative system.

Jiang Zemin pointed out in the report, "Joint stock system is a way of organizing capital in modern enterprises rather than be associated with any social system", "which can be used under both capitalism and socialism", and that "we cannot make a blanket statement that all joint stock enterprises are either public or private, for what really matters is which sector holds controlling shares. If the state or a collective holds a controlling number of the shares, it is clearly a form of public ownership, conducive to expanding the area controlled by public capital and enhancing the dominant role of public ownership." Jiang Zemin has made a very good point. Isn't it good if we draw in more investment from social and private capital to contribute to the state sector of the economy?

While drafting the 15th National Congress report, we had discussed the nature of joint stock cooperative system for rather long before it was finally defined as an organizational form of enterprises that pools labor and capital of workers as well as a form of collective ownership. At that time joint stock cooperative system was also met with some opposition due to a hotchpotch of loose definitions. It was wrong to think that the introduction of joint stock cooperative system is to promote privatization and capitalism, which however has been corrected by the 15th National Congress of the CPC. It stated very clearly that under socialism we can surely develop the collective sector of the economy to pool labor and capital of workers. Workers also hold shares of the enterprises, and therefore people won't worry about these enterprises being privatized.

The joint stock cooperative system is quite similar to the previous advanced agricultural production cooperatives, which also pooled labor and capital of workers, but the idea of "joint stock" hadn't emerged then yet. As for the joint stock cooperative system, as a form of collective ownership, it not only applies to rural areas, but to township enterprises and small SOEs as well. It was then a very promising way to achieve public ownership. At that time, I supported it and believed that it would be practiced for at least 20 years. But it should be noted that the pooling of worker's labor and capital here is very different from share-holding companies owned by capitalists, because in the latter, capitalists hire labor to work for them, which constitutes private ownership rather than public ownership.

Now, 10 years have passed since the convening of the 15th National Congress of the CPC. The decline in the proportion of the public sector and that in the private sector is an inevitable tendency. In the primary stage of socialism, public ownership should be the mainstay and different sectors of the economy develop side by side. It is inevitable that the the private sector, starting from almost zero, will increase dramatically whereas the public sector and the state sector relatively slowly. As a result, the proportion of the private sector would rise and that of the public sector and state sector decline. However, anything should be controlled within a certain bound, just like what Jiang Zemin pointed out, "Surely, there should be a limit or precondition for the decline in the public sector, that is, public ownership must be the mainstay of the economy and the state sector must play a leading role." The joint stock system was not the monopoly of private ownership. It will still be a form of public ownership as long as the state holds controlling shares. However, if state shares are reduced beyond that limit, the enterprises would be in jeopardy because it will be nothing different from these enterprises being privatized.

As for the forms of public ownership, the 15th National Congress report has specifically mentioned two, namely, joint stock system and joint stock cooperative system, which are both necessary means to achieve public ownership. However, I'm afraid that we shouldn't just have these two ways. The joint stock system is very important but not necessarily the most important of all. As for joint stock cooperative system, it was originally designed to pool labor and capital of workers who hold equal shares. But if individual operators own the lion's share, the enterprise will be owned by these operators and thus the nature of the joint stock cooperative system will be totally changed. Actually, we still have many other ways to achieve public ownership, such as community ownership, mass organization collective ownership, funds, and especially public offer funds which include pensions etc.

(This is the summary of the interview of Liu Guoguang by the editor of *Literature of Chinese Communist* Party, which was published in *Literature of Chinese Communist* Party, 2009, No. 1)

The Evolving Relationship between Planning and Market over 30 years

—From the perspective of my personal experiences

1. Exploration of the relationship between planning and market inspired by "emancipation of the mind" campaigns

In the Third Plenary Session of the 11th Central Committee of the CPC, Deng

Xiaoping put forward the ideological line of "emancipating the mind and seeking truth from facts", freeing economic theoreticians from dogmatic chains. Since then, how to act according to objective economic laws under socialist conditions has become the focus of discussions among theoretical circles of economics.

Inspired by the spirit of the Third Plenary Session of the 11th Central Committee, Zhao Renwei, researcher from the Institute of Economics in Chinese Academy of Social Sciences, and I began to study this issue from the end of 1978 to the early 1979, and later co-wrote an article entitled "on the relationship between planning and market in the socialistic economy", which was later submitted to the symposium on "commodity economy and the law of value" co-chaired by Xue Muqiao and Sun Yefang in April 1979 in the name of the Chinese Academy of Social Sciences.

Having broken with the traditional idea that planning and market, which are mutually exclusive, cannot be combined in the socialist economy, this article argued in depth that planning and market in socialist economy are neither mutually exclusive nor being combined just for expediency, but instead they were integrated with each other, which was determined by the nature of socialist economy. In order to coordinate the economic development of all sectors and regions, to safeguard public interests of the whole society and to deal with material relations correctly, we must make good use of market under planned economy, and strengthen the role of state planning in economic regulation in the meanwhile.

Having touched upon core issues of China's economic reform, this article then attracted great attention from both home and abroad and thus gave rise to widespread discussions. Hu Yaobang, then General Secretary of the Central Committee of the CPC, commented after he read this article from *"Drafts"* issued by Chinese Academy of Social Sciences, "This original article aiming to study new problems has set good examples for other theoretical researchers. In theoretical studies, we must strongly encourage such spirit before most theoretical researchers haven't been determined enough to study these new problems." And then, this full article was published in restricted periodicals of Party School of the Central Committee of the CPC, State Development Planning Commission (SDPC) and Chinese Academy of Social Sciences (CASS) as well as key domestic newspapers.

Besides, the International Atlantic Economic Association (IAES) contacted Hu Qiaomu, then President of Chinese Academy of Social Sciences, and asked him to deliver the message to us that we are welcome to submit the revised version of this article to its annual meeting. Later, Helmont Shuster, then executive President of IAES told Hu Qiaomu in the telegram that this article has "won great applause" in the annual meeting and that it is believed to "have great significance in the academic research". He also said that they have decided to publish the full article of this paper along with the one by James Edward Meade, the Nobel laureate, in the *Atlantic Economic Journal*, December, 1979 (as for other articles in the annual meeting, they are only allowed to publish their abstracts).

Despite its great impact at that time, this article still has its own limitations due to historical conditions—it is still within the framework of planned economy that we suggested planning and market can and must be combined. After the article was published, Deng Xiaoping remarked, while meeting Frank, B. Gibney, the vice-chairman of the Compilation Committee of Encyclopedia Britannica, Inc. of the United States, "Why can't we develop a market economy under socialism? While maintaining a planned economy as the mainstay of our economic system, we are also introducing a market economy, but it is a socialist market economy." Deng Xiaoping is the first leader of the Central Committee that ever put forward the concept of market economy. His such remarks were not made public until around 1990. As a matter of fact, he still believed that we should "focus on planned economy" while making these remarks. Later, even in the Third Plenary Session of the 12th Central Committee of the CPC in 1984, when the party issued an epoch-making statement that "socialist economy is a planned commodity economy", it was still added that "the planned commodity economy", "generally speaking", is "a planned economy that China has been practicing". In this sense, we still had a long way to go before the transition from a traditional theoretical framework of "planned economy" to a new one, i.e., the system of socialist market economy.

Nevertheless, we had already abandoned the traditional idea that planning and market are mutually exclusive and incompatible at that time. This key step has ushered in a transition from traditional planned economy to socialist market economy, which constitutes a significant victory of our party in "emancipation of the mind" campaigns under the leadership of Deng Xiaoping.

2. The narrowing of mandatory planning and expansion of guidance planning, i.e., the narrowing of management through administrative orders and expansion of management through economic means, which is how we initially carried out the economic reform.

Since then, it has been widely accepted that planned economy and regulation by market forces can be combined, which was clarified in official documents of both the Sixth Plenary Session of the 11th Central Committee of the CPC and the 12th National Congress of the CPC. However, we need to know how to combine them to manage the economy, i.e., how to apply the law of value to planned economy. We began to use less administrative orders and more economic means to manage our economy, which is how we initially carried out the economic reform.

To solve this issue, we need study how our national economy is managed. In the past, we used to adopt mandatory planning as a means of economic management. Even though Chen Yun has long since put forward "three mains and three supplements", which was progressive and correct, it was then hard to achieve under the erosive influence of "leftist" thoughts. In order to find better ways to achieve a combination between planning and market in the socialist economy, we need to study the means of economic management at first. In early September, 1982, I was asked by People's Daily, an official newspaper of the CPC, to write an article entitled "the Orientation of the Economic Restructuring", in which I proposed that we should adopt three different ways of economic management while dealing with the relationship between planning and market in socialist economy.

We should apply mandatory planning to production and allocation of major products concerning the overall economic situation; we should apply guidance planning to production and sale of general products; we must guarantee free production and sale of various daily-use goods, small wares and other subsidiary agricultural products while carrying out regulation by market forces. Besides, I also suggested that we should gradually narrow the scope of mandatory planning and expand the role of guidance planning, since the buyer's market has gradually formed, the price has been rationalized and some progress has been made with economic adjustment. I even proposed that guidance planning is a means of economic regulation, in which regulation by planning is achieved through regulation by market forces. I also added that we must study the mechanism of guidance planning while preserving and improving on the three economic management forms. It constitutes one of the toughest issues concerning the relationship between planning and market in the socialist economy as well as an issue crucial for the right direction of economic reform, which therefore must be solved.

This article was submitted to the "People's Daily" before the 12th National Congress and happened to be published during the 12th National Congress. Because my suggestion that we should narrow the scope of mandatory planning gradually in the ensuing reform is inconsistent with the spirit of the 12th National Congress report concerning the role of mandatory planning, i.e., "mandatory planning, indispensable to major fields or key sectors, ensures the fulfillment of plans concerning people's livelihood", some expert from the drafting panel of the 12th National Congress documents, who believed that I've already betrayed the principle of planned economy, published a long article in the name of "commentator" in an authoritative newspaper to level criticism against me. The article said, "Mandatory planning is the primary and basic form of planned economy", "only if we apply mandatory planning to key products and enterprises could our economy be a real planned economy."

At that time, I did not know that on September 7th, 1982, Hu Qiaomu ever wrote to leaders of People's Daily to remind them that it is imprudent to publish such an article. At the close of the 12th National Congress of the CPC, I came across Hu Qiaomu when I was stepping out of the Great Hall of the People. He said to me, "If you disagree with the Central Committee on certain issues, you can report directly to them. But you shouldn't make these ideas published in the newspaper, which will have a bad impact, so you should make a self-criticism." Later, I did make a self-criticism in the Party organization of CASS, admitting that I failed to be consistent with the Central Committee of the Party, but I didn't say that my views were wrong.

China's reform kept moving forward. In the early and mid-1980s, in general, market tended to carry more weight in the economic regulation; as for regulation by planning, the role of guidance planning was inclined to increase whilst that of mandatory planning decline in economic regulation. Two years later, I was proved to be right by the Party's decisions at the Third Plenary Session of the 12th CPC Central Committee in 1984, which proposed that our socialist economy is a planned commodity economy based on public ownership. It also pointed out that to practice a planned economy does not mean to focus on mandatory planning, because guidance planning is also a means of economic management. Besides, it also suggested that we should take steps to narrow the scope of mandatory planning and expand the role of guidance planning appropriately.

Those who used to criticize me began to accept my ideas, too. It also proves that the improvement of understanding needs some time, and nobody can be always right. I guess almost everyone has ever had such experience. Take me as an example. I used to maintain that we should focus on planned economy; I also expressed reservations about the conception of "socialist economy as a planned commodity economy" before the third Plenary Session of the 12th Central Committee of the CPC. In 1982 I ever proposed, "in the first place, socialist economy should be defined as a planned economy, and properties of commodity economy are secondary to it". My previous suggestion that it might be better to term socialist economy "a planned economy with properties of commodity economy" did reflect my limitations of understanding at that time.

3. Which is more important, planning or market?

We should carry out a market-oriented reform but avoid any blind faith in market; we should persist with macroeconomic regulation by planning but avoid any blind faith in planning. From the Third Plenary Session of the 12th Central Committee of the CPC in 1984, when socialist economy was defined as a planned commodity economy, to the 14th National Congress of the CPC in 1992, when it was proposed to establish a socialist market economy, our understanding of the relationship between planning and market has undergone a significant change.

At its third Plenary Session, the 12th Central Committee proposed to define socialist economy as a planned commodity economy. However, as for which one should be attached more importance, commodity economy or planned economy, theoretical circles were quite divided and the debate had lasted for many years. Some people argued that planned economy still remained the essential characteristic of socialism whilst commodity economy was just an adjunct to it. Some people held that commodity economy should be the essential feature of socialism and that planned economy, which is not a feature, shouldn't thereby be viewed as a socialist feature at all. To sum up, some focused on planning, some market. Different understandings of the concept of planned commodity economy would surely lead to different policies.

On February 6th, 1987, eight months before the 13th National Congress of the CPC, Deng Xiaoping suggested while talking with some Central Committee leaders, "we shouldn't lay one-sided emphasis on planned economy any more". As a result, the 13th National Congress did not say which aspect we should attach more importance to, but stated, "the socialist planned commodity economy should be a system that integrates planning with the market". Besides, it also came up with the formula of "the market being regulated by the state; the enterprise being guided by market forces", with more emphasis laid on market in the triad of state, enterprise and market. It also suggested that we should shift the focus of macroeconomic regulation from direct means to indirect means.

To sum up, from the 12th National Congress to the 13th National Congress, the relationship between planning and market has evolved from "planned economy in the main and regulation by market forces as the supplement" to planning and market being on the equal footing. Afterwards, the balance was even more inclined toward commodity/market economy.

Things began to change since 1989. Given the political and economic situations at that time, Deng Xiaoping suggested that we would rather "continue to combine planned economy with regulation by market forces," which was actually a return to the policy of the 12th National Congress. From then on, we continued to use this policy till the 14th National Congress in 1992. Accordingly, we began to count more on administrative power of the Central Committee to manage the economy during that period of time, and the share of market in economic regulation had somewhat declined.

However, as the policy of "combining planned economy with regulation by market forces" did not state clearly in theory which one, planning or market, is in the main and which one serves as the supplement, the debate concerning this issue was still going on in theoretical circles in 1990 and 1991. Besides, they were also divided on the orientation of the reform. Some people embraced market-oriented reform, whereas some opposed it. The latter justified themselves by UN classification of countries. According to UN standard, centrally planned economies are considered as socialist countries and market economies as capitalist countries.

In the Seventh Plenary Session of the 13th Central Committee of the CPC in December 1990, it was revealed that Deng Xiaoping advised us not to associate planning or market with social system; In the fourth meeting of the 7th National People's Congress in 1991, the party proposed again that we should narrow the scope of mandatory planning, expand that of guidance planning, and make better use of the market mechanism.

With these subtle changes in the political climate, the debate in the academic world of economics also underwent some changes. For instance, people tended not to associate planning or market with social system any more, but began to consider them as means of regulating resource allocation. More and more people were later convinced, especially since Deng Xiaoping made the famous south China tour talks in 1992, in which he stated clearly that rather than the dividing line between socialism and capitalism, planning and market, as means of regulating economic activities, can be used both under socialism and capitalism.

Such a long debate has revealed two severe complexes concerning the relations between planning and market in theoretical circles, namely, planned economy complex and market economy complex. They both laid extreme emphasis on one side and never denied the existence of the other, and therefore people kept arguing about the issue as to which one is in the main and which one serves as the supplement.

As a matter of fact, both planning and market, as means of regulating resource allocation, have their own merits and demerits respectively. By combining planning and market in the socialist economy, we mean to bring their advantages into full play and make up for the deficiency of each other as far as possible.

In this spirit, I tried to find a way in the middle to overcome these complexes at the final stage of debate, which can be seen from several speeches or reports I ever made, such as a speech in a symposium hosted by *Qiushi* (seeking truth) Journal, an official journal of the Central Committee of the CPC, in May 1990, a speech at the second congress of "National Planning Society" in May 1995, and an academic report in the Party School of the Central Committee of the CPC in October 1991.

In order to overcome these two complexes, I proposed to persist with two things and banish two blind faiths. One of them is that we should persist with the market-oriented reform but avoid blind faith in market; the other is that we should persist with regulation by planning but avoid any blind faith in planning. To put it simply, the advantages of planning lie in its capacity of gathering necessary financial, human and material resources together in the whole society to accomplish major tasks, adjusting incomes and ensuring social equity. The strength of market lies in its capacity of promoting technical and management progress through competition to link production with demand. However, neither planning nor market is all-powerful.

Five major tasks cannot be assigned totally to the market or the the law of value alone. They are as follows: to maintain a balance between aggregate demand and aggregate supply, to make timely adjustments to major economic structures, to fight against monopoly resulting from competition, to protect ecological environment and to ensure social equity. In order to solve these issues, the state needs to intervene through state planning in the macroeconomic regulation. But plans are made by man, who will inevitably have their own limitations and thus many difficulties in overcoming some contradictions. Take the pair of contradiction between subjectivity and objectivity, a major problem in planning, as an example. First, subjective perception of things falls behind the objective development of things; second, man often have information asymmetries and limitations in collecting, transmitting and processing information and data; third, planners' observation and judgment are often influenced by social forces and interests.

All in all, owing to these limitations, planning might deviate from real situations or objective laws, leading to serious mistakes in macroeconomic management. Therefore, we need to keep improving our understanding and political awareness to adjust planning to the requirement of objective laws and real situations.

To summarize, we need persist with the market-oriented reform but avoid any blind faith in market; we need persist with macroeconomic regulation by planning but avoid any blind faith in planning. All these ideas I came up with during the period from 1990 to 1991 are in line with Deng Xiaoping's spirit concerning the relations of planning with market. Besides, they have overcome negative effects of these two complexes and thus complied with the spirit of the 14th National Congress, i.e., to establish socialist market economy subject to macroeconomic regulation.

4. "Socialist market economy", the final wording of socialist economy in the 14th National Congress. Here, the modifier "planned" is just deleted for the sake of brevity rather than removed in a real sense.

In order to establish a new system of socialist market economy, we are required to attach more importance to market and let it serve as the basic means of regulating resource allocation, so that planning and market, as both means of regulating resource allocation, can be combined in a better way. Modern market economy shouldn't oppose any economic interventions by the government or guidance from planning; rather, it must rely on them to make up for its own deficiency. The modifier "planned" (before "market economy") is just deleted for the sake of brevity rather than removed in a real sense.

In October 1992, the 14th National Congress of the CPC stated clearly that the objective of our economic restructuring is to establish a socialist market economy, which marks a great milestone in the evolution of the relationship between planning and market. It is my great honor that I participated in the drafting of the 14th National Congress document. During the nationwide campaign of studying Deng Xiaoping's South China tour talks, some new ideas concerning the relationship between planning and market and the establishment of new economic system were put forward. The drafting panel boiled these ideas down to three versions in terms of reform target: to establish a socialist commodity economy characterized by combination between planning and market, to establish a socialist planned market economy, and to establish a socialist market economy. This is exactly what Jiang Zemin ever said in the speech delivered in the Party School of the Central Committee of the CPC on 9th June, 1992.

As to these three versions, Jiang Zemin ever consulted with me before the speech in the Party School. He favored personally the version of "establishing a socialist market economy" and asked me for some advice. I approved of this version for it is brief and to the point. Besides, I also suggested that if we leave the word "planned" out, which is however of great significance for the socialist economy, "planning" would probably be neglected by people. In response to my suggestion, he said, "A planned commodity economy is equivalent to a planned market economy. Socialist economy had planning since its establishment, and everybody knows it perfectly well. Therefore, one should not infer from the missing of the word 'planned' that planning would be aborted." He also made the same remark later in a speech delivered in the Party School of the CPC. I think that he had made a good point and is therefore absolutely right. For decades, people did interpret it this way, that is, "planning" is an intrinsic nature of socialism.

By proposing to establish a socialist market economy in the 14th National congress, the Central Committee meant to let market, subject to state macroeconomic regulation, serve as the basic means of regulating resource allocation. Means of state macroeconomic regulation includes not only monetary and fiscal policies such as taxation, but also state planning. The 14th National Congress report stated clearly, "state planning is one of the important means of macroeconomic regulation". Besides, monetary and fiscal policies cannot function without the guidance of state macroeconomic planning. Macroeconomic regulation refers to regulation by state planning in a broad sense. The socialist market economy we aim to establish is neither a capitalist market economy nor a market economy in general, but a socialist one. Socialism is rich in meaning, including public ownership as the mainstay, common prosperity and "planning". Therefore, it is 100% right to define our socialist market economy as a planned market economy.

On September 19th, 1992, in order to make cadres better informed of the reform target, i.e., to establish a socialist market economy, before the 14th National Congress, several departments of the Central Committee jointly held a conference and a series of lectures, which was kicked off by my speech entitled "on several issues concerning the theory of socialist market economy". In that speech, I reviewed the tortuous evolution of people's conception of planning and market and elaborated on several focal issues. I said that in order to establish a socialist market economy, we are required to attach more importance to market and make it serve as the basic means of regulating resource allocation.

I also added, "On the basis of this, we should combine planning with market, both as means of regulating economic activities, in a more effective way. In terms of resource allocation, whenever market is capable of achieving the end, they should be given a free rein; in contrast, as for whatever issue is beyond market's reach, we should count on the government to solve it through policies and planning. Modern market economy shouldn't oppose any economic interventions by the government or guidance from planning; rather, it must rely on them to make up for its own deficiency. We should always keep this in mind during the transition of planned economy to market economy." I responded my way to the warning that we shouldn't forget that "socialism also has planning" at the critical moment of our transition to market economy.

5. The 17th National Congress of the CPC reiterated the guiding role of state planning in the macroeconomic regulation

Transition from planned economy to market economy and then to a reemphasis on the guiding role of state planning in the macroeconomic regulation is in accordance with "thesis-antithesis-synthesis" dialectics. This is not a retrogression to the previous traditional planned economy, but a higher-level combination of planning with market in the new phase of reform.

Over the past three decades, our economy has witnessed a gradual change from traditional planned economy to socialist market economy and an increasing share of market in economic regulation, which has vigorously boosted china's economy. In the circulation of all commodities, over 90% is regulated by market forces. Several years ago, it was estimated that 70% of China's economy has been marketized. In this sense, we can say that socialist market economy has been initially established. Surely, market economy has not developed enough in some aspects, such as the resource factor market, capital and financial market, etc., which still need further improvement.

However, due to lack of experience and "market infantilism", over-marketization occurred in some fields such as education, medical care and housing etc., where marketization was not supposed to occur at all. In these fields, market was so worshipped that many unnecessary bad consequences were brought about and people suffered a lot from it. Despite its superiority in encouraging competition and optimizing resource allocation, flaws inherent in the market economy and especially its negative effects on the equilibrium between aggregate supply and aggregate demand, environmental protection, resource conservation and social equity have been fully exposed three decades later.

To sum up, our economy has made unprecedented progress on the one hand; but on the other, some new social and economic problems also emerged and piled up in some aspects, such as resource and environmental protection, income distribution and people's livelihood etc. This has a lot to do with the failure of state macroeconomic planning to keep up with the process of marketization.

As aforementioned, the market economy we aim to establish is the one subject to macroeconomic regulation, just like what the 14th National Congress of the CPC proposed. Over these years, China has been trying to improve macroeconomic regulation and has thus made a lot of progress. Especially since the 14th National Congress, we have succeeded in putting inflation and deflation under control successively while implementing the short-term macroeconomic regulation. However, the guidance of state planning for both short- and long-term macroeconomic regulation has drastically declined. Plans involve mostly compilation of polices but seldom any tasks with accountability or binding quotas; local plans are divorced from central plans, with the latter unable to control the former's "GDP-Complex" (i.e., blind pursuit of GDP growth); a huge mismatch exists between plans and real work. All these facts have affected the effectiveness of macroeconomic management and thus resulted in many imbalances in social and economic development.

Given the circumstances, the 17th National Congress restated, "We will give play to the guiding role of national development plans, programs and industrial policies in macroeconomic regulation and combine the use of fiscal and monetary policies to improve macroeconomic regulation." In my point of view, it is highly purposeful for the Central Committee to reaffirm the guiding role of state planning, which has been overlooked for many years, in the 17th National Congress. It reminded us again that socialist market should have "planning".

As mentioned before, there are three major means of macroeconomic regulation—planning, fiscal and monetary policies. As industrial policy is also a means of planning and the program is also a type of plan, they both fall into the category of planning. That's why we get three major means in total. In the triad, fiscal and monetary policies should be guided by state planning. In this sense, macroeconomic regulation is inseparable from state planning and it can be said that the latter is the backbone of the former.

With both strong and weak points of the market fully exposed after the initial establishment of market economy, it is very necessary to reaffirm the important role of state macroeconomic planning while developing a socialist market economy, especially when people worship the market so much that planning has almost been dismissed as a taboo subject under the slogan of "marketization reform". For instance, it is very necessary to reemphasize the guiding role of state planning subject to macroeconomic regulation in the 17th National Congress of the CPC. Rather than "a retrogression to the traditional planned economy" as some people distorted, it is a higher-level combination of planning with market in a more advanced stage of reform.

Given the inadequate attention to this major issue in most propaganda articles calling on the people to study the 17th National Congress report, I wrote an article entitled "my understanding of some economic issues in the 17th National Congress report", in which the first point I made was "the significance of reemphasizing the guiding role of state planning in the macroeconomic regulation". Recently I wrote another article titled "A Marxist philosophical approach to sum up China's reform and opening-up over the three decades", pointing out that transition from planned economy to market economy and then to a re-emphasis on the guiding role of state planning in macroeconomic regulation is in accordance with the "thesis-antithesis-synthesis" dialectics. This is not a retrogression to the previous traditional planned economy, but a higher-level combination of planning with market in the new phase of reform.

It is not groundless for me to say so. The re-emphasis on the guiding role of state planning in macroeconomic regulation is different from the "traditional planned economy" in the following ways. First, the current state planning is not inclusive, but instead it only attends to the macroeconomic activities, whereas the micro-economic activities are assigned to the market. Second, market is the current basic means of regulating resource allocation, whilst planning is the necessary means to remedy the defects of the market. Third, the current plans do not mainly refer to administrative orders any more, but include guiding, strategic and predictive plans instead. And at the same time, these plans must serve as a guide and commit entities to complete tasks and take responsibilities when necessary.

Macroeconomic regulation under the guidance of state planning is what socialist market economy with Chinese characteristics must have and achieve. And therefore "planning" should not be excluded from the meaning of socialist market economy. In this spirit, we should try to improve state planning and macroeconomic regulation to make them serve as a guide for the development of socialist market economy in a real sense and thus to achieve a higher-level combination of planning with market.

(This article was published in *"social sciences weekly",* Oct 16, 2008)

Planning and Market in China over the past Six Decades since the Founding of PRC

—China's Exploration and Establishment of the Operational Mechanism of Socialist Economy with Chinese Characteristics

Over the six decades, our long-term economic exploration has been centering on the basic issue of planning and market since the founding of the PRC. In this long process, we have been working on issues as to how to establish socialism, what model we should follow and what system we should build in China while moving toward the goal. We have to make such exploration under such historical conditions, which is the result of combined influence of objective conditions, requirements and perceptions.

1. Transition from the new-democratic economy to the socialist planned economy

In the backward, semi-colonial and semi-feudal old China, the economic lifeblood and major means of production were controlled by foreign capitalists, feudal landlords and bureaucratic capitalists; at that time, the economy was composed of all forms of commodity-market economy based on private ownership, and natural economy widely practiced in the countryside. After the victory of New-democratic Revolution, bureaucratic capitalist enterprises used to be owned by Kuo Min Tang (KMT) government were confiscated and converted into state owned enterprises (SOEs); Western countries were deprived of all prerogatives in China; foreign-owned enterprises left by western countries on the Mainland China were gradually taken over by the state and finally transformed into SOEs through measures such as surveillance, purchase, expropriation and escrow. These two types of SOEs form the state sector of the economy, which together with cooperative sector of the economy, private capitalist economy, individual economy, and state capitalist economy, comprised the five sectors of the economy at that time.

The state sector of the economy is in essence a socialist economy based on the ownership by the whole people and run by the new-democratic country, representing the direction of the new-democratic economic development; the cooperative sector of the economy is in essence a semi-socialist economy as well as a collective economy owned by the people based on the individual ownership; private capitalist economy is in essence a private sector based on private ownership and owned by profit-seeking capitalists. Due to the special duality of private capitalist economy, our party placed restrictions on it while making use of it; individual economy refers to the scattered individually-owned agricultural and handicraft economy, accounting for over 80% of the overall national economy; state capitalist economy is the result of cooperation between state economy and private capital and thus carries some socialist elements, with the prospect of turning into a state sector of the socialist economy.

New-democratic economy cannot be skipped because it helps a rather backward China achieve socialization of production, the very foundation for socialist revolution. We must make the best of individual economy and private capitalist economy, and bring the regulatory role of commodity-market economy into play. Since it's founding in 1952, State Development Planning Commission (SDPC) had adopted various means of planning to manage the economy. However, it was still a market economy on the whole, given that five sectors of the economy developed side by side under the new-democratic economy. Nevertheless, such market economy had already developed some new features, and the system of market economy with a certain degree of regulation by planning was already formed.

Many sectors of the economy developed side by side coordinately, with the state sector of the socialist economy playing a leading role; market forces subject to state macro-control served as the basic means of regulating resource allocation; with the combination between market mechanism and many ways of planned management, the policy of "taking both pubic and private interests into account, benefiting both labor and capital, building an urban-rural partnership, promoting foreign exchanges and communications" was implemented. In this way, we can take the interests of all the parties concerned into consideration, exercise the initiatives of the vast number of farmers to develop individual economy and cooperate with one another, and make the private sector of the economy gain normal profits so as to maintain production and expand reproduction.

All these features constitute the basic characteristics of new-democratic economy in the early period of new China. Thanks to such socialist economic system in line with national conditions and solid theoretical foundations, the whole nation under the leadership of the party and the government has managed to balance the books, maintain a stable market and recover the production under extremely poor economic conditions. In the early period after the founding of the PRC, our society was prosperous and flourishing.

As our economy had basically recovered in the second half of 1952, the whole nation was to embark on a large-scale economic construction. Thereby, the Central Committee needed desperately to decide on what model China should adopt in its economic construction while discussing the formulation of the first Five-Year plan. After one and a half year's economic explorations in both practice and theory from July 1952 to the end of 1953, China unsurprisingly chose the Soviet model given the international situations and historical conditions. After its economic recovery, China was confronted with a pressing task of realizing industrialization with heavy industry lying at its core, which is the realistic motivation behind China's efforts to accelerate socialist transformation and to establish a planned economy with the state playing the leading role; in order to lay solid institutional foundations for industrialization, China must impose state monopoly on purchase and sale of products and accelerate agricultural co-operation.

As a result, our party made the policy of "one industrialization and three transformations" (transformation of agriculture, handcraft industry and capitalist industry and commerce) as the general guideline for the transitional period, and chose the model of socialist industrialization characterized by the First Five-Year Plan.

While we were achieving a transition from new-democratic market economy to socialist planned economy, carrying out socialist transformation, and establishing a socialist economic system, we did not eliminate commodity-money relations and thus avoided repeating the Soviet Union's mistakes in its first few years. Our party has made a lot of valuable explorations of the socialist ownership structure, the mechanism of economic regulation, and the market etc. Having sensed earlier that the economy under the Soviet model was too centralized, Mao Zedong put forward in his article *"Ten Major Relationships"* that a Chinese model of socialist construction should be established in line with its own national conditions.

Chen Yun proposed a model while delivering a speech in the 8th National Congress of the CPC. He suggested, "Our socialist economy would be like this: in terms of operation of the business, the industry and commerce should be mainly run by the state and the collective, but at the same time, a certain number of individual economy should be allowed to develop side by side and serve as the supplement. As for production, production of most agricultural produce and industrial products is based on plans, whilst some free production based on changes in supply and demand but subject to state planning is also allowed. That is to say, planned production is in the main, whilst free production based on changes in supply and demand but subject to state planning serves as the supplement. Therefore, our market is definitely not the capitalist free market, but a socialist unified market instead."[1] Highly praised by Mao Zedong, Chen Yun's model was accepted by the congress and some decisions were made accordingly, which can be seen from Chou En-Lai's report on the Second Five-Year plan adopted in the congress.

Thanks to the socialist transformation under the guidance of the general line for the transitional period, China has achieved in advance the transition from a market economy with a certain degree of regulation by planning to a socialist planned economy, having shortened the time span of the new-democratic society, which we had expected to be 15 years or even longer before its conversion into socialism. In general, it was basically in line with the historical trend of social development. Besides, we had to do so given the circumstances, which was the result of multiple factors.

However, in retrospect, such a major historical change in the economic system and especially the gradual transition to a centrally planned economy characterized

1 Chen Yun, *the Selected Works of Chen Yun*, vol.3, People's Publishing House, 1995, p.13.

by the unitary public sector of the economy and administrative orders revealed our ill preparations in theory for socialist construction, which thus led to a simple economic structure and great leaps forward characterized by impracticably high goals unsuitable for the real development of production forces. We have to admit that, for the political party of the proletariat in economically backward countries, it is hard to solve the problem as to "what socialism is and how to build socialism" (including how to understand and handle the relationship between planning and market) in a short period of time, and therefore, it is inevitable that we had made deviations and mistakes in the initial period of the major transformation. Anyhow, we do need to reflect on the past and draw lessons from it.

2. the establishment of socialist planned economy: achievements and limitations.

The Year of 1956 marked China's completion of transformation from a market economy with some regulation by state planning to a planned economy as well as the beginning of the period of "development of planned economy", which constitutes a major change in China's social development. In the autumn of 1955, Mao Zedong wrote in the *Editor's Notes from Socialist Upsurge in China's Countryside*, "Mankind have developed for hundreds of thousands of years, but here in China it is only today that conditions have been secured for the planned development of our economy and culture. Given these conditions, the face of our country will change from year to year." [1]

After the basic completion of socialist transformation, China embarked on a large scale-socialist construction in an all-round way. Over the decade in the socialist construction, we have brought into full play the strengths of socialist public ownership and planned economy in making overall arrangements and concentrating on accomplishing major tasks. Though rather weak in national strength at that time, China had managed to lay a preliminary foundation for

1 see *Manuscripts of Mao Zedong since the founding of the PRC*, vol.5, Beijing: Central Party Literature Press, 1991, p.503.

industrialization after having concentrated national resources to the maximum, and finally established an independent, complete industrial and economic structure in sharp contrast to a rather poor and backward China before the founding of the PRC. During this decade leading up to the "Cultural Revolution" (1966-1976), we have achieved a lot despite some severe setbacks.

Due to lack of experience in socialist construction, inadequate knowledge of our basic economic conditions and laws of economic development, as well as many local and central leaders' conceit after having won a revolutionary victory, we overestimated the role of man's will and efforts in disregard of objective economic laws, resulting in a rampancy of "leftist" thinking characterized by excessively high targets (due to a rush for quick results), arbitrary and impracticable instructions, the blow of boastful wind due to over-estimation of grain yield), and "the Communist wind" stirred up by share of the produce among production teams in communes.

Influenced by such "leftist" thinking, some people suggested abolishing commodities and currencies immediately and disregarding the law of value, with the result that enthusiasm of the vast number of peasants was severely dampened and the people and the whole country suffered a tremendous loss.

Having sensed the extreme "leftist" tendency during the "Great Leap Forward" and the "Movement of People's Commune", the Central Committee under the leadership of Mao Zedong ever held a series of meetings, trying to rectify this wrong tendency. Mao Zedong pointed out that the abolishment of commodities in the era of socialism goes against the economic law, and therefore we cannot evade these positive economic categories such as commodity and the law of value etc., but instead we should use them to serve socialism. China, then a rather underdeveloped country in terms of commodity production, should strive to promote it rather than eliminate it. He specially stressed that in order to unite hundreds of millions of peasants we must encourage commodity exchanges and that any abolishment of commerce or allocation of farm produce is to deprive peasants of their rights and property. He also noted that according to the objective law of value, we have to exchange social products at equal values rather than possess and use them without compensation.

In the winter of 1960, we began to adopt the policy of "adjustment, consolidation, enrichment and improvement" to manage the national economy. Besides, we also formulated and implemented a series of correct policies and decisive measures. Owing to these efforts, the market and free trade were once brought into full play. In order to loosen control on market and improve planning, State Development Planning Commission (SDPC) ever reintroduced a variety of ways to carry out planned management, which are as follows: First, mandatory planning, guidance planning and suggestive planning should be combined; second, planning for the collective sector should be distinguished from that for enterprises owned by the whole people, that is, direct planning should apply to enterprises owned by the whole people, whereas indirect planning should be adopted in the rural areas as well as the handicraft industry, where collective ownership is practiced; the government should only plan the purchase of farm produce for the People's Commune in the countryside, and make suggestive planning for production of grain, cotton and oil crops etc. As for supply, production and sale of handicrafts, state planning should just include that of major products vital to the national economy and people's livelihood; the rest should be delegated to local planning. As for supply, production and sale of petty goods made in handcraft workshops and native, subsidiary products made by farmers or People's Commune in the countryside, we should use supply and marketing agreements and village fair trade to promote commodity production, increase the circulation of commodities, and satisfy people's needs for production and consumption. All these should be achieved under the unified control of the commerce sector in conformity with the law of value.

Owing to such way of thinking and policy adjustments in the economic construction, our economy saw a gradual renewal of promise and prosperity. It was declared in the 3rd National Congress of the CPC, which opened at the end of 1964 and closed in early 1965, that since the task of adjusting the national economy was already basically completed, our national economy would enter a new phase of development, that is, we should build our country into a great socialist power equipped with modern agriculture, industry, national defense and science and technology.

However, soon afterwards, especially during the "Great Cultural Revolution", "leftist" thoughts and policies gained great momentum, so much so that our economic structure became very rigid and the form of planning was even more monotonous. Planned economy was considered as the essential characteristic of socialism, whereas market economy the monopoly of capitalism. So, during that period of time, people all deviated to the left in perceptions of both the relationship between socialism and commodity economy and that between planning and market.

Due to the party's "leftist" deviation in the guiding ideology since 1957, various correct measures to invigorate enterprises and develop socialist commodity economy were all dismissed as "capitalist" ones, so that the problem of excessive centralization with the economic structure cannot be solved for long within a certain historical period, and what is more, it has become even more complicated and got even worse. We must acknowledge that it is of profound significance for our country to develop a planned economy based on public ownership, which has laid a structural basis for our social development.

However, we should also notice that some deviations occurred inevitably in the early period of socialist construction. On the one hand, we were too eager to succeed. On the other, we blindly pursued a unitary public sector of the economy, neglecting the existence and development of other sectors. Besides, in terms of economic operational mechanism, we focused exclusively on planning and denied the role of commodity economy and regulation by market forces. As a result, something went seriously wrong with the guiding ideology and policies for economic construction.

Another noteworthy thing is that for the sake of socialist modernization drive, we should handle the relationship between planning and market properly and thereafter set up a reasonable and effective economic mechanism. To achieve that, we must keep enhancing our understanding and gaining wider experience, which will surely take time. In 1962 Mao Zedong ever said, "It takes time before we come to understand the law of socialist construction. We must value practice, gain more experience out of nothing and achieve a knowledge leap, moving from the realm of necessity to the realm of freedom and growing from knowing nothing of the socialist construction to finally freeing from chains by gradually overcoming blindness and understanding objective laws."[1] So, historical development requires us to make new explorations of the relationship between planning and market in both theory and practice by learning from previous practice.

3. Transition from a socialist planned economy to a socialist market economy

Having established the policy of reform and opening up in the 3rd Plenary Session of the 11th Central Committee of the CPC, China embarked on a historical structural reform, striving to achieve transition from a socialist planned economy to a socialist market economy. In a sense, it is a summing-up of the experience and valuable lessons from the first thirty years' explorations since the founding of the PRC, in which we have been fumbling for a socialist economic system in line with China's national conditions. At the very beginning of the new exploration, quite a few people mistook economic reform as a way of improving on the previous method of economic management. However, it was not long before they realized that the crux of the matter is the economic structure and mechanism, and thereby their understanding of the reform was heightened to a new level. People have since then realized that the reform should center on the issue as to how to deal with the relationship between planning and market. As a matter of fact, we need make further efforts to deal with the relationship between planning and market on a new starting line.

1 *The Collected Works of Mao Zedong*, vol. 8, Beijing: People's Publishing House, 1999, p.300.

A new historical reform is the sublation of planned economy, which can be manifested in the following two aspects: on the one hand, the already established economic structure and system is to be preserved for improvement; on the other, deviations and errors in such structure or system are to be corrected. Deng Xiaoping ever pointed out very clearly the importance and toughness of this issue. He said, "How should we handle the relationship between planning and market? If we handle it properly, it will greatly benefit economic development; if we don't, things will go bad." [1]How to understand and handle the relations between planning and market under socialist conditions has hereby become an issue vital to the overall situation in economic restructuring. So, our understanding of this issue was further deepened during the explorations.

In the *Resolution Clarifying Certain Questions in the History of the Party Since the Foundation of the People's Republic of China* adopted in the Sixth Plenary Session of the 11th Central Committee in 1981, it was established that commodity production and exchanges do exist in the socialist society but by then it hadn't come up with the term of "commodity economy" yet. At that time, commodity economy as a whole was still held exclusive to the capitalist society based on private ownership. Even in 1982 when the 12th National Congress of the CPC stated clearly the principle of "planned economy in the main and regulation by market forces as the supplement", it was still hard for the Central Committee to come up with the concept of "commodity economy". Although Deng Xiaoping ever said in November 1979 that "market economy can be developed under socialism" while meeting American delegations in China, it was then not made public. Therefore, the concepts of "commodity economy" and "market economy" were still considered as taboo subjects. It was Not until 1984, when *"The Decision on Economic Restructuring"* was adopted in the Third Plenary Session of the 12th Central Committee of the CPC, that the party put forward for the first time,

1 *the Selected Works of Deng Xiaoping*, volume 3, Beijing: People's Publishing House, 1993, p.17.

"Socialist economy is a planned commodity economy based on public ownership", which constitutes a great breakthrough in the theory of socialist economy.

Since then, people interpreted the concept of "planned commodity economy" differently, with some laying emphasis on "planned economy" whereas some "commodity economy". Before the 13th National Congress of the CPC in 1987, Deng Xiaoping suggested while talking with some Central Committee leaders, "we shouldn't lay one-sided emphasis on planned economy any more". Thereby, the 13th National Congress did not say which one is more important, but stated, "the socialist planned commodity economy should be a system that integrates planning with the market". Besides, it also came up with the formula of "the market being regulated by the state; the enterprise being guided by market forces".

To sum up, from the 12th National Congress to the 13th National Congress, the relationship between planning and market has evolved from "planned economy in the main and regulation by market forces as the supplement" to planning and market being on the equal footing. Afterwards, the balance was even more inclined toward commodity/market economy.

Our initial practice shows that this mechanism did invigorate our economy on the one hand; but on the other, it also resulted in the loss of macroeconomic control such as the overlarge-scale capital construction, soaring prices and inflation etc., due to weak planning, failure to establish an indirect regulatory mechanism in a real sense and prolonged overheated economy etc.

Given the political and economic situations at that time, Deng Xiaoping suggested that we would rather "continue to combine planned economy with regulation by market forces," which was actually a retrogression to the policy of the 12th National Congress. From then on, we continued to use this policy till the 14th National Congress in 1992. Accordingly, we began to count more on administrative power of the Central Committee to manage the economy during that period of time, and the share of market in economic regulation had somewhat declined.

In the 14th National Congress of the CPC in October 1992, it was clearly stated that our economic restructuring aims to establish a socialist market economy, a great milestone in the evolution of the relations between planning and market. In the beginning of 1992, Deng Xiaoping said, "the proportion of planning to market is not the essential difference between socialism and capitalism". Besides, he also pointed out that neither planning nor market is the dividing line between socialism and capitalism but instead they can be used both under socialism and capitalism.[1]

Both Planning and market have their own merits and demerits. The strength of market lies in its capacity of promoting technical and management progress through competition to link production with demand. However, market is not all-powerful. The following five major tasks cannot be assigned totally to the market or the law of value alone: to maintain a balance between aggregate demand and supply, to make timely adjustments to major economic structures, to fight against monopoly resulting from competition, to protect ecological environment and to ensure social equity. In order to solve these issues, the state needs to intervene in the economy through state macroeconomic planning.

The advantages of planning lie in its capacity of concentrating on accomplishing some great things, reorienting the economic development when necessary, adjusting incomes and maintaining social equity. But plans are made by man, who will inevitably have their own limitations and thus many difficulties in overcoming some contradictions, such as the contradiction between subjectivity and objectivity, contradictions among different interests, etc. In view of these circumstances, we need to improve our planning on the one hand and try to make up for the deficiency of planning by means of market forces on the other.

In practical work, we should give full play to their merits, avoid their weakness and make them complement with each other. It is wrong to have blind faith in either of them and make them mutually exclusive.

In the 14th National Congress, the party officially proposed to establish a

1 *The Selected Works of Deng Xiaoping*, volume 3, Beijing: People's Publishing House, 1993, p. 373.

"socialist market economy", excluding "planned" from the wording. On June 9th, 1992, Jiang Zemin, then General Secretary of the Central Committee of the CPC, ever spoke of three types of reform target in the speech delivered in the Party School of the Central Committee of the CPC, namely, to establish a socialist commodity economy characterized by the combination between planning and market, to establish a socialist planned market economy, and to establish a socialist market economy. He favored personally the "socialist market economy". He said, "A planned commodity economy is equivalent to a planned market economy. Socialist economy had planning since its establishment, and everybody knows it perfectly well. Therefore, one should not infer from the missing of the word "planned" that planning would be aborted." [1] I think that Jiang Zemin has made a very good and correct point. The modifier "planned" is just deleted for the sake of brevity rather than removed in a real sense, as "planning" is an intrinsic nature of socialism.

The 14th National Congress of the CPC put forward the establishment of socialist market economy as the objective of economic restructuring. From then on, conscious efforts were made to establish the socialist market economy. According to the strategic plans made by the 14th National Congress of the CPC, "*the Decision of the Central Committee of the Communist Party of China on Some Issues concerning the Establishment of the Socialist Market Economy*" ("*the Decision*" in short) was adopted in the Third Plenary Session of the 14th Central Committee of the CPC. In line with China's national conditions, "*the Decision*" made the objective and basic principles of economic restructuring established in the 14th national Congress of the CPC more specific and systematic, elaborating on several major principles, policies and contents of the system of socialist market economy.

"*The Decision*" has mapped out plans for reform tasks in the 1990's and laid

1 the selected works of Jiang Zemin, volume 1, Beijing: People's Publishing House, 2006, p.202

out a framework for socialist market economy, ranging from micro-foundations to macroeconomic management, from urban reform to rural development, from economic operational mechanism to scientific and educational system, from the use of economic means to the building of legal system, from production and distribution to circulation and consumption, etc.

4. Development and Improvement of socialist market economy

Over the past three decades since the reform and opening-up, we have made many ground-breaking achievements in theory and thus benefited a lot from them in practice. The initial establishment of socialist market economy has given rise to China's economic boom and many spectacular achievements.

Our economic restructuring has already completed the 'breakthrough' stage and 'expansion' stage over the past three decades since the reform and opening-up, with essential elements of commodity economy having been fully developed, economic agents of market economy more mature, and market mechanism brought into full play. Within just three decades, we've initially established the socialist market economy. However, our economic growth was still based on an extensive mode and therefore a lot of things needed to be improved. That is to say, we are still in the stage of "system building" characterized by an extensive mode of economic growth; we still have a long list of tasks to be completed before we move on to the next stage of "system improvement" characterized by an intensive mode of economic growth.

So, I figure that such economic feature in this particular phase is the very reason why the 16th National Congress of the CPC established the "improvement of the socialist market economy" as one of "the major tasks for economic development and reform in the first two decades in the 21st Century". Having summarized very carefully China's achievements and development over the three decades since the reform and opening-up and our party's work since the 16th National Congress, the 17th National Congress of the CPC stated very clearly that we should strive to build a moderately prosperous society in all respects. It also stressed that in order to achieve the economic development goal, the key is to make significant progress in the transformation of economic development pattern and the improvement of socialist market economy. Besides, it also highlighted the necessity of accelerating the improvement of the socialist market economy

In my point of view, on the basis of 60 years' explorations, we should develop a more scientific and precise understanding of features and functions of planning under socialist market economy, which would be an important aspect for the improvement of the socialist market economy. To view it in perspective, both positive and negative aspects of market have been fully exposed since the initial establishment of market economy. Inherent flaws of market economy have gradually come to the surface despite its superiority in stimulating competition and optimizing resource allocation. Especially when it is required to achieve a balance between aggregate demand and aggregate supply, conserve resources, protect the environment and ensure social equity, market seemed to be at the end of its tether.

So far, people have already had a better understanding of the historical role of market economy and market mechanism as well as the relations between market economy and modernization. However, market fundamentalism, i.e., blind worship of market mechanism and market economy, also arose in the meanwhile. Quite a few people infected with market "infantilism" worshipped market economy so much that they even thought market economy could solve everything and thus attributed all current problems to the inadequacy of "marketization reform". Some people even openly advocated that China copy the European and U.S. model of free market economy; Some people denied completely the role of planning, dismissing it as an synonym for "conservatism" or "leftism"; Some people opposed market to planning, claiming that a pure liberalization is the natural call of the market, and that "the invisible hand is of paramount importance in the market economy", and therefore it should "play the dominant role" whereas "the visible hand" should "quit". [1]

1 Zhang Jian, "Socialist Market Economy is the Optimal Choice", *Economic Information Daily*, June, 24, 2009

Under the corrosive influence of these wrong thoughts, over-marketization has occurred in many fields, such as education, medical care and housing etc., which should have been avoided. As a matter of fact, even western capitalist countries dare not carry out 100% marketization in these fields. It turned out that over-marketization in these fields had led to many bad consequences in people's life.

Since the 14th National Congress, we have succeeded in controlling inflation and deflation successively while implementing the short-term macroeconomic regulation. However, the guidance of state planning for macroeconomic activities tends to be dwindling gradually. Plans involve mostly compilation of polices but seldom any tasks with accountability or binding quotas; local plans are divorced from central ones, with the latter unable to control the former's blind pursuit of GDP growth; a huge mismatch exists between plans and real work. As a result, state planning now is rather weak and even dispensable. We have been chanting the slogan of "overcoming GDP Complex, expansion of domestic demand, industrial upgrading and independent innovation" for years but bore little fruit, which actually has something to do with the weakening of state macroeconomic regulation resulting from poor accountability and low binding force of state planning.

The 17th National Congress restated, "We will give play to the guiding role of national development plans, programs and industrial policies in macroeconomic regulation and combine the use of fiscal and monetary policies to improve macroeconomic regulation."[1] In my point of view, it is highly purposeful for the Central Committee to reaffirm the guiding role of state planning, which has been overlooked for many years, in the 17th National Congress. It reminded us again that socialist market should have "planning". Macroeconomic regulation guided by state planning is what socialist market economy with Chinese characteristics must include and achieve.

1 *Collection of Selected Major Documents Over the Three Decades Since the Reform and Opening up* Ⅱ , Beijing: Central Party Literature Press,2008, p.1762.

Therefore, we should make a conscious effort to regulate the economy by macroeconomic state planning in a scientific way, and in the meanwhile allow the law of value and market forces to dictate the economy where it should go, i.e., a spontaneous regulation of the economy. The 17th National Congress highlighted that we should accelerate the improvement of socialist market economy in many aspects. I think a correct understanding of planning under socialist market economy concerns the operational mechanism of socialist market economy as a whole. And now, It's high time to reinforce the role of macroeconomic planned regulation and stress the regulatory role of state planning and its leading role in macroeconomic regulation while continuing to maintain market forces as the basic means of regulating resource allocation.

We must fully understand the status of planning in the socialist market economy. As we all know, there are several major means of macroeconomic regulation: fiscal policy, monetary policy and planning. Only a few market economies set up planned agencies so as to make predictive plans, but they seldom use planning as a means of economic regulation. However, as a great socialist power, China should necessarily use planning as a means of macroeconomic regulation. Industrial policies are also a means of planning, the same is true with programs and development plans. So, we just have three means of macroeconomic regulation in total as mentioned before. The report of the 14th National Congress of the CPC has stated very clearly, "state planning is one of the important means of macroeconomic regulation." [1]

In the triad, planning should serve as a guide for both fiscal and monetary policies, and fiscal and monetary policies need the guidance of planning as well. State planning is inseparable from the macroeconomic regulation, with the former serving as the backbone of the latter. State planning covers annual plans and

1 Collection of Documents of the 14th National Congress of the Communist Party of China. Beijing: People's Publishing House, 1992, p.23.

medium-to-long term plans such as Five-Year Plans, Ten-Year Plans. Annual plans include targets for economic growth, total investment volume, fiscal budgets, credit volume, foreign exchange revenues and expenditures, unemployment rate, the rate of price rise, and population growth rate etc. They are all made annually by the State Council and approved by the National People's Congress, and therefore they should have the force of law and executive effectiveness. These medium-to-long programs and annual plans are all supposed to play a guiding role in macroeconomic regulation and have the binding force, i.e., committing entities to complete their tasks. When it comes to the crunch, some entity should be held accountable and take legal responsibilities. Only in this way can state planning play the guiding role in macroeconomic regulation in a real sense.

The 17th Central Committee of the CPC reemphasized the guiding role of state planning in the macroeconomic regulation, which is not a retrogression to the traditional planned economy as some people distorted. The reasons are as follows: First, the current state planning is not inclusive, but instead it only attends to the macroeconomic activities, whereas the micro-economic activities are assigned to the market. Second, market is the current basic means of regulating resource allocation, whilst planning is the necessary means to remedy the defects of market. Third, the current plans do not mainly refer to administrative orders any more, but include guiding, strategic and predictive plans instead. And at the same time, these plans must serve as a guide and commit entities to complete tasks and to take responsibilities when necessary. Transition from planned economy to market economy and the renewed emphasis on the guiding role of state planning in the macroeconomic regulation are in line with the "thesis-antithesis-synthesis" dialectics. Rather than a retrogression to the previous traditional planned economy, it is a higher-level synthesis of planning and market in the new stage of economic reform. Therefore, a harmony needs to be achieved between planning and market, and this is what a harmonious socialist should have.

Looking back at the past 60 years of New China, I strongly believe that the spiral development of socialist economy with Chinese characteristics conforms to the basic trend of historical development. If we regard our economic construction before reform and opening-up as a "thesis", our reform and opening-up would be called an "anti-thesis", i.e., the negation of the thesis. Over the past six decades, this pair of thesis and antithesis has opened a new situation and brought about new conflicts as well. Now it's time to propose a new "antithesis" to the previous 'antithesis' and form a new thesis, that is to say, to negate the previous negation and thus achieve a new and higher-level synthesis. Rather than a retrogression, such a synthesis will be achieved on a higher level, pushing things forward to reach a higher level. Now we have reached a critical stage to decide whether we can maintain a correct outlook for development and thus achieve that synthesis. A good synthesis will promise China a bright future, maintaining and projecting the superiorities of socialist market economy.

(I owed a great debt of gratitude to Mao Liyan, a researcher from the Academic Division of Marxist Studies, CASS, for his great assistance to me while I was writing this article. This article was entitled "Planning and Market in China over the Six Decades Since the Founding of the PRC" when it was included into the *Collection of studies concerning the history of 60-year-old China since the founding of the PRC* by the CCCPC Party Literature Research Office. It was also published in the academic journal *Contemporary China History Studies*, entitled as "China's Exploration and establishment of the economic mechanism of socialism with Chinese characteristics". This article was originally published in *Contemporary China History Studies, 2009: 5)*

Part III

China's Socialist Market Economy: an Organic Unity between "Socialism" and "Market Economy"

An Organic Unity between "Market Economy" and "Socialism" —A development road that China should rightfully take

I am greatly honored and grateful to accept the "Economics Award for Outstanding Contribution in the 21st Century".

I am already 87 years old. As an eyewitness of New China's twists and turns during its socialist construction, I have the great honor to have ever participated in many major discussions about economic theories ever since the reform and opening-up, the making of some major decisions vital to the reform and opening-up, and the drafting of many central documents and medium-to-long-term plans as well.

In my award-winning article entitled "A Marxist philosophical approach to sum up China's reform and opening-up over the three decades", I, a witness of China's reform and opening-up, tried to use some basic ideas and methods of

Marxist philosophy to sum up China's reform and opening-up over the three decades, striving to break some fresh ground. In order to make my point brief, objective, comprehensive, and to the point, I proposed to analyze China's reform and opening-up from the following 11 aspects, which I hope would be almost inclusive.

I analyzed in this article that China's reform and opening-up has undergone a round of negation of negation, i.e., thesis-antithesis-synthesis. We must apply an antithesis to the previous thesis so as to achieve a higher-level synthesis. To view the reform and opening-up over the past three decades in a dialectic way, we need fully acknowledge our great achievements during this period of time on the one hand, and face up to existent problems and potential risks on the other, such as the contradiction between the productive forces and the relations of production, that between the economic basis and superstructure, internal contradictions within the productive forces, those within the relations of production and the contradiction between social consciousness and social being etc. To sum up, we need to achieve an organic unity between market economy and socialism.

Socialist market economy has two-fold meanings. One is "socialism" with its focus on the relations of production; the other is "market economy" with its emphasis on the productive forces. Within an organic unity, neither aspect should be overemphasized one over the other. Success or failure of the reform is dictated by the consolidation of socialist relations of production. If the reform fails, it is not the productive forces that fail, but socialist relations of production, which thus leads to polarization and emergence of a new bourgeoisie. Deng Xiaoping called it a failure of reform. It is not everything that is either capitalist or socialist, such as the productive forces and some generality shared by the relations of production. However, as for distinctive characteristics of different relations of production, we must find out which category they fall into, capitalist or socialist. So, we must make a concrete analysis of a concrete problem.

In this article, I applied the law of "negation of negation" and historical materialism to the analysis of reform. I proposed to push the reform further forward by "achieving a higher-level synthesis" and offered some suggestions on the deepening of reform under new circumstances within the framework of Marxist economics.

First, we should view planning and market as an organic unity. I have always been insisting on dividing one into two and seeing them in perspective rather than lay one-sided emphasis on any of them. In the initial period of reform and opening-up, market was demonized by some people. However, I was among the very few people who supported the market-oriented reform very boldly at that time. By the time when market economy was basically established and a lot of problems emerged in the market, I had begun to pay particular attention to market flaws and advocated reasonable and effective government interventions in the economy. I have always been insisting on the combination between planning and market, believing that in every phase--though with different focuses—we all aim to make the invisible hand and the visible hand complement with each other and bring their due roles into full play.

Neither planning nor market forces alone would be sufficient to regulate the economy. It is inevitable for the market forces to serve as a basic means of regulating resource allocation, but we shouldn't hold blind faith in the market economy which has many limitations. While carrying out the market-oriented reform, the government must implement macroeconomic regulation properly and effectively. As socialist market economy is complete in its meaning, we must reinforce macroeconomic planned regulation and the guiding role of state planning in the macroeconomic regulation while carrying on the market-oriented reform. Under socialist market economy, it is very necessary that we must strengthen the guiding role of state planning in the macroeconomic regulation. We cannot exclude "planning" from the meaning of socialist market economy.

Second, we should pay attention to both efficiency and equity. Aside from the relationship between planning and market, the relations between efficiency and equity is another focus of people's attention during the reform. In the initial period of reform and opening-up when equity took precedence over efficiency, I approved of “giving priority to efficiency” so as to break away from the indiscriminate egalitarianism. Three decades later, when social equity has become a more pressing task than efficiency and tended to affected efficiency and stability, I advocated paying attention to both efficiency and equity with more emphasis on social equity. I believed that the invisible hand alone cannot guarantee social equity and coordinated development. Rather, we should try to guard against polarization and thus avoid the failure of reform. Given the unsound legal system in current China, any disregard for socialism or common prosperity while establishing the market economy is bound for the so-called “crony market economy”.

Third, we should integrate ownership with distribution relations. When it comes to adjusting income distribution relations and reducing the gap between the rich and the poor, we tend to focus on distribution relations and especially redistribution such as taxation and transfer payments etc. to enhance social security and improve the livelihood of the low-income people, which are absolutely necessary. However, it is far from enough to just focus on distribution and redistribution, as it is impossible to reverse the widening of gap between the rich and the poor at its source. Rather, we also need to take other perspectives into consideration as well, such as ownership structure and property system etc. That is to say, we also need slow down the decline in the proportion of the public sector and the rise in that of the private sector, and strive to prevent private ownership from replacing public ownership and becoming the mainstay. Only in this way can we eventually prevent income inequality from widening and the trend of polarization from worsening.

Fourthly, we should view emancipation of the mind and the reform and opening-up as a dialectical unity. There are two different views concerning emancipation of mind. The first view is that we should emancipate the mind under the guidance of Marxism and scientific socialism with a view to achieving the self-improvement of socialism during the reform and opening-up. The other view is emancipation of the mind under the guidance of neo-liberalization and democratic socialism. We cannot naively think that whatever efforts to emancipate the mind would end up guiding and advancing our reform and opening-up in the right direction, but instead we should be cautious of any attempts to mislead the reform and opening-up under the disguise of emancipating the mind.

It is not anti-reform to view the reform in perspective, reflect on both our gains and losses during the reform, and try to sum up experience and draw lessons from it. Rather, only in this way can we always hold onto the right direction of reform and remove hidden dangers in time. And the best way is to nip an evil in the bud and take preventive measures rather than cover up mistakes or whitewash errors. Three decades later when we review the reform and opening-up, we have found out that it has just completed a negation of negation, that is, a round of "thesis-antithesis-synthesis".

Now it is high time for us to apply a new antithesis to new problems. In other words, it is high time to solve problems and contradictions in reality so as to achieve a higher-level synthesis in both reform and opening-up and the undertaking of building socialism. Specifically speaking, in terms of the economic mechanism, we should carry on the market-oriented reform and reemphasize the role of state macroeconomic planned regulation; in terms of ownership structure, we should reemphasize the status of public ownership as the mainstay of the economy while developing many kinds of ownership side by side, that is to say, we should develop both the public sector and the private sector of the economy unwaveringly; in terms of distribution relations, we should change our policy from "encouraging some people to get rich first" to "attaching greater importance to social equity". All these are exactly what "China Model" or "Beijing Consensus" means! China's success has demonstrated its uniqueness in experience, model and road.

However, for a rather long period of time since the reform and opening-up, some people just noticed the trend of bourgeois liberalization in the political field rather than in the economic field, as problems in the latter hadn't been that serious at that time. Notwithstanding this, privatization, full marketization and the idea of "government as the night watchman" are all typical phenomena of bourgeois liberalization in the field of economy. To prevent the trend of bourgeois liberalization in the economic field is to prevent the status of public ownership as the mainstay of the economy from being affected. If that happens, the political field would also fall victim to it, because economic basis determines superstructure and social being social consciousness. Those who thought that ideological problems won't exist in the economic field are politically naive.

In order to uphold the right direction of reform, the most pressing task is to draw a clear line of demarcation between us and neo-liberalism. Neo-liberalists did not insist on one dividing into two, but placed one-sided emphasis on just one aspect instead. They advocate that "the invisible hand" should "exclusively" dictate the economy where it goes, opposing government interventions and state control over market. The core theory and value of neo-liberalism is marketization, privatization and liberalization; accordingly, neoliberalism schemes to deny public ownership, socialism and state intervention. It is also called "market fundamentalism". So how will it end up? It will surely lead to "Crony Capitalism" and extremely serious, unbearable income inequality. Therefore, neoliberalism is not the gospel at all, but a nuisance. We must try hard to fight against it since the very beginning of the reform.

In terms of global strategies, neoliberalism promotes self-regulation of market, privatization of SOEs, free trade, free flow of capital, and liberalization etc. Neoliberalism justified itself by benefiting the world with global integration in terms of politics, economy and culture led by superpowers, i.e., global capitalization, which however served as their theoretical tools of undermining the interests of developing countries and socialist countries and influencing public opinions. As a matter of fact, it did not benefit developing countries too much either.

As early as in the 1990s, many Latin American countries began to practice liberalization, privatization, and self-regulation of the global financial system and ended up with severe problems. Having realized these problems, they abandoned decisively the "Europe- and U.S.-style free market model" and turned to the left. Russia, whose economy failed to recover after having applied the so-called "shock therapy" advertised by neo-liberalism, also came to and realized its mistakes. Just as Professor William K. Tabb from New York University of the United States pointed out, "As far as its promised goal is concerned, neo-liberalism has already failed. It failed to bring any high economic growth, to wipe out poverty, and to stabilize the economy. It turned out that even in its prime time, the economic growth slowed down, the poverty rate increased and the economic and financial crisis grew into an epidemic."

The global financial crisis triggered by the subprime mortgage crisis is the very bad result of laissez-faire policies. Western large capital, financial capital and fictitious capital all feed on such a system; Western powers such as the United States even leveraged their huge capital to push for the same system in developing countries for their own convenience; in the 1970s and 1980s, Margaret Thatcher and Ronald Reagan stepped into power successively, who gave neoliberalism a big boost. Since then, neoliberalism reigned the western world for almost 30 years. However, this financial crisis put an abrupt end to the myth of neo-liberalism. After the financial crisis broke out, many capitalist countries had to rely on Keynesian ideas such as state intervention, and socialist means such as planning etc. Surely, it does not mean the end of neoliberalism. Once the economy recovers, it might rise again from the ashes. Cartels and especially big financial corps would still boast about neoliberalism and continue to use it to poison and bewitch people.

In face of this turbulent global economic crisis, Chinese government has taken many major measures to stabilize its economy and thus yielded good results, which again demonstrated strongly that state macroeconomic regulation is crucial to socialist market economy. The "invisible hand", i.e., market forces, should not be allowed to dictate the economy in many key industries or fields, including major fields concerning the people's livelihood such as education, medical care, housing, social security and income distribution etc., and capital constructions such as transportation, resource development, environmental protection, and rural infrastructure etc. Besides, we cannot count on the free market alone to expand domestic demand, adjust the economic structure and achieve the balance between aggregate supply and aggregate demand etc., either. Having realized its true color and malicious intention, more and more people have refused to believe the neo-liberalist myth of "almighty market" or "laissez-faire economy".

(This is the speech I made in the award ceremony of *China Economics Award for Outstanding Contribution in the 21st Century.* This article was published in *Chinese Social Sciences Weekly*. June 29th, 2010)

Pursuing a Socialist Market Economy in the Reform Instead of a Capitalist One

Journalist (Zhong Weizhi): You have won the first China Economics Award for Outstanding Contribution this March, congratulations! As one of the most influential economists in China, why did you publicize your article entitled "A conversation about problems in the study of economics teaching" through the Internet?

Liu Guoguang: This article should be traced back to a small talk between a young man from Research Center for Social Sciences Development in HEIs, Ministry of Education, and I in July 2005. He just came to have an idle talk with me, which however developed into a long conversation covering quite many issues, I guess, around 8 topics. He noted our conversation down, sorted them out, and wrote the first draft. Since the research center runs a newspaper, he had this article published immediately. In the meanwhile, he also posted it on several websites, but I didn't know it beforehand. To be honest, I did not know the Internet well and had no idea what impact that would bring. Anyway, it didn't do any harm, so I did not oppose it, either.

Journalist: Just to the opposite, this article has had a huge impact after it was posted.

Liu Guoguang: You can tell that quite many people did agree with me on these issues. Some people made phone calls to talk about this, whilst some held meetings to discuss it. As for the Internet thing, I said that I was not against it, but I had never expected to gain anything from it. But it turned out to be a great hit, which really caught me by surprise. I don't think it is out of some personal influence, but instead, these issues do concern the people deeply.

Journalist: In your article, you mentioned some people and things. For example, you criticized some economists who "audaciously suggested that western economics be regarded as our mainstream economics".

Liu Guoguang: Although some harsh words have already been removed from the article later published in the *Theoretical Front in Higher Education* (2005, No.9), and *Economic Research Journal* (2005, No.10), it still inevitably offended many people, most of whom are my friends in academia. But I just told the truth and never meant to make any offence. Those people or things I quoted were not groundless. As for whether it is appropriate or not, different people have different ideas. But we cannot deny the facts that did exist. Anyway, I still admire and respect them as scholars very much. We just disagreed on some issues, which doesn't matter.

Journalist: as early as in 1979, you ever elaborated on the relations between planning and market. On the eve of the 14th National congress of the CPC in 1992 you proposed to replace administrative planning with market forces as the major means of regulating resource allocation. However, some people were very confused by your acceptance speech in that award ceremony. Why would you, an economist with such a deep insight into the theory of socialist market economy, criticize the marketization reform so harshly?

Liu Guoguang: I have expounded many times on the relations between planning and market, which is probably a problem that might take a century or so to solve. I just repeated these old ideas in my acceptance speech on that day. I said that we should "carry on the market-oriented reform" but avoid any blind faith in the imperfect market. I talked a lot about the disadvantages of planned economy and the merits of market economy, at least not less than others. After all, our perception keeps developing. But some people claimed that they would never be wrong. I don't think I will be always right and nobody can actually be.

Having sensed many problems in planned economy during the past, we came to realize gradually that we should establish market economy. Planned economy cannot guarantee efficiency or provide incentives, whereas market economy, as a major means of regulating resource allocation, must be established as it is an inevitable trend in the course of history. Shortly after we carried out the reform and opening-up, I only sensed that something was wrong with planned economy and that regulation by market forces was needed. However, at that time planned economy was still in the main and regulation by market forces only served as the supplement. In late 1980s or early 1990s, after repeated reflections and studies of experience from both home and abroad, I came to realize the important role of market economy, began to believe that the market-oriented reform will work, and finally embraced the idea of "establishing a socialist market economy". It shows that I am not that quick-minded, however, I think, it does conform with the objective development of human mind. While I was "converted" to the market-oriented reform, I also warned people not to have any blind faith in the market. Besides, we should attach great importance to the law of value, but in the meanwhile we shouldn't believe that it would be capable of achieving everything and thus assign everything to the market. Even now I still think so, I am just retelling the old story. There is nothing new! I think all the old-timers know why.

Journalist: So, just as some people put it, you still insist that planned economy hasn't been completely out of date yet. Is that right?

Liu Guoguang: From what I mentioned above, you can tell I did not mean that. Since I am already "converted" to the market-oriented reform and that I approved of establishing a socialist market economy, I would definitely consider market forces as the basic and major means of regulating resource allocation and socialist market economy as a new economic system. At least in the whole primary stage of socialism, "planned economy" will not work. Nothing can be more obvious than that.

However, we cannot mix up "planned economy" as an economic system with "regulation by planning" under the market economy (here, planning, in a broad sense, includes strategic and guidance planning, necessary economic management and regulation by the government, etc.). In that speech, I said, "While adhering to the market-oriented reform, the government must intervene effectively in the economy to rectify the defects of market under the guidance of necessary planning." And this is what I mean. There is absolutely nothing that indicates that "planned economy" as an economic system hasn't been out of date yet!

When I proposed to replace planned economy with market economy as a major means of regulating resource allocation, I also talked about the limitations of market. I made a list of things that must be attended to by the government rather than by the law of value or market alone.

I think that at least the following things cannot be dictated by the law of value alone.

The first one is to balance aggregate supply and aggregate demand. If we leave this matter to the law of value alone, the economy is bound for cyclical fluctuations and repeated crises. The second thing is the major restructuring in terms of agriculture, industry, heavy industry, light industry, primary, secondary and tertiary industries, consumption and accumulation, processing industry and basic industry, etc. We aim to achieve the rationalization, modernization and supererogation of the industrial structure at little cost in the short run, say, one, two, or three decade(s). It is not unlikely to achieve major restructuring spontaneously through market alone in allocating human and material resources, but it would probably take rather long at a higher price with many repeated crises before it is accomplished. We cannot afford it. The third thing concerns fair competition. The belief that market guarantees fair competition is a sheer fantasy. Even in the period of laissez-faire capitalism, fair competition cannot be ensured because the market rule of "big fish swallowing little fish" (i.e., the strong bullying the weak) will definitely lead to monopoly, that is to say, unfair competition. That's why some capitalist nations are also making the anti-trust law or competition law.

The fourth thing concerns ecological balance, environmental protection and "external dis-economy". "External dis-economy" is a phenomenon in which enterprises might benefit from certain development pattern, which, however, might cause damages to natural resources and ecological environment, such as air and water pollution. These short-term benefits are detrimental to social interests and even the survival of mankind in the long run. So, market is not capable of solving these problems. The fifth one is the relationship between equity and efficiency. The market alone cannot guarantee social equity in a real sense, but just an exchange of products with equal values instead, which only ensures that people get equal compensations. In this sense, it does promote efficiency and social progress, however, the spontaneous regulation by market alone would inevitably lead to social polarization and a dramatic gap between the rich and the poor. While we were introducing the market mechanism, some symptoms had already developed, causing anxiety among people and dampening their enthusiasm. In response to this, the government should take some measures to prevent this from deteriorating. Since we are now calling for a harmonious society, it is even more necessary to make up for the deficiency of market economy.

Later, I found similar arguments in some western economic literature, so my opinions are not brand new.

Journalist: So, you have been insisting on these ideas in recent years. As we know, Chen Yun ever compared the relationship between planning and market to that between the "cage" and "birds" since the Third Plenary Session of the 11th Central Committee of the CPC. Do you think this "bird-cage" is still necessary under market economy?

Liu Guoguang: Chen Yun made a vivid analogy. Even though the word "bird-cage" does not sound good to ears, we should fully acknowledge its role. Isn't the budget of government, a plan of restrictions on government revenues and expenses, a "cage"? Isn't the control on aggregate supplies of money and credit a "cage"? Isn't the program for major projects a "cage"? Besides, the cage varies in size and flexibility. It can be made of different materials, such as steel or plastic. So, mandatory planning is rigid whereas guidance planning is flexible. All in all, we cannot overlook the necessary role of "cage", i.e., government management and planned coordination, while carrying out the market-oriented reform and developing a socialist market economy.

Now, in the Chinese version for the "11th Five-Year Plan", "jihua"(plan) was reworded into "guihua" (program). However, the latter is also a kind of plan, though a long-term one, which refers to the strategic and guidance plan rather than mandatory one. It should play a guiding role, but in the meanwhile, mandatory planning is also necessary to some major projects, which therefore cannot be eliminated. As the so-called market-oriented reform intrinsically includes the reform of planned economy and that of government management system, planning should be adjusted to the development of market economy and government control and management should be strengthened as well.

In my opinion, a pure market economy is not what our reform aims to achieve. Even in the western capitalist countries, the meaning of the so-called "pure" market economy is also changing. For example, due to government intervention through policies or planning, their current market economy is not as pure and typical as that in the 19th century any more. But there are still some people who suggested naively that we should implement full "marketization". We carried out a market-oriented reform after some mistakes were made due to blind faith in planning. Therefore, to draw lessons from prior experiences, we mustn't have any blind faith in market, either; rather, we should emphasize the role of state planning, macroeconomic regulation and necessary government intervention in the market-oriented reform. Otherwise, we would make many detours.

Journalist: But economic circles and ideological circles held different opinions about some problems in the current reform, such as the source of corruption. Some scholars attributed marketization and capitalization of power to excessive power that the government has in regulating resource allocation and too much room the government has been given to intervene in microeconomic activities, which is the hotbed of corruption and rent seeking. According to these scholars, administrative planning should be totally eradicated in a pure market economy, and therefore it would be almost impossible for the "cronies" of government officials to seek personal gains by pulling strings. How does this theory sound to you?

Liu Guoguang: This problem is very important and complicated as well, which should be analyzed from the following aspects.

First, you said just now that the "excessive" power that the government has in regulating resource allocation is the villain. Sure, it is inappropriate for any government to have too large power especially in regulating resource allocation, because such government might overstep the boundaries and attend to things that are supposed to be the job of market. Likewise, it might be also inappropriate for any government to have too small power in regulating resource allocation or too little room for economic intervention, too, in which case the government would function inadequately and shun responsibilities. The government, one of the three main agents in the economy (governments, firms, households/individuals), which stands for the interests of public interests, must have considerable social resources at its disposal to regulate resource allocation; but at the same time, there is no denying that the government should try as far as possible to follow market rules and keep its regulation within certain bounds for the sake of benefiting public interests.

Second, the occurrence of corruption has nothing directly to do with the amount of power that a government has in regulating resource allocation. Large or small, a government is still likely to commit corruptions. An unsound legal system and inadequate democratic supervision, incapable of binding government officials effectively, will surely result in corruption. However, rather than a rooted cause for corruption, the amount of power that a government has in regulating resource allocation does affect the degree of corruption. In order to uproot corruption, we need to improve our legal system and democratic supervision so as to carry out a political structural reform. And this is the right cure!

Third, apart from an unsound legal system and lack of democratic supervision, market is also a hotbed of corruption and capitalization and marketization of power. Here I want to clarify that corruption and capitalization and marketization of power are not any flaws inherent in planned economy, but problems that developed and even got worse ever since the market-oriented reform. Under planned economy, there used to be no capitalization nor marketization of power. I am not trying to gloss over the planned economy, which though did have many flaws, such as extreme rigidity, incapability of arousing people's enthusiasm in work, bureaucracy, abuse of power, corruption etc.

At that time the government did have huge power in regulating resource allocation, but corruptions were very rare, just occurring in "cracks" or at the fringe of planned economy, not to mention capitalization or marketization of power, which just popped up and got worse recently. I'm afraid it has something to do with the introduction of market, because without market there would be no capital and thus no capitalization or marketization of power. It is inadequate or far-fetched to explain that market is still not developed enough or the reform is not radical enough, which though does make some sense. Rather, it would sound more reasonable to attribute it to the imperfect and somewhat twisted market, which however is an inevitable result of marketization reform. Therefore, in order to reduce the cost of introducing market, the government must intervene and play its due role in the economic management to rectify the situation and remedy the defects of market.

Fourthly, we cannot confuse economic regulation, intervention and planning by the government with government officials' abuse of power such as power-for-money deal, collusion between government officials and businessmen, and capitalization and marketization of power etc. They are two entirely different things. That is to say, we cannot deprive the government of the right to regulate resource allocation or deny its role in economic management (through planning in a broad sense), just because excessive power the government has in regulating resource allocation makes it possible for corruption and rent seeking to happen.

As abovementioned, in order to fight against corruption, capitalization and marketization of power, we should start with political structural reform, striving to improve democracy and legal system step by step. Now I' d like to add another thing. That is, we should also strive to rectify mistakes and remedy defects of market. In order to achieve that, we must strengthen the role of state/government management or planning (in a broad sense). Therefore, I said in the acceptance speech, "While adhering to the market-oriented reform, the government must intervene effectively in the economy to rectify the defects of market under the guidance of necessary planning." As far as I know, many readers know what I really mean and agree with me, but some people just insisted that I schemed to restore a planned economy. I can really do nothing about them! Let them be!

Journalist: you mean you still support the market-oriented reform? But some people ever pointed out that you had been recently suggesting "less emphasis on market economy", is that true?

Liu Guoguang: "Socialist market economy" is a complete concept and an organic unity as well. In my acceptance speech, I raised one of my concerns, that is, I am afraid relatively more emphasis has been placed on market economy and relatively less on socialism these years. When it comes to socialism, we tended to attach relatively more importance to the development of the productive forces, i.e., efficiency, and relatively less to common prosperity, i.e., social equity.

Please note that here I used the word "relatively", which has a real and precise meaning. "Relatively more" does not mean "absolutely more", and "relatively less" does not mean "absolutely less", either. We should not mix up the logical senses of the two. By saying so, I just wanted to remind that we didn't pay due attention to socialism while interpreting the concept of "socialist market economy", which however does not mean that we've laid too much emphasis on market economy. Rather, we should attach even further importance to market economy, if the government does have too much power in regulating resource allocation and is indeed given too much room for intervention in micro-economic activities.

It is not fair to say that we have never attached any importance to socialism these years, though we just have paid relatively less attention to it. Although we have achieved a huge success in the reform, such as an economic boom, the improvement of people's lives in general, etc., many problems also arose at the same time due to relatively less emphasis on socialism, such as the worsening of social contradictions, the dramatic widening of the gap between the rich and the poor, the trend of polarization, and the upsurge in corruption and capitalization of power. We should stop this from deteriorating, since such trend is conflicting with the reform, i.e., the self-improvement of socialism. Therefore, more emphasis should be placed on socialism, which is in line with the direction of our reform and meets people's expectations. Sure, market economy is still not developed enough, and in this sense we should stress it more. As long as we keep to socialism, the more emphasis on market economy the better.

This is exactly what I mean. Both socialism and market economy deserve more attention, but now we need place relatively more emphasis on socialism. I am deeply moved by many readers, who wrote to me to express their approval and understanding. I do not know how come I offended the "reformists", who criticized me for having concluded that more emphasis was placed on market economy and less on socialism. I ever said, "Here comes a deviation. So, what should we do? Should we thereby attach less importance to market economy? My answer is 'No'." But dear sir, since I also said No, why did you still distort my words and create so much logical confusion? On a second thought, I wouldn't blame anybody, but myself. Even though I have paid particular attention to the choice of word, my explanation is not sufficient and clear enough so that I was misunderstood by some people in the logic sense. I owed a debt of gratitude to this gentleman, who had so kindly "given me a break". He said, "I did not deny him because he has just won the prize." Oh, I really don't know how to thank him.

Journalist: In your article "A conversation about problems in the study of economics teaching", you criticized "western mainstream thoughts especially neo-liberalistic economics", arguing that neo-liberalistic economics has misguided

China's economic reform and development. Some people thereby thought that you seemed to be retreating from the marketization reform.

Liu Guoguang: Does criticism of neo-liberalism mean "a retreat from the marketization reform" or "disapproval of the reform"? What a label! As for neo-liberalistic economics, there are many scientific things reflecting the general law of modern market economy that we should learn from, such as monetarism represented by Milton Friedman and new classical macroeconomics represented by Robert Lucas, Jr. These things weren't criticized. However, on the whole, its theoretical premises and core conceptions, such as "human beings are selfish by nature", "private ownership will be eternal" and "the all-powerful market always knows best", etc. (I've listed them in that article), are not suitable for socialist China, and therefore neo-liberalism cannot be regarded as a mainstream theory in China or the guiding ideology for its economic reform and development.

Only the developing Marxism that keeps pace with the times is capable of guiding China's economics teaching and economic decision-making. I wonder how come they concluded that my comments on neo-liberalism suggested "a retreat from the marketization reform" or "anti-reform"! Most criticisms of neo-liberalism from Chinese economists were well-grounded academic studies or reviews, which wouldn't be reversed just by some casual, absurd charges! Persuasive academic research might stand some chances. Besides, some upright western economists are also levelling criticism at neo-liberalism. We all know what devastating effects neo-liberalism has ever had on the former Soviet Union and Latin America. Given these circumstances, Chinese scholars did have some political and ideological concerns, worrying that core conceptions of neo-liberalism would affect our economic thoughts and decision-making. Nobody has, nevertheless, ever said that our reform decision-making was shaped by neo-liberalism, which so far hasn't been that capable.

However, these concerns and worries were neither groundless nor superfluous, for individualism, privatization and market fundamentalism etc. have penetrated into China's social and economic life and are even gaining more momentum. In previous articles, I ever pointed out that some people, who disliked any criticism against neo-liberalism, worshiped neo-liberalism so much that they compared neo-liberalism as a basket discriminating against nothing. Well, those people, who embraced the core conceptions of neo-liberalism, just set themselves up, and nobody else is to blame. However, someone has now gone so far to forbid others to criticize neo-liberalism just because he has stepped forward and admitted that he had been converted to it! He who criticized neo-liberalism would be labelled as an advocate of "retreat from the marketization reform" or "anti-reform"! How ridiculous!

They not only applied the label of "anti-reform" to critics of neo-liberalism, but also applied it randomly, spreading rumors that a wave of anti-reform has recently emerged. We have to admit that the huge success of our reform did give rise to divided interests—very few people suddenly came into money; most gained some benefits; some people's interests were damaged. And it is very natural for the people, including the academia, to diverge in opinions about the reform, and the same is true when people criticized those wrong and negative aspects. So, dissenting opinions are no equal to "anti-reform".

By reflecting on the reform, we mean to correct negative things and carry forward positive sides in the process of reform, and thus advance our reform in the right direction. So, "reflection on the reform" should not be equated with "anti-reform". If many common people and scholars were labelled "anti-reformists" and thereby pushed to the opposite camp, it would be hard to imagine the bad consequences! Therefore, we must unite whoever is ready to contribute to China's social progress and whoever is working on it, and try to make everyone embrace the reform. But how? In order to make the reform benefit us all, we should pursue a socialist market economy in the reform instead of a capitalist one.

(This article is the transcript of my interview by Zhong Zhiwei, a journalist from newspaper *the Economic Observer*, on November 8th & 25th, 2005. The Original title of this article is "Reflection on the Reform ***Isn't*** Anti-reform", published in the *Economic Observer*, December 12th, 2005.)

A Brief Discussion of the "Marketization Reform"
—in what direction china's reform must and mustn't head

Recently, discussions about China's reform are getting increasingly heated. Some people called it "the third great debate", but as for what the previous two debates are, people held different opinions. Under no circumstances this debate is less intense. But something weird is that the views of one side can be seen or heard in the mainstream media where those of the other hardly can. Rather, the latter's opinions were circulated very widely on the Internet. Another interesting thing is that one side of the debate kept attacking the other side but forbade them to argue back. The other side surely did not care what they said, arguing back that truth can defend itself in whatever argument. Actually, the first side just wanted themselves to be heard, expecting the other side to make their mouths shut. Since the reform and opening-up has been so deepened and the Internet technology so advanced, I'm afraid their schemes to gag the others would fail. But one-sided reportage on the mainstream media does deserve pondering. Why did that happen? Surely, such problem of partiality has been somewhat corrected, thanks to the Internet.

As to the nature of this great debate, people were also divided sharply. Some people called it a debate concerning "anti-reform VS unwavering adherence to the reform", which was, however, severely disputed. Because one cannot forcefully apply the label of "anti-reform" to so many common people and scholars who just reflected on the reform, or just call it "a wave of anti-reform and denial of reform", either. Obviously, it is inconsistent with the spirit reflected in President Hu Jintao's recent remarks that we should "make sure the reform be embraced by the people in a real sense".

So, what is this debate about? Many people including some scholars believed that the most controversial issue is not whether to adhere to the reform or not, but in what direction our reform should head instead. Should we advance our reform in the direction of the self-improvement of socialism, a creative idea invented by

Deng Xiaoping, or "steer China to capitalism under the disguise of embracing the reform and opening-up"? Should we uphold the basic socialist economic system in which public ownership is the mainstay and different economic sectors develop side by side or adopt capitalist privatization in the reform? Should we pursue a socialist market economy or a capitalist market economy? or should it be called "marketization reform"?

It is "another ideological debate between capitalism and socialism" which cannot be evaded at all. He who wants to avoid this issue is too naive. If they use capitalist ideology as a weapon to attack you, but try to paralyze your mind with de-ideologizing ideas and persuade you out of socialist ideology, what will you think? Definitely, in terms of crucial matters concerning the fate of the whole nation and people, tricks like "de-ideologizing" or non-politicization can only work on those without any knowledge of Marxism.

Now I would like to analyze why the first side applied the label of "anti-reform" or "denial of reform" to the other side while disguising themselves as "steadfast defenders of the reform". Actually it is very simple to understand. First, in present-day China where the reform is in full swing, "anti-reform" is regarded as the most heinous crime, quite similar to the deadly "sin" of "anti-cultural revolution" in the period of "Cultural Revolution". At least, the so-called "anti-reformists" were already put on the defensive. Second, they attempted to cover up their real intention of steering China toward pure privatization, marketization, polarization and capitalism under the disguise of embracing the reform and opening-up. For instance, in the recent New Western Hills Conference, some people said, "what cannot be stated explicitly", "what are unspeakable" or "what cannot be brought to light" has to be spoken "in an evasive manner". Actually, some people have revealed much bigger ambitions not only in the economic field, but also in the political one. To spell it out, they even schemed to overthrow the communist party, which I wouldn't explain in detail here.

Some people asked me why so many people began to reflect on the reform. Is it because the reform got stuck and would not carry on? My answer is "No". Despite some disturbances or problems, our reform is still moving on. An official said that even though this or that problem had emerged in the process of reform, it had nothing to do with the direction of reform. Such remark is both right and wrong. In general, the central committee is upholding socialism in the reform, without major deviations from it. However, many aspects of the reform were sidetracked. For example, in terms of ownership, the status of public ownership as the mainstay of the economy was somewhat challenged; in terms of distribution, social equity cannot be totally guaranteed etc. In order to get rid of these disturbances, the Central Committee put forward "the Scientific Outlook on Development" and the idea of "building a harmonious society". However, the situation is too hard to rectify. These disturbances affecting the right direction of reform, i.e., socialism, are an objective reality. And it is very natural and necessary for the common people and scholars to reflect on them and offer suggestions for improvement. So they shouldn't be labelled "anti-reform" randomly.

What is more, with the deepening and complication of the reform since the 1990s, the old balance among different interests in our society has shifted. Some people's living standards and social status declined relatively or absolutely, which caused them to resent these social phenomena that undermined their interests and brought about the widening of the gap between the poor and the rich as well as deviations from socialism. They just wanted to overcome these problems rather than oppose the reform. These people include the vulnerable and the poor, most of whom are workers or peasants, the bulk of the great masses. Even though they might have overreacted due to biased opinions, we should still try to educate and unite them to embrace the reform. But some people have ridiculously labelled them as "anti-reformists". As a revered and distinguished Chinese economist put it, they are really shooting irresponsible criticism at random!

Some people called China's reform as a marketization reform. If marketization is regarded as a short form of our reform, it can be barely accepted. But we need be aware that this wording is very questionable. If it is regarded as a full name of our reform rather than a short form, that is to say, if China's reform is defined as "marketization reform", it wouldn't be more wrong than that.

As Deng Xiaoping put it, our reform aims to achieve the self-improvement of China's socialist system, including the establishment of socialist market economy. However, it should be noted that China's reform, which is supposed to cover many fields such as politics, economy, society, culture and the government etc., aims to achieve the self-improvement of socialism in every field, so it cannot be generally called "marketization reform". The structural reform should also be adjusted to the needs of socialist market economy rather than the principle of "marketization". Even in the economic field, we are not to carry out a 100% "marketization reform", but to establish a socialist market economy, which requires us to make market forces, subject to state macroeconomic regulation, serve as the basic means of regulating resource allocation. So the oversimplified wording— "marketization reform" failed to include all these meanings. Besides, there is still a modifier "socialist" and a precondition "(subject to) state macroeconomic regulation" before the term "market economy". These are words in black and white carrying substantial meanings in the document of the Third Plenary Session of the 14th Central Committee of the CPC, rather than an empty talk.

Now let's talk about the modifier "socialist" at first. While advertising "marketization reform", some people deliberately dropped the modifier "socialist". Some people mentioned "socialist" briefly and pretentiously just for the sake of covering up their real intentions, reducing the due role of "socialist" to something unimportant or distorting it's meaning randomly. I ever said that the modifier "socialist" has substantial and precise meanings, which should not be taken as an empty word. Deng Xiaoping ever said of the two fundamental principles of socialism that we must adhere to, i.e., public ownership as the mainstay with many kinds of ownership developing side by side and common prosperity without polarization. However, some people maliciously removed and killed these two basic principles of socialism while advertising "marketization reform". And what is more, they even deliberately dropped the most fundamental one concerning the basic socialist economic system, i.e. public ownership as the mainstay of the economy. But instead, words like "the private sector has already become 'the very foundation of national economy" or 'the economic mainstay'" are flooding some media and meetings. I guess it might be the real meaning of "deepening the marketization reform"! (the private sector is allowed to develop side by side with the public sector, which is predicated on the principle that public ownership is the mainstay; but the Central Committee has never stated "the private sector is the economic mainstay"!)

Next, I would like to talk about its precondition—"(subject to) state macroeconomic regulation", which is also very important. Despite its important role in regulating resource allocation and especially its superiority in allocation of competitive resources, market economy has many flaws and limitations in maintaining a balance between aggregate supply and aggregate demand, dealing with the relations between competition and monopoly, protecting the environment, conserving resources, and ensuring social equity, and so on (I used to talk a lot about the merits and demerits of market economy, which many textbooks also cover, so I would not repeat it here; as for "marketization-reformists" who only preferred to the positive side of the market economy and turned a blind eye to its negative effects, I would spare my comments here, too).

Therefore, we should count on state intervention, management and macroeconomic regulation to correct, restrain and remedy these defects of market. That is to say, we should use "the visible hand" to supplement "the invisible hand". Moreover, as a socialist country, it is even more necessary to strengthen state macroeconomic regulation and adjustment of government functions, due to its nature of socialism, public ownership as the mainstay of the economy, the objective possibility of unitary planning on the whole socialist society, and its superiority in concentrating resources on accomplishing great things under socialism.

The basic role that market forces play in regulating resource allocation is conditioned by state macroeconomic regulation, however, it does not mean that all resource allocation would be totally regulated by market. Actually, allocation of some key resources have to be regulated by the state, which is also very self-evident. All in all, we should respect market and avoid any blind faith in it. Likewise, we should not have blind faith in planning, either, which however does not mean that we should abandon the other means of controlling economic activities. Currently, under the slogan of "marketization reform", worship of market has run so wild that planning has almost been considered as a taboo subject.

Given these circumstances, I noted the necessity of reinforcing state intervention in the economy and regulation by planning while developing the socialist market economy. How come it is misinterpreted as "a retreat to the old planned economy"? Those who advertised "marketization reform" imposed a label on us, wishfully thinking that our mouth would be thus kept shut. I am afraid they couldn't have their way.

Besides, I also want to add a few points. State macroeconomic regulation mainly includes regulation by planning, regulation through taxation, and financial regulation. As for China's state macroeconomic regulation, land regulation is newly added, which actually also falls into the category of regulation by planning. All these types of regulation are conscious ex-ante regulation, involving centralized decision-making; whereas regulation by market forces is spontaneous ex-post regulation, involving decentralized decision-making. Such blind and delayed regulation is bound for many bad consequences, which must be corrected by state macroeconomic regulation and regulation by planning, as both ways of carrying out conscious, ex-ante regulation involving centralized decision-making.

That explains why Deng Xiaoping said that planning and market forces, as both means of controlling economic activities, could be used under both socialism and capitalism. So, why can't we use planning, a means of carrying out conscious, ex-ante regulation involving centralized decision-making, to remedy these defects of the market economy under socialist market economy? Some people suggested letting market dictate the economy where it goes, that is to say, applying full marketization to the national economy. Besides, they even advised to apply marketization to social, cultural and political activities, to exclude planning from socialist market economy and to dismiss it as a taboo subject. I think, they are more than naïve to have blind faith in market economy; rather, they are conceiving some ulterior schemes!

Of course, it was ever pointed out that planning as a means of economic regulation under socialist market economy mainly refers to guidance and strategic planning rather than mandatory planning. Now the Chinese version of the "Eleventh Five-Year Plan" (2006-2010) is reworded from "the Eleventh Five-Year 'jihua' (plan)" into "the Eleventh Five-Year 'guihua' (program)", but program is still a kind of plan, or more precisely, a guiding and strategic plan. As to the role of guidance planning and strategic planning in the market economy, I've already clarified it long since. But ever since the very word was replaced (in the Chinese version), the slightest nuance of change was thereafter so ridiculously hyped up! What a good harvest from the "marketization reform"!

Besides, guidance and strategic planning must live up to its name. If it only exists in name without providing any guidance in a real sense, what will be the point of making so many efforts to draft, discuss, and censor the Five-Year Plan before it is finally passed? So, we must emphasize the guiding role of plans or programs. Besides, plans are also required to set necessary targets, projects or mandatory tasks, such as some medium-to-long term plans for huge projects, breaking disruptive technologies and environmental governance etc., and some short-term plans including counter-cyclical investment plans, regulation measures to iron out the cycle (including fiscal and monetary policies) etc. All these need to prescribe mandatory tasks with binding force. In this sense, mandatory planning should not be excluded. Currently, plans tend to be formulated just for the sake of compiling policies, rarely including compulsory targets or tasks requiring accountability, so they are rather optional. It is very necessary to improve them.

To summarize, China's reform aiming to achieve the self-improvement of the socialist system and to establish a socialist market economy is absolutely more than a "marketization reform". Check documents of the Central Committee, the Constitution, and Party Constitution, and you will surely find the word "marketization reform" nowhere! Besides, you will find that the "reform and opening-up" is always associated with "the Four Cardinal Principles"; before "market economy", there must be a modifier "socialist"; "socialism" always goes hand in hand with "public ownership as the mainstay". In sharp contrast, those who advertised "marketization reform" deliberately dropped these key words in almost every occasion. But as for some government officials who did occasionally say the word "marketization reform", I think they must be using it only as a short form rather than a full name. Given that this wording tends to misguide our reform and the fact that it might be manipulated by advocates of "marketization reform", I suggest that party leaders avoid using it in case they fall into their traps.

"Marketization Reform" shouldn't be the full Name of China's Reform

—An interview with Liu Guoguang, a distinguished Chinese economist

Our reform aims to achieve the self-improvement of the socialist system, including the establishment of socialist market economy. China's reform, which is supposed to cover many fields such as politics, economy, society, culture and the government etc., aims to achieve the self-improvement of socialism in every field, so it cannot be generally called "marketization reform", nor should the principle of marketization apply to all. Even the economic field cannot be 100% marketized, as the economic reform aims to establish a socialist market economy and let market forces, subject to state macroeconomic regulation, serve as the basic means of regulating resource allocation. However, the simplified wording of "marketization reform" fails to cover all these meanings.

(Journalist Guo Jinhui reported from Beijing)

The Editor's Note

Over a period of time, the reform has set off a heated discussion. Our newspaper has published a series of in-depth interviews with many distinguished scholars, including Yaoyang, Huasheng, Li Jiange, Liu Shijin and Xu Xiaonian etc., providing many insightful and rational analyses of issues concerning the

reform.

We believe that the reform is still the common understanding of the whole society despite many controversies. The reform is an objective reality as well as the result of historical awareness.

Our experience since the Third Plenary Session of the 11th Central Committee has demonstrated, "the reform and opening up is the path to a stronger China as well as the historical decision crucial to the fate of modern China. It is the most distinctive characteristic of New China as well. If we hadn't carried out the reform and opening-up, there would be no socialism with Chinese characteristics". Combination of socialism with market economy is a great pioneering undertaking. In order to achieve that, "we need make active explorations and bold experiments, showing respect to people's pioneering spirit; we need deepen the reform to solve deeper contradictions and fundamental problems that may arise during structural transformation; we need open up more widely to the outside world and absorb and use for reference the advanced technology and managerial expertise of foreign countries including developed capitalist ones." If we did not carry out the reform, many problems would be insoluble. "It would be more difficult and complicated to advance the reform further. We must press ahead boldly and strive to make significant progress in institutional innovation, never flinching from difficulty." "In every historical stage of socialist society, we need carry out reform at appropriate times to constantly give impetus to the self-improvement and self-development of the socialist system so as to meet the requirements for economic and social development. Only thus can we imbue the socialist system with vigor and vitality."

These remarks, which have been kept in key documents of the CPC in the new stage, are also our invaluable experience gathered while seeking to rejuvenate the Chinese nation. In this sense, it is a result of historical awareness.

Reform is a process of self-improvement. In every historical stage, we need accomplish new historical missions, which requires us to keep deepening the reform. As President Hu Jintao ever stated, in order to make our economy grow rapidly and soundly, we should give full play to the basic role of market forces in regulating resource allocation and in the meanwhile strive to reinforce and improve macroeconomic regulation; we should seize every opportunity to advance the reform and step up our efforts in it practically, but at the same time, we should also seek to improve the scientific soundness of policy-making and coherence among policies and measures with a view to balancing the interests of all aspects and taking their concerns into consideration in the process of reform. Such dialectic thinking has profound significance for our reform.

Speaking of this debate, you have to know the opinions of Liu Guoguang, a famous economist, whose ideas carry a lot of weight. In our interview with him recently, Professor Liu elaborated on his previous views and added some new points, which are basically coherent.

British philosopher Bertrand Russell ever said, "Never try to discourage thinking, for you are sure to succeed." Such quote will apply to whatever argument is responsible and based on reasoning, regardless of how intense the debate is.

Journalist from *China Business News*: This debate over reform has lasted for over two years. Some people called it the third great debate since the reform and opening-up. What do you think sets apart this debate from the previous ones?

Liu Guoguang: This debate is no less intense than the previous two. But something weird is that the views of one side can be seen or heard in the mainstream media where those of the other hardly can. But the latter's views are circulated so widely on the Internet that they have already had very huge impact.

Journalist: what do you think is at the heart of the debate?

Liu Guoguang: As to the nature of this great debate, people were also divided sharply. Some people called it a debate concerning "anti-reform VS unwavering adherence to the reform", which was, however, severely disputed. Because one cannot forcefully apply the label of "anti-reform" to so many common people and scholars who just reflected on the reform, or just call it "a wave of anti-reform and denial of reform", either.

It was mostly believed that the most controversial issue is not whether to adhere to the reform or not, but in what direction our reform should head instead. Should we uphold the basic socialist economic system in which public ownership is the mainstay and many types of ownership develop side by side to achieve the self-improvement of socialism or just seek privatization in the reform? Should we pursue a socialist market economy or just simply called the reform "marketization reform"?

Journalist: Not long ago you pointed out in an article that two different outlooks on reform would inevitably compete with each other. Besides, you also made it very clear that ideological issues would unavoidably be involved. But it seems to be somewhat contradicting Deng Xiaoping's "black cat and white cat theory"[1] and his idea of "regardless of whether it is capitalism or socialism". Could you explain that?

Liu Guoguang: To start with, I need to clarify that Deng Xiaoping's idea of "regardless of whether it is capitalism or socialism" was relevant to the relations between planning and market. Planning and market forces, both as means of controlling economic activities, can be used under both capitalism and socialism. Neither planning nor market is the essential characteristic of socialism or capitalism. Actually, Deng Xiaoping did not mean that all the aspects of the reform should recognize no boundaries between capitalism and socialism. If not so, why did he bother to emphasize the necessity of adhering to the "Four Cardinal Principles"? Why did he bother to repeatedly stress the importance of upholding socialism and maintaining the status of public ownership as the mainstay of the economy? Why did he bother to place the modifier "socialist" before "Three Favorables"[2]? So, we should understand Deng Xiaoping's theory as a whole and

1 It is one of the most famous maxims of Deng Xiaoping, dating back to the years before the Cultural Revolution. He said, "It doesn't matter whether a cat is white or black, as long as it catches mice."

2 "Three Favorables" are whether it promotes the growth of the productive forces in a socialist society, increases the overall strength of the socialist state and raises the people's living standards).

try to put it in perspective.

Next, we must realize that the other side is actually replacing the socialist ideology with the capitalist one such as "privatization" and "pure marketization" under the disguise of "de-ideologization", which we will be absolutely zero tolerant of. Tricks such as "de-ideologization" and "non-politicization" played on crucial matters concerning the fate of the whole nation and people can only work on those without any knowledge of Marxism.

Journalist: From your academic background, we can tell that you are one of the economists promoting the idea of market economy very early. Now some people said that you led the campaign of "anti-marketization-reform", believing that you were to retrieve the old planned economy. How come they viewed you this way?

Liu Guoguang: Do you know why one side of the debate labelled the other side "anti-reform" and disguised themselves as "steadfast defenders of the reform"? It is very simple to understand.

First, in present-day China where the reform is in full swing, "anti-reform" is regarded as the most heinous crime, quite similar to the deadly "sin" of "anti-cultural revolution" in the period of "Cultural Revolution". At least, the so-called "anti-reformists" were already put on the defensive. Second, they attempted to cover up their real intention of steering China to pure privatization and marketization under the disguise of embracing the reform and opening-up.

Journalist: Why did you participate in the debate since you are already in your eighties? Why are you so concerned about it?

Liu Guoguang: Seriously, I had not intended to. My research in recent years was mainly focused on macroeconomics, with more emphasis on economic operation and development. In the awarding ceremony of *China Economics Award for Outstanding Contribution* in March 2005, I made a brief speech, which unexpectedly triggered some disputes. Besides, in June 2005, I talked about several issues in the current economics teaching sheer by chance, which received great attention after the article was posted on the Internet. This is how I got involved in the debate. But at the very beginning, I was kind of forced to respond to it. Gradually I came to realize that the direction of reform is indeed a big issue.

Journalist: why did so many people begin to reflect on the reform recently? Is it because the reform got stuck and would not carry on due to too many problems, just like some people said?

Liu Guoguang: I do not think so. Despite some disturbances, our reform still keeps moving forward. Some problems did arise in our reform, such as the drain of state assets in SOE reform, which is the very reason some people got rich overnight, and "three big mountains", namely, education, medical care and housing.

Some people said that the direction of reform shouldn't be to blame for this or that problem in the reform, that is to say, all the current problems had nothing to do with the direction of reform. I think it is both right and wrong. In general, we are upholding socialism in the reform. But as far as its implementation is concerned, many aspects of the reform have been sidetracked. For example, in terms of ownership, the status of public ownership as the mainstay of the economy was somewhat challenged. Evidently, local state-owned enterprises have almost been sold out, among which quite a lot were sold in extremely low prices or just given away. Now central SOEs are to be sold, too, and some people are even suggesting a bid on some enterprises concerning the lifeblood of the national economy. Currently, nobody can tell the precise proportion of the public sector. In NPC & CPPCC sessions, some committee members and deputies proposed to reveal these statistics, but there weren't any follow-ups.

Take distribution as another example. Witnessing the widening of the gap between the rich and the poor, people began to worry about the trend of polarization. All this indicates that the reform was being sidetracked. If some people think these problems have nothing to do with "marketization", that is sheer nonsense!

In my opinion, it is for the very purpose of removing these disturbances and advancing our reform in a more correct direction that the Central Committee put forward "the Scientific Outlook on Development" and the idea of "building a harmonious society". However, the situation is too hard to be completely rectified. These disturbances affecting the right direction of reform, i.e., socialism, are an objective reality. So, it is not right to say that nothing is wrong with the direction of reform.

Journalist: Do you think these disturbances are the rooted cause for the problems in the current reform?

Liu Guoguang: Surely, the reform hasn't been fully carried out in some aspects; the reform is still not complete enough. All these factors might lead to problems in the reform. But we cannot overlook the disruptive influence of these disturbances on the right direction of reform, i.e., socialism. And therefore, people began to reflect on these problems in the reform, such as corruption, social problems and many problems in the restructuring of SOEs, etc., and then offered some suggestions for improvement. These people shouldn't be labelled as "anti-reformists" just because they exercised their rights. This is the first reason that people reflected on the reform.

Second, with the deepening and complication of the reform since the 1990s, the old balance among different interests in our society has shifted. Some people became better-off; some got extremely rich overnight; many people's lives were improved; a considerable number of people's lives were barely improved; some people's interests were damaged; some were even reduced to poverty and vulnerability. It is very natural for these people, whose living standards and social status declined relatively or absolutely, to resent these social phenomena that undermined their interests and brought about the widening of the gap between the poor and the rich as well as deviations from socialism. They just expected something to be done to overcome some problems with some aspects of the reform rather than oppose the reform.

These people include the vulnerable and the poor, most of whom are workers or peasants making up the bulk of the great masses. Even though they might have overreacted due to biased opinions, we should still try to educate and unite them to embrace the reform rather than drive them to the anti-reform camp. But some people have ridiculously labelled them as "anti-reformists". As a respected and distinguished Chinese economist put it, they are really shooting irresponsible criticism at random!

Journalist: Some people attributed many problems that arose during the reform to the inadequacy of "marketization reform", and therefore they suggested strengthening the "marketization reform". How do you like the "marketization reform"?

Liu Guoguang: some people called China's reform a "marketization reform". If it is just regarded as a short form for our reform, it can be barely accepted. But this wording is very questionable. If it is regarded as the full name of our reform rather than a short form, that is to say, if China's reform is defined as a "marketization reform", it wouldn't be more wrong than that.

Our reform aims to achieve the self-improvement of China's socialist system, including the establishment of socialist market economy. However, it should be noted that China's reform, which is supposed to cover many fields such as politics, economy, society, culture and the government etc., aims to achieve the self-improvement of socialism in every field, so it cannot be generally called "marketization reform", and the principle of "marketization" does not apply to all, either.

Even the economic field cannot be 100% marketized, as the economic reform aims to establish a socialist market economy and let market forces, subject to state macroeconomic regulation, serve as the basic means of regulating resource allocation. However, the simplified wording of "marketization reform" fails to cover all these meanings. Besides, there is still a modifier "socialist" before the term "market economy", with "subject to state macroeconomic regulation" serving as its precondition. These are words in black and white carrying substantial meanings in the document of the Third Plenary Session of the 14th Central Committee of the CPC, rather than an empty talk.

Journalist: In your acceptance speech for the "China Economics Award for Outstanding Contribution", you commented that more emphasis had been placed on market economy and less on socialism these years. When it comes to socialism, we tended to attach relatively more importance to the development of the productive forces, i.e., efficiency, and relatively less to common prosperity, i.e., social equity. Did you realize this earlier? How should we understand the socialist market economy?

Liu Guoguang: "socialist market economy" is a complete concept and an organic unity as well. Some people deliberately dropped the word "socialist" or reduced it to something dispensable while talking about the "marketization reform". However, I don't believe that the modifier "socialist" is an empty word, as Deng Xiaoping has repeatedly emphasized the two fundamental principles of socialism, i.e., public ownership as the mainstay with many kinds of ownership developing side by side and common prosperity without polarization.

However, some people maliciously removed and killed these two basic principles of socialism while advertising "marketization reform", attempting to make people accept the "marketization reform" before they even know it. And what's more, they even deliberately dropped the most fundamental principle, i.e. public ownership as the mainstay of the economy. But instead, words like "the private sector has already become 'the very foundation of national economy" or 'the economic mainstay'" are flooding some media and meetings. I guess it might be the real meaning of deepening the "marketization reform". We are sure to develop the private sector, which is however conditioned by the status of public ownership as the mainstay of the economy. However, the Central Committee has never stated that the private sector should be the economic mainstay.

"Subject to state macroeconomic regulation" is the precondition for the socialist market economy. Market economy does play an important role in regulating resource allocation and have a sharp edge in allocating competitive resources; besides, in response to price fluctuations, economic agents can make judgments and decisions on their own. All these are indeed the advantages of market economy, however, it does have many flaws and limitations in achieving the overall macro-economic equilibrium, handling the relations between monopoly and competition, protecting environment, conserving resources, and ensuring social equity, etc.

Under these circumstances, we cannot do without state intervention or government control. We need count on macroeconomic regulation to correct market faults, restrain market behaviors and remedy the defects of market economy. In other words, the "visible hand" is made to complement the "invisible hand".

Especially in socialist China, the dominant role of socialist public ownership makes it possible for China to achieve unitary planning and enables its society to concentrate on accomplishing great things. Therefore, it will be more necessary for us to reinforce state macroeconomic regulation and government intervention. It is only subject to state macroeconomic regulation that market forces can play a basic role in regulating resource allocation, which suggests that not all the resources would be allocated by the market. Rather, allocation of some key resources have to be regulated by the state, which is also very self-evident.

All in all, we should respect market and avoid any blind faith in it. At the same time, we should not have blind faith in planning either, but it does not mean that we should abandon the other means of controlling economic activities. Currently, under "the slogan of marketization reform", the market is so worshipped that planning has almost been considered as a taboo subject. It was under such circumstances that I noted the necessity of reinforcing state intervention and regulation by planning while developing a socialist market economy. How come it has now become "an attempt to retrieve the old planned economy"? Those who advertised the "marketization reform" just wanted to impose a label on us. I am afraid they couldn't have their way.

State macroeconomic regulation mainly includes regulation by planning, regulation through taxation, and financial regulation. As for China's state macroeconomic regulation, land-use regulation is also included, which actually falls into the category of regulation by planning. The current investment regulation cannot do without land-use regulation. All these types of regulation are conscious, ex-ante regulation, involving centralized decision-making; whereas regulation by market forces is spontaneous, ex-post regulation, involving decentralized decision-making. Such spontaneous, decentralized, ex-post regulation will surely bring about many bad consequences, which therefore must be corrected by state macroeconomic regulation and regulation by planning, i.e., government intervention. Some people suggested letting market forces dictate the economy where it goes, and even applying marketization to politics and culture. Their schemes to exclude planning from the socialist market economy and social life and to dismiss it as a taboo subject, I think, are more than naïve.

To summarize, China's reform aiming to achieve the self-improvement of the socialist system and to establish a socialist market economy is absolutely more than a "marketization reform". Check documents of the Central Committee, the Constitution, and Party Constitution, and you will surely find the word "marketization reform" nowhere! Besides, you will find that the "reform and opening-up" is always associated with "the Four Cardinal Principles"; before "market economy", there must be a modifier "socialist"; "socialism" always goes hand in hand with "public ownership as the mainstay". In sharp contrast, those who advertised "marketization reform" deliberately dropped these key words in almost every occasion. As for some government officials who did occasionally say the word "marketization reform", I think they must be using it only as a short form rather than a full name. However, by doing so, they would easily be used by those advocates of "marketization reform" and thus misguide the reform.

Journalist: The biggest difference between the Chinese version of the "Eleventh Five-Year Plan (jihua in Chinese)" and the previous ones is that jihua (plan) has been reworded into "guihua" (program). Some people considered it as a huge progress, a good harvest from the "marketization reform". What do you think of it?

Liu Guoguang: Even though (in the Chinese wording) "jihua" (plan) is reworded into "guihua" (program), the program is still a kind of plan, or more precisely, a guiding and strategic plan. I pointed out earlier that planning, as a means of regulation under socialist market economy mainly refers to guidance and strategic planning rather than mandatory planning. But ever since the very word was replaced (in the Chinese version), the slightest nuance of change was thereafter so ridiculously hyped up! Actually, it does not make any sense to do so, as both "guihua" and "jihua" mean the same, and the English version is still the "Eleventh Five-Year Plan"! what a joke from the "marketization reform"!

Journalist: Recently you have studied systematically all the previous Five-Year Plans. What characteristics do you think plans under socialist market economy should have?

Liu Guoguang: Even though plans under socialist market economy mainly refers to strategic plans, they must provide guidance as well. If it only exists in name without providing any guidance, what will be the point of making so many efforts to draft, discuss, and censor the Five-Year Plan before it is finally passed?

So, it is still very necessary to emphasize the guiding role of plans or programs. Such plans should not only serve as a guide for policy-making, but also set necessary targets, projects or mandatory tasks, such as some medium-to-long term plans including programs for huge projects, breaking disruptive technologies and environmental governance etc., and some short-term plans including counter-cyclical investment plans to iron out the cycle. All measures such as fiscal and monetary policies etc. need contain mandatory tasks with binding force. In this sense, mandatory planning should not be excluded.

Currently, plans tend to be formulated just for the sake of compiling policies, rarely including compulsory targets or tasks requiring accountability, so they are rather optional. It is very necessary to improve them.

(This is the summary of Guo Jinhui's interview with me in May 2006. Guo Jinhui is a journalist from *"China Business News"*. This article, which was originally intended to be published in the newspaper *China Business News*, was held by senior censors sent by Publicity Department of the CCP Shanghai Municipal Committee to the newspaper office. Afterwards, I submitted the same article to the *Digest of Marxism* run by CASS, with the content unchanged at all.

On the 7th volume in 2006, It was published and the *"Digest of Marxism"* did not say that my article contains anything inappropriate. Here, I've attached Guo Jinhui's letter which specifically explains why the interview was not published in the newspaper *"China Business News"* and the transcript of his interview with me. Please read them for reference.)

The Right Direction of China's Reform and Opening-up —China's market-oriented reform aiming to achieve the self-improvement of socialism

The current popular saying that "if we did not carry out the reform and opening-up, we would find ourselves in a blind alley" is not accurate and complete enough. From the very beginning, our reform was market-oriented, but it was also firmly believed at the same time that it is the self-improvement of socialism. The 14th National Congress of the CPC stated clearly that our reform aims to establish a socialist market economy instead of a capitalist one. Deng Xiaoping also repeatedly emphasized public ownership as the mainstay of the economy and common prosperity without polarization as the two basic principles of socialism, which, I think, the 18th National Congress report should use as the criterion to tell and determine in which direction our reform should head.

In early February, many media all quoted one of Deng Xiaoping's famous remarks in his South China Tour talks out of context, "if we did not carry out the reform and opening-up, we would find ourselves in a blind alley." It has caught people's wide attention and "filled people with great enthusiasm"; in the meanwhile, it also stirred wide discussions among the people on the street and on the Internet.

30 years' reform and opening-up has witnessed the increase of China's national strength, which is undoubtedly a huge step forward. However, with the deepening of the reform, some deeper contradictions also came to the surface and got even worse. Indeed, only if we persist in the reform and opening-up would it be

possible for China to head off risks and promise a bright future. Otherwise, we would get nowhere.

Reform can head in many directions. However, as to which direction it should head toward, socialism or capitalism, it is a big question.

At the beginning of the reform, we stressed that "the reform is the self-improvement of the socialist system" and that "adherence to the Four Cardinal Principles" and "adherence to the reform and opening-up" are "two basic points" with equal importance. At that time, everybody was cheerful and ready to embrace the reform.

But now, the "self-improvement of the socialist system" is seldom mentioned, and "adherence to the Four Cardinal Principles" is also neglected or not mentioned at all. Even if touched upon occasionally, it was not treated that seriously any more. So, many people began to have some misgivings about the current "reform".

Given the situation, it seems very necessary to repeat the warning that "if we did not carry out the reform and opening-up, we would find ourselves in a blind alley." However, the current popular saying is not precise or complete enough. Reform can head in different directions. What direction our reform should take, socialism or capitalism, needs to be made crystal clear. Mikhail Gorbachev ever adhered to the reform too, but how did Soviet Union end up? The former head of Agitprop of the Soviet Union ever said, "with even a brief look at the history of our reform, one would find that Gorbachev's reform has actually undergone the following phases: implementation of strategies on acceleration of development, advances in science and technology, expansion of democracy (i.e., practice of democratic socialism), and elimination of socialism."

Mikhail Titarenko, Chairman of the Russia-China Friendship Association remarked, "Under the disguise of reform, Gorbachev's 'reform' is actually a plan to sabotage and even disintegrate the USSR." Deng Xiaoping also pointed out, "Certain individuals pretended to support the reform and opening-up in an attempt to lead the country towards capitalism. They are only trying vainly to change the nature of our society." Therefore, we cannot simply say that "if we do not carry out the reform and opening-up, we would find ourselves in a blind alley". It would be more precise to say that if we do not carry out the reform in the direction of socialism, we would find ourselves in a blind alley; likewise, if we carry out the reform in the direction of capitalism, we would find ourselves in a blind alley, too.

Therefore, we should not blindly say that "if we do not carry out the reform and opening-up, we would find ourselves in a blind alley", for it tends to misguide our reform. Having referred to the transcript of Deng Xiaoping's South China tour talks in 1992, we found out that these words were not uttered out of context, but with an important precondition. He said,

> "In upholding the line, principles and policies formulated since the Third Plenary Session of the Eleventh Central Committee of the CPC, it is essential to adhere to the principle of 'one central task and two basic points'. If we did not adhere to socialism, implement the policies of reform and opening-up, develop the economy and raise people's living standards, we would find ourselves in a blind alley."

Therefore, rather than quote Deng Xiaoping's words out of context, we should see the whole picture and try to grasp the spirit of Deng Xiaoping's speech.

While talking about the reform and opening-up, if some people deliberately evaded or downplayed the "Four Cardinal Principles" or socialism, distorted the meaning of socialism, and quoted Deng Xiaoping's words out of context, such as "if we do not carry out the reform and opening-up, we would find ourselves in a dead alley", they must be guiding the reform and opening-up astray towards capitalism, maliciously or unconsciously.

I hope that the 18th National Congress report could elaborate on this spirit with great clarity, leaving no room to those who had an axe to grind.

This issue is crucial to the fate of socialist China and over a billion people.

It is correct that our reform has been market-oriented since the very beginning; in the meanwhile, it was also firmly believed that our reform is the self-improvement of the socialist system. The 14th National Congress stated clearly that our reform aims to establish a socialist market economy instead of a capitalist one. Deng Xiaoping has stated very clearly what essential characteristics and basic principles set socialism apart from capitalism. He said, "What sets socialism apart from capitalism is common prosperity without polarization."[1] "The greatest superiority of socialism is that it enables all the people to prosper; common prosperity is an essential characteristic of socialism." [2]

In order to achieve common prosperity, the essential characteristic that differentiates socialism from capitalism, we need to maintain the dominant role of public ownership. "So long as public ownership is the mainstay, polarization can be avoided"[3], and common prosperity will be finally achieved. That explains why Deng Xiaoping has repeatedly stressed public ownership as the mainstay of the economy and common prosperity without polarization as the two basic principles. Approximately, he repeated it at least five times in different occasions, "public ownership as the mainstay and common prosperity without polarization are the two fundamental socialist principles that we must adhere to."[4]

The two fundamental socialist principles and the relationship between the two principles, i.e., "so long as public ownership is the economic mainstay, polarization can be avoided", invented by Deng Xiaoping, constitute the essence of the theory of socialism with Chinese characteristics, which are in line with with Marxism and Mao Zedong thought as well. Therefore, the 18th National Congress report should use these two principles as the criterion to tell and determine in which direction our reform should head.

According to the first fundamental socialist principle that Deng Xiaoping put forward, the 18th National Congress report should not only reaffirm the necessity of adhering to the Four Cardinal Principles, but also reiterate the importance of

1 *the Selected Works of Deng Xiaoping*, vol. 3, p.123.

2 *Chronology of Deng Xiaoping's Career (1975-1977),* p.1324.

3 *The selected works of Deng Xiaoping*, vol.3, p.149.

4 *The Chorology of Deng Xiaoping's Career (1975-1997)*, p.1033, 1069, 1075, 1078, 1091.

upholding unswervingly the basic socialist economic system in which public ownership is the mainstay and the public sector of the economy plays a leading role just as the Constitution stipulates. Currently, the share of public assets in operating assets is far lower than the lower bound, resulting in the loss of its superiority; the leading role and control of the state sector concerning the lifeblood of national economy has been dramatically crippled. In view of this, we should stop any policies or decrees from violating the Constitution, and try to resist and reduce any negative influence of them.

A famous scholar pointed out bluntly that since our basic economic system prescribed in the Constitution hasn't been abolished yet, policies of pushing SOEs to be privatized and encouraging private capital to enter the key fields concerning the lifeblood of national economy are "not only a violation of the supreme law of the PRC, but a sign of the radical change of our state system". Robert Bruce Zoellick, President of the World Bank (2007-2012), ever called on China in his report to drastically cut down the number of State-owned enterprises. According to the English version of the report, China's SOEs' share of gross industrial output should be reduced from 27% in 2010 to 10% till 2030. In fact, behind this plot was very few liberalistic bureaucratic elites in China, who attempted to rely on international capital to suppress the tide of anti-privatization at home.

In a senior forum held in the Diaoyutai State Guesthouse, Beijing on March 17, some specially invited "distinguished scholar" stepped forward to defend the World Bank report, "I strongly welcome some suggestions offered by the World Bank report, as SOEs have in fact become one of the largest obstacles hindering China's further progress. The proportion of SOEs should be reduced to around 10% in the next five to ten years." He is even more desperate to achieve this than the World Bank, ten to fifteen years ahead of the timetable set by the World Bank report! In the plan for China's privatization designed by rightist bourgeois elites from home and abroad, the proportion of China's SOEs in the national economy they suggested is even much smaller than the share of state-owned monopoly capital that some modern capitalist countries have ever reached.

In the 1980s, we ever inspected French SOEs and found that their turnover accounted for 21% of GDP and 42% of gross industrial output; value added accounted for 28% of GDP. By way of comparison, we can tell how strongly these so-called experts from home and abroad desired to convert China to capitalism! I believe that the Communist Party of China, as a real Marxist party, will solve this problem properly in the 18th National Congress of the CPC.

According to the second fundamental socialist principle that Deng Xiaoping put forward, the report of the 18th National Congress of the CPC should point out that in the past three decades, we devoted most time and energy to making a large cake, i.e., GDP growth while focusing on economic development, and still haven't had the time to divide the cake equitably. As a result, the gap between the rich and the poor kept widening and the trend of polarization got even worse. Therefore, in the following period of time, we should strive to correct this by placing greater emphasis on the equitable division of the cake. That is to say, we should regard the equitable division of the cake, namely, people's livelihood and income distribution as our first priority in the economic development.

In order to display the great determination of the CPC in achieving common prosperity without polarization, I suggest that the 18th National Congress report should emphatically expound on Deng Xiaoping's expositions concerning this aspect, never trying to evade Deng's repeated warning that "if our policies lead to polarization, we would end up with failure". We should promote local models of successful explorations in common prosperity embraced by local people and avoid argumentum ad hominem. However, in order to reverse the trend of polarization and achieve common prosperity, the 18th National Congress report should, in theory, suggest transcending these local models, which are mainly focused on distribution and redistribution of income and welfare, because, aside from distribution and redistribution, we need also adjust ownership structure and property relations in accordance with Deng Xiaoping's ideas concerning the relations between the two fundamental principles of socialism. That is to say, in order to solve the problem at its source, we have to still count on the basic economic system in which public ownership is the mainstay.

[Note: I ever talked about these main points in a speech I made in the first meeting of the executive committee at CSM (China's Society of Macroeconomics) on March 24th, 2012, and another speech in the 22nd Annual Meeting of China's Economic Law Research Society in Wuhan University on April 12th, 2012. This article was published in the journal of *Economics Information*, 2012, No. 7.]

Characteristics of China's Socialist Market Economy —marking the 20th anniversary of the target for China's economic restructuring

In 1992, the 14th National Congress firstly proposed that the reform aims to establish a socialist market economy, which is a great milestone in our history since the reform and opening-up. Till now, socialist market economy has been practiced in China for two decades. It is of great practical significance and academic value to review the origin and development of our reform target, i.e., to establish a socialist market economy. In order to celebrate the 20th anniversary of the target for China's economic restructuring, our newspaper interviewed Liu Guoguang, a distinguished scholar and committee member of CASS, who ever participated in the drafting of the central documents of the 14th National Congress.

1. The origin of reform target, i.e., to establish a socialist market economy

Journalist from *Chinese Social Sciences Today*: How was the concept of "socialist market economy" put forward creatively two decades ago?

Liu Guoguang: It was the great result of China's 14 years' explorations of reform and opening-up. Since 1978, China has begun to carry out the reform and opening-up and placed more emphasis on regulation by market forces, having moved a long way forward. Till 1984, the Third Plenary Session of the 12th Central Committee of the CPC proposed that socialist economy is "a planned commodity economy based on pubic ownership", a major step towards building the theory of socialist market economy. In 1987, the 13th National Congress stated, "the socialist planned commodity economy should be a system that integrates planning with the market." Besides, it also came up with the formula of "the market being regulated by the state; the enterprise being guided by market forces", with more emphasis laid on market in the triad of state, market and enterprise. During his inspection tour of the southern coastal cities of China in early 1992, Deng Xiaoping made it very clear that planning and market are not the differentiating features of social system, but the means of controlling economic activities that could be used both under socialism and capitalism instead. Besides, he also reiterated, "market economy can also be practiced under socialism".

Before the convention of the 14th National Congress, the drafting panel summarized three types of target for economic restructuring: to establish a socialist commodity economy characterized by the combination of planning and market, to establish a socialist planned market economy, and to establish a socialist market economy. The first wording is an improved version of the policies of both the Third Plenary Session of the 12th Central Committee and the 13th National Congress; The second and third versions are newly created. At last, the 14th National Congress report decided on the third one, which is brief and to the point. And the second and the third mean actually the same thing.

Jiang Zemin, then General Secretary of the Central Committee of the CPC, talked about the relationship between socialist market economy and planning in his speech delivered in the Party School of the Central Committee of the CPC on June 9th, 1992. He said, "Socialist economy had planning since its establishment, and everybody knows it perfectly well. Therefore, one should not infer from the missing of the word "planned" that planning would be aborted." [1]

In this way, the spirit of the 14th National Congress concerning the reform target is very complete. "Socialist market economy" is in essence a "planned market economy". The exclusion of the word "planned" from the wording of reform target

1 *Collection of Selected Major Documents Over the Three Decades Since the Reform and Opening up* Ⅰ, Beijing: Central Party Literature Press,2008, p.647.

at that time was mainly due to the reason that traditional planned economy was then very deep-rooted in people's mind and that the concept of market economy hadn't been that penetrating yet. In order to enhance the image of market in people's mind and encourage them to embrace the concept of "market economy", the word "planned" was deliberately omitted; but the substantial modifier "socialist" that carries great weight was placed before "market economy", because "socialism had planning since the very beginning".

2. Viewing planning and market in perspective

Journalist: So far, to what extent has China's economy been marketized? How deep is our understanding of the market?

Liu Guoguang: A few years ago, it was estimated that, in general, 70% of China's economy has been marketized. In this sense, we can say that socialist market economy has been initially established. Surely, market economy has not developed that much in some aspects, such as resource factor markets, capital and financial markets, etc., so it still needs further improvement. However, due to lack of experience, over-marketization also occurred in some fields such as education, medical care and housing etc. Though both under-marketization and over-marketization still deserve attention, they are not mainstream issues in the period of transition from traditional planned economy to market economy any more. So far, all positive and negative effects of market have been fully exposed. The market has great superiorities in encouraging competition and optimizing resource allocation; besides, it also has many inherent limitations in maintaining the balance between aggregate supply and aggregate demand, conserving natural resources, protecting the environment, and ensuring social equity, in which market seems to be at its end of tether. This has a lot to do with the inherent flaws of market and the failure of state macroeconomic regulation by planning to keep up with the process of marketization.

Market economy has been carried out in China for two decades, but planning seemed to have faded away. Due to historical reasons, we used to overvalue planned economy. However, things have changed with the passage of time. Some people have gone from one extreme to another, i.e., from holding blind faith in planning to blindly worshipping market, resulting in market fundamentalism and market infantilism. They believed that market can solve all the problems, attributing all problems to the inadequacy of "marketization reform". Some people thought that marketization was not complete enough due to too much state intervention and that planning was not worth mentioning since the marketization reform is being carried out. Some people even suggested that China copy European and US models of free market and adopt pure liberalization. These people kept selling the ideas of anti-socialism and anti-planning proposed by Friedrich Hayek, Austrian capitalist economist. Actually, both planning and market have their own merits and demerits. We should respect market instead of having blind faith in it. At the same time, we shouldn't neglect or have blind faith in planning, either.

To put it simply, the advantages of planning lie in its capacity of gathering necessary financial, human and material resources together in the whole society to accomplish some great things, adjusting incomes and maintaining social equity. The strengths of market lie in its capacity of promoting progress in technology and management through competition to link production with demand. However, neither planning nor market is all-powerful. Five major tasks cannot be assigned totally to market or the law of value alone. They are as follows: to achieve the balance between aggregate demand and aggregate supply, to make timely adjustments to major economic structures, to fight against monopoly resulting from competition, to protect ecological environment and to ensure social equity. In order to solve these issues, the state needs to carry out macroeconomic regulation through state planning. But plans are made by man, who will inevitably have their own limitations and thus many difficulties in overcoming some contradictions.

Take the pair of contradiction between subjectivity and objectivity, a major problem in planning, as an example. First, subjective perception of things falls behind the objective development of things; second, man often have information asymmetries and limitations in collecting, transmitting and processing information and data; third, planners' observation and judgment are often influenced by social forces and interests. All in all, owing to these limitations, planning might deviate from real situations or objective laws, leading to serious mistakes in macroeconomic management. Therefore, we need to keep improving our understanding and awareness, adjusting our planning to the requirement of objective laws and circumstances.

To summarize, we need carry out the market-oriented reform but avoid any blind faith in market; we need persist with macroeconomic regulation by planning but avoid any blind faith in planning. All these things I kept talking about are in line with Deng Xiaoping's ideas that both planning and market can be used under socialism; besides, they all conform to the spirit of the 14th National Congress of the CPC concerning the reform target.

3. A higher-level combination between planning and market

Journalist: How to achieve a combination between planning and market on a higher level?

Liu Guoguang: Marxism holds that the national economy should achieve balanced, proportionate development in communal production. To put it another way, national economy should develop in a sustained, sound and coordinated way, which, however does not mean a traditional planned economy regulated by administrative and mandatory planning. Over the three decades, based on our national conditions in the primary stage of socialism, we have overcome limitations of planned economy by carrying out a market-oriented reform, and begun to establish a socialist market economy two decades ago. However, at the same time we should always respect the economic law of balanced, proportionate development under public ownership. This explains why we should reinforce the guiding role of state planning in macroeconomic regulation.

The 17th National Congress stated, "We will give play to the guiding role of national development plans, programs and industrial policies in macroeconomic regulation and combine the use of fiscal and monetary policies to improve macroeconomic regulation." Some people misinterpreted the emphasis on "the guiding role of state planning in macroeconomic regulation" as a retrogression to "traditional planned economy", which is quite wrong. Actually it is a higher-level combination between planning and market. The reasons are as follows: First, the current state planning is not inclusive, but instead it only attends to the macroeconomic activities, whereas the micro-economic activities are assigned to market. Second, market is the current basic means of regulating resource allocation, whilst planning is the necessary means to remedy the defects of market. Third, current plans do not mainly refer to administrative orders any more, but include guiding, strategic and predictive plans instead. And at the same time, these plans must serve as a guide and commit entities to complete tasks and to take responsibilities when necessary. That is to say, these plans also need contain some mandatory tasks rather than be shelved after they are made.

At present, in some aspects of the economic field, some local plans did not contain any tasks with binding quotas or accountability; some local plans are divorced from central ones; most of the plans are just focused on the compilation of policies. All these indicate that people are gradually downplaying the role of planning, which needs to be rectified.

4. What sets socialist market economy apart from capitalist one?

—State planning being the "backbone" of macroeconomic regulation

Journalist: Some people held that macroeconomic regulation is the essential feature that differentiates socialist market economy from capitalist one. What do you think of it? Are there any differences between macroeconomic regulation under socialist market economy and that under capitalist market economy?

Liu Guoguang: The 14th National Congress report pointed out that, socialist market economy is a type of market economy subject to state macroeconomic regulation, in which market serves as the basic means of regulating resource allocation. It was ever mistaken by some people as the distinctive feature of socialist market economy. However, macroeconomic regulation is also carried out in capitalist market economies, so it is not the essential characteristic that sets socialist market economy apart from capitalist one. Rather, planning, or more precisely, the role of planning in macroeconomic regulation is the thing that really matters. State planning plays a guiding role in the macroeconomic regulation, which is a distinctive feature of our socialist market economy.

As early as in Bashan Cruise Meeting[1] in 1985, , Hungarian economist Junos kornai put forward the so-called "BII" model, i.e., "the model of market economy subject to macroeconomic regulation", which was then echoed by French economist Albert O. Hirschman, who said that France was also using this model. Under capitalist market economy, macroeconomic regulation was mainly implemented through fiscal and monetary policies. In very few market economies such as Japan, South Korea, France, some organizations like "Economic Planning Agency" were ever set up to make predictive plans occasionally. However, most market economies such as the United States and UK don't regulate the economy through planning.

A colleague of mine (from CASS) who attended the Bashan Cruise Meeting wrote an article entitled "Economic Restructuring and Macroeconomic Management"[2], pointing out that we should draw a dividing line between the socialist market economy subject to macroeconomic regulation and the capitalist market economy in which macroeconomic regulation is also used. Since socialist market economy has already been set as the reform target, we must uphold the fundamental socialist principles, i.e., public ownership as the mainstay of the economy and common prosperity; in the meanwhile, we must carry on state planning which serves as a guide for socialist market economy as well. In this sense, socialist macroeconomic regulation can also be implemented through another means, that is, state planning. To put it another way, for a socialist country

1 Note: This meeting was held in the *Bashan* cruise headed for Wuhan, China, in which many famous economists all participated, so it was named Bashan Cruise Meeting.

2 See *Collected works of Liu Guoguang*, vol.4, pp.232-234.

in which public ownership is the mainstay, it is very necessary to use planning as another means to implement macroeconomic regulation, aside from fiscal and monetary policies. Therefore, we still need regulation by state planning while establishing the system of socialist market economy. For example, we still make annual plans and Five-Year Plans etc. and keep such a large organization as National Development and Reform Commission as well.

The 14th National Congress report also stated clearly, "State planning is one of the important means of macroeconomic regulation". Socialist market economy is bound together with the socialist basic economic system. In the tripartite of fiscal policies, monetary policies and planning, planning serves as a guide for fiscal and monetary policies, and fiscal and monetary policies also need guidance from state planning. So state planning is inseparable from macroeconomic regulation; or to put it anther way, the former is the "backbone" of the latter. This is another characteristic of socialist market economy setting the macroeconomic regulation under socialist market economy apart from that under capitalist one.

5. Adhering to the basic economic system in the primary stage of socialism

Journalist: what are the fundamental differences between socialist market economy and capitalist one?

Liu Guoguang: The first and foremost difference between them is the basic economic system. The 14th National Congress report stated very clearly, "socialist market economy is bound together with the socialist basic economic system". The cornerstone of our socialist market economy is the basic economic system in the primary stage of socialism in which public ownership is the mainstay and other kinds of ownership develop side by side. Without the basic economic system, there would be no socialist market economy. In contrast, the cornerstone of capitalist market economy is capitalist private ownership. This is the most fundamental difference.

In its Fifth Plenary Session, it is highly purposeful for the 17th Central Committee of the CPC to propose that "we should uphold and improve the socialist basic economic system". A lot of evidence shows that the trend of privatization does exist and pose a threat. Advocates of privatization requires the state sector to withdraw not only completely from competitive fields, but also from key industries and fields concerning the lifeblood of the national economy and to give place to the private sector.

In the capitalist market economy, the state sector mainly provides services that private enterprises won't do, only serving as a supplement to the private sector to make up for the deficiency of market mechanism. However, in the socialist market economy, the state sector, indispensable to sustained, sound and coordinated economic development, is established for the sake of consolidating and improving the socialist system. Therefore, the state sector should cover these key industries and fields concerning the lifeline of the national economy, such as energy, transportation, communications, finance, infrastructure and pillar industries, and have "absolute control" or "fairly strong control" over them; enterprises should be wholly or partially owned by the state, with the state holding an absolutely or relatively controlling number of shares, so that the national economy could be regulated by state planning. As for competitive fields and industries crucial to social equity and justice, we should also regard them as "major" fields or "key" industries and strive to do a good job, though they do not matter too much to economic regulation by the government.

Surely, we should open competitive fields to private enterprises, encouraging them to compete fairly with each other and with SOEs as well. Besides, we should ensure and give play to the positive role of the private sector in competitive markets at both institutional and policy level. We should also fully acknowledge all contributions that the non-public sector including the private sector has made to the development of the productive forces. However, the private sector has duality. On the one hand, it benefits the development of the productive forces; on the other, it involves exploitation. Therefore, we should not only guide them to run the business legally and seek growth healthily, but restrict their unhealthy and illegal operations as well as their range of business.

It should be noted that as for strategic fields and natural monopoly industries concerning the lifeblood of the national economy and vital to the national security, the crux of the matter is not whether they are monopolized or not, but under whose control they are instead. More capable of standing for strategic interests of the state and social public interests, public enterprises are in general in a better position than private ones to run these special fields and industries. Surely, administrative monopoly should nevertheless be overcome. In terms of distribution of income, SOE reform is currently focused on the readjustment of senior executives' incomes and prevention of SOE interests from being departmentalized or privatized since the "marketization reform". However, one thing that deserves our attention is that these problems did not emerge before the marketization reform, which has great implications for relevant studies.

6. The direction of reform and opening-up

Journalist: Deng Xiaoping stressed in his South China Tour Talks two decades ago that if we did not carry out the reform and opening-up, "we would find ourselves in a dead alley". Now it has been widely quoted. What do you think of it?

Liu Guoguang: First and Foremost, we should never quote the great man's words out of context. To fully understand Deng Xiaoping's remarks concerning the so-called "dead alley", we should notice that these words were uttered with a very important precondition. He said, "In upholding the line, principles and policies formulated since the Third Plenary Session of the Eleventh Central Committee of the CPC, it is essential to adhere to the principle of 'one central task and two basic points'. If we did not adhere to socialism, implement the policies of reform and opening-up, develop the economy and raise living standards, we would find ourselves in a blind alley." Strictly speaking, it is imprecise and partial to say that "if we did not carry out the reform and opening-up, we would find ourselves in a blind alley", which doesn't tally with the spirit of Deng Xiaoping's talks. This issue is so critical that it determines the direction of our reform and opening-up and even the fate of our socialist country and over a billion people.

Journalist: Could you please talk about the direction of reform and opening-up in detail?

Liu Guoguang: Reform can head in different directions, say, capitalism or socialism. We should always keep a check on the direction of our reform. Deng Xiaoping ever pointed out, "Certain individuals, pretending to support the policy of reform and opening-up, attempt to lead the country towards capitalism. They are only trying vainly to change the nature of our society." Our reform has been market-oriented since the very beginning; in the meanwhile, it was also firmly believed that our reform is the self-improvement of the socialist system. The 14th National Congress stated clearly that our reform aims to establish a socialist market economy instead of a capitalist one. Deng Xiaoping has mentioned at least five times the two fundamental principles of socialism, namely, public ownership as the mainstay of the economy and common prosperity without polarization. Such original idea of Deng Xiaoping is the very essence of the theory of socialism with Chinese characteristics.

But now, while talking about the reform and opening-up, the "self-improvement of the socialist system" is seldom mentioned, and "adherence to the Four Cardinal Principles" is neglected or not mentioned, either. Sometimes, it was just mentioned in passing. Therefore, it is very necessary to reiterate and stress the importance of adhering to the Four Cardinal Principles and maintaining the dominant role of public ownership. Currently, the share of public-owned assets in operating assets has declined, and the leading role and control of the state sector concerning the lifeblood of national economy has been drastically undermined.

In the 1980s, we ever inspected French SOEs and found that their turnover accounted for 21% of GDP and 42% of gross industrial output; value added accounted for 28% of GDP. As we can see, the proportion of China's SOEs in the national economy is even much smaller than that of state-owned monopoly capital some modern capitalist countries have ever reached.

In the past three decades, we devoted most time and energy to making a bigger cake and thus haven't had the time to divide the cake equitably, with the result that the gap between the rich and the poor kept widening and the trend of polarization got even worse. Therefore, we should put the equitable division of the cake higher on our lists of priorities in the next period of time.

(This article is the summary of an interview with me by Zhang Wenqi, a journalist from *Chinese Social Sciences Today*. It was published in *Chinese Social Sciences Today,* September 12th, *2012)*

Part IV

Socialist Market Economy does Have Planning

Planning and Public Ownership as the Mainstay of the Economy —the two fundamental characteristics setting socialist market economy apart from capitalist market economy

It has been 20 years since the 14th National Congress proposed to establish a socialist market economy in 1992. Over the two decades, it is very obvious that huge achievements have been made since the establishment of new economic system, but at the same time it also led to many problems which need to be corrected or improved. Here, I would like to analyze the issues as to how to deal with the relations between planning and market and how to consolidate the foundation of socialist market economy (i.e., the basic economic system in the primary stage of socialism). Any idea in this article is open to discussion.

1. Planning under socialist market economy

Marxism holds that the national economy should achieve balanced, proportionate development. To put it another way, national economy should develop in a sustained, sound and coordinated way, which, however, does not mean a traditional planned economy regulated by administrative and mandatory planning. Since the reform and opening-up, we have overcome limitations of planned economy and established a socialist market economy based on our national conditions in the primary stage of socialism. However, in the meanwhile, we should also respect the economic law of balanced, proportionate development under public ownership. Scholars in political economics should particularly bear it in mind.

In line with the spirit of Deng Xiaoping's South China tour talks, i.e., "planning and market, as both means of controlling economic activities, can be used", the 14th National Congress of the CPC proposed in 1992 that our reform aims to establish a socialist market economy. At that time, there were three types of target for the reform: to establish a socialist commodity economy characterized by the combination of planning and market, to establish a socialist planned market economy, and to establish a socialist market economy. At last, our party decided on the third version, "to establish a socialist market economy".

Jiang Zemin, then General Secretary of the CPC Central Committee explained why this version excludes the word "planned". He said, "A planned commodity economy is equivalent to a planned market economy. Socialist economy had planning since its establishment, and everybody knows it perfectly well. Therefore, one should not infer from the missing of the word planned that planning would be aborted." [1]The exclusion of the word "planned" from the wording of reform target at that time was mainly due to the reason that traditional planned economy was then very deep-rooted in people's mind and that the concept of market economy hasn't been that penetrating yet.

In order to enhance the image of market in people's mind and encourage

1 *Collection of Selected Major Documents Over the Three Decades Since the Reform and Opening up I*, Beijing: Central Party Literature Press, 2008, p.647.

them to embrace the concept of "market economy", the word "planned" was deliberately omitted; but the substantial modifier "socialist" that carries great weight was placed before "market economy", because "socialism has already had planning since its establishment". In this way, the spirit of the 14th National Congress concerning the reform target is very complete. As a member of the drafting panel of the central document, I felt it is very right for the Central Committee to put so much effort into this.

Until now, market economy has been carried out in China for two decades, during which planning has faded away. Due to historical reasons, we used to overvalue the planned economy. However, things have changed with the passage of time. Some people have gone from one extreme to another, i.e., from holding blind faith in planning to blindly worshipping market. They even said that planning wouldn't be needed any more. In some aspects of the economic field, the guidance of state planning for macroeconomic activities has dwindled; some local plans or programs failed to commit entities to complete tasks and to take responsibilities when necessary; some local plans are divorced from central ones, blindly pursuing higher GDP growth, so much so that these plans or programs have ceased to serve as the guide. All these have affected the effectiveness of macroeconomic management, leading to many imbalances in social and economic development.

Under the circumstances, it is very necessary to reaffirm that socialist market economy also has planning. Given that the role of planning has been downplayed both in practice and ideological thinking, the 17th National Congress restated "the guiding role of national development plans, programs and industrial policies in macroeconomic regulation". Therefore, we should not only implement this major policy in practice, but highlight the important role of planning under socialist market economy while publicizing the theory of socialist market economy.

There is no denying that socialist market economy must have a sound macroeconomic regulation system. In Bashan Cruise meetings in 1985 in which issues of macroeconomic management were widely discussed between economists from all over the world, Hungarian economist Junos kornai suggested that China should establish a market economy subject to macroeconomic regulation, which was then echoed by French economist Alber O. Hirschman, who said that France was also using the very model. It suggests that macroeconomic regulation, which is also practiced in capitalist countries, is not exclusive to socialist economies. But what sets socialist market economy subject to macroeconomic regulation from the capitalist market economy in which macroeconomic regulation is also practiced? Aside from its basic economic system, planning or guidance from state planning, is another distinctive feature of socialist market economy.

In quite a few market economies, such as Japan, South Korea and France, organizations like "Economic Planning Agency" were ever set up to make predictive plans occasionally. In most market economies such as USA and UK, they only use fiscal and monetary policies instead of planning as a means to regulate economy. However, in contrast, it is very necessary and probable for China, as a great socialist power with public ownership as the mainstay, to use planning as a means of macroeconomic regulation to guide the balanced, proportionate development of the national economy, which is the superiority of socialist market economy.

There are several means of macroeconomic regulation, among which planning, fiscal policies and monetary policies are the most important. The 14th National Congress report specifically pointed out, "State planning is an important means of macroeconomic planning," however, fiscal and monetary policies were not mentioned. It is not because they are not important at all, but instead, they are under the guidance of state macroeconomic planning. To sum up, macroeconomic regulation is inseparable from state planning, with the latter being the backbone of the former. Market economy subject to macroeconomic regulation can also be called a market economy subject to macroeconomic regulation by state planning, which is the distinctive characteristic that sets socialist market economy apart from capitalist market economy.

2. How to consolidate the foundation of socialist market economy

Another fundamental difference between socialist market economy and capitalist market economy is the basic economic system. The former is founded on the basic economic system in the primary stage of socialism, in which public ownership is the mainstay and other kinds of ownership develop side by side, whereas the latter is grounded on the basic economic system dominated by private ownership. The basic economic system of socialism is the prerequisite for socialist market economy.

The Fifth Plenary Session of the 17th Central Committee reiterated that we should "uphold and improve the socialist basic economic system". Therefore, we must avoid both privatization and the system that just has a unitary public sector, which is one of the "four important distinctions"[1] proposed in the Fourth Plenary Session of the 17th Central Committee of the CPC. At present, we need to find out which trend is more serious, "privatization" or "a system that just has a unitary public sector", so as to mitigate its negative effects more effectively. The latter is the result of people's belief in the past that sufficiently large communes under exclusive public ownership should be the best form of socialism, but now very few people think in that way except some radical "leftists". This is indeed an important distinction we must make. Notwithstanding this, a lot of evidence shows that the ill trend of privatization poses a more serious threat. Marxist political economics cannot afford to ignore this.

It is right that Marxism did not judge the nature of ownership only by the proportion of ownership; however, according to Marxism, complete disregard

1 "Four important distinctions" was proposed at the Fourth Plenary Session of the 17th Central Committee of the CPC. It stated, "we must consciously make a clear distinction between Marxism and anti-Marxism, between the basic economic system in which public ownership is the mainstay and many types of ownership develop side by side on the one hand and privatization or a system that only has a unitary public sector on the other, between socialist democracy with Chinese characteristics and the capitalist-style democracy of the West, and between socialist ideas and culture on the one hand and corrupt feudalist and capitalist ideas and culture on the other."

for the proportion of ownership is not recommended, either. If the proportion of the public sector in national economy keeps declining to almost zero, the nature of socialism would be changed. According to statistics newly released by NBS (National Bureau of statistics of PRC), the proportion of the public sector (esp. the state sector) in the national economy is still declining; in the macro-level, there was no such a trend of "guo jin min tui" (the state advances whereas the private sector retreats); In the micro-level, it is mostly "guo tui min jin" (the state retreats whilst the private sector advances); besides, "guo jin min tui", occurring in rare cases just for the sake of resource allocation, also makes sense. Our party has been insisting that there should be a limit to the reduction in the proportion of the public sector, that is, public ownership must remain the mainstay of the economy. But quite a few people have begun to doubt it. One way to remove their doubts is to make statistics known to the public. It is incumbent on the Marxist political economics to remove people's doubts and increase their confidence in the basic economic system in the primary stage of socialism.

As the basic economic system dictates, public ownership should be the mainstay of the economy and the state sector play a leading role. Therefore, the state needs to control the lifeline of the national economy and the state sector's control, influence and competitiveness must be enhanced. In capitalist societies, the state sector mainly provides services that private enterprises won't do, only serving as a supplement to the private sector to make up for the deficiency of market mechanism. However, in socialist societies, the state sector, indispensable to sustained, sound and coordinated economic development, is established for the sake of consolidating and improving the socialist system.

Therefore, the state sector should cover these key industries and fields concerning the lifeline of the national economy, such as energy, transportation, communications, finance, infrastructure and pillar industries, and have "absolute control" or "fairly strong control" over them; enterprises should be wholly or partially owned by the state, with the state holding an absolutely or relatively controlling number of shares. All these are prescribed and emphasized by the documents of Central Committee. The state sector must maintain control on these fields or industries so that the national economy could be regulated by state planning and thus develop in a more sustained, sound and coordinated way.

Besides, the state sector is obligated to ensure social equity and justice as well. As for competitive fields and industries crucial to social equity and justice, we should also regard them as "major" fields or "key" industries and strive to do a good job, though they do not matter too much to economic regulation by the government. Therefore, in order to stabilize employment, create more jobs, ensure social welfare, provide public services, increase transfer payments and guarantee social equity through redistribution, we need not only maintain the state sector's control on the major fields concerning the lifeline of the national economy characterized by natural monopoly, but bring its role into play in the competitive fields.

Why can't SOEs enter the competitive fields? Why do all the profits have to be gained exclusively by private enterprises? The Central Committee has always been insisting that state-owned capital move in and out of the competitive fields based on rational choices so as to bring their competitiveness into full play, rather than withdraw completely from them, just like what neo-liberalist elites and its followers who are "inside the system" *(ti zhi nei)* kept preaching! Of course, in order to encourage fair competition, these competitive fields should be open to all. All these things should be made crystal clear in the textbooks on political economics.

Advocates of privatization require the state sector to withdraw not only completely from competitive fields, but also from major fields and key industries concerning the lifeline of the national economy. They often labelled the state sector as "monopoly enterprises or industries" due to its control on these industries or its sharp edge over its rivals. They often levelled random criticism at SOEs, condemning that they colluded with the government to exercise monopoly. Besides, they even reduced all state-owned capital to "bureaucratic monopoly capital".

It should be noted that what really matters is not whether these industries concerning the lifeline of the national economy and vital to the national security are monopolized or not, but who controls them instead. More capable of standing for strategic interests of the state and social public interests, public enterprises are in general in a better position than private ones to run these special sectors and industries.

Defects of administrative monopoly should be eradicated. Its solutions are nothing different from those employed in the reform of common SOEs, such as separation of government administration from both enterprise management and state assets, corporatization, establishment of modern corporate structure, reform of income distribution system, improvement of legal and supervision systems, etc. In terms of income distribution, the current reform of SOEs is mainly focused on the re-commitment of SOEs to turn in profits to the state treasury, the readjustment of senior executive's high pay (some of them have exorbitant pays), and the prevention of SOE interests from being departmentalized or privatized since the "marketization reform". Besides, we should further improve the Staff and Workers Representatives Congress (SWRC) system to make it truly represent the interests of the working people. If employees were allowed to supervise during SOE reorganization in a real sense, tragedies like Tonghua (Jilin province, China) Iron and Steel Group riot would have probably be avoided.

The private sector is also part of the basic economic system in the primary stage of socialism, and therefore we should expound on the positive role that the non-public sector including the private sector has played in promoting the development of the productive forces in China. However, the private sector also has duality: it not only benefits the development of productive forces, but involves exploitation. In view of this, we should not only guide them to run the business legally and healthily, but also restrict their unhealthy and illegal operations as well as their range of business. These key industries concerning the lifeline of the national economy and vital to public interests must be controlled by the public sector, because the private sector, caring nothing but profits, would widen the gap between the rich and the poor and thus undermine national economic security.

(This article was originally entitled "Two Fundamental Differences between Socialist Market Economy and Capitalist Market economy", published in *HongQi Wengao (Red Flag Manuscript)*, 2010, No.21)

Planning: Socialist Market Economy's Forte

1. Lessons from the global economic crisis

These years many people tended to consider market economy practiced in western capitalist countries as a modern, standard, and mature market economy. In other words, they believe that modern capitalism has already overcome its internal contradictions and thus no cyclical economic fluctuations, i.e., economic crisis, would occur. According to them, Marxist analysis of capitalism has already been out of date. However, a financial crisis broke out recently in the United States and spread to the world very rapidly, which suggests that the nature of capitalism isn't changed at all, and that Marxist analysis of capitalism still works.

Since the end of 1970s, neo-liberalism sprang up in the western world. Neo-liberalists believe that people should not put capitalism to blame for all these problems; rather, too much state intervention, they think, is the villain. Their theory is that so long as state intervention is weakened, capitalism would regain vitality. Neo-liberalism and market fundamentalism kept running wild in the western world for three decades. As a result, the poor became even poorer and the rich even richer; the economy had to be maintained by debt-fuelled consumption and financial speculation, resulting in financial tsunami and global financial crisis. Capitalism can hardly overcome contradictions between socialized mass production and private ownership of the means of production, resulting in many imbalances among all sectors, between aggregate supply and aggregate demand, and between virtual economy and real economy, which manifest themselves in the current crisis. For rather long in the past, many people did not take them seriously; but at present, almost nobody dare continue to overlook them .

Currently, a buzzword in the United States is "bailout". To put it in our way, it is just the "strengthening of state macroeconomic regulation". The feverish worship of market has been cooled down in western countries. Nowadays, western leaders are at such a loss in the economic crisis that some of them even resort to the classic work "Das Kapital" for solutions. So, we should review Marxist analysis of capitalism more than ever to deepen our understanding of the current world.

These years, we also tended to overestimate the strengths of market and overlook its weaknesses. Accordingly, the strengths of planning have been severely undervalued and ignored, which deserves our reflection.

2. with distinctive merits and demerits, planning and market being both indispensable

Deng Xiaoping firstly pointed out that, planning and market, both as means of regulating resource allocation rather than essential characteristics of any social system, can be used under both socialism and capitalism. [1]

Both Planning and market have their own merits and demerits. The strengths of market lie in its capacity of promoting progress in technology and management through competition to link production with demand. However, market is not all-powerful. Five major tasks cannot be assigned totally to the market or the the law of value alone. They are as follows: to maintain a balance between aggregate demand and supply, to make timely adjustments to major economic structures, to fight against monopoly resulting from competition, to protect ecological environment and to ensure social equity.

The advantages of planning lie in its capacity of concentrating resources on accomplishing some great things, reorienting the economic development when necessary, adjusting incomes and ensuring social equity. But plans are made by man, who will inevitably have their own limitations and thus many difficulties in overcoming some contradictions, such as the contradiction between subjectivity and objectivity, contradictions among different interests, etc. In view of these, we

1 *The Selected Works of Deng Xiaoping*, vol.3, People's Publishing House, 1993, p.373.

need to improve planning on the one hand and try to use market to make up for the deficiency of planning on the other.

In practice, we should give full play to their strengths, avoid their weaknesses and make them complement with each other. It is wrong to have blind faith in either of them and make them conflict with each other.

3. "Planning" — an intrinsic nature of "socialist market economy"

Many people believe that the establishment of socialist market economy means the total denial and abandonment of planning. However, it is not right to think so.

It was the 14th National Congress of the CPC that proposed to establish a socialist market economy. Not long before that, Jiang Zemin consulted with me about the relationship between socialist market economy and planning. He said to me, "A planned commodity economy is equivalent to a planned market economy. Socialist economy had planning since its establishment, and everybody knows it perfectly well. Therefore, one should not infer from the missing of the word 'planned' that planning would be aborted." He also made the same remark in a speech delivered in the Party School of the CPC on June 9th, 1992. [1]He is absolutely correct in saying so. For decades, people did interpret it this way, as "planning" is an intrinsic nature of socialist market economy.

By proposing to establish a socialist market economy in the 14th National congress, the Central Committee meant to let market forces, subject to state macroeconomic regulation, serve as the basic means of regulating resource allocation. Means of state macroeconomic regulation includes not only monetary and fiscal policies, but also state planning. The 14th National Congress report stated clearly, "state planning is one of the important means of macroeconomic regulation"[2]. The socialist market economy we aim to establish is neither a capitalist market economy nor a market economy in general, but a socialist one

1 *The Selected Works of Jiang Zemin,* vol.1, Beijing: People's Publishing House, 2006, p.202.

2 *Collection of Selected Major Documents Over the Three Decades Since the Reform and Opening up I*, Beijing: Central Party Literature Press, 2008, p.660.

with planning.

Please note two most important differences between socialist market economy and capitalist market economy. The first difference is public ownership as the mainstay and common prosperity; in other words, it stands for the interests of the people; the second one is "planning", which makes up for the deficiency of market in guarding against a volatile economy and ensuring that the interests of the people will be served. Therefore, it is absolutely right to define socialist market economy as a planned market economy.

In 1992 I ever said, "modern market economy shouldn't oppose any economic interventions by the government or guidance from planning; rather, it must rely on them to make up for its own deficiency; and we should always keep this in mind during the transition of planned economy to market economy." [1]These words rather serve as a reminder that "socialist market economy also has planning" at the juncture of our economic transition to market economy!

4. Bad consequences of macroeconomic regulation by planning failing to keep up with the process of marketization

Over the past three decades, our economy has witnessed a gradual change from traditional planned economy to socialist market economy and an increasing share of market in economic regulation, which has vigorously boosted China's economy. In the circulation of all commodities, over 90% is regulated by market forces. Several years ago, it was estimated that 70% of China's economy had been marketized. In this sense, we can say that socialist market economy has been initially established.

Since the initial establishment of market economy, both positive and negative aspects of the market have been fully exposed. Inherent flaws of market economy have gradually come to the surface despite its superiority in stimulating competition and optimizing resource allocation. Especially when it is required

1 *Collected Works of Liu Guoguang*, vol. 7, Beijing: China Social Sciences Press, 2006, p.130.

to achieve a balance between aggregate demand and aggregate supply, conserve resources, protect the environment and ensure social equity, market seemed to be at the end of its tether.

However, quite a few people infected with "market infantilism" worshipped market so much that over-marketization occurred in many fields such as education, medical care and housing etc., where marketization was not supposed to occur at all. I am afraid very few, if at all, western capitalist countries have ventured to carry out a pure liberalization. Actually, over-marketization in these fields has brought about many bad consequences to the people's lives.

Market seeks profit maximization and therefore gives strong impetus to economic development, which is an advantage of market economy. However, we cannot overlook its flaws at the same time. Market tends to seek the maximization of immediate profits instead of long-term ones. In view of this, we need to count on state planning to make up for the short-sightedness of market. For example, there are an excessively large number of "sweatshops" on the brink of collapsing, which will probably bear the brunt in the economic crisis, just like what is now happening across the southeastern coastal regions. However, even if they are lucky enough to survive, they would hardly try to conduct indigenous innovation and industrial upgrading. I'll give you another example. The Central Committee is planning to build bigger indigenous jetliners. However, based on the theory of comparative advantage which believes in free trade and free market, China should just manufacture 800 million pairs of pants because it has a comparative advantage in producing pants, while building the airplane is a comparative advantage of western capitalist countries.

The market tends to seek maximization of local and individual interests, which however will not necessarily lead to maximization of social interests. Take a paper mill for an example. It does save a sum of money by discharging untreated wastewater to the river, and its profits are thereby maximized; however, the river is polluted. Its private interests are gained at the expense of social interests. Take small coal pits for another example. They did make large fortunes by illegitimate mining, which, however has damaged severely good mineral veins. These years, natural resources and environmental problems are getting even more acute. By the way, the Melamine-tainted-baby-milk scandal in 2008 is also another typical example of such kind.

To sum up, over the past three decades since the reform and opening-up, China has no doubt made many remarkable achievements, but on the other hand, problems are also piling up, such as environmental damage, the widening gap between the rich and the poor, and urban-rural disparity etc. All these have a lot to do with the failure of state macroeconomic regulation by planning to keep up with the process of marketization.

Since the 14th National Congress, we have succeeded in controlling inflation and deflation successively while implementing the short-term macroeconomic regulation. However, the guidance of state planning for macroeconomic activities tends to be dwindling gradually. Plans involve mostly compilation of polices but seldom any tasks with accountability or binding quotas; local plans are divorced from central ones, with the latter unable to control the former's blind pursuit of GDP growth; a huge mismatch exists between plans and real work. In short, state planning is now rather weak and even dispensable. For years, we have been chanting the slogan of "overcoming GDP Complex, expanding domestic demand, pursuing indigenous innovation and industrial upgrading" but bore little fruit, which actually has something to do with the weakening of state macroeconomic regulation resulting from poor accountability and low binding force of state plans.

Wisdom comes from experience, that is to say, the more we have experienced, the more lessons we will learn: we should respect market rather than blindly worship it; at the same time, we shouldn't blindly worship or neglect planning either. Due to historical reasons, we used to overvalue planning. Now things have changed with the passage of time. Some people have gone from one extreme to another: from having blind faith in planning to blindly worshipping market.

Many people defined our reform as the "marketization reform", which obviously is too narrow. Our reform, as Deng Xiaoping put it, aims to achieve the self-improvement of the socialist system, covering many fields such as politics, economy, society, culture, and the government. Therefore, we shouldn't simply call it the "marketization reform". Even in the economic field, we are not to carry out a 100% "marketization reform", but to establish a socialist market economy, under which market forces, subject to state macroeconomic regulation, serve as the basic means of regulating resource allocation. So the oversimplified wording—"marketization reform" —failed to include all these meanings. None of the major party documents has ever defined our reform so simply as "marketization reform"!

5. Reemphasis on the guiding role of state planning in the macroeconomic regulation in the 17th National Congress

Now it's time for us to reinforce the role of macroeconomic regulation by planning and to emphasize the leading role of state planning in macroeconomic regulation while maintaining market forces as the basic means of regulating resource allocation.

the 17th National Congress restated, "We will give play to the guiding role of national development plans, programs and industrial policies in macroeconomic regulation and combine the use of fiscal and monetary policies to improve macroeconomic regulation."[1] In my point of view, it is highly purposeful for the Central Committee to reaffirm the guiding role of state planning, which has been overlooked for many years, in the 17th National Congress. It reminded us again that socialist market should have "planning". Macroeconomic regulation guided by state planning is what socialist market economy with Chinese characteristics must include and achieve.

The 17th Central Committee of the CPC reemphasized the guiding role of state planning in the macroeconomic regulation, which is not a retrogression to the traditional planned economy as some people distorted. The reasons are as follows: First, the current state planning is not inclusive, but instead it only attends to the

1 *Collection of Selected Major Documents Over the Three Decades Since the Reform and Opening up II*, Beijing: Central Party Literature Press,2008, p.1762.

macroeconomic activities, whereas the micro-economic activities are assigned to the market. Second, market is currently the basic means of regulating resource allocation, whilst planning is the necessary means to remedy the defects of market. Third, the current plans do not mainly refer to administrative orders any more, but include guiding, strategic and predictive plans instead. And at the same time, these plans must serve as a guide and commit entities to complete tasks and to take responsibilities when necessary.

Transition from planned economy to market economy and the renewed emphasis on the guiding role of state planning in the macroeconomic regulation are in line with the "thesis-antithesis-synthesis" dialectics. Rather than a retrogression to the previous traditional planned economy, it is a higher-level synthesis of planning and market in the new stage of economic reform.

Therefore, we need to achieve harmony between planning and market, and this is what a harmonious socialist should have.

6. Public ownership as the mainstay of the economy, the very precondition for both macroeconomic regulation by planning and common prosperity

As mentioned before, socialist market economy and capitalist market economy are sharply different in the following two aspects: one is planning and the other is that it stands for the interests of the people. Public ownership as the mainstay of the economy is the prerequisite for both of them.

The 14th National Congress pointed out, "Socialist market economy is bound together with the socialist basic economic system". [1]Socialist basic economic system is a structure in which public ownership is the mainstay and other kinds of ownership develop side by side. Here, it is extremely important to lay emphasis on public ownership as the mainstay of the economy. If the proportion of the public sector is too small, it would be difficult to carry forward state macroeconomic regulation by planning. In order to ensure that everyone has access to medical

---

1 *Collection of Selected Major Documents Over the Three Decades Since the Reform and Opening up I*, Beijing: Central Party Literature Press, 2008, P.660.

care, the state wants to grant subsidies to the medical establishment. However, the previous public health care system has been destroyed, many medical and health organizations especially grass-roots ones having been privatized. Does it mean that the government is to subsidize private medical enterprises?!

Since centrally-administered enterprises have become the locomotive of economic growth, the saying that public enterprises are bound to yield low results can not hold water. Surely, we still need further deepen our reform in terms of SOE management, striving to maintain a reasonable income gap between SOE leaders and employees and to crack down on corruption within SOEs. Now the government has initialized the Northeast Area Revitalization Plan (i.e. to revitalize the old northeast industrial bases). We all know that old industrial bases had ever contributed massively to China's economy, but in times of great need the government just cast them off. And what's more, after their collapse, it was believed that these old industrial bases should have themselves to blame due to their low efficiency. But now, the government has made the right decision. Better late than never.

Now when it comes to the causes of the widening gap between the rich and the poor, people would at first associate them with urban-rural disparity, local disparity, industrial monopoly, corruption, uneven distribution of public goods, and delayed redistribution etc. All these are good reasons, but not the most fundamental ones.

According to Marxism, ownership determines distribution and property disparity tends to affect the income gap the most. Even Paul Anthony Samuelson, a western capitalist economist, had to acknowledge that uneven wealth determines income inequality the most, whereas individual capabilities do not make any big difference. He also said that property ownership is the number one factor determining the income gap, with individual capabilities, education, training, opportunities and health coming next to it one after another.[1] Aside from factors mentioned above, changes in ownership structure, i.e., the decline in the

1 see Samuelson, Paul A., *Economics: An Introductory Analysis.*

proportion of the public sector, the rise in that of private sector and the spread of privatization of public assets, also constitute another fundamental cause of the widening of income inequality over the three decades since the reform and opening-up.

But it is not dogmatism to stress that public ownership is the mainstay of the economy. Actually, it is so essential that we cannot afford to overlook it; otherwise, we would end up with polarization and fail to make the fruits of reform shared by all the people. Besides, taxation, transfer payments and means of improving social welfare are also very necessary to narrow the income gap and now they are well under way. However, we cannot totally count on them to reverse the trend at its source.

Take Sweden, a model country for capitalist welfare states, as an example, its long-term policy of using taxation to redistribute income and wealth still bore little fruit. According to the latest research result from Research Institute of Industrial Economics in 2007, the concentration of wealth in Sweden is roughly the same as that in the United States. If man of means who have emigrated are also counted, such as the President of the IKEA Group, the wealth possessed by the minority rich Swedish only accounting for 1% of the whole population of Sweden, is 40% more than the total private wealth of the whole Sweden. In this sense, its concentration of wealth is even probably much higher than that of the United States.

Deng Xiaoping emphasized, "So long as public ownership remains the mainstay of our economy, polarization can be avoided"[1]. It is neither empty talk nor cliché.

7. Greater necessity of reinforcing government planning in the face of the global crisis

In the face of the global economic crisis, the Central Committee of the CPC

1 *the Selected Works of Dent Xiaoping*, Vol. 3, Beijing: People's Publishing House, 1993, p.149.

has decisively started a 4 trillion RMB fund to stimulate the economy. All these economic incentives, be it construction of infrastructure such as railway, highway and energy, or rural construction or ecological enhancement projects, cannot do without planning. Since it costs such a huge amount of money, we must make the most of it to yield the best results. So, careful planning is a must! It proves that macroeconomic regulation guided by state planning is indispensable to socialist market economy. Even in a non-crisis period, we would not allow market, i.e., "the invisible hand" to dictate some key fields of the national economy, not to mention in the crises. At such time of emergency, the government must reinforce macroeconomic planning.

As everybody knows, Thomas Friedman, a famous American columnist, is a representative of neo-liberalism in the U.S. media. His masterpiece *"The World Is Flat",* mainly focused on globalization and extreme marketization, has been translated into Chinese and was published last year. It has become a big influence in China, and even some top leaders read it, too. This year when Friedman visited Guangdong province of China, he can't help exclaiming if only the United States "could just be China for a day" after he found the large-scale promotion of the renewable electricity generation in Guangdong province. After such exclamation, he continued to say, "I mean, just, just, just one day. You know, I mean, where we could actually, you know, authorize the right solutions, and I do think there is a sense of that, on, on everything from the economy to environment... I want my democracy to work with the same authority, focus and stick-to-it-iveness."

It shows that, even Thomas Friedman, a hard-core advocate of marketization, has to admit that market is not all-powerful. The biggest strength of our socialist market economy lies in our capability of concentrating resources on accomplishing great things by planning, such as harnessing alternative energies, narrowing the gap between the rich and the poor, promoting industrial upgrading, protecting the natural environment, land governance, etc. They are the very things that Friedman wanted the United State to have! However, we should also draw strengths from them and bring ours into full play rather than abandon them!

(Du Jianguo, an editor of the journal "Green Leaf", dictated my words and sorted them out into an article, which was published in *Green Leaf*, 2009, Vol. 1)

Macroeconomic Regulation by Planning to Keep up with the Process of Marketization

To look back on the history of reform and opening-up over the three decades, I would like to start from an academic conference in September 1985. In this conference, a Hungarian scholar believed that socialist economy can be operated in two ways, namely, administrative regulation and regulation by market forces, and that each can also be subdivided into two types. So, there are four models altogether as follows: (1) direct administrative regulation, i.e., administrative regulation by mandatory planning; (2) indirect administrative regulation, i.e., regulation by guidance planning; (3) free market regulation, i.e., a pure free market; (4) regulation by market forces subject to macro-control. The fourth one did influence our economic restructuring. For example, conceptions like "letting market forces serve as the basic means of regulating resource allocation" and "establishing a socialist market economy" that the 14th National Congress put forward were deeply inspired by the last one.

CASS economic scholars attending the conference noted that three conditions must be met if we were to finally decide on "regulation by market forces subject to macro-control" as the model for socialist economic restructuring. First, we must adhere to the principle of socialism, which is the only way to tell socialist market economy from capitalist market economy, because regulation by market forces subject to macro-control applies to both, rather than exclusive to socialism. Second, we must reform our ownership structure radically to suite the new economic system. Third, a complete system dictates that the decision-making power must be defined very clearly in some relations such as centralization vs decentralization, central government vs local government, state vs enterprise, plan vs production etc. We should say that, in theory, these conditions were all met in the economic restructuring afterwards.

With regard to the principle of socialism, the 14th National Congress has stated clearly that the market economy we aim to establish is a socialist one, instead of a capitalist one. The word "socialist" that Jiang Zemin particularly emphasized is not superfluous, as socialist market economy is neither a common market economy adopted by capitalist countries, nor a marketization reform in a broad sense, but regulation by market forces subject to macro-control under socialism.

As regards the ownership structure, party documents ranging from the 14th National Congress to the 17th National Congress all affirmed that socialist market economy is bound together with the socialist basic economic system. The socialist basic economic system is a structure in which public ownership is the mainstay and other kinds of ownership develop side by side. As a result, the relationship among all kinds of ownership is clarified.

As for the power of decision-making, the 14th National Congress stressed that state planning is also an important means of macroeconomic regulation. Before that, three models were ever put forward: to combine planning with market, to establish a planned market economy, and to establish a socialist market economy. And we finally decided on the third one, "to establish a socialist market economy". The reason why we excluded the modifier "planned" from the wording is that planning is an intrinsic nature of the socialist economy, which would ensure a balance between centralization and decentralization in the system of socialist market economy.

Even though the aforementioned three conditions are all met in theory, they are more complicated in practice. For example, some people said, "since we've decided to practice a market economy, there is no need to say it is socialist or capitalist; since it is a market economy, there shouldn't be a modifier 'socialist'." If such advice is taken, China's economy would recognize no boundaries between capitalism and socialism. Besides, some people even suggested, "since we've decided to practice a market economy, there is no need to divide our economy into the public sector and the private sector any more." He is suggesting that the socialist basic economic system, in which public ownership is the mainstay and all kinds of ownership develop side by side, should be cast away and that we should pursue 100% privatization! How ridiculous! Some people also said, "market economy means small government with less intervention. The government just functions as a night watchman, maintaining order in the market." Though Deng Xiaoping, who believed that disputes would complicate matters and waste a lot of time with the result that nothing would be accomplished, suggested no contention or arguing, the hot debate among these people still went on. In recent years, these ideas have already had very deep and far-reaching influence in some experimental regions, which therefore need practical solutions.

Over the past three decades, China has witnessed a gradual change from traditional planned economy to socialist market economy and thus an increasing share of market in economic regulation, which has vigorously boosted its economic growth. Surely, market economy has not developed enough in some aspects, such as resource factor markets, capital and financial markets, etc., which still needs further improvement. However, due to lack of experience, over-marketization and especially market infantilism, occurred in some fields such as education, medical care and housing etc. So far, all positive and negative effects of the market have been fully exposed. Despite its strengths in encouraging competition, optimizing resource allocation, and promoting economic progress and benefits, its inherent defects, especially its failures to maintain a balance between aggregate demand and aggregate supply, to preserve natural resources, to protect the environment, and to ensure social equity in terms of income distribution, have been fully exposed.

To sum up, over the three decades, unprecedented economic progress has been made on the one hand, while new problems concerning resource conservation, environmental protection, income distribution and people's livelihood also arose on the other, which has a lot to do with the failure of state macroeconomic regulation by planning to keep up with the process of marketization.

The market economy China aims to establish is the one subject to macroeconomic regulation, which has already been written into the 14th

National Congress document. State planning is one of the important means of macroeconomic regulation. As for other important means, such as fiscal and monetary policies, they all need to be implemented under the guidance of state planning. During these years, we kept improving macroeconomic regulation and succeeded in controlling inflation and deflation in the short run. However, the guidance of state planning for short- and long-term macroeconomic activities has drastically dwindled. Plans involve mostly compilation of polices but seldom any tasks with accountability or binding quotas; local plans are divorced from central ones, with the latter unable to control the former's blind pursuit of GDP growth. All these facts have affected the effectiveness of macroeconomic management and thus resulted in many economic imbalances.

In view of this, the 17th National Congress reaffirmed the guiding role of national development plans, programs and industrial policies in macroeconomic regulation that has been neglected for many years, which I believe is strongly purposeful. It reminds us again that socialist market economy should have planning. Rather than a retrogression to the traditional planned economy just like what some people distorted, China is to achieve a higher-level combination between planning and market in a new stage of reform by placing more emphasis on the regulatory role of planning in the market economy.

The reasons are as follows: First, the current state planning is not inclusive, but instead it only attends to the macroeconomic activities, whereas the micro-economic activities are already assigned to market. Second, market is currently the basic means of regulating resource allocation, whilst planning is the necessary means to remedy the defects of market. Third, current plans do not mainly refer to administrative orders any more, but include guiding, strategic and predictive plans instead. And at the same time, these plans must serve as a guide and commit entities to complete tasks and to take responsibilities when necessary. So, macroeconomic regulation under the guidance of state planning is the very thing that makes socialist market economy with Chinese characteristics so characteristic!

Therefore, we should strive to improve state planning and macroeconomic regulation so as to make them guide the development of socialist market economy in a real sense and thus to achieve a higher-level combination between planning and market forces.

(This is a speech I made in a panel discussion among economists marking the 30th anniversary of the reform and opening-up organized by China Development Research Foundation.)

On Strengthening the Guiding Role of State Planning before the Formulation of the Twelfth Five-Year Plan

Over the past three decades, China has witnessed a gradual change from traditional planned economy to socialist market economy and thus an increasing share of market in economic regulation, which has vigorously boosted its economic growth. In the circulation of all commodities, over 90% is regulated by market forces. Several years ago, it was estimated that 70% of China's economy had been marketized. In this sense, we can say that socialist market economy has been initially established. To some extent, we can also say that the reform, i.e., transformation from highly centralized planned economy to socialist market economy has been basically completed. Surely, market economy has not developed enough in some aspects, such as the resource factor market, capital and financial market, etc., which still need further improvement. However, due to lack of experience and "market infantilism", over-marketization occurred in some fields such as education, medical care and housing etc., where marketization was not supposed to occur at all. Though both under-marketization and over-marketization still deserve attention, they are not mainstream issues in the period of transition from traditional planned economy to market economy any more.

Since the initial establishment of market economy, both positive and negative aspects of the market have been fully exposed. Though market economy has succeeded in stimulating competition and optimizing resource allocation, its inherent flaws also came to the surface in the meanwhile. Especially when it comes to the matters concerning overall economic equilibrium, resource reservation, environmental protection and social equity, market seemed to be at the end of its tether. This has a lot to do with the inherent defects of market economy and the failure of state macroeconomic regulation by planning to keep up with the process of marketization.

In the early 1990s, I ever said in a meeting that both planning and market have their own advantages and disadvantages. Therefore, I suggested that we should respect market but avoid blind faith in it, and that at the same time we should neither blindly worship nor neglect planning. Due to historical reasons, we used to overvalue the planned economy. However, things have changed with the passage of time. Some people have gone from one extreme to another, i.e., from holding blind faith in planning to blindly worshipping market, resulting in market fundamentalism and market infantilism. They believed that the market can solve all the problems, and therefore attributed all problems to the inadequacy of "marketization reform". Some people even suggested that China copy European and US models of free market. And what's more, some people believed that since we were carrying out the marketization reform, there was no need to mention planning any longer.

Some people even hyped up the minor change in the Chinese wording of the 11th Five-Year Plan, i.e., from the 11th Five-Year "jihua" (plan) to the 11th Five-Year "guihua" (program), talking exaggeratedly that we have been much closer to market economy and farther away from planned economy. How ridiculous! Actually, program is also a type of plan. In whatever words we clothe these plans, be it annual plans, five-year plans (programs) or ten-year plans (programs), they are all plans. As for the 12th Five-Year Plan we are now working on, it is also a plan though it is called "guihua" in Chinese.

The market economy we aim to establish is the market economy subject to macroeconomic regulation, just like what the 14th National Congress of the CPC proposed. Over these years, China has been trying to improve macroeconomic regulation and thus has made a lot of progress. Especially since the 14th National Congress, we have succeeded in putting inflation and deflation under control successively while implementing the short-term macroeconomic regulation. However, the guidance of state planning for both short- and long-term macroeconomic regulation has drastically declined. Plans involve mostly compilation of polices but seldom include any tasks with accountability or binding quotas; local plans are divorced from central ones, with the latter unable to control the former's severe "GDP Complex" (i.e., blind pursuit of GDP growth); a huge mismatch exists between plans and real work. All these facts have affected the effectiveness of macroeconomic management, resulting in many imbalances in social and economic development.

Macroeconomic regulation is also practiced in the capitalist market economy, mainly by means of fiscal and monetary policies. So what is the difference between the macroeconomic regulation in the capitalist market economy and that in the socialist market economy? As early as in Bashan Cruise meeting in 1985, Hungarian economist Junos kornai put forward the so-called "B-II model", i.e., "regulation by market forces subject to macro-control", which was then echoed by French economist Albert O. Hirschman, who said that France was also using this model.

A colleague of mine (from CASS) who attended the meeting wrote an article about the Bashan Cruise Meeting, pointing out that we should draw a dividing line between the socialist market economy subject to macroeconomic regulation and the capitalist market economy in which macroeconomic regulation is also used. Since socialist market economy has already been set as the reform target, we must uphold the fundamental socialist principles, i.e., public ownership as the mainstay and common prosperity, and never abandon state planning which serves as a guide for socialist market economy. In this sense, socialist macroeconomic regulation can also be implemented through another means, that is, state planning. In very few market economies such as Japan, South Korea, France, some organizations like "Economic Planning Agency" are set up to make predictive plans occasionally. Whereas in most market economies such as the United States and UK, planning was not used to regulate their economy.

However, as a socialist country, it is necessary and probable for us to use planning as another means to implement macroeconomic regulation. And therefore, we still preserve state planning while developing socialist market economy. For example, we still make annual plans and Five-Year Plans etc. and keep such a large organization as National Development and Reform Commission as well.

Along with the proposition that we should establish a socialist market economy, the 14th National Congress report also stated clearly, “State planning is one of the important means of macroeconomic regulation”. In the tripartite of fiscal policies, monetary policies and planning, planning serves as the guide to fiscal and monetary policies, and fiscal and monetary policies also need guidance from state planning. So state planning is inseparable from macroeconomic regulation; or to put it another way, the former is the “backbone” of the latter. This is the very essential feature that sets the macroeconomic regulation under socialist market economy apart from that under capitalist one.

Under the circumstances, the 17th National Congress restated, “We will give play to the guiding role of national development plans, programs and industrial policies in macroeconomic regulation and combine the use of fiscal and monetary policies to improve macroeconomic regulation.” I believe that it is very purposeful for the central committee to reemphasize the guiding role of state planning that has been neglected for many years, which is not empty words at all. It reminds us again that socialist market economy should have planning. With both strong and weak points of market fully exposed after the initial establishment of market economy, it is very necessary to reaffirm the important role of state macroeconomic planning while developing a socialist market economy, especially when people worshipped market so much that planning had almost been dismissed as a taboo subject under the slogan of “marketization reform”. For instance, it is very necessary to reemphasize the guiding role of state planning in macroeconomic regulation in the 17th National Congress of the CPC. It reminded us again that socialist market economy should be a planed market economy.

Actually, the idea that socialist market economy should have planning is not my invention; As early as June 9th, 1992, four months before the convention of the 14th National Congress, Jiang Zemin said so while talking about the relationship between socialist market economy and planning in his speech delivered in the Party School of the Central Committee. He said, "A planned commodity economy is equivalent to a planned market economy. Socialist economy had planning since its establishment, and everybody knows it perfectly well. Therefore, one should not infer from the missing of the word 'planned' that planning would be aborted."[1] However, many people forgot these remarks or neglected it on purpose.

Here, I would also like to recommend an article written by Professor Ji Baocheng from Renmin University of China entitled "On Political Economics teaching and research", which also provided an insightful analysis of this issue.

> Now, we are called upon to have a 'Scientific Outlook on Development'. Recently, President Hu Jintao proposed that we should take overall consideration as its fundamental approach while expounding on the "Scientific Outlook on Development" in the Party School of the Central Committee of the CPC. So what is "overall consideration"? How to support it in theory in economics? How about "the necessity of the distribution of social labor in definite proportions" in Marxist political economics? This law is really "long time no see"! Why? Because we have reduced planned economy and planning almost to nothing, so much so that nobody dared to say the word "planning". Even though Deng Xiaoping has set right planning

1 Jiang Zemin, "On China's Establishment of a Socialist Market Economy", *Selected Works of Jiang Zemin*, Volume 1, People's Publishing House, 2006, p.202.

> in his South China Tour Talks by mentioning both planning and market as means of controlling economic activities and that there is planning under capitalism and there is market under socialism too, many people still dare not talk about planning and even avoid it like plague. How weird! ... How can we achieve overall consideration without planning? How come planning was abandoned just out of some unaccountable fear? But it does exist in our real work! Have a look at our textbooks on Political Economics and see whether there is anything involving the necessity of planning or its theoretical basis, or the law of distribution of social labor in definite proportions. I sense that very few people tend to talk about it.

In theory, we have explained clearly why socialist market economy should have planning; in practice, the 17th National Congress of the CPC has reaffirmed the guiding role of state planning in the macroeconomic regulation. Does it mean "a retrogression to the traditional planned economy", just like what some people accused of? I don't think so. As a matter of fact, it is a combination between planning and market on a higher level.

It is not groundless to say so. The renewed emphasis on the guiding role of state planning in the macroeconomic regulation in the 17th National Congress is nothing similar to the "traditional planned economy". The reasons are as follows: First, the current state planning is not inclusive, but instead it only attends to the macroeconomic activities, whereas the micro-economic activities are assigned to market. Second, market is the current basic means of regulating resource allocation, whilst planning is the necessary means to remedy the defects of the market. Third, current plans do not mainly refer to administrative orders any more, but include guiding, strategic and predictive plans instead. And at the same time, these plans must serve as a guide and commit entities to complete tasks and to take responsibilities when necessary. That is to say, these plans also need contain some mandatory tasks rather than be shelved after they are made.

The 12th "Five-Year Plan" is the first medium-to-long term plan that we have ever formulated and implemented since the 17th National Congress, which has profound implications for the transformation of our economic development patterns and solutions to problems with social relations. We need to act in the spirit of the 17th National Congress, striving to improve state planning and macroeconomic regulation, making state planning live up to the role that it has been given, i.e., the guide for our economic and social development. During the "12th Five-Year Plan (2011-2015)" period, we need to transform our economic development pattern and maintain a moderate economic growth; we need to promote the development of both the public sector and the private sector while consolidating the socialist basic economic system; we need to reverse the trend of polarization while attaching more importance to social equity.

In order to achieve all these, we mustn't rely exclusively on market economy, but also resort to state macroeconomic regulation by planning as well. A noteworthy thing here is that macroeconomic regulation by planning must be controlled by the Central Committee and local plans must be subject to central plans. I approve of some people' suggestion that local governments should stop making any inclusive national development plans driven by and centered on GDP growth, but seek to make local plans for their own economic and social development in proportion to local financial resources and transfer payments granted by the central government so as to reinforce the role of local governments in market supervision, social management and public service.

Besides, we should also preserve the government's function of regulating resource allocation, especially in major structural adjustment and infrastructure construction etc. Even capitalist countries have never forsworn the use of the so-called "socialist policies" such as nationalization, not to mention socialist countries! So, we shouldn't make market dictate the economy where it goes, but combine it with planning instead.

(This is my speech in "China's Macroeconomics Symposium" on April 24th, 2010, which was published in *Finance & Trade Economics*, 2010, No.7)

Planning and Market: both Required in the Circulation Industry

1. Significant changes in the circulation industry since the reform and opening-up

China's economic restructuring has been oriented towards market since its very beginning, aiming to achieve a gradual transition from traditional planned economy to socialist market economy. For over three decades since the reform and opening-up, China has witnessed tremendous changes in the circulation industry in the following aspects.

First, circulation is growing very rapidly. Since the reform and opening-up, our total volume of retail sales scored double-digit growth year after year. From 1978 to 2009, China's total volume of retail sales has increased from 1.5 trillion RMB to 12.5 trillion RMB, vaunting into the third place among the world. From 1980 to 2009, our sales of means of production have increased from 44.9 billion RMB to 28.5 trillion RMB.

Second, the circulation network has been basically formed. A commodity circulation network has extended in all directions both in urban and rural areas, various commodity markets flourishing unprecedentedly. The business model has undergone a radical change from the previous monotonous one to an open, multi-level, competition-driven model with less red tape.

Third, many forms of business operation exist side by side. It took us only 20 years to create various forms of business operation, which however took western capitalist countries nearly a century to do so. Now we have more than 30 forms of business operation in either physical stores or virtual ones, with even more new forms being constantly added either in retail or wholesale. The circulation system has grown from an exclusive state sector to a structure in which many types of economic sectors develop side by side, such as state-holding enterprise, joint-stock company, private enterprise, Sino-foreign joint venture, Sino-foreign co-operative joint venture, and wholly foreign-owned enterprise, which have jointly promoted the sustainable development of China's circulation industry.

In the meanwhile, circulation modernization drive is gaining momentum. China has witnessed the emergence of chain store business, modern logistics and E-commerce and the wide use of modern information technology, such as digital information, purchase, transportation, storage and operation, which have been widely used in cities.

Thanks to all the abovementioned and other gratifying progress along with the rapid increase and expansion of circulation enterprises, a lot of surplus labor in the countryside and unemployed workers in urban areas were all placed and social pressures arising from unemployment were thereby alleviated. All these achievements are joint efforts of working personnel in the circulation industry under the leadership of the communist party, which deserves great applause and elaboration.

2. Circulation industry having come to prominence as a basic, leading industry under socialist market economy

More than a decade ago, in a symposium on circulation system marking the 20th anniversary of the reform and opening-up hosted by State Bureau of Internal Trade, I proposed that commerce should be upgraded to the status of a leading industry, which still works even now. Since the reform and opening-up, buyers have gradually gained the upper hand, whereas sellers used to have an advantage over buyers. Now, the buyer's market has already been formed. A cycle of market operation starts from circulation industry, which incorporates immediate and potential needs into consumer behavior, and then another cycle begins...In this sense, circulation industry has already grown into a leading industry under socialist market economy.

Our economy has shifted from the previous resource-constrained economy to the current market economy, from the previous supply-constrained economy to the current demand-constrained one. The status of circulation industry has thereby been elevated. Now it's time for it to rise to a leading industry. Besides, we should also realize that against the backdrop of economic globalization, circulation is an indicator of a nation's development and social prosperity, a barometer of a nation's overall national strength and people's living standards and an endless stimulus to launch the market and boost both demand and supply. With the improvement of socialist market economy and industrial restructuring, consumption has contributed more and more to the economic growth. Please note that our government, in the face of the spread and worsening of the global financial crisis, has adopted proactive and expansionary fiscal policies and appropriate monetary policies to expand domestic demand and to increase investment as means of economic incentives. What our government has done is absolutely necessary.

However, expansion of investment demand is not enough to propel domestic demand. After all, investment demand is unlikely to be met without satisfying the ultimate demand of consumption, which would probably result in surplus productivity and an increase in the inventory; and it is utterly unnecessary to manufacture goods for the sake of a larger inventory. Therefore, we should tap into consumption demand through many channels, especially rural market demand with huge potentials, rather than an exclusive focus on investment demand. Thanks to the positive impact of investment multiplier, the increasing effective demand stimulated by investment spending would lead to more consumption, which cannot be realized without circulation. So, it is incumbent on our circulation industry to further tap into consumption demand through many channels.

All in all, circulation industry shoulders the major responsibility of expanding domestic demand, which has gradually come to prominence as a basic, leading industry.

3. In order to develop circulation industry and achieve structural upgrading, we need to improve the mechanism of macroeconomic management and combine planning with market.

Since the reform and opening-up, we have made tremendous progress while striving to establish the socialist market economy, and managed to make market forces, subject to state macroeconomic regulation, serve as the basic means of regulating resource allocation. Until now, market economy has been carried out in China for two decades, but planning seemed to have faded away. In the past, traditional planned economy was overvalued due to historical reasons. However, things have changed with the passage of time. Some people have gone from one extreme to another, i.e., from holding blind faith in planning to blindly worshipping market. In theoretical conception, planning has almost become a taboo subject. In terms of macroeconomic regulation, the guidance of state planning for macroeconomic activities has drastically dwindled; some local plans or programs fail to commit entities to complete tasks and to take responsibilities when necessary; some local plans are divorced from central ones, with the latter unable to control the former's "GDP Complex" (i.e., blind pursuit of higher GDP growth); a huge mismatch exists between plans and real work. All these have affected the effectiveness of macroeconomic management, leading to many imbalances in social and economic development.

In this case, it is very necessary to reaffirm that socialist market economy also has planning. Given that the role of planning was downplayed and marginalized both in practice and ideological thinking, the 17th National Congress restated that we would give play to "the guiding role of national development plans, programs and industrial policies in macroeconomic regulation". So, those industrial policies for the development of circulation industry also play a guiding role in macroeconomic regulation. To sum up, we should not only implement this major policy put forward by the 17th National Congress practically, but also reemphasize the important role of planning under socialist market economy while publicizing the theory of socialist market economy. In order to develop circulation industry, we should not only emphasize the role of the market mechanism, but also make good use of the means of macro-economic regulation.

In Bashan Cruise meetings in 1985, Hungarian economist Junos kornai suggested that China should practice a market economy subject to macroeconomic regulation, which however is not exclusive to the socialist economy, because macroeconomic regulation can also be carried out in capitalist market economies. But what sets socialist market economy subject to macroeconomic regulation from the capitalist market economy in which macroeconomic regulation is also used?

Aside from its basic economic system, planning, or guidance from state planning, is another distinctive feature of socialist market economy.

In quite a few market economies, such as Japan, South Korea and France, organizations like "Economic Planning Agency" were ever set up to make predictive plans occasionally. In most market economies such as USA and UK, they only use fiscal and monetary policies instead of planning as a means to regulate economy. However, in contrast, it is very necessary and probable for China, as a great socialist power with the public sector of the economy as the mainstay, to use several means of macroeconomic regulation, among which planning, fiscal policies and monetary policies are the most important. The 14th National Congress report specifically pointed out, "State planning is an important means of macroeconomic planning," without highlighting the importance of fiscal and monetary policies. It is not because they are not important at all, but instead, they are under the guidance of state macroeconomic planning. To sum up, macroeconomic regulation is inseparable from state planning, with the latter as the backbone of the former. Market economy subject to macroeconomic regulation can also be called a market economy subject to state macroeconomic regulation by planning, which is the distinctive characteristic that sets socialist market economy form the capitalist one.

The guidance of state planning in macroeconomic regulation is not equivalent to the "traditional planned economy". In theory, we have explained clearly why socialist market economy should have planning; in practice, the 17th National Congress of the CPC has reemphasized the guidance of state planning for macroeconomic regulation. Does it mean "a retrogression to the traditional planned economy", just like what some people accused of? I don't think so. As a matter of fact, it is a better combination between planning and market on a higher level.

The reasons are as follows. First, the current state planning is not inclusive, but instead it only attends to the macroeconomic activities, whereas the micro-economic activities are assigned to the market. Second, market is the current basic means of regulating resource allocation, whilst planning is the necessary means to remedy the defects of the market. Third, the current plans do not mainly refer to administrative orders any more, but include guiding, strategic and predictive plans instead. And at the same time, these plans must serve as a guide and commit entities to complete tasks and to take responsibilities when necessary. That is to say, these plans also need contain some mandatory tasks rather than be shelved after they are made.

The 12th "Five-Year Plan" is the first medium-to-long term plan that we have ever formulated and implemented since the 17th National Congress, which has profound implications for the transformation of our economic development patterns and solutions to problems in social relations. We need to implement the policy of the 17th National Congress practically, striving to improve state planning and macroeconomic regulation and to bring their guiding roles into full play in the national economic development. During the "12th Five-Year Plan (2011-2015)" period, we need to transform our economic development patterns and maintain a moderate economic growth; we need to promote the development of both the public sector and the private sector while consolidating the socialist basic economic system; we need to reverse the trend of polarization while attaching more importance to social equity.

In order to achieve all these, we mustn't rely exclusively on market economy, but also resort to state macroeconomic regulation by planning as well. The same is true with the circulation industry. A noteworthy thing here is that macroeconomic regulation by planning must be controlled by the Central Committee and local plans must be subject to central plans. I approve of some people' suggestion that local governments should stop making any inclusive national development plans driven by and centered on GDP growth; rather, they should make local plans for their own economic and social development in proportion to local financial resources and transfer payments granted by the central government, and reinforce local governments' roles in market supervision, social management and public service.

Besides, we should also preserve the government's function of regulating resource allocation, especially when it comes to major structural adjustment and infrastructure construction etc. Even capitalist countries have never forsworn the use of the so-called "socialist policies" such as nationalization, not to mention socialist countries! So, we shouldn't make market forces dictate the economy, but combine it with planning instead.

(This article was published in *Trade & Economy*, May, 2011)

Part V

The Basic Economic System in the Primary Stage of Socialism
—the foundation of Socialist Market Economy

Consolidation of the Basic Economic System in the Primary Stage of Socialism
—the foundation of socialist market economy

One of the fundamental differences between socialist market economy and the capitalist one is the basic economic system. The former is founded on the basic economic system in the primary stage of socialism, in which public ownership is the mainstay and other kinds of ownership develop side by side, whereas the latter is grounded on the basic economic system dominated by private ownership. The basic economic system is the prerequisite for socialist market economy.

The Fifth Plenary Session of the 17th Central Committee reiterated that we should "uphold and improve the socialist basic economic system". Therefore, we must avoid both privatization and the system that just has a unitary public sector, which is one of the "four important distinctions" proposed in the Fourth

Plenary Session of the 17th Central Committee of the CPC. Currently, we need to find out which trend is more serious, "privatization" or "a system that just has a unitary public sector". The latter is the result of people's belief in the past that sufficiently large communes under exclusive public ownership should be the best form of socialism., but now very few people think in that way except some radical "leftists". Nevertheless, a lot of evidence shows that the ill trend of privatization does exist and pose a serious threat. Marxist political economics cannot afford to ignore this. If these two ill trends were dealt with the same amount of punishment indiscriminately, it is nothing different from cutting the more serious trend of privatization slack.

It is right that Marxism did not judge the nature of ownership only by the proportion of ownership; but according to Marxism, complete disregard for the proportion of ownership is not recommended, either. If the proportion of public ownership in national economy keeps declining to almost zero, is it still socialism? Recently even Commissioner of the NBS (National Bureau of Statistics of PRC) also kept saying that the proportion of the public sector (esp. the state sector) is declining whereas the private sector rising.

In the macro-level, there was no such a trend of "guo jin min tui" (the state advances whereas the private sector retreats) in China's economy just like what some people claimed; In the micro-level, it is mostly "guo tui min jin" (the state retreats whilst the private sector advances). That is to say, in most cases, the public sector retreats whilst the private sector advances. However, "guo jin min tui" only occurs in rare cases for the sake of resource allocation, which also makes sense. So, on the whole, the public sector is declining whereas the private sector rising.

But what is the lowest bound? Now, quite a few people have begun to doubt the status of public ownership, and some scholars even came to the conclusion that public ownership was not the mainstay of the economy any more. If it is true, the basic economic system prescribed in the Constitution would be in imminent danger. Under the circumstances, we need to turn the tide as soon as possible.

As the basic economic system dictates, public ownership should be the mainstay of the economy and the state sector play a leading role. Therefore, the state needs to control the lifeline of the national economy and the state sector's control, influence and competitiveness must be enhanced. In capitalist societies, the state sector mainly provides services that private enterprises won't do, only serving as a supplement to the private sector to make up for the deficiency of market mechanism. However, in socialist societies, the state sector, indispensable to sustained, sound and coordinated economic development, is established for the sake of consolidating and improving the socialist system. Therefore, the state sector should cover these key industries and fields concerning the lifeline of the national economy, such as energy, transportation, communications, finance, infrastructure and pillar industries, and have "absolute control" or "fairly strong control" over them; enterprises should be wholly or partially owned by the state, with the state holding an absolutely or relatively controlling number of shares. All these are prescribed and emphasized by the documents of the Central Committee. The state sector must maintain control on these fields or industries so that the national economy could be regulated by state planning and thus develop in a more sustained, sound and coordinated way.

Besides, the state sector is obligated to ensure social equity and justice as well. As for competitive fields and industries crucial to social equity and justice, we should also regard them as "major" fields or "key" industries and strive to do a good job, though they do not matter too much to economic regulation by the government. Therefore, in order to stabilize employment, create more jobs, ensure social welfare, provide public services, increase transfer payments and guarantee social equity through redistribution, we need not only maintain the state sector's control on the major fields concerning the lifeline of the national economy characterized by natural monopoly, but bring its role into play in the competitive fields.

Why can't SOEs enter the competitive fields? Why should all the profits be gained exclusively by private enterprises? The Central Committee has always been insisting that state-owned capital move in and out of the competitive fields based on rational choices so as to bring their competitiveness into full play, rather than withdraw completely from these competitive fields, just like what neo-liberalist elites and its followers who are "inside the system" (*ti zhi nei*) kept preaching! Of course, to encourage fair competition, these competitive fields should be open to all. All these things should be made crystal clear in the textbooks on political economics.

Advocates of privatization requires the state sector to withdraw not only completely from competitive fields, but also from major fields and key industries concerning the lifeline of the national economy. They often labelled the state sector as "monopoly enterprises or industries" due to its control on these industries or its sharp edge over its rivals. They often levelled random criticism at SOEs, condemning that they colluded with the government to exercise monopoly. Besides, they even reduced all state-owned capital to "bureaucratic monopoly capital".

Some people proposed that one way to reform monopoly industries is to create favorable conditions for private enterprises' entry into these profitable industries, which is exactly what advocates of privatization have been desiring for. However, what really matters is not whether these industries concerning the lifeline of the national economy and vital to the national security are monopolized or not, but instead who controls them. More capable of standing for strategic interests of the state and social public interests, public enterprises are in general in a better position than private ones to run these special sectors and industries.

Surely, we should also carry out a reform in state-owned monopoly enterprises to eradicate administrative monopoly. As for the way it should be reformed, its is almost the same as common SOEs, such as separation of government administration from both enterprise management and state assets, corporatization, establishment of modern corporate structure, reform of income distribution system, improvement of legal and supervision systems, etc. In terms of income distribution, the current reform of SOEs is mainly focused on the recommitment of

SOEs to turn in profits to the state treasury, the readjustment of senior executive's high pay (some of them have exorbitant pays), and the prevention of SOE interests from being departmentalized or privatized since the "marketization reform". Besides, we should further improve the Staff and Workers Representatives Congress (SWRC) system to make it truly represent the interests of the working people. If employees were allowed to supervise during SOE reorganization in a real sense, tragedies like Tonghua (Jilin province, China) Iron and Steel Group riot would have probably be avoided.

The private sector is also part of the basic economic system in the primary stage of socialism, and therefore we should expound on the positive role that the non-public sector including the private sector has played in promoting the development of the productive forces in China and create favorable conditions for its development. However, the private sector also has duality: it not only benefits the development of productive forces, but involves exploitation. Notwithstanding this, the façade of exploitation is still tolerated in the primary stage of socialism, but the development of the private sector should be restricted. As its exploiting and profit-seeking nature has resulted in a series of bad consequences such as disputes between employers and employees, polarization, etc., Marxist political economics cannot overlook this aspect.

Due to the duality of both the private sector and owners of private enterprises, we should not only guide them to run the business legally and healthily, but restrain them from operating unhealthily or illegally and restrict their range of business. For example, they shouldn't be allowed to control key industries concerning the lifeline of the national economy or monopoly industries. As these industries have always been producing high profits and are vital to the interests of both our country and the public, they must be controlled by the public sector rather than serve as milk cows for the private sector in order to prevent the gap between the rich and the poor from widening. Even Sun Yat-Sen (1866-1925), the great forerunner of China's democratic revolution, also called on his men to restrict capital, not to mention socialism!

(This article was published in *China SOE,* 2011, No. 1)

Reflection on Several Issues Concerning the Basic Economic System in the Primary Stage of Socialism

1. Formation of the theory of "the primary stage of socialism" & the origin of the basic economic system

The theory of the primary stage of socialism was originated from Marxism. Karl Marx and Friedrich Engels said that communist society should be divided into two phases and that socialism was the primary stage of communism. Russia, under the leadership of Vladimir Lenin, has ever undergone an era of new economic policy, which is equivalent to the primary stage of socialism. In China, Mao Tse-tung divided socialism into "underdeveloped phase" and "developed phase"[1]. The former is also equivalent to the primary stage of socialism. After a detailed analysis of the basic theory of "the primary stage of socialism", we would easily find out that it is the further development of Marxist ideas concerning the future stages of social development.

There are two premises for the theory of the primary stage of socialism. First, in given conditions, economically and culturally underdeveloped countries can move on to socialism before capitalism is fully developed; Second, under no circumstances will the development of the productive forces be skipped. These are what Karl Marx and Friedrich Engels have been advocating consistently. The formation of the theory of "the primary stage of socialism" since the Third Plenary Session of the 11th Central Committee of the CPC is the concrete application of the Marxist theory of permanent revolution and the "two-stages" theory of revolution. Relevant ideas from Marxism, Leninism and Maoism have laid major theoretical foundations for the proposition of the theory of "the primary stage of socialism" by the party after the Third Plenary Session of the 11th Central Committee.

1 See *Selected Works of Mao Zedong*, vol. 8, People's Publishing House, 1999, p.116.

Now let's find out how the theory of the primary stage of socialism has been officially established. In *the Resolution Clarifying Certain Questions in the History of the Party Since the Foundation of the People's Republic of China* adopted in the Six Plenary Session of the 11th CPC Central Committee in 1981, it was proposed for the first time that we were still in the primary stage of socialism. And then in the 13th National Congress of the CPC in 1987, the theory of the primary stage of socialism was officially established. Before the 13th National Congress, Deng Xiaoping ever said, "The 13th National Congress of the CPC is supposed to explain what stage of socialism China is currently in, that is, the primary stage of socialism. Socialism is the primary stage of communism, but China is still in the primary stage of socialism, that is, the underdeveloped stage. In everything we do we must proceed from this reality, and all planning must be consistent with it."[1] Till September 1997, the 15th National Congress of the CPC formulated the party's basic program for the primary stage of socialism, providing insights into what socialist economy, politics and culture with Chinese characteristics in the primary stage really mean and how to achieve them.

In the primary stage of socialism, our party kept deepening their understanding as to what ownership structure and basic economic system we should establish. In July 1981, *Certain Policy Provisions Regarding the Non-agricultural Individual Economy in Cities and Rural Towns* was promulgated by the State Council. In 1982, the 12th National Congress of the CPC stressed that the socialist state sector plays a leading role in the national economy, and proposed for the first time in the document that individual economy is encouraged to develop and even extend to the rural areas. In January 1987, the Central Committee issued the document entitled *To Deepen the Rural Reform*, prescribing that we should "allow for the existence of the private sector, enhance management, promote the beneficial, abolish the harmful, and guide its development step by step". On the one hand, private enterprises are hereby legitimized; on the other, the document also pointed

1 See Selected Works of Deng Xiaoping, Vol. 3, People's Publishing House, 1993, p.252.

out that private enterprises, contradictory to the public sector, do have defects and limitations and thus we should adjust and restrict them properly.

In 1987, the 13th National Congress report officially acknowledged the legitimate existence and development of the private sector for the first time, proposing that the private sector is "a necessary and valuable supplement to the public sector". In 1992, the 14th National Congress report stated, "public ownership including ownership by the whole people and collective ownership is the mainstay of the economy, with individual economy, the private sector of the economy and the foreign sector of the economy serving as a complement. That is to say, many sectors of the economy will develop side by side in a long term."

It is in the 15th National Congress report in 1997 that the concept of "the basic economic system in the primary stage of socialism" was officially put forward for the first time. The document said, "The system in which public ownership is the mainstay and other kinds of ownership develop side by side is our basic economic system in the primary stage of socialism." Besides, it also added, "The non-public sector is an integral part of the socialist market economy." That is to say, we should step up efforts to elevate the non-public sector from a marginal role to an important role. So far, the basic economic system in the primary stage of socialism has been officially established.

In 2002, the 16th National Congress of the CPC stated that we should "unwaveringly consolidate and develop the public sector of the economy" and "unswervingly encourage, support and guide the development of the non-public sector". In 2007, the 17th National Congress of the CPC reiterated that we should "uphold and improve the basic economic system in which public ownership is the mainstay and other kinds of ownership develop side by side". In 2010, the Fifth Plenary Session of the 17th Central Committee proposed that we should adhere to the basic socialist economic system, avoiding both privatization and a system in which we just have a unitary public sector. The latter two, especially the trend of privatization, are the very reasons why the Central Committee came up with these policies, which is a crucial matter deserving our attention.

2. The basis for our basic economic system in the primary stage of socialism

The basic economic system determines the nature of a society and its direction of development. To be more specific, ownership of the means of production is the only criterion that determines the nature of a society and its direction of development. Private ownership of the means of production had been playing the key role in every society before the birth of socialism. Public ownership of the means of production is the essential feature that sets the socialist system from other ones in the human history. So why should China uphold the basic economic system in which public ownership is the mainstay and other kinds of ownership develop side by side?

Since we are a socialist country, we must base our socialist economic system on public ownership of the means of production. The Constitution of the PRC states, "The basis of the socialist economic system of the People's Republic of China is socialist public ownership of the means of production, namely, ownership by the whole people and collective ownership by the working people... China should uphold the basic economic system in which public ownership is the mainstay and other kinds of ownership develop side by side in the primary stage of socialism." [1]Therefore, we should try to distinct "the socialist economic system" from "the basic economic system in the primary stage of socialism". The former is the heart of the latter. "The socialist economic system" based on public ownership does not include the non-public sector; whereas the basic economic system in the primary stage of socialism includes the non-public sector, and public ownership must be the mainstay of the economy.

The "socialist economic system", persisting from the primary stage of socialism through other future stages of socialism, keeps growing and developing for further improvements. However, the basic economic system in the primary stage of socialism is just a reflection of features in this particular period of time.

1 See: *Constitution of the PRC* (revised version 2004), Chapter 1, General Principle, Article 6.

We can imagine that the non-public sector would not possibly be replaced by the public sector soon after the primary stage came to an end. Even after we move on to the intermediate stage of socialism, the non-public sector would not suddenly disappear into nowhere but only shrink gradually, whilst the public sector keeps expanding. Until the advanced stage of socialism when socialist economy will be almost complete and mature, the system of exploitation and private ownership of the means of production would eventually retire from the stage of history.

The national conditions of China in the primary stage of socialism dictate the basic economic system in the primary stage of socialism in which the non-public sector is allowed to exist and many types of ownership develops side by side. Actually, we have moderately low productivity, but with a large population; we have rather less new jobs available; our economy is far lagged behind that of developed countries; our principal contradiction is the one between the ever-growing material and cultural needs of the people and the low level of production; the fundamental task of socialism is to "emancipate the mind and develop the productive forces". Therefore, as long as the sector of the economy meets the "Three Favorables"[1] , it would be allowed and even encouraged to develop. As a result, individual economy, the private sector of the economy, and the foreign sector of the economy, provided that they meet the "three criteria", should be part of the basic economic system in the primary stage of socialism and an integral part of socialist market economy.

We are still in the primary stage of socialism, which is the theoretical and practical basis for the basic economic system of socialism. But please be aware that the primary stage would come to an end at a due time and that it is impossible to be an eternal existence. Deng Xiaoping said in his South China Tour Talks in 1992, "We have to adhere to the basic line for the primary stage of socialism for

1 "Three favorables", proposed by Deng Xiaoping in South China Tour talks in 1992, refer to whether it promotes the growth of the productive forces in a socialist society, increases the overall strength of the socialist state and raises the people's living standard.

a hundred years, with no vacillation."[1] So, 100 years later, this is the deadline we should meet in the socialist modernization drive. According to Deng Xiaoping's blueprint, the primary stage started from the year of 1956 when socialism was initially established in China and would end in the 2050s or 2060s. Afterwards, we should be prepared for the intermediate stage of socialism. Given the dramatic growth of productivity and the rapid progress of science and technology in China, we would probably complete the primary stage ahead of time, that is, less than one hundred years. Here, I just want to remind people that we should not just be busy with catching up, but pause from time to time to look far ahead. We should always bear in mind the long-term goal, firstly socialism and then communism. In different periods within the primary stage, the party should be well prepared for any new problems and make due adjustments or changes to guard against any possible deviations from the socialist road. Our party should never forget the ultimate goal of our party and the purpose of serving the people.

3. Consolidation of the role of public ownership as the mainstay being the first priority for the basic economic system

Socialist system is based on socialist public ownership, and the basic economic system in the primary stage of socialism is based on and preconditioned by the status of public ownership as the mainstay of the economy. Therefore, to consolidate such role of public ownership is our first priority while upholding the basic economic system in the primary stage of socialism.

"The mainstay status of public ownership is mainly reflected in the predominance of public-owned assets. The predominance here not only refers to the quantity, but also the quality."[2] However, many people nowadays began to doubt it, especially the aspect of quantity. According to statistics newly released by NBS (National Bureau of statistics of PRC), the proportion of the public sector (esp. the state sector) in the national economy is still declining; in the

1 "*Selected works of Deng Xiaoping*, Vol. 3, People's Publishing House, 1993, p.370.

2 *Selected Collection of Major Documents since the 15th National Congress I*, People's Publishing House, 2000, P.21.

macro-level, there was no such a trend of "guo jin min tui" (the state advances whereas the private sector retreats); In the micro-level, it is mostly "guo tui min jin" (the state retreats whilst the private sector advances); besides, "guo jin min tui", occurring in rare cases just for the sake of resource allocation, also makes sense. Our party has been insisting, "there should be a limit to the reduction in the proportion of the public sector, that is, public ownership must remain the mainstay of the economy."[1] One of the ways to remove people's doubts is to provide them with statistics , which is the duty of Marxist political economics so as to increase people's confidence in the basic economic system in the primary stage of socialism.

Actually, the predominance of public assets should be more reflected in its quality. That is to say, the state should control the means of production in industries or fields concerning the economic lifeblood, the overall strategic situation and the direction of national economic development rather than insignificant ones; the state should control the advanced, guiding and dominant means of production that keep improving and expanding rather than backward ones. Only in this way can public assets control the economic lifeblood, play a leading role in the national economy, have more power in control and decision-making, set a good example and give a boost to the economic development.

As the basic economic system dictates, public ownership should be the mainstay of the economy and the state sector play a leading role. Therefore, the state needs to control the lifeline of the national economy and the state sector's control, influence and competitiveness must be enhanced. In capitalist societies, the state sector mainly provides services that private enterprises won't do, only serving as a supplement to the private sector to make up for the deficiency of market mechanism. However, in socialist societies, the state sector, indispensable to sustained, sound and coordinated economic development, is established for the sake of consolidating and improving the socialist system. Therefore, the state

1 *Selected Works of Jiang Zemin*, volume 3, People's Publishing House, 2006, p.72.

sector should cover these key industries and fields concerning the lifeline of the national economy, such as energy, transportation, communications, finance, infrastructure and pillar industries, and have "absolute control" or "fairly strong control" over them; enterprises should be wholly or partially owned by the state, with "the state holding an absolutely or relatively controlling number of shares".[1] All these are prescribed and emphasized by the documents of the Central Committee. The state sector must maintain control on these fields or industries so that the national economy could be regulated by state planning and thus develop in a more sustained, sound and coordinated way.

As to what fields should be under the control of the state sector, one opinion is worthy of our attention and study. It holds that the state sector mainly shoulders the following two social responsibilities: to help the government with economic regulation and to ensure social equity and justice. The former applies to both socialist countries and modern capitalist market economies, whereas the latter is exclusive to socialist countries. "According to the western mainstream economics, the state sector does benefit economic regulation by the government in given conditions. However, practice of privatization in OECD members proves that the government can still regulate the economy effectively through monetary, fiscal and industrial policies and commercial means, even though basic monopoly industries are already privatized or the proportion of the state sector has been reduced to below 10%. Nevertheless, social equity and justice can not be guaranteed by economies with high-level privatization and mixed economies mainly characterized by privatization."

China's reform aiming to establish a socialist market economy should rightfully include efforts to ensure, realize and enhance social equity and justice while striving to strengthen the control of the state sector and bring its leading role into play. As for state-owned assets in competitive fields and industries crucial to

1 *Selected Collection of Major Documents since the 15th National Congress II*, Beijing: People's Publishing House, 2003, p.2587.

social equity and justice, we should also regard them as "key" state-owned assets and strive to do a good job, though they do not matter too much to economic regulation by the government; otherwise, the reform would be out of control such as the large drain of state assets and rampant large-scale "transfer".[1]

Since the state sector is obligated to ensure social equity and justice, the state should guarantee effective investment in public service, infrastructure and major industries. Therefore, many forms of investment and operation in labor-intensive fields with a view to solving the problem of unemployment can also be considered as alternatives. We should guarantee the healthy development of SOEs not only in monopoly fields but in competitive fields; we should give play to its role of stabilizing employment, creating more jobs, ensuring social welfare and providing public services; we should enhance the country's economic strength to provide more transfer payments to enhance redistribution. Why can't competitive SOEs enter the competitive fields? Why should all the profits be gained exclusively by private enterprises? That's why the Central Committee has always been insisting that state-owned capital move in and out of the competitive fields based on rational choices and its competitiveness should be brought into full play. And that's why the Central Committee would never allow the state sector to withdraw completely from "competitive fields", just like what the hard core of neo-liberalism and its followers who are "inside the system"(*ti zhi nei*) kept preaching!

China, as a great socialist power, can not refer to the so-called "international experience" of privatization from capitalist countries while setting the lower bound for the proportion of the state sector. But instead, factors as to whether social equity and stability would be guaranteed and even enhanced should be rightfully taken into consideration. Therefore, it is very necessary for us to study further the scope of the state sector's control.

4. To handle the relationship between the public sector and the non-public

1 Xia Xiaolin, "Following up the Scaling-Down of the Non-State Investment", *China Business Times*, January 31st, 2007.

sector correctly

When it comes to the basic economic system, the private sector of the economy, an integral part of the non-public sector of the economy, should never be avoided. The non-public sector develops side by side with with the public sector, which constitutes our basic economic system in the primary stage of socialism. We cannot do without the non-public sector now and even throughout the primary stage of socialism due to its crucial, positive role in promoting our economic development, creating more jobs, increasing financial revenues, and meeting needs from all aspects of the society. Therefore, we must encourage, support and guide the economic development of the non-public sector, rather than ignore, discriminate against or even reject it. That's why the party and the government have consistently attached great importance to the non-public sector including the private sector, which can be demonstrated by its policies concerning the non-public sector over these years. For instance, the non-public sector was defined as "a supplement to the public sector of the economy" in both the 13th and 14th National Congress of the CPC; it was elevated to "an integral part of the socialist market economy" in the Second Session of the Ninth National People's Congress of the PRC; and in the 16th National Congress of the CPC, it was proposed that we should "unswervingly encourage, support and guide the development of the non-public sector" while unwaveringly consolidating and developing the public sector of the economy.

However, we should try to distinct the nature of the private sector of the economy from its role. So long as the means of production is privately owned involving employment and exploitation, the private sector of the economy will never be socialist by nature. However, as to its role, we should study it against specific historic conditions. In the primary stage of socialism when it meets the needs of the development of the productive forces, it still plays a positive role so that it is considered as an integral part of the socialist market economy. However, it cannot be defined as a component of socialist economy, because it is not socialist by nature. But some theoreticians sneakily replaced "(the non-public sector as) an integral part of the socialist market economy" with "(the non-public sector as) an integral part of the socialist economy", claiming that "the private sector" "has already become" or "is expected to replace the public sector and become" the mainstay of the socialist economy. They have obviously overstepped the boundary set by the Constitution of the PRC concerning the basic economic system!

To sum up, we must neither overlook or discriminate against it, nor flatter or cover for it. So, in what ways should we treat it so that it would conform to the basic socialist economic system? No doubt, we should continue to unswervingly develop the private sector of the economy, trying to bring its flexibility and positive roles in promoting productive forces into full play; at the same time, we should also endeavor to overcome any negative influence on social and economic development arising from exploitation. For instance, some owners of private enterprises bribed government officials, evaded taxes, lowered workers' wages, worsened employees' working conditions, produced counterfeit goods, destroyed natural resources and environment, embezzled state property and defrauded in other cases etc. All these ills should be uprooted by means of education, supervision and the rule of law. I guess, out of duties and conscience of "builders of the socialist undertaking", most owners of private enterprises would agree to do so, for it would only benefit their own development, but not the other way around.

While encouraging and supporting the development of the private sector, we should also guide its development correctly by prescribing specifically what fields it should and should not enter. For example, as far as competitive fields are concerned, we should give green light to the private sector and try to remove all barriers to their access. Especially those fields allowing for foreign investment should be also open to domestic investment. However, as for those key sectors and major fields concerning the lifeblood of the national economy, the private sector would only be given the permit conditionally or restrictively in case that it would dominate and manipulate these major fields and key sectors so much so that the control of the state sector would be undermined. The private sector has been given enough room to invest in competitive fields and also allowed to purchase shares and share profitable gains from some key sectors concerning the lifeblood of the national economy, so that private owners should be gratified. As "builders of the socialist undertaking" and "the new class of the society", owners of private enterprises would probably not covet the "mainstay" of the socialist economy on their part. However, some neo-liberalist elites did overtly or covertly push them to this end. So, we should educate private enterprise owners not to blindly follow these elites.

All in all, we should develop the non-public sector including the private sector unswervingly, but at the same time we must unwaveringly consolidate and develop the public sector of the economy, too. More importantly, the prerequisite for such side-by-side development is that the public sector serves as the mainstay and the state sector plays the leading role. Only in this way can we consolidate and develop the basic socialist economic system and maintain a permanent, invincible position.

5. The basic economic system dictates that socialist market economy should have planning

According to Marxism, the national economy should achieve balanced, proportionate development in communal production, i.e., social production based on public ownership. Here, "balanced, proportionate development" is not equivalent to a traditional planned economy regulated by administrative, mandatory planning. Since the reform and opening-up, we have overcome the limitations of traditional planned economy and established a socialist market economy consistent with the basic economic system in the primary stage of socialism; and such basic economic system is predicated on the status of public ownership as the mainstay of the economy. Therefore, in order to develop socialist market economy, we mustn't abandon the economic law of "balanced, proportionate development".

In 1992, the 14th National Congress of the CPC proposed that the reform aimed to establish a "socialist market economy", without including the modifier "planned" in the version, which Jiang Zemin, then General Secretary of the CPC Central Committee, accounted for at that time. He said, "Socialist economy had planning since its establishment, and everybody knows it perfectly well. Therefore, one should not infer from the missing of the word "planned" that planning would be aborted." [1]The exclusion of the modifier "planned" from the wording of reform target at that time was mainly due to the reason that traditional planned economy was then very deep-rooted in people's mind and that the concept of market economy hasn't been that penetrating yet. In order to enhance the image of market in people's mind and encourage them to embrace the concept of "market economy", the word "planned" was deliberately omitted; but the substantial modifier "socialist" that carries great weight was placed before "market economy", because "socialism has had planning since the very beginning". In this way, with both "being based on public ownership" and having "planning", the spirit of the 14th National Congress concerning the reform target is very complete.

A sound macroeconomic regulation system is something that socialist market economy must have, which is surely very correct. However, market economy subject to macroeconomic regulation, which is also practiced in capitalist states, is not exclusive to socialist countries at all. But what sets socialist market economy subject to macroeconomic regulation from the capitalist market economy in which macroeconomic regulation is also used? Aside from its basic economic system, planning, or guidance from state planning, is another distinctive feature of socialist market economy because public ownership as the mainstay of the economy is the very foundation of the socialist market economy.

In quite a few market economies, such as Japan, South Korea and France, organizations like "Economic Planning Agency" were ever set up to make predictive plans occasionally. In most market economies such as USA and UK,

1 Jiang Zemin, "On China's Establishment of a Socialist Market Economy", *Selected Works of Jiang Zemin*, Volume 1, Beijing: People's Publishing House, 2006, p.202.

they only use fiscal and monetary policies instead of planning as a means to regulate economy. However, in contrast, it is very necessary and probable for China, as a great socialist power with public ownership as the mainstay of the economy, to use planning as a means of macroeconomic regulation to guide balanced, proportionate development of the national economy. It not only conforms to the Marxist economic law of balanced, proportionate development, but constitutes the superiority of socialist market economy as well.

There are several means of macroeconomic regulation, among which planning, fiscal policies and monetary policies are the most important. The 14th National Congress report specifically pointed out, "State planning is an important means of macroeconomic planning," [1]without highlighting the importance of fiscal and monetary policies. It is not because they are not important at all, but instead, they are under the guidance of state macroeconomic planning. Besides, the guidance of state planning for macroeconomic regulation was also emphasized in the 17th National Congress report. To sum up, macroeconomic regulation is inseparable from state planning, with the latter as the backbone of the former. Market economy subject to macroeconomic regulation can also be called a market economy subject to state macroeconomic regulation by planning, which is the distinctive characteristic that sets socialist market economy apart from the capitalist one.

The 17th Central Committee of the CPC reemphasized the guiding role of state planning in the macroeconomic regulation, which is not a retrogression to the traditional planned economy as some people distorted. The reasons are as follows: First, the current state planning is not inclusive, but instead it only attends to the macroeconomic activities, whereas the micro-economic activities are assigned to the market. Second, market is the current basic means of regulating resource allocation, whilst planning is the necessary means to remedy the defects of the

1 *Documents of the 14th National Congress of the Communist Party of China.* Beijing: People's Publishing House, 1992, p.23.

market. Third, the current plans do not mainly refer to administrative orders any more, but include guiding, strategic and predictive plans instead. And at the same time, these plans must serve as a guide and commit entities to complete tasks and to take responsibilities when necessary. Transition from planned economy to market economy and the renewed emphasis on the guiding role of state planning in the macroeconomic regulation are in line with the "thesis-antithesis-synthesis" dialectics. Rather than a retrogression to the previous traditional planned economy, it is a higher-level synthesis of planning and market in the new stage of economic reform.

6. Only adherence to the basic economic system can save us from polarization

Over more than three decades since the reform and opening-up, people's living standard has been generally improved on the one hand, but, on the other, the tendency of polarization in terms of income distribution got worse. When it comes to the cause of the widening gap between the rich and the poor, people would associate it firstly with the expansion of urban-rural disparity and regional imbalances, industrial monopoly, corruption, uneven supply of public goods, and delayed redistribution and readjustment etc. All these reasons do make sense and we are supposed to handle them one by one, but they are not the rooted cause for inequitable distribution. Rather, they are usually overlooked.

Unequal distribution of income is formed in primary distribution, and the core issue that influences primary distribution the most is the relations between labor and capital, which is closely linked with the basic relations of production or property relations. According to Marxism, distribution is determined by ownership and distribution relations are determined by property relations. Therefore, property disparity tends to affect the income gap the most. Paul Anthony Samuelson, a famous western economist, also acknowledged that wealth determines income inequity the most.[1] Aside from factors mentioned above, the decline in the

1 Samuelson, Paul A. (1948) *Economics: An Introductory Analysis.*

proportion of the public sector, the rise in that of the private sector, privatization and quick concentration of wealth in the hands of the very few people are the most fundamental causes for the widening of income inequality and the tendency of polarization over more than three decades since the reform and opening-up.

At the very beginning of our reform and opening-up, we just had a unitary public sector, due to the policies of "encouraging some people to get rich first" and "giving priority to efficiency" since the reform and opening-up, the non-public sector dominated by private ownership will surely outgrow that of the public sector, with the result that many kinds of ownership would develop side by side, which will benefit the economic development as a whole. However, if such momentum keeps going, "problems would become a full-blown crisis at some point", and "polarization would emerge automatically"[1] (by Deng Xiaoping). With the decline in the proportion of the public sector and the rise in that of the private sector, less income and wealth would be distributed according to work and more according to factors of production (mainly capital).

Some people even came to the conclusion that distribution according to production factors (capital) has already replaced distribution according to work as the dominant mode of distribution for the national economy.[2] Based on the law of capital accumulation and the general process of market economic development, it can be inferred that as private property rights expand, the share of capital income would relatively increase and that of labor income would relatively decline, resulting in the widening of the gap between the rich and the poor and the worsening of the trend of polarization. Besides, it can also be proved by statistics about the share of labor income and that of capital income in China's national income.

When it comes to adjusting income distribution relations and narrowing the

1 *Chronology of Deng Xiaoping's Career* (1975-1997) *II*, Beijing: Central Party Literature Press, 2004, p.1364.

2 Wu Li, Wen Rui, "My Perspective on Changes in Distribution of Income Since 1992", *China Business Times*, May 26th, 2006.

gap between the rich and the poor, people tend to check the system of distribution first, especially means of redistribution such as taxation and transfer payments so as to enhance social security and public welfare, and improve the livelihood of low-income people. These measures are absolutely necessary and we've already begun to take them. However, they are still far from enough, and we need further step up efforts to implement them. Actually, it is impossible to reverse the widening of the gap between the rich and the poor by just focusing on distribution and redistribution. Besides, we also need check our ownership structure, property system, the basic relations of production and the basic economic system. Only by reinforcing the status of public ownership as the mainstay of the economy can we possibly prevent the income gap from widening and finally achieve common prosperity. Therefore, only if the public sector of the economy expands, the situation of distribution would probably be improved. To sum up, we need reverse the decline in the proportion of the public sector and the rise in that of the private sector, striving to prevent private ownership from replacing public ownership and becoming the mainstay of the economy. Only thus can we eventually avoid income polarization from happening! Just as Deng Xiaoping ever put it, "so long as public ownership remains the mainstay of the economy, polarization will be avoided.[1]

He also added, "If basic means of production is owned by the state or the collective, i.e., public-owned, "a new bourgeoisie would not emerge".[2] This inference pointed out that in the primary stage of socialism, private property rights would be tolerated and non-labor factors (mainly capital) allowed to have a rightful share only if public ownership is the mainstay of the economy and distribution according to work constitutes the major mode of distribution. We would have zero tolerance for private ownership's replacement of public ownership as the mainstay of the economy; we must also strive to reverse the

1 *Selected Works of Deng Xiaoping*, Volume 3, Beijing: People's Publishing House, 1993, p.149.

2 ibid, p.123.

trend of distribution according to capital taking the place of distribution according to work as the major mode of distribution. Besides, we must also control the free flow of private capital into profitable industries and sectors concerning the lifeblood of the national economy, which might result in the further widening of income gap and property disparity. So long as public ownership is the mainstay of the economy and distribution according to work constitutes the dominant mode of distribution, the gap between the rich and the poor would be controlled within proper bounds and stopped from reaching the limit, i.e., polarization, and hence common prosperity would be eventfully achieved. Otherwise, polarization and social split will inevitably happen.

Therefore, in order to reform radically distribution system and reverse the widening of the gap between the rich and the poor, we must take necessary measures or policies to implement the two Constitutional principles, i.e., public ownership as the mainstay of the economy and distribution according to work as the dominant distribution mode.

(It was published in *Economics Information*, 2011, No. 7)

Reflections on Several Issues Concerning the Relations between Distribution and Ownership

Focus on relations of production and distribution relations constitutes an important component of Deng Xiaoping's theory on the reform. We should see the widening trend of the gap between the rich and the poor in current China in perspective and realize that the change of ownership structure is the most rooted cause. In both real economic life and ideology, the tendency of "privatization" does exist, threatening the mainstay status of public ownership; the public sector was said to have lower efficiency, which has proved to be a false proposition; many people embraced the so-called "guo tui min jin" (the state retreats while the private sector advances) and tried to implement it, which we would overlook at our peril. In order to strengthen the state sector's control, we need study further the number, organization and structure of the SOEs, checks and balances, supervision and public involvement in the reform decision-making process. In the current stage, we should continue to develop the private sector and give full play to its positive roles while unswervingly upholding and developing the public sector as the economic mainstay. Only in this way can we consolidate and develop the basic economic system of socialism and maintain its everlasting invincible position.

1. Deng Xiaoping's focus on income distribution

It has been noticed that Deng Xiaoping attached great importance to income distribution in his theory of socialist reform. For example, he started his analysis of the essence of socialism from the perspective of the productive forces by defining it as "liberation and development of the productive forces", and then provided us a deep insight into the essence of socialism by defining it from the relations of production, namely, socialism intends to "eliminate both exploitation and polarization and finally achieve common prosperity". Here, elimination of polarization with a view to achieving common prosperity, which turns out to be an issue of distribution, can only be reflected on the distribution of social income and wealth.

Besides, Deng Xiaoping has mentioned repeatedly that socialism has "two basic principles" or "two crucial aspects". One is the basic economic system in which public ownership is the mainstay and many kinds of ownership develop side by side", the other one is "common prosperity without polarization". The second "crucial aspect" or "basic principle" is also an issue of distribution, which is telling the same story as the essence of socialism, "elimination of polarization and the ultimate achievement of prosperity for all".

Deng Xiaoping has made many consistent remarks concerning the nature and fundamental principles of socialism. Many things he talked about actually constitute some essentials of socialism, such as liberation and development of the productive forces, public ownership as the mainstay of the economy, and elimination of polarization etc. That is to say, it will not be called "Socialism" without them. However, among all these essentials, Deng Xiaoping laid particular emphasis on the relations of production and distribution relations. For example, we should surely develop the productive forces to complete the task of socialist reform, but it will hardly succeed if we just focus on the development of the productive forces and undervalue efforts to develop and improve the relations of production, which can be well proved by one of Deng Xiaoping's famous words, "If our policies lead to polarization, we would end up with failure".[1] And no matter how fast GDP grows, the conclusion will always be the same. So, we can see the vital role of distribution relations in Deng Xiaoping's theory of socialist reform!

The failure of reform that Deng Xiaoping warned of does not refer to the failure of a general reform, but the debacle of socialist reform, or its incapability of keeping to the right socialist direction. Socialism intrinsically includes elimination of polarization and the ultimate achievement of prosperity for all, however, the accumulated wealth would probably fall into the hands of the very few people with the rapid development of the productive forces. Although the national economic strength has been greatly enhanced, GDP has grown dramatically and stayed high on a particular level for rather long, "this amount of wealth would probably make less than 10% of the people prosper while over 90% people still cannot benefit from it."[2] So, most of the people would be left outside the process of reform. Though it can be called a success of reform, it is definitely no success for the socialist reform, but the capitalist reform instead.

Very obviously, elimination of polarization and realization of common prosperity is the simplest and the most direct goal of socialism, the very essential feature that sets socialism apart from capitalism, socialist reform from capitalist one.

"Liberation and development of the productive forces" is also part and parcel of socialism. Socialism is not poverty and should never be satisfied with the level of underdevelopment, which is common sense. Any new mode of social

1 *Selected Works of Deng Xiaoping, volume 3*, Beijing: People's Publishing House, 1993, p.111.

2 ibid, p.64.

production attempting to remove barriers to the development of the productive forces, including the capitalist mode of production, can liberate and develop the productive forces. However, not each of them is capable of "eliminating polarization and achieving common prosperity; rather, only the socialist mode of production can do. Due to the backward productive forces and economic underdevelopment, it is very correct and logical for China to add "liberation and development of the productive forces" to the list of essential requirements of socialism in the primary stage of socialism, however it is not the ultimate goal of socialism. As a matter of fact, the ultimate goal of socialism is man's development, which manifests itself in the economic field as "common prosperity". In his theory concerning the essence of socialism, Deng Xiaoping emphasizes specifically "common prosperity" by saying, "the greatest superiority of socialism is common prosperity, a great reflection of the essence of socialism"[1]. Therefore, we should never just focus on the development of the productive forces and neglect any adjustment to the relations of production or distribution relations while studying Deng Xiaoping's theory concerning the essence of socialism.

Deng Xiaoping also values socialist distribution, which is the fruit of his painstaking work in building socialism in his lifetime. In his remaining years, his ideas concerning this aspect even gushed forth more freely. He said to his little brother Deng Ken not long before his death, "How to make 1.2 billion people prosper and how to distribute the wealth among them after that is a big headache, which seems to be much harder to deal with than the problem of development. We cannot take the issue of income distribution lightly. Even though we strive to guard against polarization, it would emerge automatically anyway." [2]

Surely, Deng Xiaoping does not just emphasize socialist distribution relations, i.e., elimination of polarization, he also attaches greater importance to the socialist

1 *Selected Works of Deng Xiaoping*, vol. 3, Beijing: People's Publishing House, 1993, p.364.

2 *Chronology of Deng Xiaoping's Career (1975-1997) II*, Beijing: Central Party Literature Press.

relations of production linked with distribution, especially ownership relations. He views public ownership as the mainstay of the economy as the prerequisite for non-polarization. He said, "so long as public ownership remains the mainstay of the economy, polarization would be avoided."[1] "If basic means of production is owned by the state or the collective, i.e., public-owned", "a new bourgeoisie would never emerge even by the time when GDP per capita reaches several thousands dollars"[2]. Distribution relations are determined by ownership relations, which constitutes one important rule of Marxist political economics, is of extremely great significance in both theoretical and policy levels, which however tends to be overlooked. Later in this article, I would elaborate on this again. Here, I just want to call people's attention to it and suggest them learning it.

2. To evaluate correctly the widening of income inequality in current China

Since the reform and opening-up, our party, in the spirit of Deng Xiaoping's thoughts, have overcome indiscriminate egalitarianism (the egalitarian tendency used to be very serious in China despite the principle of distribution according to work, which, though, did produce some good effects.) by "encouraging some people in some regions to get rich first and then helping others to catch up to achieve common prosperity". Thanks to approximately three decades' practice of reform, different income brackets have been formed in China's society, but the goal of common prosperity hasn't been achieved after some people and some regions got rich first. It is temporarily beneficial to the economic development, but at the same time it also gives rise to many deep social contradictions causing great concerns among people and hot debates among scholars.

One of the points at issue is whether the gap between the rich and the poor has been so widened that polarization has emerged. Deng Xiaoping has repeatedly warned people that polarization would possibly happen if some condition is met, which is just an assumption rather than a prophecy. After Deng heightened this

1 *Selected Works of Deng Xiaoping*, volume 3, Beijing: People's Publishing House, 1993, p.149.

2 ibid, pp.90-91.

to a prominently high political level, this issue became very sensitive and such debate became more heated, too. Each side stuck to his own argument, so it is hard for either side to be convinced by the other.

As to whether income polarization has emerged in current China, there are mainly two opposing opinions. Those who believed that it has already emerged are very concerned about the fate of the whole country, using many facts, statistics, and even internationally recognized standards as supporting evidence, such as Gini Coefficient, S80/S20 ratio and S90/S10 ratio etc. Besides, they also tried to convince people into believing that Deng Xiaoping's "prophecy" about polarization has come true by providing some examples as to how some people wallowed in luxury whereas some people lived in extreme poverty. So, they suggested that something should be done as quickly as possible to rectify the current situation. In contrast, those who don't think polarization has emerged argued that even though the rich are getting much richer, the poor is not getting even poorer. According to them, thanks to the reform, the rising tide has raised all the ships together, that is to say, people's lives have been improved in general; besides, the so-called internationally recognized standards don't apply to China. So, they came to the conclusion that the expansion of Gini Coefficient is an inevitable result of market economy, and that the so-called "emergence of polarization" was just fabricated to thwart the reform.

Obviously, the two opposing opinions stand for two different interest groups. One stands for capital, wealth and opinions of some elites; the other stands for the great masses mainly made up of workers and peasants. Though I, as a social being, cannot be totally free from any interest groups' influence, I have tried my best to reduce such influence to the minimum. So I have always been very cautious about words as to whether income polarization has emerged in China.

In 2003, I pointed out in the article "A Focus on the Issue of Income Distribution in the study of the Macroeconomic Situation", "Currently, our Gini Coefficient is around 0.45...and still remains on the rising side of the inverted

U-shaped curve. With the development of market economy, Gini coefficient will continue to rise. Therefore, we cannot force a reduction or impose the policy of equitable distribution all at once, but instead we should increase the weight of equity gradually. That is to say, we should at first slow down the expansion of Gini coefficient, and then reduce the Gini Coefficient moderately so as to achieve a transition from the policy of "giving priority to efficiency with due consideration to equity" to that of "paying attention to both efficiency and equity". [1]

I said in my article entitled "Attaching Further Importance to Social Equity" (April, 2005), "If income gap reaches the limit someday, it might be caused by polarization. However, we haven't gone that far now, so we should neither say that income polarization has emerged (which is the prerequisite for the failure of reform according to Deng Xiaoping), nor state that the income gap has already reached the limit. Our Gini coefficient is now still on the rise. So we should take some precautious measures before it is too late. Otherwise, polarization would soon emerge and our income gap would soon reach the limit." [2]

Even now I still think so. Why did I take a middle course (I believed that the gap between the rich and poor hadn't reached the limit and that polarization hadn't emerged yet) and still suggest that we must take the problem seriously and strive to solve it in time? Why didn't I favor either of them? It is based on the following considerations.

Polarization was defined by Karl Marx in his *Das Kapital* as an inevitable result of the general rule of capitalist accumulation, with accumulation of wealth at one pole and accumulation of misery at the opposite one. Wealth accumulation is an endless process of expansion, whereas misery at the other pole undergoes a transition from "absolute misery" to "relative misery". "Absolute misery" is the result of separation of capital from labor. Labor is the only thing that workers can provide; capital is exclusively owned by capitalists. So, for the sake of

1 *Collected Works of Liu Guoguang*, volume 10, Beijing: China Social Sciences Press, 2006, p.510.

2 ibid, p.588.

profit maximization, capitalists would naturally take advantage of their capital and fierce competition among workers to lower workers' wages and worsen their working conditions as far as possible, which has a lot to do with a relative surplus of labor force and a large industrial reserve army. So, the working class's misery is in direct proportion to their physical torment during work, which causes the accumulation of "absolute misery". However, due to an increase in productivity, growing protests from workers, and welfare programs that capitalist governments have to run, the absolute level of workers' wages and welfare was indeed improved. But as far as the proportion of labor to capital is concerned, no favorable changes have indeed taken place in the interests of the working class; on the contrary, it is becoming even more beneficial to the accumulation of capital and wealth and hence has thrown the working class into "relative misery" rather than "absolute misery". As a result, with accumulation of wealth at the one pole and accumulation of misery at the other, the trend of polarization will continue to exist. A study has demonstrated with a lot of evidence that many countries, be developed countries with parliamentary systems or developing countries with parliamentary systems, are "rife with the phenomena of polarization" against the backdrop of privatization, marketization, democratization and globalization.

There is no denying that China is different from them, but the transition of the working class's conditions from "absolute misery" to "relative misery" in these countries does provide us with a new angle. While striving to prove that polarization has already occurred in China, some Chinese scholars failed to notice that the population of absolutely poor people in China's rural land has reduced from 250 million to 21.48 million (228 million less than before) and the headcount ratio (HCR) from 30% to 2.3%, which is the gratifying fruits of the development of the productive forces and poverty alleviation initiatives by the government. In this regard, the widening of the gap between the rich and the poor has been slowed down to some extent. But we cannot infer from this that China's income gap has been narrowed, because the poverty line also rises to the economic growth.

Based on China's calculus, there are tens of millions of people living below the poverty line, but according to the international standard such population is 200 million. Therefore, the decline in the population of Chinese people who live in absolute poverty based on our calculus does not mean that the relative gap between the rich and the poor is not expanding. Some people said that the tide of economic growth would rise all ships, i.e., people's income, and therefore some people become extremely rich whereas some fairly rich. So they came to the conclusion that it would be unlikely for polarization to occur in China.[1]

However, this assumption contradicts the objective law that the tendency of polarization will continue to exist regardless of the transition of workers' conditions from "absolute misery" to "relative misery" (under market economy and wage labor) with the development of the productive forces. Especially in China, some mistaken policies in educational, health care, housing, and SOE reforms and some damages to local residents' interests due to land requisition, house demolition and relocation have given rise to the emergence of a poor class and made the bad situation even worse, that is, "the poor is getting much poorer whilst the rich much richer" (remarks by Li Jinhua, then Auditor General of China). Surely, our government is striving to solve this problem, but we still cannot let our guard down.

Here, I would like to reemphasize that such tendency does not mean that polarization has already occurred. Can Gini coefficient be used to tell whether polarization has emerged or not? Some people said the Gini coefficient did not apply to China for some reason and thus it does not make too much sense to use it as a measurement. But it so contradicts their consistent support for China's integration with the global economy!

Gini Coefficient, as a measure of inequality in terms of income distribution, is a neutral index that the countries all over the world have been using since the Second World War. In 1964, our Gini Coefficient was 0.184; it was 0.2 in 1978, and 0.26 in 1980; by 1990, it has exceeded 0.4. How fast it has expanded! We

1 *Economic Observer*, March 18th, 2007.

would overlook such dramatic rise at our peril! Our Gini coefficient has exceeded that of many capitalist developed countries, but it hasn't been so seriously high as that of some extremely turbulent developing countries in Latin America. Most capitalist developed countries, which used to be colonial empires and now are running multinational corporations across the globe, have indeed managed to alleviate social contradictions by using some of the surplus values extracted from all over the world to cover welfare of domestic workers. This is also one of the reasons why their Gini coefficient has reduced to a value even lower than us. Notwithstanding this, we still need reflect upon our own problems and try to find out the reasons why the Gini coefficient of a socialist country has overtaken that of capitalist developed countries.

On the other hand, I do appreciate some experts' views that we cannot apply mechanically the Gini coefficient to our country due to the complexity of structural factors. For example, 0.4 is set as the international warning line, which means a country should go on alert when its Gini coefficient exceeds it. However, I think, we should not apply such standard mechanically!

I pointed out in the article entitled *A Focus on the Issue of Income Distribution in the study of the Macroeconomic Situation*, Based on experiences of many countries, 0.4 is set as the warning line to monitor and control income inequality, which is quite of universal significance. However, national conditions vary from country to country, with their residents holding different concepts of social equity and having varying degrees of endurance for high income inequality.

Take China as an example, whose urban and rural residents are both counted in its calculus of Gini Coefficient. In China, the widening of the income gap between urban and rural residents is obviously faster than the expansion of income inequality within urban areas and that within the rural areas. From 1978 to 2000, Gini Coefficient within the urban areas has increased from 0.16 to 0.32, and that within the countryside from 0.21 to 0.35, all being well kept below the internationally recognized warning line. However, in sharp contrast, the income gap between urban and rural residents is way larger than that: from

1980 to 2000, the Gini Coefficient has seen a rapid increase from 0.341 to 0.417, which was already above the international warning line. Currently, the income inequality between urban and rural residents is very large, with the ratio of city dwellers' income to rural farmers' income being 3.1:1, and even larger (5:1-6:1) if differentiated welfare subsidies were also counted. So, it can be inferred that urban and rural residents belong to two entirely different income groups or consumer groups. The formation of the huge income gap between urban and rural residents due to historical reasons has made it hard for rural residents to keep up with city dwellers in a short time, and thus enabled them to take even more.

Therefore, our warning line might as well be set higher than the international one.[1] (It has long since been universally recognized in academia of economics that urban-rural disparity does affect the Gini Coefficient. But word came via the Internet that some economist claimed that it was his own invention and applied for Nobel Prize on account of this. If it is true, it is really absurd and funny!)

In view of the influence of such structural factor on the Gini Coefficient of China, I highlighted in my article entitled *Attaching Further Importance to Social Equity* that we must neither say that polarization has already occurred nor declare that income gap has reached the limit, because Chinese residents are still capable of enduring more, i.e., a larger Gini Coefficient. However, it does not mean that the expansion of income inequality is not important. Just to the opposite, we should take measures to curb this trend. And then I warned people that during the time when Gini Coefficient is on the rapid rise, polarization would probably occur and the income gap might reach the limit very soon unless powerful measures are taken in time. Therefore, it is not right to say that we should wait until the time is ripe to solve this problem given that the expansion of Gini Coefficient is an inevitable result of the development of market economy.

According to the blueprint designed by Deng Xiaoping, approximately at the

1 *Collected Works of Liu Guoguang*, volume 7, Beijing: China Social Sciences Press, 2006, pp.505-506.

turn of the 21st century, it will be time that those people who got rich first should help others to catch up and thus achieve common prosperity, that is, by that time, we should set about narrowing the gap between the rich and the poor.[1] Such timeline seemed to be a little bit optimistic. However, after nearly three decades' reform and development, our economic strength and financial power has currently been great enough to accelerate this timetable.

Since the first goal of "encouraging some people in some regions to get rich first" has been realized so soon, why should it take us a very long time to achieve the second goal of "encouraging those who got rich first to help others to catch up so as to achieve common prosperity"? For China, as a socialist country, it is hard to explain that away. Obviously, those who hold such view are defending for the accumulation of wealth at one pole, which would lead to the foreseeable aggravation of social contradictions.

Aside from these considerations, there is another reason for me to take a moderately middle course, that is, I have great confidence in the correct political line of the CPC, under whose leadership our reform and opening-up is carried out. The widening of income inequality and the gap between the rich and the poor since the reform and opening-up is partly the result of our lack of experience while implementing the correct policy of "encouraging some people in some regions to get rich first". We just focused on the prosperity of some people and haven't had the time to think out ways to make the fruits of reform shared by all. Besides, it also has something to do with various wrong social thoughts (I will elaborate on this later).

The Central Committee of the CPC has always been keeping to the socialist road while carrying out the reform. A lot of remarkable achievements have been made in the development of social production, invigoration of market and the improvement of macroeconomic regulation and people's lives, which is obvious to all. So, even though there was something wrong with income distribution during

1 *Selected Works of Deng Xiaoping*, volume 3, Beijing: People's Publishing House, 1993, p.374.

the reform, we should never say that Deng Xiaoping's "prophecy" has come true or the reform has failed. It is neither true nor fair to say so. The party has always been accountable to the people; especially since the 16th National Congress of the CPC, the party, in the spirit of caring for the people's interests, has come up with the "Scientific Outlook on Development" putting people first and the idea of "building a harmonious society", pledging to "make the people share in the fruits of reform".

In response to the ever-growing social contradictions, the party has begun to "attach more importance to social equity" after the policy of "giving priority to efficiency with due consideration to equity" gradually retired. Besides, the party has set about solving the problem of inequitable distribution through taxation reform and transfer payments; the party has taken proactive measures to solve prominent problems in some aspects vital to the interests of people, such as medical care services, education charges, residential housing, land requisition, and house demolition and relocation etc. In May 2006, the Central Committee of the CPC convened a special meeting on the reform of income distribution. These major steps by the Central Committee, I believe, would alleviate the widening of the gap between the rich and the poor and reverse the trend of polarization provided that they are implemented conscientiously and effectively.

A multitude of things need to be done to adjust distribution relations and promote social equity. Most importantly, the CPC and the government should take the lead; besides, it also needs cooperation from the whole society in all aspects, including ideology and public opinion. Therefore, it is no good for the solution if we are too obsessed with the problem of polarization, though it is indeed the researchers' duty to warn people of the tendency. That explains why I took a moderately middle course with some preference.

3. Changes in the ownership structure—the most rooted cause for the widening of the gap between the rich and the poor

At the end of the first section in this article, I elaborated on an important point made by Deng Xiaoping in terms of income distribution. He said, "so long as pubic ownership remains the mainstay of the economy, polarization will be avoided", which reflects a key principle in Marxist political economics, "relations of production (especially ownership relations) determine distribution relations." In order to drive the point home, we need to find out at first the causes of the widening of the gap between the rich and the poor and especially the most fundamental one.

Many explanations were already made as to what causes the widening of the gap between the rich and the poor.

Some people said that the widening of the gap between the rich and the poor is the price that we have to pay during "the marketization reform", which is not wrong. Owing to fierce competition and the law of "the survival the fittest" in the process of marketization, the income gap kept widening, which, in a sense, does help improve efficiency and develop the economy. This is the positive side of market economy. However, the development of market economy and especially the law of capital accumulation would inevitably lead to a large gap between the rich and the poor and polarization, which is an ironclad law of the market. This trend will be unstoppable under market economy and will not be alleviated unless the government carries out effective economic intervention.

Besides, some people attributed the widening of the gap between the rich and the poor to "the inadequacy of marketization and immature market economy", which is however incorrect.

Do they mean a mature market economy guarantees lower income inequality? It turned out not to be true. As a matter of fact, the tendency of wealth being concentrated in the hands of the very few people is becoming even more apparent with the development of market economy. A quote earlier in the article said that developed market economies are "rife with the phenomena of polarization". UN Human Development Report 2006 said, "According to statistics last updated, the gap between the rich and the poor around the globe is still expanding, be it between countries or within a country." Since the 1970s, major capitalist market economies such as the UK, the USA and Japan are excessively relying on the market mechanism and private property rights, resulting in higher concentration of wealth, worsening of income inequality and degeneration of social equity. Besides, in developed welfare market economies, the situation of wealth and income distribution is also deteriorating. However, all these facts cannot verify the hypothesis that the worsening of income inequality and polarization would be automatically solved if market economy is mature and developed enough. Therefore, those who claimed that the problem would be solved if "marketization reform" is fully implemented are just armchair strategists.

Many scholars have analyzed the reasons of the worsening of income inequality in China very specifically from different perspectives, but it is hard to boil them down into several categories. Here I would like to list some and analyze them briefly one by one.

The "dual urban-rural economic structure" model;

The "regional imbalance" model

The "industrial imbalance" model (including some industrial monopoly);

The model of "corruption, power-for-money deals, and dishonest practices"

The model of "policy imbalance between regions and shortage of public goods"

The model of "inadequate regulation in redistribution (taxation, social security and welfare)"

...

Here, I just named a few reasons of inequitable distribution. All of them have contributed to China's widening of the gap between the rich and the poor. It can be seen that these causes are quite overlapping.

Urban-rural disparity is a major cause of the widening of the gap between the rich and the poor. As mentioned before, the Gini Coefficient in urban areas and that in rural ones are both 0.3-0.4, whereas the country's Gini index (including both urban and rural areas) is over 0.45. Though the expansion of urban-rural gap has been alleviated after the government adopted the policy of building a new socialist countryside to support and benefit agriculture, rural areas and farmers, the change is still far from being complete and radical.

Regional imbalance is to a larger extent related to urban-rural disparity. In the map of China, the east is dotted with many prosperous cities; while in the west, most places are vast rural areas. Thanks to regional balance policies, the expansion of regional disparity has been slowed down, but the gap still kept widening.

Industrial imbalance mainly refers to inequitable distribution of income resulting from natural or administrative monopoly in some industries. In the era of planned economy, there was also industrial monopoly in China, but high pay and corruption in monopoly industries were very rare. However, since the reform and opening-up, some monopoly industries were ill influenced by the concept of market interests. Especially since the taxation reform in 1994, the enterprises can have all the after-profits at their own disposal but there is no supervision over the use of these profits, which has thus given rise to high pay, bonus, and welfare in some monopoly industries. So, monopoly should not be to blame. In order to solve these problems, we should reform income distribution radically and improve supervision within monopoly enterprises. Besides, it is also urgent that we take some measures to remove people's dissatisfaction with some excessively high income in monopoly industries, though the problem isn't serious enough to affect the overall situation of income distribution. However, some people deliberately diverted people's attention from the rooted cause of inequitable distribution and manipulated them into opposing the necessary control of the state sector on a few major fields and key industries concerning the lifeblood of the national economy so as to prepare the way for privatization. We should increase vigilance and strive to thwart their ambitions.

Corruption, power-for-money deals, and dishonest practices are the core issues arousing public indignation over inequitable distribution of income, therefore we should use both legal means and moral standards to fight against them more boldly and resolutely. Such illegitimate income is hard to be included in the official calculation of Gini Coefficient. Even though some dark income and grey income occasionally amounted to several hundred million or several billion RMB, they just made up a small part in the national income and thereby would not make a big difference. However, some people made a great deal about this problem by viewing it as another cause for income inequality, scheming to divert people's attention from the rooted cause of income distribution. So, we need make our eyes wide open to thwart such plot. At the same time, we also need fight against corruption while studying the issue of inequitable distribution.

Policy imbalance between regions, which can further affect urban-rural disparity, regional imbalance, and industrial imbalance, is on the list of our priorities during the government reform. We should go all out to transform government functions, striving to enhance public service, increase the supply of public goods and attach equal importance to economic development and social service rather than just focus on the former. However, the call for equal importance to social service does not mean that the government should back off from economic management, just like what neo-liberalists advertised. State intervention is anyhow conducive to both sufficient supply and equitable distribution of public goods.

It is known that redistribution is indispensable to the adjustment of distribution relations. However, redistribution tends to be delayed and fails to cover everything, which constitutes a major cause for inequitable distribution. Our government has been advocating that efficiency should be the first priority in the primary distribution and equity would be given precedence in redistribution. So, the government mainly counted on redistribution, especially taxation and transfer payments to achieve social equity. However, only a very small proportion of national income could be regulated in redistribution, whilst the bulk of the national income was apportioned in the primary distribution. That is to say, inequitable distribution largely occurs in primary distribution. For example, capital income is high in proportion to labor income within enterprises; senior managers got high pays, whilst employees got paid with fairly low wages; monopoly industries had far more profits than common industries, etc. Therefore, great importance should be attached to social equity even in the primary distribution, which are more often than not neglected.

The key issue that affects income distribution the most is the relations between capital and labor, which is closely related to the basic social production relations or property relations. In recent years, many Marxist economists have elaborated on it in their study of income distribution[1]. Property ownership tends to affect income gap the most.

However, some people failed to notice that, talking with great relish that people vary in contribution due to different capabilities, that is to say, the more one contributes, the more income he should get; the less one contributes, the less he should get. It seems that income is only determined by individual capability, knowledge and contribution. Marxism does not deny the contribution of individual capability (such as complex labor). In the *Critique of the Gotha Programme*, Marx also took this factor into consideration while elaborating on the principle of distribution according to work.

However, even western mainstream scholars in economics also recognized that property relations affected income distribution the most, admitting that private property disparity is the rooted cause of income inequality. Paul Adam Samuelson, a neo-classical generalist, ever said, "income gap is mainly caused by wealth disparity...in comparison with wealth, individual capability is too insignificant." He also added that "property ownership is the number one cause of income gap, what comes next to it in the declining order of importance is individual capability, education, training, opportunity, and health."

We believe that such argument made by this distinguished western economist is fair and scientific, but such point will be even clearer if we explain it with Marxist political economics. According to Marxism, production determines distribution and distribution of any consumer goods is determined by allocation of production conditions, which reflects the nature of the mode and the relations of production. Varying relations of production lead to different distribution relations and modes.

1 See Deng Bing's speech entitled "A Study on the causes of Polarization in China and its Solutions" in *Wu You Zhi Xiang* Literary Club on August 6th, 2006; Yang Chengxun, "To Trace the Rooted Cause of Inequitable distribution from the Perspective of Ownership Relations", *Economics Study of Shanghai School*, 2004, No. 11.

Therefore, what fits capitalist private ownership is distribution according to factors of production (mainly capital and the price of labor), and what suits socialist public ownership is distribution according to work.

These are two different modes of distribution conforming to different modes of social production. So how about the mode of distribution in the primary stage of socialism? Based on Marxist theories and the 15th Central Committee of the CPC report, our Constitution stipulates that in the primary stage of socialism we must adhere to the basic economic system in which public ownership is the mainstay and different economic sectors develop side by side, and the system of distribution under which distribution according to work is dominant and a variety of modes of distribution coexist.

At the very beginning of the reform and opening-up, we just had an exclusive public sector, and the non-public sector almost started from zero. As a result, the growth of the non-public sector is sure to overtake that of the public sector, and only in this way can different economic sectors develop side by side. This is conducive to the development of the economy as a whole. Therefore, the non-public sector will inevitably grow faster than the public sector over a fairly long period of time, resulting in an increase in the proportion of the non-public sector in the national economy and a relative decline in that of the public sector. At the same time, distribution according to work carries less weight than before, and accordingly distribution according to production factors carries relatively more weight than before. Some people even came to the conclusion that distribution according to production factors has already replaced distribution according to work as the dominant mode of distribution for the national economy.[1] It can be inferred from the general law of capitalist market economy and the real development of our market economy that, with the relative expansion of private property rights, such distribution mode would cause a relative increase in the

1 Wu Li, Wen Rui, "My Perspective on Changes in Distribution of Income Since 1992", *China Business Times*, May 26th, 2006.

share of capital income and a relative decline in the share of labor income, and thus the widening of income gap. This explains why absolute wealth goes hand in hand with relative poverty.

We have already begun to check our system of distribution and especially means of redistribution such as taxation to adjust distribution relations and narrow the gap between the rich and the poor, which is very necessary but still far from enough. Besides, we need also check our basic relations of production and the basic economic system. Only in this way can we eventually prevent the gap between the rich and the poor from widening and approaching the limit, i.e., polarization, and finally achieve common prosperity. That also explains why Deng Xiaoping said, "So long as public ownership remains the mainstay of the economy, polarization will be avoided." Besides, he also added, "If basic means of production is owned by the state or the collective, i.e., public-owned", "a new bourgeoisie would not emerge".

This penetrating thesis pointed out that in the primary stage of socialism, private property rights are tolerated and non-labor factors (mainly capital) are allowed to have a rightful share only if public ownership plays the dominant role. So long as public ownership remains the mainstay of the economy, the gap between the rich and the poor would be controlled within proper bounds and kept from reaching the limit, i.e., polarization, and hence common prosperity would be eventfully achieved. Otherwise, polarization will inevitably occur.

Therefore, over a certain period of time in the primary stage of socialism, the private sector is sure to outgrow the public sector, and it is also very necessary and beneficial for the private sector to expand gradually. However, anything should be controlled within a certain bound, just like what Jiang Zemin pointed out, "Surely, there should be a limit or precondition for the decline in the public sector, that is, public ownership must remain the mainstay of the economy and the state sector must play the leading role."[1] As the private sector grows to a certain point, it'll

1 *Selected Works of Jiang Zemin,* Volume 3, Beijing: People's Publishing House, 2006, p.72.

be time we re-evaluate its share and expansion and try to keep it from affecting the mainstay status of the public sector and the leading role of the state sector, so that both sectors could develop side by side harmoniously in a sound, healthy, and orderly way.

With further progress in our reform and opening-up, our ownership structure has undergone great changes from an exclusive public sector to a side-by-side development of many economic sectors. So, has the decline of the public sector and the expansion of the private sector already touched bottom and begun to affect the mainstay status of public ownership yet? It is another sensitive issue since it concerns the basic economic system stipulated by the Constitution. China's theoretical circles are quite divided on this issue.

4. Several evaluations of changes in China's ownership structure

The 15th National Congress report finalized the definition of the basic economic system in the primary stage of socialism, that is, a system in which public ownership is the mainstay and other kinds of ownership develop side by side. The report also prescribes clearly that the status of public ownership as the mainstay of the economy is mainly manifested in the predominance of public assets, the state sector's control on the lifeblood of the national economy and its leading role in the economic development.

This report has specifically pointed out that as long as we keep public ownership as the mainstay of the economy, ensure state control over the lifeblood of the national economy, and manage to enhance the dominance and competitiveness of the state sector, the nature of socialism would remain unchanged regardless of the decline in the proportion of the state sector.

However, there is a precondition for the above conclusion, namely, predominance of public assets in quantity and the state sector's control on the national economy. But what if public ownership fails to maintain the predominance?

What does "predominance" in quantity here refer to? What is the minimum of the proportion of the state sector or the public sector? These ambiguities in the report gave rise to different interpretations.

In general, they are as follows:

(1) Some people asserted that the private sector had already dominated the economy in place of the public sector and became the mainstay of the economy, and the latter had reduced to a supplementary role. They justified themselves by the following statistics: All-China Federation of Industry & Commerce announced that the private sector, the foreign sector and the economy in Hong Kong, Macau and Taiwan accounted for 65% of China's GDP in 2005; Veteran experts from National Bureau of Statistics estimated that the ratio of the public sector to the private sector was 39:61 in 2005.

(2) Some people maintained that public ownership is still the mainstay of the economy despite the decline in the public sector. Their conclusion is based on the following statistics: by the end of 2004, public assets still accounted for 56% in all paid-in capita; according to estimates by some veteran experts from National Bureau of Statistics, in 2005, the ratio of the public sector to the private sector in terms of paid-in capital of secondary and tertiary industries was 53:47, public assets still making up the majority and thus still maintaining the predominance. They believed that, with state-owned assets accounting for over 70% of the overall social assets, the state sector is still predominant in key industries concerning the lifeblood of the national economy and still maintained very strong control over the national economy.

(3) Based on the following facts, some people concluded that China's ownership structure was at the crossing road. In terms of the proportion of the assets, public assets and private assets, roughly half and half, are on an equal footing. (It is measured that from 1985 to 2005 the ratio of public assets to private assets declined from 94.09:5.91 to 48.8:50.9.) As far as its rightful control on the lifeblood of the national economy is concerned, the state sector still played the leading role in key fields and basic industries (in terms of paid-in capital, the public sector accounted for 64% in key basic industries and highly monopolized industries in 2005); however, its control on the crucial manufacturing industry characterized by high-level marketization, high profits, and fierce competition is

rather weak; in many cities or provinces, especially those developed coastal areas, the percentage of public assets has reduced to below 50%. The predominance of public assets and the state sector's control on the national economy has drastically declined so that the status of public ownership as the mainstay of the economy has shown some sign of weakening.

However, these three opinions are all grounded on unofficial data. Unfortunately, the government didn't issue any complete or precise data concerning the ratio of the public sector to the private sector, either. So, it is hard to tell exactly the current situation of our ownership structure.

Some economists and academic institutions held that the status of public ownership as the mainstay of the economy was mainly reflected in its control on the national economy rather than its predominance in quantity, denying that the state sector's control is conditioned by the predominance of public assets (in quantity). Therefore, they didn't think it is necessary to set the proportion of the public sector or that of the private sector precisely in state plans, and hence the government needn't or issue such data. If we are to follow such advice, we couldn't see our current ownership structure in perspective and thus would fail to take correct measures to protect the basic socialist economic system.

The Central Committee has been upholding the basic economic system in which public ownership is the mainstay and many economic sectors develop side by side, which was also reiterated in the 16th National Congress, the third and fifth plenary sessions of the 16th Central Committee, and many economic conferences held by the Central Committee. Every department of the government should work hard to achieve this. Some people suggested that the NPC should supervise and check up on our basic economic system to examine whether public ownership still remain the mainstay of the economy. I think these suggestions are worth considering.

5. Tendency of privatization affecting the mainstay status of public ownership: at the practical level

People's opinions about whether the status of public ownership as the mainstay of the economy has been weakened are not only based on their own evaluations or judgment of the proportion of the public sector and the state sector's control on the national economy, but have something to do with their detection of the rise of a certain trend in the process of China's economic reform. As a matter of fact, we did notice such a trend in real economic life. Even though most people tried to avoid calling it "privatization", it is what it is. Besides, some people did promote the idea of "privatization" publicly without scruples.

The rise of privatization manifests itself in the following two aspects. At the practical level, they distorted our party's reform policies, scheming to mislead us towards privatization and trying every trick in the book to push its implementation. In the ideological sense, they advertised privatization under the disguise of our party's slogan of "emancipating the mind". Surely, these two aspects also interacted with each other.

Over these years, reforms of state-owned and collectively-owned enterprises have proved in general to be very healthy, smooth and successful, which have contributed a lot to the economic development, social progress, social stability and solidarity. But at the same time, they also gave rise to some problems. Some people had been trying to distort reform policies or measures made by the CPC Central Committee to serve privatization by every conceivable means.

For example, no sooner had the Central Committee proposed that our economic restructuring aimed to establish a socialist market economy than some people began to sell the idea that China must practice privatization because the market economy China aims to establish is incompatible with public ownership.

Shortly after the Central Committee put forward the modern corporate system characterized by "clearly established ownership, well-defined powers and responsibilities, separation of government administration from enterprise management as well as scientific management", some people began to criticize public ownership for being unclearly defined and existing just in name, claiming that only if they are owned by the natural person (i.e., privatization) can its property rights be clearly defined.

No sooner had the Central Committee proposed that the joint stock system, as a way of fulfilling public ownership, can be used to enhance the predominance of public assets and the status of public ownership as the mainstay of the economy than some people began to privatize SOEs under the disguise of joint stock system.

Shortly after the Central Committee came up with the policy of encouraging the joint stock cooperative system characterized by cooperation among workers in both labor and capital, some people tried to make operators hold the lion's share and promote ownership concentration in individuals, scheming to change the nature of the joint stock cooperative system from collective ownership to private one.

Shortly after the Central Committee proposed that strategic adjustments should be made to the overextended public sector so as to enhance the leading role of the state sector, some people replaced maliciously the policy of encouraging "state-owned assets to move in and out of a certain field based on rational choices" with that of "*Guo tui min jin*" (the state retreats whilst the private sector advances).

Shortly after the Central Committee adopted the strategy of "*zhua da fang xiao*" (managing large SOEs well while relaxing control over small ones) in SOE reform and encouraged to adopt flexible ways to invigorate the small and medium-sized state-owned enterprises, some people held onto the idea of selling out SOEs and started a wave of selling SOEs at extremely low prices or even giving them away.

This evil trend was very abnormal. "We did not have solid theoretical foundations for the SOE reform or any prior experience to draw from. Everything seemed to have be done in a swarm. Some local SOEs had been almost sold out when top officials wanted to know how far SOE restructuring has gone." "There are almost no local state-owned assets left when regulations on transfer of state-owned assets are officially announced."[1] "The Central Committee's policies

1 *Sanlian Life Weekly*, December 11, 2003.

concerning the restructuring of enterprises and transfer of ownership had been "adapted" by local entities beyond recognition. For instance, some SOE leaders have sold or acquired the enterprises without authorization, taken them by force or trickery, or even got them without a penny, having almost drained state assets and deprived workers of many rights.[1]

These ills in the reform of SOEs were mainly incurred by very few people's embezzlement of state assets, which are illegal or do not conform to norms or regulations. The Central Committee and relevant departments kept drawing lessons, promoting legislation and improving policies and made constantly greater efforts to correct errors or deviations with a view to keeping our reform on the right track. Some people likened such huge misappropriation of state assets to a "feast", but it is obviously not correct to summarize the SOE reform in such a way. However, instead of sporadic occurrence, such phenomenon was rather rampant at that time. Many cases did indicate some signs of a free feast, so, in a sense, it is not an exaggeration. An article published on Xinhua net commented, "No one can tell exactly how many SOEs had been restructured illegally or against rules or regulations." However, when the history of the PRC is written some day, it needs to be accounted for. As for whether it could, it all depends on the intensity of the administration's efforts or capabilities.

Due to the reform, a group of people became rich overnight on the one hand; on the other, just as a famous economist put it, the success of reform had to be achieved at the expense of the interests of a group of people, that is, 30 million veteran workers. How lame and wicked justification! Luckily, a Hong Kong scholar with a clear conscience has noticed it. Actually, mainland scholars knew more of the real situation in China than Professor Lang Xianping did. But Professor Lang managed to grasp crucial matters and hit home, such as privatization, MBO etc. It was reported that over 90% netizens approved of

1 *Xinhua net*, July 31st, 2005.

Professor Lang's view[1], opposing privatization and any schemes to deny the mainstay status of public ownership, which in a sense showed that the people embraced the socialist road in the reform and opposed the capitalist one.

At the practical level, the process of privatization and adjustment to ownership structure has been artificially accelerated and even distorted, on which both people and top leaders have begun to reflect deeply. The slogan of "no more selling" was heard shouting among the people! Top leaders also began to work on regulations to standardize such process.

6. Tendency of privatization threatening the mainstay status of public ownership: at the ideological and theoretical level

For several years, the ideology of privatization had been running even more wild and with a more variety on the theoretical level. Here I shall just make a few comments. In socialist China whose Constitution prescribes that public ownership is the mainstay of the economy, how dare someone openly advertise the idea of "privatization being the right road"! And what is more, his book entitled *Privatization: SOE Reform can never Evade,* which publicized the idea of "privatization of SOEs being the core (of SOE reform)", was even kept in the shelves of Xinhua bookstore for sales for rather long! There is really plenty of freedom of speech and freedom of the press in China!

Influenced by such ideology, someone even advocated openly that the private sector should be the mainstay of China's economy. He said, "In the future, most investment would be drawn from private capital and the private sector of the economy would be the mainstay."

Someone even did not mince words about his scheme of promoting privatization. He audaciously urged people to "remove obstacles (to privatization) by eradicating traditional ideologies". He said, "In whatever names, the private sector (including privately-run enterprises or organizations, private-owned assets), non-public sector or non-state sector, they all proved one thing, i.e., privatization,

1 *Economic Daily*, August 3rd, 2005.

just from different perspectives." "Due to the ill influence of traditional ideologies, privatization was interfered with by the unaccountable play of words," added he. In the meanwhile, another person claimed, "keeping public ownership as the mainstay of the economy suggests that our society's understanding of socialism is just on a par with that of the Soviet Union under the rule of Joseph Stalin." He dismissed the stipulation of the Constitution of the PRC and the Constitution of the CPC concerning the mainstay status of public ownership as "the vestige of traditional socialist concepts", which has denied totally the essential characteristic and the fundamental principle of socialism, i.e., the establishment of public ownership and elimination of exploitation.

By contrast, some advocates of privatization, who said in private that privatization is a foregone conclusion, tended to sell the idea or plan of privatization evasively. In public, whenever they finished advertising the idea of privatization, they would add automatically, "it is absolutely no privatization", or "it's just another form of public ownership". Some famous economist misled the public by defining private joint-stock companies and common non-public joint-stock companies as "new forms of public ownership". Some people coined the word "indirect public ownership", claiming that "indirect public ownership" should take the place of "direct public ownership" as the economic mainstay through redistribution of taxation, and that capitalist countries such as the United States were also using this method to "realize socialism". To disguise capitalism as socialism is sheer deception of both themselves and others! How unbelievable!

Another opinion came from a "prophecy". An "unassuming" prophet predicted that it was still too early to conclude that the private sector had already become the economic mainstay, but it surely would as it developed. It was cited from an article published on a journal attached to some party school, which was led by a distinguished economist. It said, "We used to say that the private sector is a useful supplement to the state sector, but now we have found out that someday their relationship would be turned upside down as market economy develops along the course that it should, that is, the state sector would be a useful supplement to the private sector." How arrogant and grand sounding! They seemed to be laughing smugly at the 1.3 billion Chinese people and looking on coldly, saying, "Someday, you would sure lose the stronghold of public ownership". Or they seem to be provoking the administrators gloatingly, "and then, what can you do with it?"

Besides, there is also another view supportive of privatization under the disguise of studies on essential characteristics of socialism and selection of socialist patterns. On the eve of the 15th National Congress of the CPC, some people invented the formula of "socialism = social equity + market economy". This ambiguous formula even applies to social democracy and capitalism, denying public ownership and elimination of exploitation as one of the essential characteristics and fundamental principles of socialism. Some people said recently that it was not right for us to keep public ownership and distribution according to work as essential characteristics of socialism for so long, but instead they should be replaced by "common prosperity, social harmony, equity and justice". Though the latter are very important, they would still fail to form socialism without public ownership or elimination of exploitation.

Advocates of such theory had never said a single word about the mainstay status of public ownership while introducing the five characteristics of the "socialist pattern of the people". Someone omitted the phrase of "elimination of exploitation" while citing Deng Xiaoping's remarks about the essence of socialism. He said, "Deng Xiaoping said that the essence of socialism is liberation and development of the productive forces, elimination of polarization and the ultimate achievement of prosperity for all." We all know that the establishment of public ownership is to "eliminate exploitation", which helps explain why Deng Xiaoping has repeatedly listed "public ownership as the mainstay of the economy" as one of the major principles of socialism. However, he defined socialist ownership by quoting Deng Xiaoping's words out of context and evaded key words such as "public ownership" and "elimination of exploitation", claiming that both public ownership and private ownership are socialist ownerships! It is so lacking in rigor!

Finally, there is also another theory embracing privatization and opposing public ownership under the disguise of Marxism. They schemed to beguile people with the distorted Marxist idea of "re-establishing individual property". In the past people kept misunderstanding Marx in this regard, but later those misunderstandings all cleared up. Recently, in *Yanhuang Chunqiu* (*China Through the Ages*) (2007, No.6), a monthly journal in China, some scholars such as Xie Tao misinterpreted Marx's idea of "re-establishing individual property on the basis of collective ownership of the means of production", into "an even distribution of wealth on the basis of individual private property", that is to say, "every natural person possesses an equal share of the means of production", distortedly classifying private ownership as Marx's ideas.

Actually, Friedrich Engels has long since clarified such idea of Marx in his book *Anti-Duhring*, as far as the re-establishment of individual property based on social ownership of the means of production is concerned, "Anyone who knows Germany would know that social ownership involves land and other means of production whereas individual property refers to products including consuming goods."[1] Turning a blind eye to these insightful analyses, people like Xie Tao levelled attacks at socialism with Chinese characteristics, which is the result of efforts by several generations of Chinese leaders, and justified themselves with the distorted idea of Marx, reducing socialism with Chinese characteristics to a social democracy focusing on the re-establishment of individual property. They said that "the re-establishment of individual property" was "the general line and policy of China's reform and opening-up". Their ill intention of privatization was so self-evident that any further comments would be superfluous.

You see, how rampant the tendency of privatization has already been! China respects people's freedom of speech and embraces the co-existence of and contention among a variety of schools of thoughts. But China would never

1 *Marx and Engels: Selected works* (volume 3), Beijing: People's Publishing House, p.473.

practice pluralism or Glasnost just like what the Soviet Union did in its reform led by by Mikhail Gorbachev, which will probably lead to people's ideological confusion and thus mislead our reform and opening-up. It's time that we deal with it.

7. "Low efficiency in the public sector": a pseudo-proposition

Those scheming to steer China's reform towards privatization were mostly based on some lame models, among which the proposition of "low efficiency in the public sector" was cited the most.

However, this feeble model had actually been criticized a lot in many articles and books. For example, Zuo Dapei, author of the book *No More Selling*, refuted forcibly and sensibly in this book many false views with sufficient evidence and great rigor, such as "SOE ownership existing just in name", "as everyone is born selfish, operators will run business very well only if they become owners", "excessively high costs incurred by supervision over SOE", etc. So far, advocates of "privatization" haven't justified themselves with any sound evidence, but they still insisted on low efficiency in the public sector and claimed that it would speak for itself. It seems that they did not intend to argue with you at all.

However, there are many books about efficiency within the public or private sector or arguments against "low efficiency in the public sector", so I would not elaborate on these issues any more. I just want to make a brief analysis of some aspects for readers' attention.

(1) It is indisputable that the public sector is more superior to the private one in terms of social and economic benefits at the macro-level, such as economic growth, job security, social welfare etc. For instance, for a fairly long period of time, economies dominated by the public sector kept growing faster than those by the private sector; the former have managed to build their own countries, which used to be backward and poor, into industrialized powers or industrialized powers-to-be; the former have defeated strong fascist powers, etc. They all provided good evidence of the public sector's superiorities.

(2) It is known that at the microeconomic level, when an enterprise is big enough, owners and operators should be separated, that is, the position of entrepreneur would be subdivided into boss (shareholder) and professional executive. The public sector can also adopt the model of principal-agent to improve the incentive and restraint mechanism. It has proven that the public sector does not necessarily need so many levels of capital operation as private joint stock companies do. According to the result of an empirical research by Joseph E. Stiglitz, a famous American economist, no evidence, be it statistics or examples of facts, shows that the public sector has lower efficiency than the private sector. This conclusion can be well demonstrated by SOEs with fairly high efficiency (including monopoly and competitive sectors) in France, Italy, Singapore, etc. Besides, sound evidence can also be found in China's SOEs whose operational performances have been dramatically enhanced in recent years.

(3) Some people used some cases of poor management of SOEs, an increase in the number of loss-making SOEs and a widespread decline in economic benefits within SOEs since the reform and opening-up especially in the middle and late 1990s, as evidence of low efficiency in the public sector, refusing to mention any causes for such phenomena. For example, some investment funds that used to be allocated by the state were later issued by banks in the form of loans, which might lead to a potential lack of fund or large deficits in many enterprises; an excessively large amount of surplus labor burdened the society with a heavy load; taxes levied on SOEs largely exceeded those on the private and foreign-owned enterprises, etc. During the reform, SOEs have paid a high price so as to secure social and economic stability but later ended up weighing down the society as a cumbersome burden. The decline in SOE benefits due to these special reasons is just a momentary thing, which can be overcome and solved through some measures and has nothing to do with ownership at all. However, advocates of privatization refused to mention these, but just cited them to prove that SOEs have low efficiency and justified their scheme of privatizing them. How far-fetched and absurd!

(4) What is more intolerable is that some people generalized from isolated incidents such as the decline in benefits and drain of state assets due to some SOE leaders' corruption, dismissing all China's SOEs as "crony capitalism"! And what is more, a major newspaper from southern China even suggested that all state-owned assets be privatized so as to eradicate "crony capitalism", which is obviously a distortion and slander of the state sector of our economy as a whole.

First, it does not tally with the fact that employees and a great majority of leaders of SOEs performed their duties conscientiously. The rise of cronies of powerful officials cannot be neglected, but it is just the result of power-for-money, collusion between government officials and businessmen, and shady deals rather than something inherent within the state sector. Second, those who reduced the nature of SOEs to crony capitalism had never tried to figure out why corruption was very rare in the era of planned economy whilst corruption runs wild at present. The first reason is that we used to have strict regulations on SOEs. For example, we ever formulated *the Charter of the Anshan Iron and Steel Company* in 1960s based on our lessons and experience in terms of SOE management; in 1980s, an inspection team was ever sent overseas to learn from foreign enterprises only to find that Japan, the United States and Europe were also learning from *the Charter of the Anshan Iron and Steel Company*. Very interestingly, we brought their experience back again to China to enrich our charter. [1]

The other reason is that some unhealthy tendencies in the past did not influence the general climate too much. For example, people still took the interests of the collective very seriously, not just for the sake of their own interests, which is in sharp contrast with the currently pervasive ideas due to the corrosive influence of neo-liberalism such as "every man for himself, and the devil take the hindmost", "man were born selfish" and "economic man" etc. With such tendency running so wild, some leaders of SOEs didn't stand up to the test. Some SOE managers, who anticipated privatization, turned SOEs into a total mess, which were however

1 http://bbs.people.com.cn, August 3rd, 2007.

supposed to yield good results. These top executives forced the government to permit them to acquire these enterprises at an extremely low price so as to achieve their end of privatization. Besides, some party leaders colluded with some SOE managers to seize high profits from the privatization of SOEs. Actually, under the influence of these partial ideas such as "men were born selfish" and "economic man", many people undertook dirty deals at the expense of the interests of our country and people in the name of reform. For example, the farce of Management Buy-outs (MBO) was indeed based on and nurtured by the popularized theories such as "economic man" and "men were born selfish" etc.

(5) The heated debate on "low efficiency in the public sector" has reached a deadlock, with neither side ready to listen or compromise. However, it does not mean that both of them are right. After all, in a debate, there is always one side standing for the truth, and the other being wrong. Notwithstanding this, either side does stand for a particular interest group: one stands for capital, wealth, corrupted bureaucrats, and unconscientious scholars; the other the great masses mainly composed of farmers and workers. Therefore, it is natural that the two sides are hard to be convinced by each other. But what really counts is that departments responsible for publicizing theories and executive branches must know exactly which side they should and shouldn't support.

8. On the so-called "*guo tui min jin*" ("the state retreats while the private sector advances")

We should strategically readjust the layout of the state sector, allow the state-owned capital to move in and out of certain fields based on rational choices and focus on something while setting others aside to strengthen the state sector's control on the national economy and keep public ownership as the mainstay of the economy. These decisions were made in the 15th National Congress of the CPC and the fourth Plenary Session of the 15th Central Committee of the CPC. As I mentioned earlier, soon after the Central Committee came up with these policies, some people misinterpreted them as "guo tui min jin", the upside-down version of "guo jin min tui". That is to say, they suggested that the state sector should retire from the competitive fields, and the private sector cover for it. Even though such misinterpretation has been censured and corrected officially, it still popped up from time to time. For example, on March 1st, 2006, a major Beijing newspaper published an article written by the director of some institute, who said, "the current reform of SOEs requires that most SOEs must withdraw strategically and be transformed into non-state-owned enterprises". He even asserted that such tendency "will be irreversible and inevitable". Later, after some readers wrote to question such opinion, the editor-in-chief apologized, "Due to slack censorship, we failed to discern these inappropriate opinions." However, this director had publicized the idea of "guo tui min jin" for more than once before that. For example, on August 2nd, 2005, he ever said in an article published on the website of Chinanews (Chinanews.com.cn) that "guo tui min jin" is an inevitable result of market economy while paraphrasing a piece of news from Ta Kung Pao (May 2nd ,2005), a newspaper in China. He said, "as the market economy develops, state-owned enterprises would inevitably withdraw in a large scale". On August 7th, 2005, he reiterated in a meeting in Jiamusi, Heilongjiang province of China, that the so-called SOE reform means that state-owned enterprises should be transformed into non-state-owned ones."

So, from which fields should state-owned enterprises retreat? This director has made his point very clear, that is, from competitive fields. On January 16th, 2004, Xinhua net quoted his comments, "There is no competition between state-owned enterprises and other enterprises. But if competition occurs, SOEs should be sensible enough to withdraw," because "SOEs cannot catch up with non-state-owned enterprises in terms of efficiency and hence are less competitive than their opponents".

Should the state sector withdraw from competitive fields? In China, 95% of the industry involve intense competition. If SOEs are forced to withdraw from these competitive fields, it is nothing different from eradication of all state-owned enterprises from the industry. Besides, should all these strategic SOEs and key SOEs concerning the people's livelihood withdraw completely from these competitive fields? If the SOE with a sharp edge is capable enough to yield profits, why do we have to let private owners take the money? Even some western upright scholars did not agree with such biased opinion that "SOEs are less competitive than private enterprises". Besides, it is also conducive to ensuring equity and justice in distribution of social wealth if those SOEs in competitive fields turn in their profits to the state to fund production and social welfare.

Not only many people from the academia advocated that SOEs or state-owned assets should not withdraw completely from competitive fields, but the Central Committee also made it very clear in its policies. The report of the 15th National Congress of the CPC stated that in other fields (which mainly refers to competitive fields), SOEs should undergo asset reorganization and structural adjustment to strengthen their priorities and raise the overall quality of state assets. It was also stated in the third Plenary Session of the 16th Central Committee of the CPC that, in other industries or fields beyond the control of the state sector (also mainly competitive fields), SOEs should undergo restructuring and reorganization so as to compete fairly with their rivals. So, it was not required officially that the state sector must withdraw from these fields. Actually, it means that the state sector should "improve the quality of state assets", "respect the law of 'survival of the fittest'", and "strengthen its focus" to compete with its rivals fairly in the competitive fields.

So, we cannot come to the blanket conclusion that the state sector should retreat from all competitive fields (the so-called "*guo tui*"), for SOEs also need advance in some occasions. Now, let's move on to the so-called "*min jin*" ("the private sector advances"). Private enterprises are the natural major players in market competition. It goes without saying that private enterprises should gain free access to competitive fields. How about key industries or fields? The 15th National Congress of the CPC stipulated that the state sector must dominate key industries and sectors concerning the lifeblood of the national economy. So will private capital be allowed to enter these key industries or sectors? According to the State Council document on policies of encouraging and supporting the development of the non-public sector issued in 2005, the non-public sector is also allowed to enter monopoly industries and fields. These industries include electric power, telecommunications, railway, civil aviation and oil etc.; and these fields include mineral resources tapping, public utilities, infrastructure, and construction of science, technology and industry for national defense, etc. All these documents and regulations have demonstrated the party's magnanimity toward the non-public sector by giving them access to key industries and fields concerning the lifeblood of national economy.

However, some people didn't approve of it. They argued that giving the non-public sector access to many fields concerning the lifeblood of the national economy ran against the policy that "the state sector should control the lifeblood of national economy" issued by the 15th National Congress of the CPC. They believed that such policy would affect and even change the leading role of the state sector in the national economy and the mainstay status of public ownership. They have already expressed such concerns to authorities concerned in the hope that they would back down and rescind the policy.

I think that a moderate existence of the private sector in key industries and fields concerning the lifeblood of the national economy is in line with the spirit of the 15th National Congress of the CPC and conforms to the direction of SOE reform, as it does help to attract more social capital, expand public assets, strengthen the control of the state sector and diversify the sources of investment. Therefore, private capital can be allowed to own minority stake in these key industries or fields, but will never be tolerated to take controlling shares or fund exclusively in case the state sector's control on these industries or sectors would be affected; besides, we should also reinforce supervision over the enterprises and institutions to which private capital has gained access.

Currently in China, private capital is not strong enough; even if private capital expands, the state would just absorb it rather than mainly count on it to develop these key industries or sectors. As for high profits from these major industries and key fields, they are mostly equivalent to monopoly differential rents, which should be rightfully turned in to the state treasury based on theories from both home and abroad. Therefore, the government should restrain and reduce private equity dividends in these industries or fields so that such private capital could at most obtain equal profits as common competitive industries do. It also complies with Sun Yat-sen's idea of "restricting private capital". So it is understandable that the CPC referred to Sun Yat-sen's correct thinking that "private capital can never control the people's livelihood" and adjusted it to our national conditions in the primary stage of socialism. To restrict private capital from obtaining excess monopoly profits in key industries or sectors concerning the people's livelihood is not contradicting Sun Yat-sen's position.

After the government further classified a loosening of the previous restrictions on the non-public sector's access to certain fields, some officials and economists misinterpreted the policy from a wrong perspective. Denying the leading role of the state sector, they demanded that the private sector should be on an equal footing with the state sector in key fields. Some people even suggested that state capital should withdraw from all industries except public services before a certain deadline. Such opinions began to be heard from influential schools and universities and some departments of senior research institutes when the Central Committee was formulating the policy of further encouraging the development of the non-public sector last year, and even louder in the first half of 2005; and moreover, they were heard very often in mainstream media and forums. Against such backdrop, senior government officials in charge stepped in successively and clarified the following things: First, monopoly industries and sectors should be dominated by the state sector, which is determined by the nature of our economic system; second, structural adjustments of the state sector shouldn't be considered as the policy of forcing it to withdraw from all competitive fields; lastly, structural adjustments of the state sector mustn't be viewed as the policy of making centrally-administered enterprises advance and local SOEs retreat. Rather, a group of strong, highly competitive enterprises with distinctive local flavors and strengths must be developed.

Even after government officials in charge have repeatedly made clear their positions, voice of protest and criticism against the policy that SOEs are encouraged to expand and grow stronger in key fields can still be heard "inside the system" (*ti zhi nei*). They openly asserted that the state should withdraw completely from all industries; some articles even sang the praises of Ronald H. Coase's theory concerning China's reform, which boils down the key to the success of China's reform into "communist party plus property rights", claiming that if the state is to withdraw completely from all industries, it would be the magnificent feat of the Communist Party of China!

As a matter of fact, top decision-makers have made their positions very clear, having corrected some people's mistaken belief that "both private capital and state capital can gain equal access to monopoly industries", and censored some officials and economists' opinions that the state should withdraw completely from all industries. Notwithstanding these efforts, "the spirit of the resolution of the Third Plenary Session of the 16th Central Committee, namely, to keep public ownership as the mainstay of the economy, to maintain the leading role of the state sector and to develop the non-public sector of the economy, still failed to be fully acknowledged and implemented in a real sense."[1] Now, such ideology was still affecting the reform in real work, so we cannot afford to overlook it.

For example, *China's Macroeconomic Analysis* revealed the plan of some department on how much state capital would be transferred and how much state holdings would be sold off.[2] It aimed to dilute state shares owned by listed state-owned companies in many key and non-key fields by lowering the minimum percentage of state holdings. According to some reviews, such plan indicated that state capital would be reduced drastically in key fields, and that the state would withdraw from almost all competitive fields. It is imprudent to suggest

1 See: "joint stock system to rekindle private enterprises' hope of becoming bigger and stronger", *China Business Times, July 11th*, 2005.

2 See: *China's Macroeconomic Analysis*, 2005, No. 11.

that state holdings should be sold off in large quantities, and we must be on high alert against its repercussions (non-listed SOEs and other SOEs would be also affected). Besides, it also pointed out that the situation of state-owned industries, be it monopoly industry or competitive industry, has gradually taken a favorable turn, and that assets, output, and especially profits and tax contribution have dramatically increased despite the decline in the number of state-owned enterprises, which proves that reforms of ownership and SOEs under socialism are both very promising. Given such circumstance, it should be re-evaluated whether the state should continue with a large-scale withdrawal. Surely, there are still many problems with the layout of state-owned assets and the structure of SOEs, which therefore still need proper adjustments through the flow of capital.

9. What fields should be put under the state sector's control?

One of the themes of *The Guiding Opinions of SASAC (State-owned Assets Supervision and Administration Commission) about Promoting the Adjustment of State-owned Capital and the Reorganization of State-owned Enterprises* issued on December 18th, 2006 is to promote the concentration of state-owned capital in major industries and key fields, to enhance the state sector's control and to bring its leading role into play. These major industries and key fields include industries concerning state security, major infrastructure, major mineral resources, industries providing key public goods and services, and key enterprises in pillar industries and high technology industries. As for state-owned capital beyond these major industries or key fields, it should be allowed to move in and out of certain industries or fields based on rational choices so as to be transferred in accordance with the law.

This policy gave rise to two major responses. Some people believed that most industries, including the seven industries in which state capital must hold majority shares such as war industry and the nine major industries over which state capital must maintain a rather strong control such as machinery manufacturing industry, cover both competitive fields and non-competitive fields, in which SOEs are not the sole qualified players. They also argued that since these industries involved competition, it was illogical for them to be controlled by state-owned capital. According to them, erection of monopoly thresholds by state-owned enterprises is a violation of the principle of fair market competition; "to strengthen the control of the state sector has no legal basis"; the government has no right to claim monopoly over certain fields without any permission from the representative assembly, and so on. However, we insist that we must strengthen the control of the state sector and ensure that it must dominate major industries and key fields concerning the lifeblood of the national economy and play a leading role in the socialist market economy, because it is stipulated by the Constitution of the PRC, our fundamental law. Therefore, this is the very legal basis. Besides, it would not violate the principle of fair market competition at all if SOEs win the game by their strength.

Another response is that if state-owned capital which does not belong to major industries or key fields is "transferred in accordance with the law", i.e., to withdraw from these industries and fields, the non-public sector would hold a controlling number of the shares of these SOEs through mergers and acquisitions. Its consequences are very worrisome. Xia Xiaolin pointed out in his article published in *China Business Times*, "According to statistics from SASAC, in 2005, assets of China's centrally-administered enterprises accounted for 41.4% in total state-owned assets amounting to 26.8 trillion RMB, and 3/4 SOEs were in competitive industries. Under some logic, if the important role of state-owned assets in ensuring social equity is to be disregarded, the rest of state-owned enterprises (58.6%) and 3/4 SOEs in competitive industries would be mostly "transferred in accordance with the law", since they do not "belong to major industries or key fields". So how would distribution of wealth and income end up if such transfer results in private assets exceeding overwhelmingly state-owned assets in China's overall assets and the skyrocketed rise in the private wealth of very few people?[1]

Xia Xiaolin's suggestion on what fields should be put under the state sector's control deserves our attention. He believed that the state sector mainly shoulders the following two social responsibilities: to help the government with economic regulation and to ensure social equity and justice. The former applies to both socialist countries and modern capitalist market economies, whereas the latter is exclusive to socialist countries. "According to the western mainstream economics, the state sector facilitates economic regulation by the government in given conditions. However, practice of privatization in OECD members proves that the government can still regulate the economy effectively through monetary, fiscal and industrial policies and commercial means, even though basic monopoly industries are already privatized or the proportion of the state sector has been reduced to below 10%. Nevertheless, social equity and justice can not be guaranteed by economies with high-level privatization and mixed economies mainly characterized by privatization."

"China's reform aiming to establish a socialist market economy should rightfully include efforts to ensure, realize and enhance social equity and justice while striving to enhance the control of state assess and bring its leading role into play". As for state-owned assets in competitive fields and industries crucial to social equity and justice, we should also regard them as "key" state-owned assets and strive to do a good job, though they do not matter too much to economic regulation by the government; otherwise, the reform would be out of control such as the large drain of state assets and rampant large-scale "transfer".[2] Therefore, to put aside the criterion of being "major industries" or "key fields", we have good reasons to believe that state-owned enterprises and state-holding enterprises even in competitive fields should also be within the range of the state sector's control,

1 Xia Xiaolin, "Following up the Scaling Down of the Non-State Investment", *China Business Times*, January 31st, 2007.

2 Xia Xiaolin, "Following up the Scaling-Down of the Non-State Investment", *China Business Times*, January 31st, 2007.

and efforts to maintain and develop these enterprises are also "proper choices".

Since the state sector is obligated to ensure social equity and justice, the state should guarantee effective investment in public service, infrastructure and major industries. Therefore, many forms of investment and operation in labor-intensive fields with a view to solving the problem of unemployment can also be considered as some alternatives. We should guarantee the healthy development of SOEs not only in monopoly fields but in competitive fields; we should give play to its role of stabilizing employment, creating more jobs, ensuring social welfare and providing public services; we should enhance the country's economic strength to provide more transfer payments in redistribution. Besides, the state mustn't step out of economic management just like what some neo-liberalists had been advertising. China, as a great socialist country, must not refer to the so-called "international experience" of privatization from capitalist countries while setting a lower bound for the proportion of the state sector. But instead, factors as to whether social equity and stability would be guaranteed, achieved and even enhanced should be rightfully taken into consideration. Therefore, it is very necessary for us to study further the scope of the state sector's control.

Having gathered opinions from many quarters, I'd like to offer some suggestions as to how to strengthen the state sector's control. They are briefly stated as follows:

(1) SOEs should be contracted, which, however, does not mean that the less the better.

In the initial period of reform, due to the fact that SOEs are overextended, it is necessary to scale back the number of SOEs and make greater efforts to improve the quality of SOEs and provide more room for non-state sectors. However, it does not mean that the less SOEs the better. These years, some officials and scholars suggested that China should "avoid opening new SOEs to 'ease the heavy load weighing on the state so that the state could be more than equal to the task of running a minimum number of SOEs'. In this way, 'these few SOEs would be quite well-off and live at ease, rather than maintain a precarious living and gloom about their future like what they do nowadays'."

As for how to reform the ownership structure, people from both "inside" and "outside the system" have repeatedly voiced their opinions, "in terms of the reform of ownership structure, China should either aim to make natural person property (private property) become the mainstay of market economy within 15 to 30 years, or set the proportion of the state sector within the range of 7% to 10% just like what the United States and European countries do (however, the director of SASAC research center pointed out that SOEs only account for 5% in the national economy of western capitalist countries), or copy the paradigm of Russia and Eastern European countries in the era of Boris Yeltsin after their goal of realizing socialism was abandoned."

The excessively large-scale reduction in the proportion of the state sector that these people suggested has far exceeded the limit that Jiang Zemin ever talked of, that is, the status of public ownership as the mainstay of the economy and the leading role of the state sector can never be affected. Since the founding of SASAC in 2003, the number of centrally-administered enterprises has already reduced from 196 to 157. It was revealed that in the next round of SOE reorganization, the number of China's centrally-administered enterprises would reduce by at least one third. SASAC aims to reduce the number of centrally administered enterprises to 80-100 by the end of 2010 through reorganization and readjustment, among which 30 to 50 enterprises would be expected to be globally competitive. However, it did not say specifically how many SOEs on earth China, a large socialist country with a large population and a large-scale economy, should have and how many of them should be centrally administered ones.

Let's have a look at Russia, which has already become capitalism and whose leader, Vladimir Putin, is no doubt a defender of private ownership. However, he announced in August 2004 that 1063 large Russian SOEs would be state-owned strategic enterprises under the direct control of the President and the government would have no right to privatize them. Here comes the question: since both China and Russia have large centrally-administered enterprises, why has Russia, which embraces and practices privatization, preserved a lot more SOEs than socialist China? If some incomparable factors are excluded, does it show that some Chinese officials are inclined to believe that the less SOEs the better and that China's SOEs deserve to "be more at ease"? Or does it indicate any other intentions harbored by just a few Chinese officials that we had better not state explicitly?

(2) Both central and local governments should control a group of powerful SOEs.

The head of relevant department pointed out that we shouldn't misinterpret structural adjustment of the state sector and state-owned asset reorganization as a policy of encouraging the centrally-administered enterprises to advance and local enterprises to retreat, but instead a group of large, strongly competitive, local SOEs with distinctive local flavors and strengths must be preserved as pillars of local economy. China is so large that the population and land of many provinces or municipalities is even larger than that of a European country. Some people ever recommended that in order to reorganize local SOEs, one or even numerous Temasek-modeled holding companies should be set up in each province, municipality, or autonomous region, or one company of such kind is to be jointly built by many provinces, municipalities or autonomous regions. I think it is plausible. Singapore has set us a good example. Since a country as small as Singapore with such a small population has already succeeded, why can't we? Not long ago, many things went wrong in local SOE restructuring, and therefore it'll now be a good opportunity to straighten out these problems through a new "restructuring" of state-owned enterprises.

(3) The decision-making of the reform of the state sector should be checked, balanced, and supervised by the People's Congress at all levels. Some people have repeatedly suggested doing so and even came up with some specific proposals. In terms of the reform of SOEs, not only labor union has no real power, but the People's Congress has scarcely exercised their power of review and supervision conscientiously. As a result, only very few people in administrative organs have

the final say on how many SOEs should be left. If the fate of state-owned assets is put into the hands of these few people, it would probably lead to irrational decisions and the drain of state assets. “Property Law of the PRC” aiming to protect private poverty has already been passed. However, “the Law of State-owned Assets of the PRC”, aiming to protect public property, hasn’t yet. As a matter of fact, it was started many years ago, even earlier than the drafting of the “Property Law of the PRC”. Now, people are still expecting the Law of State-owned Assets to be enacted in the hope that the People’s Congress at all levels would be empowered to review any proposals on SOE property right change just like what the representative assembly of market economies such as UK, Russia, Poland and Japan, etc. do.

(4) The public should get more involved in the reform of SOE property right.

Such reform is not only a high-level theoretical issue, but also involves public policies concerning the interests of all sides. Therefore, not only elites like officials and scholars but also the public should participate in the discussion of the matter and even the decision-making process. Someone from a research institute of state-owned assets believed that it was a latent rule that the pubic shouldn’t get involved in the discussion of such matter, and that the heated discussion initiated by Lang Xianping has actually “triggered off people’s discontent with the drain of state-owned capital and social inequity, which is actually a scheme of anti-reform”. The elites who said so all dismissed the great masses as good-for-nothing. As for the reform of SOE property right, the public have the right to know, speak and supervise. It is very dangerous to have all the power concentrated in the hands of just a few elites. It was reported that Wang Daohan (27 March 1915 – 24 December 2005), the former president of the Association for Relations Across the Taiwan Straits (ARATS), said on his deathbed, “I do not think foreign forces are capable of stirring up any big troubles, but domestic ones are my big concern.” “Elites, social elites,” added he. Such words were based on his long-term observation and study of the Soviet union’s decaying Communist Party and cadres.

Communist Party leaders and social elites are mainly to blame for the Soviet Union's dissolution. They took advantage of their power and social and political influence to seek private gains, turning themselves into privileged stratum seizing social wealth. They are not only uninterested in improving the socialist system, but tried every trick to distort it. Because only through the radical change of the socialist system based on public ownership, could their vested interests be legitimized. The fact that around 80% leaders or socialites of new Russia used to be communist party cadres, government officials and social elites in Soviet Union would suffice to prove that. [1]

10. The right path to the development of the private sector

When it comes to the basic economic system, one cannot evade the private sector, part and parcel of the non-public sector of the economy. The side-by-side development of the non-public sector together with public ownership as the mainstay constitutes our basic economic system in the primary stage of socialism. We cannot do without the non-public sector now and even throughout the primary stage of socialism due to its crucial, positive role in promoting our economic development, creating more jobs, increasing financial revenues, and meeting needs from all sides of the society. Therefore, we must encourage, support and guide the economic development of the non-public sector, rather than ignore, discriminate against or even reject it. That's why the party and the government have consistently attached great importance to the non-public sector including the private sector, which can be demonstrated by its policies concerning the non-public sector over these years. For instance, the non-public sector was defined as "a supplement " in both the 13th and 14th National Congress of the CPC; it was elevated to "an integral part of the socialist market economy" in the Second Session of the Ninth National People's Congress of the PRC; and in the 16th National Congress of the CPC, it was proposed that we should "unswervingly encourage, support and guide the development of the non-public sector while

1 *Hong Kong Economic Journal*, June 23rd, 2007.

unwaveringly consolidating and developing the public sector of the economy."

China's non-public sector of the economy includes two parts. The first part is individual economy, which only owns a few means of production. It contributes to the social wealth through their owners' hard work, involving no exploitation of labor. In this sense, it is just a result of individual independent labor. The of such business in our national economy is very small, and even in the future, it is unlikely to grow too much. According to SAIC (State Administration for Industry & Commerce, People's Republic of China) statistics, the number of individual business even dropped occasionally in recent years, however its growth has already picked up now. The other part includes the private sector and the foreign sector. Since the reform and opening-up, many private owners answered the call of the Central Committee, i.e., the policy of encouraging some people to get rich first, and ventured into business. These private owners have contributed a lot to the national economic development, social stability and the enriching of people's material life after so many years' painstaking efforts in starting and expanding their business. So, they deserve the credit and fair judgment from the whole society. Currently, private enterprises had great difficulty in financing, with both heavy tax and especially non-tax burdens weighing on them. It is very urgent that departments concerned should solve these problems practically.

The private sector of the economy is different from individual economy. Likewise, private enterprise owners are also different from the so-called new social class including management and technical personnel and freelancers. Though all of them are "builders of socialism", self-employed workers, management and technical personnel, and freelancers etc., different from private owners, do not exploit other people; in contrast, private enterprise owners hire workers for the sake of production and operation of their business, and hence these owners become the exploiters and the employees the exploited. As private enterprises serve the socialist drive of modernization, such exploitation in the process of production and operation is under the protection of our law. On the one hand, the private sector of the economy promotes the development of the productive forces, but on the other hand, it also seeks surplus value and involves exploitation. Exploitation inherent in private ownership would inevitably lead to social contradictions, which are so penetrating that their effects can be felt in almost every field such as politics, economy, society, culture, morality and interpersonal relationship. The duality of private ownership in the primary stage of socialism is an objective necessity, so we must face up to it rather than avoid it. However, we should try to distinct the nature of the private sector from its role. So long as the means of production is privately owned involving the exploitation of labor, the private sector of the economy will never be socialist by nature. However, as to its role, we should study it against specific historic conditions. In the primary stage of socialism when it meets the needs of the development of the productive forces, it still plays a positive role so that it is considered as an integral part of the socialist market economy. However, it cannot be defined as a component of socialist economy, because it is not socialist by nature.

Some people said, "People within the non-public sector of the economy are not the national bourgeoisie any more". It is definitely right, because self-employed workers within the non-public sector have never ever belonged to the bourgeoisie. But which class should private enterprise owners who employ and exploit workers fall into? I'm afraid they can only be categorized as the bourgeoisie and nothing else. Surely, according to its roles, they can also be considered as "builders of socialism" or "new social class". This is a very scientific analysis based on the principle of seeking truth from facts, tolerating no fake or false information.

We should treat the private sector of the economy in the primary stage of socialism correctly in the following two ways. On the one hand, we should not discriminate against or look down upon it; on the other hand, we should neither flatter nor cover up for it. Nowadays, there do exist discrimination or neglect of private enterprises especially in financing. Take large banks' discrimination against small and medium-sized enterprises (mainly private enterprises) as an example. They often favored large enterprises rather than small ones; they often despised the poor and curried favor with the rich; they also tended to discriminate against private enterprises and favor public assets. Besides, these enterprises also suffered from an increase in the so-called three types of enterprise expenditure (including contributions, apportion expenses, entertainment expenses) and blackmail from a few government officials, the latter having already become the latent rule that enterprises have to obey. But some enterprises did use this as a way to evade or reduce legitimate taxes. This is one extreme that we should avoid.

At the same time, we should also avoid going to the other extreme, that is, we shouldn't blindly flatter or cover up for it. According to an article published on the website of *People's Daily* on April 19th, 2006, many local government officials misinterpreted our party's policy of supporting private enterprises by "flattering, fawning on and coaxing" them. They lavished praises on and curried favor with them, and even offered party memberships as a gift to them, to name but a few. It was reported that in the capital city of a province in the southeast China, where common people cannot afford the medical bills, local government generously set up special funds for some chosen private entrepreneurs' health check-up and remedial rest, which had "fully demonstrated the party and the government's concern for private entrepreneurs". Some senior officials exonerated a few enterprise owners from the "sins" that they did commit and guaranteed that the department concerned would not make enquiries any more. Some theoreticians even sneakily replaced the policy of "non-public sector as an integral part of socialist market economy" with that of "non-public sector as an integral part of socialist economy", believing that the private sector "has become" or "should become" the mainstay of socialist economy and take the place of the public sector. This has obviously overstepped the boundaries prescribed in the Constitution of PRC in terms of the basic economic system.

Since we are not supposed to discriminate against, look down on, flatter or cover up for the private sector of the economy, how should we treat it so that it would accord with the requirements of the basic socialist economic system? No doubt, we should continue to unswervingly develop the private sector, bringing its flexibility and positive roles of promoting the development of the productive forces into full play; at the same time, we should also try to avoid any negative effects on social and economic development caused by exploitation. For instance, some owners of private enterprises evaded taxes, lowered workers' wages, worsened employees' working conditions, produced counterfeit goods, destroyed natural resources and environment, embezzled state property, and defrauded in other cases etc. All these ills should be eliminated by means of education, supervision and law. I guess, out of duties and conscience of "builders of the socialist undertaking", most owners of private enterprises would agree to do so as it would only benefit their own development, but not the other way around.

While encouraging and supporting the development of the private sector, we should also guide them correctly by prescribing specifically what fields it should and should not enter. For example, as to competitive fields, we should give green light to private enterprises and try to remove all barriers to their access. Especially those fields allowing for foreign investment should be more open to domestic investment. However, as to those major industries and key fields concerning the lifeblood of the national economy, private capital would only be permitted conditionally or in a restricted way in case that it would dominate and manipulate these industries or fields and thus undermine the state sector's control. The private sector has been given enough room for its investment in competitive fields and also allowed to invest in some key fields concerning the lifeblood of the national economy and share profitable gains. So, owners of private enterprises, as "builders of the socialist undertaking" and "the new class of the society", would probably be content and not crave for the dominant position in the socialist economy on their part. However, some neo-liberalist elites did overtly or covertly push them to this end. So, we should educate private enterprise owners not to blindly follow these elites.

All in all, we should develop the non-public sector including the private sector unwaveringly, but at the same time we must uphold and develop the public sector unswervingly, too, with public ownership as the mainstay of the economy and the state sector playing the leading role in the economy. Only in this way can we consolidate and develop the basic economic system of socialism and maintain a strong foothold.

This article aims to state clearly that we should not only focus on distribution especially redistribution such as taxes and transfer payments, but check our basic relations of production, i.e., ownership relations, as well as the basic economic system in order to adjust the relations of income distribution and reduce the gap between the rich and the poor. Only in this way can we eventually prevent the gap between the rich and the poor from widening. Therefore, this article provided a detailed analysis of the current situation of China's ownership structure, and pointed out the necessity and urgency of keeping public ownership as the mainstay of the economy and upholding the basic socialist economic system in a real sense.

After this article was submitted to leaders of the Central Committee, *HongQi WenGao* (Red Flag Manuscript) editorial department, *Qiushi* ("seeking truth") *Journal* wrote to me, "according to the instruction from CCPPD (the Publicity Department of the Communist Party of China), your article submitted to the leaders of the Central Committee entitled 'Reflections on Several Issues Concerning Distribution Relations and Ownership Relations' would be published in our journal." Later, the abridged version of the article was published in the journal (2007, vol. 24). (The article above is the full article published in *Social Sciences in China,* 2007, No.6.)

Part VI

The Goal of Socialist Market Economy

—to pay attention to both equity and efficiency with more emphasis on social equity so as to achieve common prosperity

A Transition to "Paying Attention to Both Efficiency and Equity"

Since the reform and opening up, we have abandoned the policy of indiscriminate egalitarianism and begun to adopt both distribution according to work and distribution according to production factors with a view to encouraging some people in some regions to get rich first and then to help others to catch up to achieve common prosperity. Besides, income distribution has also undergone great changes. On the one hand, incomes of residents have widely increased and their lives have been improved a lot; on the other hand, income disparity has been expanded and the gap between the rich and the poor was gradually widened as well accordingly.

According to the National Bureau of Statistics, our Gini coefficient in 1990 is 0.343, 0.389 in 1995 and 0.417 in 2000. We should notice that the Gini coefficient in 2000 has already exceeded the international warning line of 0.4, which deserves our attention. Based on experiences of many countries, 0.4 was set as the warning line to monitor and control the income inequality, which is quite of universal significance. However, national conditions vary from country to country, with their residents holding different concepts of social equity and having varying degrees of endurance for high income inequality.

Take China as an example, whose urban and rural residents are both counted in the calculus of the Gini Coefficient. The widening of the income gap between urban and rural residents is obviously faster than the expansion of income inequality within urban areas and that within the rural areas. From 1978 to 2000, the Gini Coefficient within the urban areas has increased from 0.16 to 0.32, and that within the rural areas from 0.21 to 0.35, all being well kept below the internationally recognized warning line. However, in sharp contrast, the income gap between urban and rural residents is far larger than that: from 1980 to 2000, the Gini Coefficient has seen a rapid increase from 0.341 to 0.417, which has already exceeded the international warning line.

Currently, the income inequality between urban and rural residents is very large, with the ratio of city dwellers' income to rural farmers' income being 3.1:1, and even larger (5:1-6:1) if differentiated welfare subsidies were also counted (according to international experience, when income per capita reaches 800-1000 dollars, the ratio of city dwellers' income and rural resident income is 1.7:1). so, it can be inferred that urban and rural residents belong to two entirely different income groups or consumer groups. Even though our urban-rural income inequality is very unreasonable and we have been striving to close it, the formation of the huge income gap between urban and rural residents due to historical reasons has made it hard for rural residents to keep up with city dwellers in a short time, and thus enabled them to take even more. Therefore, our warning line might as well be set higher than the international one. As for how much higher it could be raised, it is worth studying.

Putting aside the issue of international warning line, let's discuss the degree of our resident income inequality. Is it proper and within reasonable bounds? Or is it so large that polarization has emerged? Those who held positive answers to the first one were mainly based on official statistics of residents' normal income; Those who said yes to the second one took abnormal income and the gap between the rich and the poor into consideration.

Generally speaking, it is quite natural that distribution according to work or production factors has given rise to the widening of income gap in the primary distribution with the deepening of marketization. Besides, it also promotes the growth of economic benefits. However, the problem is that the widening of income gap is also caused by many unreasonable, nonstandard or illegal factors rather than the sheer result of rational decisions. And hence comes abnormal income. Especially in the primary distribution, there are many unfair competitions, among which the typical ones are monopoly in all kinds of forms, market disorder such as production and sale of counterfeit goods, smuggling, and tax fraud, and various forms of corruption within power hierarchy such as rent-seeking, rent-setting, power-for-money deal, embezzlement and bribe-taking etc. All these result in many illegal incomes and thus a group of nouveau riches.

As the concept and rules of market economy are slowly filtering into people's minds, high incomes and the widening of income gap through legal means have been gradually understood and accepted by people. What irritates people is the grey income "off the books" and illegal black income. As all these abnormal incomes are obtained through informal or illegal means and very well hidden, statistics of normal income distribution usually fail to include them. However, these abnormal incomes, accounting for a considerable percentage of the resident income, are a major cause of the widening of the income gap that we cannot afford to ignore.

By some measure, the Gini coefficient is 0.397 if abnormal or illegal income is excluded; however, if we take abnormal and illegal incomes into consideration, including monopoly rent, gains from illegal operations, rent gained by government officials, gains from tax fraud, misappropriation and embezzlement of public fund, our Gini coefficient will reach around 0.45. By another measure, from 1998 to 1999, our Gini coefficient is approximately 0.3 to 0.4 if abnormal or illegal income is excluded, which is within reasonable limits; however, if abnormal or illegal income is taken into account, the Gini coefficient will reach 0.4 to 0.5, a rather large range. It proves that these abnormal incomes are a big influence to be reckoned with. Some people ever suggested that the government should prioritize abnormal or illegal incomes in distribution of income. I agree with them.

Now that the gap between the rich and the poor keeps expanding, should we re-evaluate the principle of "giving priority to efficiency with due consideration to equity" which has been adopted since the reform and opening-up? It seems to be already on the agenda of economists.

Since the reform and opening up, theoreticians and the government have successively promoted the idea of "giving priority to efficiency with due consideration to equity" so as to solve the problem of low efficiency resulting from indiscriminate egalitarianism, to establish a market economy, and to promote efficiency and economic development through distribution according to work or production factors. Therefore, this guiding ideology will work throughout the whole historic period from traditional planned economy to the complete establishment of socialist market economy. Even though market economy has been initially established, it is still incomplete, and therefore it seems unnecessary to adjust this principle of distribution.

However, some people believed that even by the time the socialist market economy is completely established, the principle of "giving priority to efficiency with due consideration to equity" would still "conform to real social development and the requirement of social equity, and therefore it must be carried though". It seems to them that the guiding principle of income distribution, which just applies to a given period of time, is an unfailing rule throughout the whole era of market economy. As a matter of fact, it is inconsistent with historical facts. Some mature market economies did not have such principle. Quite to the contrary, they took several measures to guarantee social equity, trying to reduce income inequality and to maintain their Gini Coefficient within a reasonable range, i.e., between 0.3 and 0.4, so as to alleviate social contradictions (for example, Britain, France, and Germany etc.).

Especially in North European nations widely recognized as highly developed market economies, colossal fiscal houses were set up to push forward great plans on narrowing the gap between the rich and the poor. In 2002, Norway's Gini coefficient is 0.258, that of Sweden 0.250 and that of Finland 0.256, ranking as nations with the smallest income gap in the world. Even though people tended to believe that enormous public expenditure would burden the economy by hindering its economic growth and competitiveness, it turned out that the economy of northern European countries is not lagged behind at all. A survey showed that these countries ranked among the first ones in the 72 industrious countries in terms of economic performance, business and government efficiency and were still climbing.

Regardless of high taxation, many large multinational enterprises such as Nokia, Ericsson, Volvo and ABB etc. still emerged. These countries giving priority to equity could still achieve high efficiency. Surely China hasn't been so developed as these market economies, so we couldn't blindly copy their welfare policies. However, they did remind us that we should not hold onto the slogan of "giving priority to efficiency with due consideration to equity" as the only guiding principle of distribution in market economy. As for whether such wording is accurate enough or keeping pace with the times, it is still open for discussion.

With the establishment of incentive mechanisms in distribution of income and wealth, the principle of "giving priority to efficiency with due consideration to equity" aimed to make a large cake by encouraging some people to get rich first through honest work and lawful business operations and then to help others to catch up to achieve common prosperity. Till now the principle has been carried out for a period of time and some people did get rich first. Some made a fortune through honest work and lawful business operations, whilst some through unusual means. But both of them failed to help "others" with medium or low income to catch up to achieve common prosperity; and what's more, some people were laid off and their absolute income even fell.

Because equity is viewed secondary to efficiency, those who lived at the bottom of society will still be vulnerable even though people showed great concerns to them. The long-term shortage of funds for compulsory education and frequent school dropouts in rural areas are very good proof to this. Due to the policy preference in favor of efficiency, many local enterprises just focused on local interests, such as blind pursuit of mechanization and automatization, improper handling of the capital-labor substitution, only to harm the interests of small and medium sized enterprises, the private sector and the tertiary industry and worsen the situation of job market. As a result, "equity was neglected all the more and leaders would be gratified to see no civil unrest". No wonder the Gini coefficient keeps increasing very sharply year by year.

The reasons why soaring Gini coefficient and the dramatic widening of income gap are getting from bad to worse are as follows: At first, domestic demand has been seriously affected. Even though the rich have a lot of money, their incremental consumption is always less than incremental income; in sharp contrast, the poor couldn't afford to buy things. As a result, lack of effective demand has become the bottleneck of economic growth. Second, people were dissatisfied with a considerable number of abnormal income and its contribution to the widening of income gap and thus their enthusiasm in work or production were dampened and efficiency lowered; unemployment has rendered many resources idle and the efficiency of macroeconomic resource allocation was thus lowered. Third, it has given rise to social unrest to some extent

Therefore, it is very necessary to recall Deng Xiaoping's advice several years ago. After efficiency has been relatively ensured, equity will gradually come to the fore. As early as in 1992, Deng Xiaoping had already had the foresight to set a timetable for the solution of income inequality. He said, "we need to work out when and on what basis we should put the problem on the table. I think, at the end of this century when a moderately prosperous society is built we should try to solve it."

By the end of the 20th century our people were in general better off, but at the same time, income inequality also came to the fore. Just as Deng Xiaoping put it, it is time that we should put the problem on the table and try to solve it; besides, conditions are also basically ripe for that. On the one hand, our economic and financial power has been greatly enhanced over two decades; on the other hand, an excessively large income gap has become a major issue affecting social class relations and social stability.

Surely, by calling for the solution of income inequality, we do not mean to neglect efficiency or obliterate the income gap. In the current phase when our productive forces are still less developed, we still need to carry the market-oriented reform through to the end and implement distribution according to work or production factors to improve efficiency. Currently, our Gini coefficient is around 0.45. According to other countries' experience, it is only when GDP per capita reaches around 1500 dollars that the Gini coefficient will begin to fall. Currently, our GDP per capita is only about 1000 dollars, so our Gini coefficient is still on the rising side of the inverted U-shaped curve. With the deepening of market economy, our Gini coefficient is still inclined to rise. Therefore, we should not force the Gini coefficient to fall abruptly for the sake of equitable distribution, but instead we should increase the weight of equity gradually by slowing down the expansion of Gini coefficient at first and then reducing the Gini coefficient properly. Only in this way could we achieve the transition of distribution policy from "giving priority to efficiency with due consideration to equity" to "paying attention to both efficiency and equity" or "achieving an optimal combination of equity and efficiency".

It is estimated that GDP per capita will reach around 1500 dollars by 2010, and above 3000 dollars by 2020 when we build a moderately prosperous society in all respects. By that time, the Gini coefficient would begin to decline and our system of socialist market economy would be almost complete. And then it will be time that this slogan should retire. If we have to have it replaced with another slogan, I guess, "paying attention to both equity and efficiency", will not be questioned by most upright men.

As for how to slow down the expansion of income gap and then to further reduce it, theorists have offered many good suggestions after discussions, which I will not repeat. Here I would like to focus on the following three issues.

First, I would like to talk about the assignment of primary distribution and redistribution respectively. It is widely believed that primary distribution should focus on efficiency and be regulated by market; whereas redistribution should focus on equity and be regulated by the government. However, in the primary distribution, the government also needs to step in, as some expansion of income gap in the primary distribution is the result of imperfect and flawed market. For example, high incomes of employees from monopoly industries should be supervised and restricted by the government. Due to their monopoly over superior resources, these monopoly industries could gain surplus profits, some of which would be converted into high incomes of their own employees. Market access barriers to some industries should be removed as quickly as possible and the mechanism of competition brought into full play to achieve equalization of profit rates.

In order to achieve that, we need set up an effective competition mechanism in conformity with market economy rules in natural monopolies. Product prices, income distribution plans, remuneration standards, etc. of monopoly enterprises or industries that must be kept within a given historical period of time should be supervised and controlled by the government.

Besides, unemployment in cities and towns has become a major cause for the widening of income gap; and the fact that many farmers got jobs from industry and other types of enterprises has contributed a lot to income inequality in the countryside. Currently, the urgent task is to develop the labor-intensive industry, which is also an effective way to solve the problem of unemployment over the long run. This is even more true of small and medium-sized enterprises, non-governmental enterprises and tertiary industries, which all need support from the government.

For example, the government should extend preferential policies to the labor-intensive industries with high employment, low profits or temporary deficits and various labor organizations providing flexible job opportunities. These industries' development cannot do without government support and supervision; otherwise, unemployment and poverty would get even worse. Therefore, we shouldn't solve these problems just by means of redistribution; rather, we should strive to overcome them in the link of production and primary distribution.

Second, the key to redistribution is to bring the taxation system into full play. An unsound taxation system and flawed tax laws are currently the key factors hindering the solution to the widening of income gap. The working class still constitutes the bulk of income tax payers, whereas many people with high incomes tend to defraud taxes. Therefore, we should radically reform the tax system including income tax and create favorable conditions for such a reform; we should levy property tax such as real property tax and inheritance tax; we should gradually raise income taxes on high-income tax-payers to reduce the unreasonable income gap.

Some people believed that to raise income taxes on high-income taxpayers are a "Robin Hood solution", which might affect the development of the non-public sector of the economy. However, I agree with the spokesperson for State Administration of Taxation. He said that we must impose sanctions on those high incomes obtained through unlawful operations or evasion of taxes to protect lawful operations, which not only benefits the development of the non-public sector, but improves people's awareness of paying taxes.

Besides, we should also step up efforts to increase transfer payments so as to reduce the excessively large income gap between the urban and rural areas, and between different regions. The government, together with the society, must ensure that those with very low or no income and the incapacitated can meet their basic needs. The government should allocate money regularly to ensure the functioning of social security funds. Running expenses should be more used to cover people's livelihood and public welfare; construction spending should be confined to not-for-profit public construction projects; and profitable projects should be more invested by private capital. If it is still necessary to continue with proactive fiscal policies such as to issue deficit-covering bonds, they should be more used to improve people's lives in the countryside, to increase more job opportunities in cities and towns, and to enhance social welfare etc. in order to slow down the widening of income gap.

Third, more emphasis on equity in terms of income distribution does not mean to seek income equality; what really matters is that each social class could gain equal access to opportunities. By emphasizing equal opportunities, we mean to stress equality at the starting line of life rather than that at the finish line. In China, income inequality mostly results from unequal opportunities, and inequality at the finish line usually results from inequality at the starting line. Undoubtedly, people vary in talents. But we have to admit that different education or training leads to varying levels of knowledge and expertise and thus differences in job opportunities and incomes.

How strongly low-income farmers wish their children to get educated so that they can be lifted out of poverty! A survey of households receiving minimum social security benefits in Sichuan province shows that many children from such families failed to finish 9-year compulsory education. Their parents sighed over their children's fate, "They are so young and will have a very long journey. Will they still "inherit" minimum social security benefits to eke out a living?" Migrant workers were also concerned about their children's education. Due to their low levels of literacy and numeracy, they tended to work against the most unfavorable conditions and get the lowest income. They were so heavily burdened with children's tuition fees that many of them have to let their children drop out of school. Their children were hence already lagged behind at the starting line. Now it is time to overhaul the system of compulsory education and solve the fund shortage in this respect! As long as the government can cut some unnecessary expenditure and use it to finance compulsory education, each child would probably gain access to 9-year compulsory education.

The 16th National Congress proposed to raise the proportion of the middle-income group and to increase the income of the low-income group, which actually mean the same thing. In order to change the layout of our income distribution from a pyramid to a rugby ball, the crux of the matter is still education and training. The rugby ball layout refers to the structure in which the middle-income group is in the middle of the rugby ball with the high-income group and the low-income group at both ends of the ball. Currently, the low-income group includes two types of people: tens of millions of surplus labor emigrating from the countryside to cities to find jobs and millions of urban laid-off workers flowing into the labor market. The ranks of low-income people are mainly composed of the young and the middle-aged who lose out in the job market and earn very little money due to low levels of literacy and numeracy or lack of knowledge and expertise. The key to their re-employment and ascent to the middle-income group also lies in the improvement of their basic education, vocational training and an increase in human capital investment in the low-income group, which are however hard to achieve only by the low-income group themselves. As a matter of fact, the problem of unequal opportunities at the starting line can never be solved unless the government unites all social forces to make all children, in both urban and rural areas, gain access to 9-12 compulsory education and launch wide professional training programs.

(The article is a speech I made in the Spring Forum on the analysis and forecasts of China's economic situation in 2003)

Attaching Further Importance to Social Equity

Author's Note: In 2003, I ever delivered a speech entitled "A Focus on the Issue of Income Distribution in the study of the Macroeconomic Situation" in the CASS Spring forum on the analysis and forecasts of China's economic situation. At that time, one of the focuses of our discussion was the relationship between efficiency and equity, which have already had some new developments in recent years. The fact that social equity has recently received more and more attention has something to do with the idea of "building a harmonious socialist society". Recently, I wrote an article titled "Attaching Further Importance to Social Equity" for my speech in Spring forum in 2005, as a follow-up to my speech in Spring forum in 2003. Your advice and comments are appreciated.

Social equity is a key issue in building a harmonious socialist society. If social equity can hardly be ensured, we would find it hard to make the initiative of building a harmonious socialist society proceed. Therefore, social equity must be strongly valued. One of the key issues is to deal with the relations between efficiency and social equity correctly.

1

The issue on relations between efficiency and social equity has been discussed in China for many years. A heated debate over the reform of SOE property right held in the Summer in 2004 was in a sense another discussion about the relations between efficiency and equity, in which some new developments were made. For instance, some people were enlightened by these discussions and wrote many good articles, which will improve the current relations between efficiency and equity.

Some people favored one side of the balance, i.e., efficiency. They believed that efficiency should take precedence over equity. They held that any means could be employed in the reform so long as it promotes an increase in social wealth. They gave MBO (management buy-out) as an example. They said that MBO also applied to China under the circumstances. Their theory is that it is better that SOEs are taken over and invigorated by competent managers than fall into decay just like an ice lolly that melts away in the heat. Therefore, "it is pointless to be obsessed with the issue of distribution." On the other side of balance, some people strongly opposed selling state-owned assets to a few people in a very low bid or even giving them away to make these people get rich overnight, when China hasn't got a sound legal system and lacked in genuine masters for state-owned assets!

The Reform of state-owned assets property right is not simply an academic issue, but a strong issue concerning public policies instead. Therefore, not only scholars but also the public should get involved. Great public participation in Internet discussions over the reform has demonstrated people's enhanced awareness of pubic policies. The fact that almost all the people preferred to the latter opinion shows that, regarding public opinions, the latter has taken the upper hand in the debate. In revenge, the former blamed the latter for "having triggered public discontentment with the drain of state-owned assets and inequitable distribution" by laying the "latent rule" that should have been kept from the public on the table!

Now, let's look at its policy implications. Based on researches conducted by many institutions, SASAC (State-owned Assets Supervision and Administration Commission of the State Council) has confirmed that application of MBO in the current China is very problematic, which has led to a huge drain of state-owned assets. As a result, the policy concerning MBO was radically changed. At first, MBO was "never met with any opposition" from the government, and then it was suggested that "large state-owned and state-holding enterprises had better not conduct MBO". At last, the government announced very decisively that "large SOEs are forbidden to conduct MBO", and at the same time even small and medium SOEs were only allowed to try it out in an open and just manner with drastic restrictions. This can also be considered as a response to public opinions, although the government did not say so. Even if the government did acknowledge it publicly, it would not necessarily harm the dignity of its authority; rather, it would probably gain some good reputation for reflecting the will and support of the people. All in all, at both public opinion and policy levels, the debate has rebalanced efficiency and equity by attaching more weight to equity, whereas in the past the balance was in more favor of efficiency.

2

From the perspective of dialectics, efficiency and equity form a unity of contradictions. Our common sense tells us that the more evenly income and wealth is distributed, the less enthusiastic people will be and thus the lower efficiency it would lead to; a moderate income gap will help improve efficiency if distribution procedures and rules are fair enough. To put it the other way round, if we do not strive to improve efficiency, our cake will not be big enough to guarantee social equity and thus it would be also hard to solve increasing social contradictions. However, if equity is neglected, it might cause a too wide income gap and especially unfair distribution procedures and rules. As a result, efficiency would be affected and even social stability would probably be jeopardized. Hence, it has always been hard to achieve a trade-off between equity and efficiency.

In order to alleviate contradictions among social classes, modern capitalist countries have absorbed socialist thoughts and carried out measures of social security and welfare; modern liberal states value efficiency but still have to ensure equity; modern welfare nations attach great importance to both equity and efficiency. Their level of efficiency and equity have already been rather high. As a matter of fact, measures to ensure social equity and welfare taken by some capitalist countries are more complete than those by socialist China. However, given different historic conditions, China and these countries cannot be compared.

Before the reform and opening-up, China favored absolute, indiscriminate egalitarianism, which had severely undermined efficiency. Since the market-oriented reform two decades ago, we began to attach more and more importance to efficiency, which did create income brackets and increase the income gap. The policy of "encouraging some people to get rich first" did work very well on the economy, having invigorated it in both urban and rural areas. Therefore, after more than a decade's practice, the policy of "paying due attention to both efficiency and equity", was written into the document of the 14th National Congress in 1992. However, since the Third Plenary Session of the 14th Central Committee of the CPC, the policy concerning the relations between efficiency and equity was changed into "giving priority to efficiency with due consideration to equity". In this way, "efficiency" has ascended to the status of being superior to "equity", from the previous one of being on an equal footing with "equity"; in contrast, "equity", though still very important, was viewed as secondary to "efficiency". This constitutes a major change.

Since then, this wording continued to appear in every document of the Central Committee major meetings till now. Therefore, it is the official spirit of our income distribution policies.

The communist party has always been valuing social equity and justice. But why did the communist country place equity secondary to efficiency in distribution? This was closely related to our national conditions: China had been economically backward for long so that it was hard to improve people's living standards very rapidly and solve many social contradictions all at once. Besides, it also had a lot to do with profound changes and potential trends in domestic and world situations as well as opportunities and challenges brought about by these changes in 1990s and the early 20th Century. Under the circumstances, we must spare no efforts to accrue to our national wealth and improve our overall national strength.

Therefore, Deng Xiaoping suggested in his South China Tour Talks, "We should emancipate our mind more freely, carry out reform and opening-up more boldly and build up our country more rapidly, never to lose any golden opportunities." He also emphasized, "Development is the absolute principle and the key solution to everything in China." As a result, the task of increasing national wealth and enhancing national strength came to the fore, and thus efficiency became the priority. At that time, what mainly hindered the improvement of efficiency was the vestiges of egalitarianism.

Therefore, in order to improve efficiency more rapidly and accrue to the national wealth, we must "break away from egalitarianism, create rational income differential, encourage some people to get rich first through honest labor and lawful operation", which was added in the Third Plenary Session of the 14th Central Committee document to further explain the policy of "giving priority to efficiency with due consideration to equity".

Therefore, the wording of the relations between efficiency and equity adopted by the Third Plenary Session of the 14th Central Committee was then very consistent with our real national conditions and development needs, which was therefore absolutely correct. Accordingly, it was also correct for economic theorists to elaborate on and publicize the spirit of such distribution policy. However, changes also began to take place in China's social hierarchy as its economy kept growing, and hence different voices standing for various interests began to be heard from economic theoreticians, too. For example, in order to justify the concentration of wealth into very few people's hands, some people underestimated deliberately or unconsciously the importance of social equity and justice by emphasizing or exaggerating the differences between "giving priority to" and "giving due consideration to", which is however inconsistent with the spirit of reform. As a matter of fact, the Central Committee has been emphasizing that "those who got rich first should help others to catch up," and that "polarization should be guarded against". So, the Central Committee had never meant to neglect social equity.

3

Now let's look back at the issue as to how the drain of state-owned assets has resulted in the the rise of a few nouveau riches overnight. Why were some theorists so tolerant that they even defended them? Aside from other reasons, it also had something to do with the fact that the "reform of SOE property rights" has already been launched since the 1990s. In 1992, the 14th National Congress proposed to "straighten out relations between ownership and management of enterprises". The Third Plenary Session of the 14th Central Committee proposed to create a modern corporate structure characterized by four features including "the clearly established ownership". And then the Third Plenary session of the 16th Central Committee proposed to establish a modern property right system.

With regard to the "reform of property rights", which is quite new to us, we have no prior experiences in both theory and practice, so we must learn from modern market economies. And that's why western neo-liberalist economics were then introduced to China. Actually, we have a lot to learn from western neo-liberalistic economics as to how market economy works. However, some scholars who publicized neo-liberalist economics in China deliberately twisted the property rights of SOEs, promoting overtly or covertly the idea of SOE privatization, and fabricating many "facts" of social injustice during SOE restructuring. This has been too far away from the spirit of our economic restructuring!

Therefore, we should try to suite neo-liberalist economics to our own needs and prevent it from leading China's reform and development. Not only the academic world of economics should reach such a consensus, but decision-makers in economic departments of our government also ought to bear it in mind.

4

I pointed out in the article entitled "A Focus on the Issue of Income Distribution in the Study of the Macroeconomic Situation" (2003) that the policy of "giving priority to efficiency with due consideration to equity", which just serves as a temporary guiding line in terms of income distribution in a given period of time, is not an unfailing rule throughout the whole historical period of market economy. But some people just held the opposite idea, regarding it as an eternal theme in the whole period of market economy, which is actually inconsistent with historical facts. Some mature market economies did not ever have such a guiding principle. I said in the article that its accuracy and time span still need further discussion.

After problems concerning economic development and efficiency were relatively solved, the issue of social equity has gradually come to the fore. We shall not forget the timetable Deng Xiaoping ever set up as early as in 1992 for the solution of income inequality. He envisaged with foresight that by the end of the 20th Century when China is moderately prosperous, we should put this problem on the table and try to solve it.

However, at the turn of the 21st century, we neither put the solution of income inequality on the table as what Deng Xiaoping ever predicted nor adjusted the relations between efficiency and social equity. In a preceding article, I ever hinted that Den Xiaoping's prediction might be a little optimistic by pointing out that we were then still on the rising side of the inverted U-shaped curve and that the income gap still tended to expand, which would be hard to reverse. It seems that only by 2010 when GDP per capita reaches around US $ 1500, the Gini coefficient would fall and the solution of such problem would probably be laid on the table. And then, the guiding principle of "giving priority to efficiency with due consideration to equity" might possibly give place to the slogan of "paying attention to both efficiency and equity" or "achieving an optimal combination of efficiency and equity".

At that time, some people in academia disapproved of my opinion by arguing that we mustn't reschedule the timetable for 2010 because "Chinese people's endurance for income inequality has already reached the limit", and therefore "we should get started right now". Recently, someone also wrote in the article that the income gap was said to have reached the limit ten years ago, which actually was inconsistent with China's real situation. As for whether the income gap has reached the limit of Chinese people's endurance, it is surely open for discussion as well. Still in this article, I ever said that the excessively large income gap was mainly caused by the excessively large urban-rural gap. But we have to admit that the rural-urban divide has already become an established fact due to historic reasons. Even though we desire to close the urban-rural gap, rural residents know perfectly well that it is hard for them to keep up with the living standards of city dwellers in a short period of time. In this sense, Chinese people can still take more while Gini coefficient keeps expanding.

Having thought it over, I found out that the issue as to whether income gap has reached the limit and the readjustment of the relations between efficiency and equity by attaching further importance to social equity are not on the same level. If income gap reaches the limit someday, it might probably be caused by polarization. Obviously, we haven't gone that far now, so we should neither say that polarization has emerged (which, Deng Xiaoping said, would lead to the failure of reform), nor state that income gap has already reached the limit. Now, our Gini coefficient is still on the rise. If we do not act now, polarization would probably emerge soon and the income gap would risk reaching the limit immediately.

Therefore, we must start from now on to attach further importance to social equity, readjust the relations between efficiency and equity, and give more weight to social equity. At first, we should try to slow down the expansion of income gap; and then we need reduce the absolute value of Gini coefficient progressively. Now, it is time that the policy of "giving priority to efficiency with due consideration to equity" should retire gradually and prepare the way for a gradual transition to the policy of "paying attention to both equity and efficiency" or "achieving an optimal combination of equity and efficiency".

5

So, why should it be now?

After two decades' reform and economic development, our economic aggregate and national economic strength have been greatly enhanced. China has already completed the first two tasks for economic development, i.e., doubling and quadrupling of per capita GDP, and now are striving to obtain the goal for the third step. So far, a fairly well-off society has already been built and China is now striving to build a moderately prosperous society in all respects. Therefore, China has now been fairly strong and capable enough to solve the problem of income inequality that had been amassed over a long period; that is to say, time has been basically ripe for China to work out solutions to the problem that Deng Xiaoping put forward in 1992. In other words, it is time to attach further importance to social equity.

The rapid expansion of income gap has currently become a major problem affecting social harmony and stability. Within over two decades, the Gini coefficient has multiplied by folds, growing unprecedentedly from 0.2-0.3 to 0.4-0.5. Some organizations and experts from home and abroad warned us that it has already surpassed the international warning line. Whether it is exaggerated or not, we should remain vigilant and pay particular attention to such trend. Moreover, our officially announced Gini Coefficient did not include the unreasonable, abnormal, or illegal income resented by people, because they are very hard to be counted. If included, the Gini Coefficient will grow to 0.5-0.6, over 20% higher than the official data. In this sense, we cannot take lightly the abnormal income, which has contributed a lot to the widening of the income gap. But some people still suggested that we shouldn't make a big issue about these abnormal incomes. Wouldn't it be necessary for us to put it on the first priority of income distribution policy since these unreasonable, abnormal and illegal incomes have affected income gap so badly? Not to mention any violation of criminal laws!

At the very beginning of reform, people's lives had generally been improved, and thus they all vigorously embraced the reform. So, till then the whole society hadn't been divided into many interest groups yet. However, since the 1990s, different interest groups were formed gradually: some benefited a lot from the reform; some less; and some people's interests were even hurt. That explains why some people's enthusiasm for reform has changed over time. Besides, what people expect to take from the reform also varies from class to class. For example, some people that have benefited a lot from the reform said, "the reform has to be achieved at the expense of the interests of a generation, that is, tens of thousands of veteran workers." Some people argued back and made a tit-for-tat response, "why has it to be us instead of you?"

There used to be an ill tendency of "carve-up" of SOEs, which resulted in social unrest and heavy hearts of SASAC (State-owned Assets Supervision and Administration Commission of the State Council) officials in charge. A chief leader from SASAC ever talked about such matter in the meeting on December 13th, 2004. He said, "It has brought about too much resentment. We have been emphasizing that we should give priority to efficiency with due consideration to equity since we carried out the reform. But I think we should attach more importance to equity recently. For the sake of much wider support for our reform, social equity and justice conducive to social harmony and stability should be emphasized in the long run rather than just on a temporary, short-term basis."

As for the current structure of China's society, there is no need for reticence.

China's social structure has gradually evolved into the one dominated by two major groups: the advantaged group characterized by great wealth, power and knowledge and the disadvantaged mainly composed of poor farmers, rural migrant workers, and urban laid-off workers etc. The former not only has very huge influence in formulation and implementation of public policies, but plays an important role in shaping public opinions and social discourse. However, in sharp contrast, the disadvantaged group, without due organizations or platforms to express their concerns or needs, is hard to make their voices heard in the media except for visiting a higher authority to voice their grievances.

Therefore, it is urgent that we remedy this serious defect. If we do not curb such trend, it would widen the social gap and do great harm to the building of a harmonious society. However, the advantaged group, especially the spokesmen of power and influence, claimed that "corruption is a lubricant to reform" and called power-for-money deals (whose euphemism is "officials' residual claim") as "a type of Pareto improvement", which has surely been criticized by upright scholars and public opinion standing for justice. Besides, another economist even denied the common practice of using taxation as an economic lever to distribute income and fund social welfare in modern countries and opposed a levy of higher taxes on the high-income people, dubbing it as a "Robin hood solution"! I believe that any sensible high-income people, who have some idea of progressive tax, would not approve of this!

6

Factors leading to the rapid expansion of income gap and a surge of problems concerning social distribution are very complicated, among which flaws inherent in the system, loopholes in the legal system and imperfect policies etc. are all very important. The government has made great efforts in recent years to deal with them and things started to change for the better. However, many problems of income distribution, which the government is capable of solving, haven't been solved yet, due to a vast number of cadres' lack of experience, some of whom have mistakenly understood the meaning of "with due consideration to equity", and some local officials' pursuit of self interests. Personal income from monopoly industries is many times more than that from non-monopoly ones. The problem of income inequality among those with equal qualifications or making equal efforts has been denounced by the public for many years, and the government has long since pledged to solve it. However, instead of starting from the link of primary distribution, which is the very source of monopoly profits, the government just proposed to adjust personal income tax to reduce the excessively high income from monopoly industries, which however turned out to make hardly any difference.

Personal income tax was initially intended to adjust the excessively high income and make up for the extremely low income, but some people with high incomes took advantage of loopholes in tax laws to evade high personal income tax with the result that the working class with middle or low income has made up the majority of personal income tax-payers for years, which even state leaders have stepped in and voiced their dissatisfaction. Now, the system of personal income tax which had been intended to overcome income inequality has now made the situation even worse. To put it more specifically, it has become a tool of helping the rich by robbing the poor. Now it's high time that we should step up efforts to improve the system of personal income tax. Many countries have used inheritance tax as an important tool to adjust income distribution. According to conservative estimates, the number of high-income Chinese households whose assets amount to over one million RMB has exceeded at least over ten million, which means that China has currently met the basic conditions for the levy of inheritance tax and gift tax. However, the levy of these taxes should be predicated on a set of regulations for inheritance, donation and transfer of personal income and a sound system for personal property registration and income declaration, which China should have prepared and sped up its work earlier. As a matter of fact, the government hasn't, so far, had taken the lead to work on the drafting of these regulations yet. As for when to start, nobody knows.

Allocation of state-owned assets to social security funds is a key measure to ensure social equity and welfare. Such slogan has been shouted for many years but still fails to be implemented. Till now, most of local state-owned assets have been sold out, but how much of that amount of money has been used as social security funds? Once SOE restructuring starts, laws must be made as soon as possible to prescribe the use of income from liquidation, including its use for social security funds; otherwise such huge amount of money would drain away. Some people suggested that in order to reduce the gap between the rich and the poor, state-owned assets should be allocated to SOE employees. Along with ESOP (Employee Stock Ownership Plan), such appropriation would compensate these employees' social security contributions and therefore are not implausible. However, state-owned assets are not created by SOE employees alone, but a result of all people's joint efforts. In this sense, it is more natural and reasonable to allocate SOE assets to social security funds of the whole society.

In terms of its functions, the focus of government should be shifted from economic development to public service in the reform. This reform will be conducive to both the improvement of public service and the promotion of social equity, because those who benefit from public service including education, health care etc. will mostly be the low-income group. These measures to enhance social welfare would help improve the overall quality of the people and provide more equal opportunities in both employment and social life. However, transformation of government roles and fiscal function was quite lagged behind, which has a lot to do with many local governments' overemphasis on economic development and projects for the sake of political achievements. China was ever labeled by WHO as one of the most unequal countries in terms of health care resource distribution due to its overemphasis on economic development and neglect of public services. China's proportion of education funds in GDP is very much lagged behind that of many civilized countries and its compulsory education funds are particularly insufficient, so that quite many Chinese people are shut out of the doors of modernization due to their lack of basic knowledge or expertise necessary for work. Surely, some improvements regarding this have been made but still far from satisfaction in comparison with huge economic investment.

Besides, some local governments infringed upon residents' property rights and rights to income under the disguise of economic development and reform. These years have seen more rural land expropriation, urban house demolition, wage arrears for migrant workers and impairment of people's interests during SOE restructuring, which reflects to some extent an excessively centralized government, malpractice of some officials, bureaucracy and corruption within the government etc. Now, the Central Committee has shifted its focus onto the solution of prominent problems impairing people's interests by launching an intensive anti-corruption campaign in an effort to build a clean and honest government. The Central Committee persists in carrying out a radical reform to find rooted causes of corruption and make due repairs, to speed up transformation of government functions, to strengthen institution building, and to reinforce supervision over the exercise of power and increase its checks and balances. Under the correct leadership of a determined Central Committee of the CPC, people look forward to and firmly believe that such reform would yield good results, in hope that anti-corruption campaigns will not be challenged and interfered with by greater evil influences and the upsurge in corruption within the system of transport would not happen again.

7

Most people believe that we should attach further importance to social equity and rebalance the relations between efficiency and equity by attaching more weight to equity. However, some people also worried that such an emphasis on social equity and some people's "deliberate exaggeration" of the large income gap might cause the retrieval of egalitarianism inherent in the traditional planned economy.

This worry is not groundless, for some people did ever claim that China's income gap has reached such a limit that people cannot endure any more, which I ever analyzed earlier. It is indeed not sensible to "deliberately exaggerate" the problem of income gap, but it is also understandable because different people have different perspectives. Nevertheless, we can neither ignore the possibility that the widening of income gap might lead to polarization, nor neglect potential risks of social crisis caused by serious social unfairness. Given the circumstances, it is necessary for us to keep alert and take preventive measures.

No one will want the traditional indiscriminate egalitarianism any more since our reform has reached such a height. As the concept of market economy and its operating rules are filtering into people's minds, high income and the widening of income gap resulting from honest work and lawful operation has been understood, recognized and accepted. Our people have become "more tolerant of the widening of income gap due to different salaries, technological patents, and capital gains". What really irritates people is the grey income "off the books", illegal (black) income and non-standard income resulting from an unsound legal system and imperfect policies. What they want is no more than the adjustment and correction of inequitable distribution and the improvement of redistribution leverage to narrow moderately the gap between the rich and the poor rather than jeopardize those legal and rational high incomes.

Therefore, the emphasis on social equity will not possibly lead to a retrogression to egalitarianism inherent in traditional planned economy or any shattering of our consensus established since the reform and opening-up. Currently, the vestiges of egalitarianism have been drastically reduced and confined to a very small number of state-owned organizations and industrial sectors. Besides, even within the state sector, a fairly large income gap has already emerged among different units. We still need to remove the vestiges of egalitarianism, but it is not the major aspect of the contradiction any more, which now has shifted to the other side of the balance, i.e., a too large income gap, which should be narrowed properly.

But I do have another concern. The socialist market economy that the 14th National Congress proposed to establish had been a very complete concept, but now it has been separated somehow. It seems that more emphasis has been placed on market economy and less on socialism these years. When it comes to socialism, we tended to attach relatively more importance to the development of the productive forces (efficiency), and relatively less to common prosperity (social equity). If socialism and its ultimate goal of "common prosperity" are neglected, China's market economy under both the rule of law and the rule of man would surely lead to the so-called "bad market economy", "crony market economy" or "polarization-bound market economy". Deng Xiaoping ever warned us that if the reform leads to polarization, we would end up with failure. We must and will surely prevent this from happening. There's only one solution, that is, to attach more importance to social equity.

(This article is a speech made in the Spring Forum on the analysis and forecast of China's economic situation in 2005)

Applying the Principle of "Giving Priority to Efficiency" to Wherever it is Rightfully Needed

Some new spirits were written into the documents of the Fifth Plenary Session of the 16th Central Committee of the CPC. One of them is that we should attach more importance to social equity and the previous wording of "giving priority to efficiency with due consideration to equity" has been abandoned. After a careful perusal of central documents, we may find that such wording has already been removed out of the document since the Fourth Plenary Session of the 16th Central Committee of the CPC, which shows the Central Committee's great determination of implementing a Scientific Outlook on Development and building a harmonious society. These steps have received wide support among the people. But some economic theoreticians and people from the media still continued as usual to promote the idea of "giving priority to efficiency with due consideration to equity" due to their failure of understanding thoroughly the spirit of policies issued by the Central Committee.

In order to understand more deeply the Central Committee's guiding ideology for income distribution, it is necessary for us to sort out reasons why the principle of "giving priority to efficiency with due consideration to equity" has already failed to meet the requirements of the current situation and why we should apply the principle of "giving priority to efficiency" to wherever it is rightfully needed. I believe that the major reasons are as follows:

(1) "Giving priority to efficiency with due consideration to equity" means to place efficiency in the first place and social equity secondary, which is a far cry from "attaching more importance to social equity". Therefore, this wording can only apply to a particular period in the primary stage of socialism instead of the whole period.

(2) Deng Xiaoping said, "by the end of this century (Year 2000) when we become moderately prosperous, we should lay this problem (i.e., the large gap between the rich and the poor) on the table and strive to solve it." However, if "equity" is secondary to efficiency, it would be unlikely for China to highlight and solve the problem of social inequality. It is inconsistent with Deng Xiaoping's ideas.

(3) The income gap is currently so large that social inequality has given rise to many contradictions and social disharmony, and those hidden dangers tend to explode any time. If we continue to view social equity secondary to efficiency, it would be inconsistent with our party's purpose of building a harmonious society.

(4) According to the internationally recognized standard, China's Gini coefficient has exceeded 0.45 and already overstepped the international warning line, whereas the Gini Coefficient of some developed capitalist countries such as UK, US and France is just 0.3-0.4 and that of some welfare capitalist countries such as Norway and Sweden 0.2-0.3. Currently, our Gini coefficient is not only much larger than that of capitalist countries, but the highest we've ever had. If such problem still remains unsolved and social equity continues to be viewed secondary to efficiency, how could we match the title of "socialist country"?

(5) It does not mean that the policy of "giving priority to efficiency" should be totally abandoned, but instead it should apply to wherever it is rightfully needed aside from the field of distribution. Efficiency, benefits and quality are relative to speed, investments and quantity respectively. As our party's guiding principle for transformation of economic growth pattern (i.e., development pattern)

requires, quality, benefits and efficiency should be the top priority of economic development, whilst investments, quantity and speed carry due weight. Leaders in charge of production can still apply the principle of "giving priority to efficiency" and "pay due attention to speed". That is to say, rather than driven by investment or quantity, economic growth is expected to value quality and benefits the most, which does conform to the guiding strategy that "development is the absolute principle". However, not all kinds of development are to be valued, such as the development in disregard of quality and benefits. If economy continues to grow in such an extensive way, the outcome will be very gloomy. Deng Xiaoping ever said, "if both benefits and quality are considered, there will be nothing to worry about." Therefore, the principle of "giving priority to efficiency" applies to the field of production, and it will always work.

(6) In the field of distribution, it was believed that there would be a trade-off between efficiency and equity. In other words, efficiency would be much improved if income gap is to expand within a certain scope; on the contrary, the narrowing of income gap would affect negatively the improvement of efficiency. That explains why we ever proposed to give priority to efficiency with due consideration to equity. However, it was later found out that, more than a trade-off, equity and efficiency also form a unity of contradiction from the perspective of Marxism. neither too large income gaps nor too small ones would be conducive to the improvement of efficiency. Therefore, there is no need to tell which one is in the first place and which is of secondary importance. Rather, they should be viewed as a unity of contradiction.

(7) Some people suggested that we should "give priority to efficiency" in primary distribution, and needn't attach importance to equity until the link of redistribution. Isn't social equity important in primary distribution? Isn't the excessively large personal income in monopoly industries or extremely low income in non-monopoly industries formed in primary distribution? Aren't the extremely high incomes of those senior executives from some enterprises and the extremely low incomes of those common workers formed in primary distribution?

Shouldn't primary distribution be to blame for the poor, non-rising pay of workers especially migrant workers and overexploitation of workers for more surplus value? Aren't the irrational, illegal and abnormal black incomes and grey incomes formed in primary distribution? Wouldn't distribution disorder and social inequality in primary distribution deserve our attention for any solutions? If we put these problems off and just try to solve them through means of redistribution such as taxation, it would be far from possible for China to solve the problem of inequitable distribution.

Therefore, in the field of income distribution we shouldn't chant the slogan of "giving priority to efficiency with due consideration to equity" or "attaching more importance to efficiency in primary distribution and equity in redistribution" any longer, but instead we should propose to "attach more importance to social equity", just like what the document of the Fifth Plenary Session of the 16th Central Committee stressed. Such adjustment conforms to the general trend of reform and the will of the people and helps to arouse most people's enthusiasm in reform.

(This article is the transcript of the speech made in the Autumn Forum on the analysis and forecasts of the economic situation held by CASS on October 13th, 2005. It was published in *Economic Information Daily*, October 15th, 2005)

To Divide a Cake Equitably: Harder to Achieve than to Bake a Large One

One great thing about *Recommendations for the 12th Five-Year Plan for Economic and Social Development* adopted in the Fifth Plenary Session of the 17th Central Committee is its emphasis on people's livelihood and social equity.

After a quick perusal of the full text of the fifth plenary session communique containing only 4800 words, I found four places concerning how to safeguard and improve people's livelihood. In *Recommendations for the 12th Five-Year Plan for Economic and Social Development,* "people's livelihood" is mentioned more than seven times and there are four places concerning how to adjust income distribution, which is a good reflection of greater emphasis the Communique of the Fifth Plenary Session and *Recommendations for the 13th Five-Year Plan for Economic and Social Development* have laid on people's livelihood and distribution. Premier Wen Jiabao reiterated in the Fifth Plenary Session of the 16th Central Committee, "We should not only bake a large cake, i.e., social wealth, through economic development, but divide it more equitably with a reasonable income distribution system so that the fruits of reform and development can be shared by all."

Here, I also want to talk about the cake theory, though it seems to be as simple as ABC.

Since the Third Plenary Session of the 11th Central Committee, the focus of our party's work has been shifted to economic development. But the fifth plenary session communique did not mention the "the central task of economic development", probably because the party is now more committed to society building, which however does not mean to deny the importance of economic development. Besides, it is also hard to draw a strict line between the drive of economic development and society building. Take people's livelihood and distribution as an example, they are not only categories of economic development, but highly related to society building. To put it simple, the "central task of economic development" just refers to two things: the first one is to bake a large cake, that is, to enhance our economic strength and build China into a more prosperous and powerful country; the second one is to divide the cake more equitably, that is, to distribute social goods and national income more equitably so that the fruits of development would be shared by all.

Over the past three decades, we have devoted most time and energy to baking a bigger cake rather than focus on its equitable distribution. Regardless of the one-sided emphasis, the policy still made sense to a poor China. It is quite understandable that we did not try to divide the cake equitably before it is big enough. It is said that it is the government's responsibility to bake a bigger cake and its conscience to divide it equitably. Can we infer from this logic that the government would have a bad conscience if they fail to divide the cake equitably? The answer is NO. It is true that baking a bigger cake and dividing it equitably are both responsibilities of the government, rather than just an issue of conscience. But it is almost impossible for the government to have both done in the beginning. Therefore, we should strive to bake a large cake at first, and then at a certain point begin to attach importance to both, that is to say, we should not only bake a big cake, but also try to divide it equitably.

Socialism, under which the fruits of development are shared by all rather than be divided up among the very few people, demands a bigger emphasis on the equitable division of cake. It's also a must. If the cake cannot be divided equitably, people would get increasingly dissatisfied and then their enthusiasm would be dampened, and finally it would be hard to bake a larger cake. Moreover, in order to transform economic development patterns, we must at first increase domestic demand, which is also conditioned by equitable division of cake. Or else, the majority of people would be paid less and then buy less. If that really happens, we can forget any idea of increasing domestic demand, adjusting the structure or transforming development patterns! So it is high time that we should pay attention to both the task of "baking a large cake" and that of "dividing it equitably", and lay even more emphasis on equitable division of the cake.

So we must highlight that it is the right time to solve that problem. Deng Xiaoping ever pointed out in his South China Tours Talks in 1992 that we should strive to solve the problem of income inequality by the end of last century when we become moderately prosperous. By mentioning "by the end of last century", Deng Xiaoping meant to build a basically moderately prosperous society instead of in all respects. He suggested that till then we should lay the problem on the table and strive to solve it. Actually, finding out solutions to income inequality is equivalent to finding ways to divide the cake equitably. So, at the turn of the 21st century, i.e., since 2000, we should also pay attention to equitable division of the cake and put it on the priority of economic work while striving to bake a bigger one. This is Deng Xiaoping's idea, not mine. Now, the trend of polarization is even worse than 2000. In the past few years, I kept saying that it was too early to tell whether polarization has emerged. As for the reasons, I would not explain here. However, the Gini coefficient has grown so fast over these years that it has reached around 0.5. Given the circumstances, it is even more necessary for us to place equitable division of the cake on the first priority of our economic work and view it as the core of our central task.

The Central task of economic development includes the following two aspects: to bake a bigger cake and to divide it equitably. The emphasis laid on the latter does not mean that we needn't make efforts to bake bigger cakes, but instead, we still need work on this. Our per capita GDP is currently less than one tenth of that of Japan despite the fact that our economic aggregate has overtaken that of Japan and ranks the second largest in the world. Therefore, aside from making the cake bigger, we should be more focused on the issue as to how to overcome the tendency of polarization, i.e., how to divide the cake equitably while striving to accomplish the central task of economic development. We can never say that making a big cake is the most essential task, for it is inconsistent with the nature of socialism. Capitalist countries are also trying to make big cakes which are even bigger than ours. In contrast, socialism values equitable division of the cake more. To attach more importance to social equity is the great concern of all the people, which not only conforms to the essence and purpose of socialism, but also constitutes the basis for the legitimacy of our power.

Deng Xiaoping ever said that distribution inequality was a very serious problem, which was even more difficult to handle than economic development. That is to say, to divide a cake equitably is harder to achieve than to make a large cake. I believe this is what Deng Xiaoping really means. I don't know whether everyone has ever noticed such words. After all, it is not a minor issue, and the emphasis we ever placed on it is far from enough. Therefore, the whole party should attach greater importance to this issue as it is even harder to achieve than economic development. We need to study with great care this tough issue and try to solve it. It is the duty of Marxist political economics to help us solve this problem.

The fundamental premise for Marxist Distribution theory is that distribution system is determined by ownership and distribution relations are determined by property relations, which, however, people tended to neglect. People made a long list of reasons for the widening of the gap between the rich and the poor, such as the expansion of urban-rural disparity, the worsening of regional imbalances, industrial monopoly, corruption, uneven supply of public goods, and inadequate redistribution etc., to name but a few. All these reasons make sense, but neither of them is the most fundamental one. The rooted cause of inequitable income distribution has been ignored.

Primary distribution is held accountable for distribution inequity and the core issue that influences primary distribution the most is the relations between labor and capital, which are also connected with the basic relations of production or property relations in the society. Property ownership tends to affect income gap the most. Aside from the abovementioned reasons, the change of ownership structure, i.e., the decline in the proportion of the public sector and the rise in that of the private sector is also another major cause for the widening of the gap between the rich and the poor over more than three decades since the reform and opening-up.

When it comes to adjusting income distribution relations and narrowing the gap between the rich and the poor, people tend to check the system of distribution first, especially means of redistribution such as taxation and transfer payment so as to enhance social security and public welfare, and improve the livelihood of low-income people as well. These measures are absolutely necessary and we've already begun to take them, for instance, *the Recommendations* adopted in the fifth plenary session of the 16th Central Committee has prescribed many specific measures as to how to improve people's livelihood and income distribution. However, all these measures are still far from enough, we still need further step up efforts to implement them.

Actually, it is impossible to reverse the widening of the gap between the rich and the poor by just focusing on distribution and redistribution. Besides, we also need check our ownership structure, property system, the basic relations of production and the basic economic system. Only by reinforcing the status of public ownership as the mainstay of the economy can we possibly prevent the income gap from widening, guard against the worsening of polarization trend and finally achieve common prosperity.

Just as Deng Xiaoping ever noted, "so long as public ownership remains the mainstay of the economy, polarization will be avoided". "If basic means of production is owned by the state or the collective, i.e., public-owned, a new bourgeoisie would not emerge," he added. This profound inference pointed out that in the primary stage of socialism, private property rights and distribution according to non-labor factors (mainly capital) would be tolerated only if public ownership is the mainstay of the economy and distribution according to work constitutes the major mode of distribution. We would have zero tolerance for the seizure of mainstay status by the private sector; we must strive to reverse the trend of distribution according to capital taking the place of distribution according to work as the major mode of distribution.

Policies allowing private capital to penetrate into profitable industries and sectors (including major fields and key sectors concerning the lifeline of the national economy; even Sun Yat-Sen, the pioneer of China's democratic revolution, also called on his men to restrain private capital from entering these fields), and strongly encouraging the increase of "property income"(which will cause the rich to become even richer; whereas most workers and farmers will just gain some petty profits from their meager property) can only end up with an even wider gap in both income and wealth. In the circumstances, changes must be made.

So long as public ownership is the mainstay of the economy and distribution according to work constitutes the dominant mode of distribution, the gap between the rich and the poor would never reach the limit, i.e., polarization. But instead, it would be well controlled within proper bounds and common prosperity would be eventfully achieved. Otherwise, polarization and social split will inevitably happen.

Therefore, the reform of distribution system and the reversal in the widening of the gap between the rich and the poor should be viewed from the perspective of the Constitution. We must take necessary measures or policies to implement the two constitutional principles, i.e., public ownership as the mainstay of the economy and the dominant position of distribution according to work among all distribution modes.

(This article was published in *Jianghuai Tribune*, No.6, 2010)

Thoughts on National Prosperity, Prosperity of the People, and Common Prosperity

From the end of 2010 to the early 2011, when the "Twelfth Five-Year Plan" (2011-2015) was being formulated, people held many heated discussions over "national prosperity" and "prosperity of the people". Some people said that in the past we had been seeking the policy of prospering the nation first instead of "enriching the people", resulting in the current situation of "a prosperous nation VS poor people" or "a prosperous nation VS non-rich people". Some people argued that, "prospering the nation first" has driven productive forces grow even faster than consumption and thus led to insufficient aggregate demand. Therefore, they suggested that the government should change its policy from "prospering the nation first" to "enriching the people first" during the "Twelfth Five-year Plan" period.

A few officials from the State Development Planning Commission (SDPC) proposed that what was to set the "Twelfth Five-Year Plan" apart from previous eleven "Five-Year Plans" should be its pursuit of "prosperity of the people" rather than "national prosperity" while offering suggestions on the making of the "Twelfth Five-Year Plan" (2011-2015), however, it turned out that no such words have ever appeared in the "Twelfth Five-Year Plan". I think that it is not precise for some scholars and media to oppose "national prosperity" to "prosperity of the people".

As far as "national prosperity" is concerned, our economic strength has indeed been vastly enhanced; China has overtaken Japan and become the world's second largest economy since the reform and opening-up. In this sense, the nation has indeed become much more prosperous than before. In sharp contrast, China ranks the 121st in the world in Gross National Income (GNI) per capita[1], which suggests that our nation is not that prosperous at all.

As for the pursuit of "prosperity of the people", one cannot say that Chinese people are now "non-rich" or "poor". Our people's living standards have been improved a lot, and some Chinese people are so wealthy or "filthy rich" that they can compare favorably with the richest man in the world. According to some statistics, 535,000 Chinese people's mainland assets had reached one million dollars by 2010[2] and 146 Chinese's mainland assets one billion by 2011[3].

However, most Chinese people are not very rich or even very poor. To sum up, we have insufficient domestic demand and low consumption rate on the one hand, and a second world largest luxury market on the other: some rich people wallow in luxury whereas some extremely poor people feed on waste outer leaves of cabbages scattered nearby the supermarket or open markets. In this sense, we cannot simply say "poor people" or "non-rich people".

Next, what has led to low consumption rate and insufficient domestic demand? It is not the result of the so-called policy of "prospering the nation first" "in disregard of the prosperity of the people" at all. Rather, due to the policy of "encouraging some people to get rich first", some people did prosper first but most people hadn't so far been able to catch up with them, resulting in relative or even absolute poverty. According to the UN standard, those whose income per day is lower than $1 are absolutely poor, and those whose income per day is lower than US $2 are called low-income workers. Both of these groups are poor people. It is estimated that by 2010, 150,000,000 Chinese people's income per day will be

1 See Appendix to *China Statistical Yearbook 2011,* pp. 2-13.
2 http://news.cntv.cn/20110626/101326.shtml
3 http://liftnance.people.com.cn/money/GB/15625212.html

lower than $1.[1] This is absolute poverty.

These low-income people who cannot afford things are the main cause of low consumption rate and lack of domestic demand. How about those extremely wealthy people? For example, a wealthy man ever spent as much as 4 million Yuan on just a Tibetan mastiff; and what is more, a convoy of 30 Benzes were sent to the airport just for picking up the very animal! Some people spent lavishly on fancy Bentley Grand Convertibles or private jets, each costing millions of RMB or even more. It seems that they needn't be funded by the government to stimulate consumption and expand domestic demand.

And then, let's look back at the previous policies. Was there such a policy of "prospering the nation first"? As far as I remembered, no such a policy was ever announced or implemented, but we did have the policy of "encouraging some people to get rich first". If one has to call it "enriching the people first", it is just a policy of "enriching some people first". These people are mostly private businessman or those who have chances, capabilities, resources or means to accumulate wealth. This policy has turned out to be a great hit. Thanks to this, radical changes have taken place in China's economic structure. For example, the phenomenon of "Guo Jin Min Tui" (the state retreats whilst the private sector advances) has led to a sharp increase in the proportion of the private sector from almost zero before the reform and opening-up to 65% till 2005.

The fact that the private sector has outgrown the public sector and the state sector shows that the policy we have been carrying out these years is not "prospering the nation first", but "enriching the people first (of course only some of them)" instead. In the primary stage of socialism, some private enterprises should be given a free hand so as to promote the development of the productive forces. The policy of "encouraging some people to get rich first" so as to boost the economy did make sense and was then worth a try.

At that time when this policy was announced, the slogan of "encouraging

1 http://news.qq.com/a/20100818/000255.htm

those who got rich first to help others to achieve the ultimate goal of common prosperity" was also chanted for a while. However, many years' practice shows that such goal cannot be achieved automatically though some people did prosper before others in no time. After all, against such fierce competition in the wave of marketization, it is indeed a mission almost impossible. As a matter of fact, the gap between the rich and the poor kept widening with the result that the tendency of polarization has "automatically emerged" in the process of marketization. The deadly rise of Gini coefficient, a measure of income inequality, has resulted in China becoming one of the countries with the largest Gini Coefficient.

Why hadn't China achieved the goal of common prosperity after some people had long since got rich first? It will be inadequate to explain that it takes time to divide the big cake equitably after it was being baked. Deng Xiaoping has long since pointed out that the gap between the rich and the poor will surely be widened, and in due time we need to narrow it. As for when to start, he suggested that it should be the beginning of the 21st Century, when a moderately prosperous society would have been basically built in China.

China's real economic progress shows that it took quite short for Chinese rich people to accumulate wealth due to its uniqueness in primitive accumulation of capital. Hu Run, researcher focusing on the study of wealth, ever said that in western countries, it usually took one 15 years to earn 100 million dollars, and another 10 years to turn it into 1 billion, whereas in China, it can be accomplished just within three years. But the problem is that the ultimate achievement of prosperity for all seems to be in the distant future, even though it took very short for some people to prosper before others.

In order to defend capital or great wealth, some elites said that due to the complicatedness of income distribution, it would be very long before the problem of inequitable distribution is solved, and therefore people should be patient. What a weird logic! Even Deng Xiaoping cannot tolerate it because he has urged many times to solve the problem of the widening gap between the rich and the poor, warning that the trend of polarization would probably lead to the failure of the

reform.

Why was it so easy for China to fulfill the policy of "encouraging some people to get rich first", but so hard to overcome polarization and realize social equity? I believe that one of the major reasons is that since the focus of the party's work was shifted to economic development, efficiency and GDP growth have taken precedence over social equity and distribution of social goods, with the result that some party members have gradually left behind the basic ideas of the Marxist law of social and economic development. For example, in the primary stage of socialism, the private sector should be allowed to develop, but at the same time we should never forget Vladimir Lenin's warning that small-scale production would constantly breed capitalism; private capital should be allowed to exist, but at the same time we should also bear in mind Marx's admonition that capital accumulation is bound for polarization; the contribution of owners of private enterprises to the social and economic development is supposed to be acknowledged, but at the same time we should never forget the bourgeoisie's duality and especially their profit-seeking nature, which propelled them to seek more surplus values and thus produce social polarization.

"Polarization will emerge automatically" is another famous saying of Deng Xiaoping, but some people tried their best to evade the word "polarization". Some influential people within the party have gradually left behind even the basic ideas of the Marxist laws of social and economic development. As a result, these people one-sidedly focused on the positive role of private capital in promoting the development of the productive forces, but failed to see its nature of exploitation and its negative role in producing polarization, which is incompatible with the essence of socialism. So, they did not restrict private capital while encouraging and supporting the private sector's development. This is the fundamental reason why common prosperity cannot be realized over a long period of time, the gap between the rich and the poor kept widening and the trend of polarization has emerged.

Currently, the core of income distribution is the dramatic widening of the gap between the rich and the poor and the worsening of the trend of polarization. Therefore, the crux of the matter is not the problem of "national prosperity" VS "prosperity of the people", but the contradiction between the prosperity of some people (including the nouveau rich) and non-prosperity or poverty of most people. In order to overcome or reverse the trend of polarization and the widening of the gap between the rich and the poor, we should announce that we have already fulfilled the policy of "encouraging some people to get rich first" and therefore it should be replaced by the policy of "gradual achievement of common prosperity". To sum up, we are expected to achieve a transition from "the prosperity of some people" to "common prosperity", rather than from "prospering the nation first" to "enriching the people first".

Besides, it lacks scientific evidence to oppose "national prosperity" to "prosperity of the people". This pair of concepts form a unity of opposites rather than be mutually exclusive. In some sense, they can even get along swimmingly. What does "national prosperity" mean? Yan Fu was the first one to translate Adam Smith's book entitled *The Wealth of Nations* (short for *"An Inquiry to the Nature and Causes of the Wealth of Nations"*) into Chinese (Guo Fu Lun).

As a matter of fact, Adam Smith not only discusses the income and wealth of the monarch or government (equivalent to the nation), but also that of workers, farmers and businessmen (equivalent to the people). Later, Guo Dali and Wang Yanan retranslated this book and the title of the book was rendered into *Guo Min Cai Fu De Xing Zhi He Yuan Yin De Yan Jiu* in Chinese. In this way, the meaning of the title was changed from "the wealth of a nation" ("guo fu" in Chinese) to "the wealth of the people". However, Guo Dali's Chinese version of the book still included the chapters concerning the income and wealth of the government or nation. Therefore, we can infer that *the Wealth of Nations* has two senses, namely, the wealth of a nation and that of the people. In this sense, "national prosperity" and "prosperity of the people" are not either black or white.

What does the Chinese buzzword "guo fu" (the wealth of nation) imply? In general, it refers to the government's disposable and distributable income, equivalent to the income of the monarch or the nation that Adam Smith referred to in the Chapter Five. Besides, Adam Smith also discussed the pros and cons of various taxes with a view to proving that the income of monarch (government) is not always conflicting with the income of the people. An Increase in the income of the nation does not necessarily mean a reduction in the income of the people, as the monarch and the government need maintain necessary income to protect and increase the wealth of the people.

The Wealth of Nations has devoted a good deal of space to the analysis of the nation's three basic functions, namely, to protect the society, to protect every individual in the society, to provide public service and build public welfare facilities. If we temporarily put aside the fact that the nation and the government represent the interests of the ruling class and that officials tend to spend lavishly, this book also gives us a good portrait of the relations between the income and wealth of modern nations and their people, and those between the income and wealth of the government and the people in general.

In modern countries, disposable income for their residents transferred from national disposable income are only part of government expenditure on people's livelihood such as subsidies, relief funds, social security benefits, etc. However, spending on public welfare (education, culture, medical care etc.), infrastructure, economic development, security, and administrative management is not at people's direct proposal although its benefits are shared by all. After all, government/ national disposable income and disposable income for residents are not the same.

Some people compared the proportion of disposable income for residents in the national income with that of government/national disposable income to tell which one has been achieved, "national prosperity" or "people's prosperity". This measurement does have its own analytical significance, but fails to reflect the fundamental problem of distribution relations, i.e., the gap between the rich and the poor and polarization. As mentioned before, the "resident income" is a mixed concept, as the residents include both rich and poor people. So, merely by the comparison of the proportion of resident income with that of government revenue can we hardly see any gap between the rich and the poor. In order to overcome it, we should divide the resident income into labor income (the income of labor owners) and non-labor income (the income of owners of non-labor factors especially capital) and calculate their ratio. Only in this way can the gap between the rich and the poor and the degree of polarization be reflected from the resident income. This is the very core issue of income distribution at present.

For several years, with the decline in the proportion of the public sector and the rise in that of the private sector and the prevailing trend of "appreciating capital and depreciating labor" in the process of marketization, "distribution according to work as the dominant mode of distribution" prescribed in the Constitution has been gradually replaced by "distribution according to capital as the dominant mode of distribution". Therefore, the proportion of labor income keeps falling whereas that of capital income keeps increasing. As labor income constitutes the largest part of the resident income, the decline in the proportion of labor income in GDP and the rise in that of enterprises' profits would naturally lead to a reduction in the proportion of residents' disposable income in GDP, which is however not the result of an increase in government revenue. In order to prevent the proportion of residents' disposable income from further declining, we should raise workers' remuneration and payment of low-income group. This is what really matters. That is to say, the crux matter is to adjust the proportion of labor income and that of capital income rather than that of government revenue.

The proportion of government revenue in GDP, or the so-called "tax burden", used to be a hot topic in the debate concerning "national prosperity" VS "prosperity of the people". People are quite divided on the issue as to whether tax burden is too high. In a broad sense, government revenue comprises public revenue under general budget management, special revenue funds, state-owned capital operating budget, and social insurance funds. According to the Ministry of Finance, the proportion of government revenue (in a broader sense) in GDP is 27.6% in 2007, 27.9% in 2008, 30.0% in 2009. By using the measurement in the *Government Finance Statistics Manual,* the Institute of Finance and Trade

Economics of CASS concluded that the proportion of government revenue (in a broader sense) in GDP is 31.5% in 2007, 30.9% in 2008, and 32.2% in 2009, a little higher than the statistics provided by the Ministry of Finance. According to the *Government Finance Statistics Yearbook,* the average tax burden of the 53 countries investigated is 39.9% in 2007, the average tax burden of 24 industrious countries is 45.3%, and that of 29 developing countries is 35.5%. Even if we use the higher statistics provided by CASS, i.e.,32.2% in 2009 as comparison, our tax burden is still far less than that of these industrious countries, and only slightly higher than that of these developing countries. According to the international experience, the government would be more burdened by spending on people's livelihood, public welfare and redistribution of income with the development of the productive forces. Therefore, in China, there is still a lot of room for the rise in the proportion of our government revenue, or the level of tax burden, which is also very necessary.

Therefore, the proportion of government revenue does not matter too much to the tax burden. Rather, the crux of the matter lies in whether the structure of revenue and expenditure is reasonable so that harmony could be achieved between "national prosperity" and "the prosperity of people" on the one hand and "prosperity of some people" could successfully evolve into "common prosperity" on the other. Currently, the major problem with the structure is that state revenue is mainly contributed by low-income group or working class in striking contrast with rather low spending on people's livelihood and public welfare etc.

In our current taxation system, indirect tax constitutes the major part, accounting for over 70% of total tax revenues. Consumers pay indirect taxes such as value-added tax and sales tax etc., which are included in the price of commodities and services. Even though consumers with low income needn't pay income tax, they still cannot avoid these indirect taxes hidden in the price of grain, cooking oil, salt, clothes, restaurant dinners, water, electricity and gas. As low-income group need to spend most disposable income to meet their basic needs, their percentage of indirect taxes levied is much higher than that of higher-income people.

Besides, the structure of individual income tax is also evidently unreasonable. The individual income tax is mainly targeted at labor income of wage-earners, but rarely any capital income such as dividend yield, bonus, and leasing revenue etc. The rich only paid a small part of taxes; they often have enormous hidden income, which is not included in the urban resident income. In this sense, tax fairness has been severely affected. With regard to the structure of expenditure, on the one hand, our spending on administrative management is too high, whose proportion far exceeds that of western developed countries, for example, shockingly high expenses were spent each year on public vehicles, food and entertainment, and overseas trips, which are called "three public expenditures"; on the other hand, the percentage of expenses on public services such as education, medical care and social insurance in China is obviously lower than these countries whose GDP per capita is over $3000.

The abovementioned shows that too high tax burden in our country is weighing heavily on the working class with medium and low income, who however failed to be adequately compensated or didn't get sufficient social welfare that they deserve; whereas most of the rich people's income and wealth mainly derived from capital and property was not redistributed by means of taxation. Such regressive regulation can do nothing but aggravate income inequality, which thereby needs urgent solutions.

Some scholars and experts reached a consensus and agreed that it is time for radical changes. With regard to revenues, we should levy more direct income taxes and less indirect income taxes. As for direct income tax, it should be more targeted at capital, property and other non-labor income, and people with medium and low income should pay less given family burdens. Besides, the government should levy inheritance tax and gift tax etc. With regard to expenditures, we should practice economy, cut administrative costs, spend more on people's livelihood, public welfare and transfer payments etc. In a nutshell, the government needs to resume its function of "redistributing the income and wealth and promoting social equity", the outcome of which will highly depend on its determination, policies and implementation of them. It is so urgent that we need to act now.

However, it should be noted that we cannot solely count on fiscal policies to narrow the gap between the rich and the poor and to reverse the trend of polarization. There are many causes for the widening gap between the rich and the poor, such as the urban-rural disparity, regional imbalances, industry monopoly, corruption, uneven distribution of public goods, and delayed redistribution etc., which need to be addressed one by one. But none of them is the most fundamental one.

According to Marxism, ownership determines distribution system, and property relations determine distribution relations. Property ownership tends to affect income gap the most. Therefore, the decline in the proportion of the public sector, the rise in that of the private sector, privatization and quick concentration of wealth in the hands of the very few people are the most fundamental causes of the widening of income inequality and the tendency of polarization over more than three decades since the reform and opening-up.

Due to the policy of "encouraging some people to get rich first" and that of "giving priority to efficiency", the non-public sector is sure to outgrow the public sector and state sector, with the result that many types of ownership develop side by side. Such economic structure in the primary stage of socialism is beneficial to the economic development as a whole. However, if such momentum keeps going, "problems would become a full-blown crisis at some point", and "polarization would emerge automatically"[1]. As private property rights expand, capital income would relatively increase in proportion to labor income, resulting in the widening of the gap between the rich and the poor and the worsening of the trend of polarization.

When it comes to adjusting income distribution relations and narrowing the gap

1 *Chronology of Deng Xiaoping's Career* (1975-1997) Ⅱ , Beijing: Central Party Literature Press, 2004, p.1364.

between the rich and the poor, people tend to check the system of distribution first, especially means of redistribution such as taxation and transfer payment so as to enhance social security and public welfare, and improve the livelihood of low-income people. These measures are absolutely necessary and we've already begun to take them, for instance, *the Recommendations* adopted in the fifth plenary session of the 16th Central Committee has prescribed many specific measures as to how to improve people's livelihood and income distribution. However, all these measures are still far from enough, we still need further step up efforts to implement them.

Actually, it is impossible to reverse the widening of the gap between the rich and the poor by just focusing on distribution and redistribution. Rather, we also need check our ownership structure. We need reinforce the mainstay status of public ownership and the leading role of state sector so as to reverse the decline in the proportion of the public sector, the rise in that of the private sector, and the trend of "guo tui min jin" (the state retreats while the private sector advances) and thus prevent private ownership from replacing public ownership and becoming the mainstay of the economy. This is another essential way to rebalance "national prosperity" and "prosperity of the people".

Just as Deng Xiaoping ever noted, "so long as public ownership remains the mainstay of the economy, polarization will be avoided". "If basic means of production is owned by the state or the collective, i.e., public-owned, a new bourgeoisie would not emerge," he added. This profound inference pointed out that in the primary stage of socialism, private property rights and distribution according to non-labor factors (mainly capital) would be tolerated only if public ownership is the mainstay of the economy and distribution according to work constitutes the major mode of distribution. We would have zero tolerance for the seizure of mainstay status by private ownership; we must strive to reverse the trend of distribution according to capital taking the place of distribution according to work as the major mode of distribution.

Policies allowing private capital to penetrate into profitable industries and sectors (including major fields and key sectors concerning the lifeline of the national economy), and strongly encouraging the increase of "property income" can only end up with an even wider gap in both income and wealth. Therefore, radical changes must be made.

So long as public ownership is the mainstay of the economy and distribution according to work constitutes the dominant mode of distribution, the gap between the rich and the poor would never reach the limit, i.e., polarization. But instead, it would be well controlled within proper bounds and common prosperity would be eventfully achieved. Otherwise, polarization and social split will inevitably happen.

(This article was published in *Economic Research Journal*, 2011, No. 10)

Income Distribution in the New Era of China's Reform and Opening-up

As we step into the new century, drastic widening of income inequality has raised people's concern about income distribution. We need not only continue to bake a bigger cake (social wealth), but at the same time divide the cake equitably. How to make the fruits of reform shared by all people through a reasonable income distribution system is currently a big challenge for China. I ever published several articles on income distribution, suggesting that we should gradually abandon the policy of "giving priority to efficiency with due consideration to equity" and place a greater emphasis on social equity. Now it has turned out that my views are all consistent with the final decisions of the Central Committee of the CPC. Here, I would like to sum up the evolution of our income distribution policies since the reform and opening-up, talk more about my understanding of the relations between efficiency and equity, and at last offer some suggestions on the reform of distribution system in the years to come.

Evolution of income distribution policies

Income distribution policies since the reform and opening-up have undergone gradual changes. Initially, we managed to break away from egalitarianism and resume distribution according to work as the major mode of distribution; currently, we uphold distribution according to work as the dominant mode of distribution; besides, we also allow for the coexistence of a variety of modes of distribution.

Since the completion of socialist transformation, socialist system has been established, and distribution according to work has become the basic distribution system. Even in 1975 during the period of the Cultural Revolution (1966-1976), it was still stipulated in the Constitution that we should uphold distribution according to work. However, some senior leaders of the Central Committee misinterpreted Karl Marx's exposition of distribution according to work and idealized the supply system characterized by egalitarianism during wartime. Karl Marx believed that in distribution according to labor, the principle that "value in exchange equal to or proportional to the labor value" was also based on the bourgeois "pursuit of equal rights".

During the Cultural Revolution, Zhang Chunqiao (a member of the "Gang of Four") et al. took Marx's exposition to extremes, attacking distribution according to work as the bourgeois right and dismissing socialist policies such as the wage grade system as the hotbed of a new bourgeoisie. As a result, egalitarianism ran rampant. Very ironically, such a distortion of the principle of distribution according to work did not lead to common prosperity but common poverty instead. Everybody knows it.

After the victory over the "Gang of Four", the campaign aiming to set wrong things right started by economists began with the re-evaluation of the principle of distribution according to work. At Yu Guangyuan's[1] suggestion, four national symposiums on the theory of distribution according to work were held successively from 1977 to 1978. After discussions, a consensus was reached that distribution according to work, rather than a hotbed of capitalism and the bourgeoisie, is the only road to the ultimate elimination of capitalism and the

1 A renowned Chinese economist who helped Deng Xiaoping launch his market reform in late 1970s.

bourgeoisie. Distribution according to work has never been over-implemented, but implemented inadequately instead.

At that time, the Central Committee also emphasized distribution according to work as the socialist principle, which can be confirmed by some official documents. For example, in August 1977, the 11th National Congress report stated, "With regard to ideological education, we should promote the Communist spirit of labor among the broad masses; in terms of economic policies, we should adhere to the socialist principle of distribution 'from each according to their ability, to each according to their work' and gradually expand collective welfare." Besides, the Government Work Report in the Fifth National People's Congress also expounded on this. It says, "During the whole historical period of socialism, the principles of 'he that will not work shall not eat' and 'from each according to their ability, to each according to their work' should be applied...in terms of income distribution, we should avoid a too large gap or egalitarianism; the greater the contribution, the higher the pay; the less the contribution, the lower the pay." The last example, on May 5th, 1978, the newspaper *People's Daily,* the mouthpiece for Chinese Communist party, published an article entitled "Implementation of the socialist principle of distribution according to work" written by a person from Research Office of the State Council in the name of commentator. From then on, the position of distribution according to work was officially resumed.

On December 13, 1978, five days before the Third Plenary Session of the 11th Central Committee, Deng Xiaoping proposed to "encourage some people and some regions to get rich first" on the working conference of the Central Committee. He said, "in terms of economic policy, I think we should encourage some regions, enterprises, workers and peasants to earn more and enjoy more benefits sooner than others, in proportion to their hard work and greater contributions to the society. If these people's lives are thus improved first, they will surely set good examples for 'their neighbors', influencing people from other units or regions to follow suit. In this way, the whole national economy will be pushed forward like one waver after another, and people of all nationalities would get rich over a fairly short period of time." "This is a major policy that can influence and bring along our national economy as a whole. I suggest that we think it over and study it carefully," he also added.

At that time, many people still held some doubts as to whether the policy of "encouraging some people and some regions to get rich first" would lead to polarization. *The Decision on Economic Restructuring* adopted in the Third Plenary Session of the 12th Central Committee in 1984 stated, "Only if some regions, enterprises and some people are encouraged to get rich first through hard work, would the majority of people be strongly motivated and thus more and more people brought along one wave after another to become prosperous." "To prosper through hard work" is very crucial, which is the key solution to avoid polarization. Deng Xiaoping also said repeatedly, "If we adhere to socialism and the principle of distribution according to work, the gap between the rich and the poor wouldn't be too large. Even two or three decades later when our productive forces are more developed, polarization will not emerge, either."

On January 12th, 1987, the Political Bureau of the Central Committee adopted the then No. 1 Central Document, *to Deepen the Rural Reform*, which says, "In the primary stage of socialism, individual economy and a few private enterprises will inevitably exist over a fairly long period of time in the course of the development of commodity economy." It was for the first time that the private sector was acknowledged in the Central Document. Later, one more item was added to the *Amendment to the Constitution* in 1988, which stipulated that the private sector would be allowed to exist and develop. As a matter of fact, the legitimate role of individual economy was already confirmed in the Constitution as early as in 1982.

According to Marxism, production relations determine distribution relations, and thus changes in distribution relations are sure to bring about those in distribution relations. Therefore, the 13th National Congress report in 1987 clearly stated, "The distribution mode in the primary stage of socialism cannot be unitary. We must uphold the system of distribution under which distribution according to work is dominant and a variety of modes of distribution serve as a supplement." "Under the goal of common prosperity, we should encourage some people to get rich first through their hard work and lawful operation." As to "other modes of distribution", the report has made a long list including bond interest, stock bonus, partial risk compensation for enterprise operators, and the boss's non-labor income derived from his employment of labor. By way of comparison, we can see some radical changes, for example, the current income is derived not only from "honest work" but from "lawful operation".

In 1997, the 15th National Congress report proposed to uphold "a distribution system in which distribution according to work is dominant and a variety of modes of distribution coexist", and to "combine distribution according to work with that according to factors of production", "permitting and encouraging some people to prosper before others through honest labor and lawful operation, and factors of production such as capital and technology etc. to participate in the distribution of gains." This wording is dramatically different from that of the 13th National Congress in terms of distribution in the following two ways. First, the previous wording "other modes of distribution serve as a supplement" has changed to "a variety of modes of distribution coexist". The latter was put forward for the first time in the Third Plenary Session of the 14th Central Committee in 1994.

The second difference lies in the current policy of "allowing and encouraging factors of production such as capital and technology etc. to participate in the distribution of gains". I think that, in a certain sense, operating income and technology participating in the distribution of gains are also a kind of complex labor income and thus distribution according to work can apply to them, too. According to Deng Xiaoping, if the principle of distribution according to work is applied, the gap between the rich and the poor will not be too large. However, as a type of property income, capital income is radically different from labor income. Therefore, capital and labor compete with each other for more share of gains in distribution of income. Recent years have seen a decline in the proportion of labor income, a rise in that of capital income, and the widening of the gap between the rich and the poor. This is how the policy of income distribution has evolved in general.

The origin of the slogan of "giving priority to efficiency with due consideration to equity"

In theory, efficiency and equity form a unity of opposites. Common sense tells us that the more evenly distributed, the less enthusiastic people would be and the lower efficiency it would lead to. Therefore, a proper income gap is conducive to the improvement of efficiency, if distribution procedures and rules are fair enough. To put it another way, lower efficiency would not ensure a big cake and thus social equity will not be guaranteed, so that it would be hard to solve the increasing social contradictions. However, if we do not attach importance to equity, the income gap will be too large; especially when distribution procedures and rules are not fair enough, efficiency would decline and even social stability would be in jeopardy. Therefore, neither excessively large nor too small income gap will help improve efficiency. It is hard to handle the relations between efficiency and equity properly, which we should view in a dialectical unity.

Before the reform and opening-up, efficiency was severely affected due to indiscriminate egalitarianism. Since the market-oriented reform, we began to attach more and more importance to efficiency in order to increase income gap. The policy of "encouraging some people to get rich first" did work on the economy, having invigorated it in both rural and urban areas. Over a decade later, the boiled-down wisdom, i.e., "paying due attention to both efficiency and equity", was written into the document of the 14th National Congress of the CPC in 1992. As far as I know, it is the first time that the relationship between efficiency and equity was clearly stated in the central document. Before that it was hardly mentioned, be it in central documents or academia.

But two years later, the Third Plenary Session of the 14th Central Committee came up with a new policy concerning the relations between efficiency and equity, i.e., "giving priority to efficiency with due consideration to equity". The previous policy is that we should "pay due attention to both efficiency and equity". By way of comparison, the status of efficiency has been improved, from being on a par with equity to being prioritized, whereas equity has been reduced to the secondary place though still valued. Though both versions suggested that we should pay due attention to equity, meanings have been radically changed.

From then on, till the Third Plenary Session of the 16th Central Committee, such policy appeared in every major document of the Central Committee. Over a fairly long period of time, it remained our official spirit in income distribution. Later, the 16th National Congress added something new to this policy, that is, we should "attach more importance to efficiency in primary distribution and equity in redistribution", which is another important distribution policy as well.

The communist party has always been valuing social equity and justice. But why did communist China place equity secondary to efficiency in making the policy of distribution? This is closely related to our national conditions, that is to say, our long-term backwardness made it hard for us to improve people's living standards and to solve so many social contradictions in no time. Besides, it also has a lot to do with profound changes and potential trends in domestic and world situations as well as opportunities and challenges brought about by these changes. Under the circumstances, we have to spare no efforts to accrue to our national wealth and improve our overall national strength.

Therefore, Deng Xiaoping suggested in his South China Tour Talks, "We should emancipate our mind more freely, carry out reform and opening-up more boldly and build up our country more rapidly, never to lose any golden opportunities." He also emphasized, "Development is the absolute principle and the key solution to everything in China." And then, the task of increasing national wealth and improving national strength, i.e., "baking a bigger cake", came to the fore, and efficiency became the top priority.

Besides, egalitarianism that used to be practiced in the era of planned economy still existed at that time, which was also a major obstacle to the improvement of efficiency. For example, bonuses were evenly divided among all workers, everyone took turns to be "elected" as "the progressive"; and what is more, the irrational income differential between mental and manual workers in favor of the latter was then so common that intellectuals often sighed, "burger vendors are even better-off than rocket scientists!"

Therefore, in order to improve efficiency more rapidly and accrue to the national wealth, we must "break away from egalitarianism, create rational income differential, encourage some regions and people to prosper before others through honest labor and lawful operation", which was added in the Third Plenary Session of the 14th Central Committee document to further explain the policy of "giving priority to efficiency with due consideration to equity".

To sum up, it was then very right for the Third Plenary Session of the 14th Central Committee to come up with the new policy concerning the relations between efficiency and equity and view the task of "dividing the cake equitably" secondary to "baking a big cake", which was then very consistent with our real conditions and development needs.

During this period, central documents have repeatedly emphasized, "those who prospered first should bring along those who were lagged behind to achieve common prosperity", "we should guard against polarization", which indicates no neglect of social equity at all.

To Gradually Abandon the Policy of "Giving Priority to Efficiency with due Consideration to Equity" and Place a Greater Emphasis on Social Equity

For long, I have been focusing on macroeconomic issues and seldom studied income distribution. However, since we stepped into the new century, the problem of income inequality has gradually come to the fore. Our Gini coefficient, a universally recognized measurement of income inequality, has now exceeded the international warning line 0.4. However, at the very beginning of reform and opening-up, it was just 0.2-0.3. Such a drastic rise has thereby attracted wide attention. At this critical point, I thought maybe it is time that we should abandon gradually the policy of "giving priority to efficiency with due consideration to equity".

My study pointed out that the policy of "giving priority to efficiency with due consideration to equity" just serves as a temporary guiding line in terms of income distribution in a given period of time, rather than an unfailing rule throughout the whole historical period of market economy, just like some people ever claimed. Actually, some mature market economies do not have such policies at all. In order to mitigate contradictions between social classes, modern capitalist countries also borrowed some socialist ideas such as social security and welfare. Modern liberalist countries attach great importance to efficiency and at the same time social equity has to be valued, too. Modern welfare states attach more importance to equity but efficiency is also valued, both having reached a fairly high level. Some measures to ensure social equity and welfare in some capitalist countries are indeed far more complete than those in socialist China. However, due to different histories, it is really hard to compare.

After more than two decades' development since the reform and opening-up, problems concerning economic development and efficiency have been relatively solved, that is to say, the cake has already been big enough. Now, the problem of "equitable division of the cake", i.e., social equity, has gradually come to the fore. We shall not forget the fact that Deng Xiaoping has long since put forward the "big headache", i.e., "how to distribute wealth after China becomes prosperous". As early as in 1992, he set up the timetable for the solution of income inequality with foresight. He envisaged that by the end of the 20th Century when China is moderately prosperous, we should put this problem on the table and try to solve it.

Out of these considerations, I wrote an article entitled *A Focus on the Issue of Income Distribution in the study of the Macroeconomic Situation*[1], in which

1 *Selected Works of Liu Guoguang*, vol. 10, Beijing: China Social Sciences Press, pp. 498-513.

I proposed that "the previous slogan of 'giving priority to efficiency with due consideration to equity' should gradually give place to the policy of 'paying equal attention to efficiency and equity'." I, then a member of the drafting panel for the document of the Third Plenary Session of the 16th Central Committee, also offered this suggestion to the drafting committee. At that time, I believed that our Gini Coefficient was then still on the rising side of the inverted U-shaped curve and income gap was still inclined to widen, which means the Gini Coefficient is unlikely to fall for the time being. Deng Xiaoping's prediction might be a little bit optimistic. It seems that only by 2010 when per capita income reaches $ 1,500, it will be likely for the Gini coefficient to fall and then it will be time that we solve the problem and achieve the transition of policy from "giving priority to efficiency with due consideration to equity" to "paying equal attention to efficiency and equity" or "achieving an optimal combination of efficiency and equity". Therefore, we should gradually abandon the previous policy of "giving priority to efficiency with due consideration to equity", give more weight to equity, and reduce and slow down the expansion of Gini coefficient.

In fact, my position is milder than those who offered to force a reduction in Gini coefficient, say, to 0.3, which sounds very good, but undoable. However, the Third Plenary Session of the 16th Central Committee still cannot reach a consensus, and the policy of "giving priority to efficiency with due consideration to equity" was thereby not removed from the document.

After this meeting, I kept pondering over the problem of income distribution. I was also met with some criticism from the academia since then. For example, some people argued that it would be too late to put it off to 2010 to solve the problem of income inequality and readjust the relations between efficiency and equity, because "Chinese people's endurance for income inequality has already reached the limit", and therefore "we should get started right now". Recently, someone also wrote in the article that income gap was said to have reached the limit ten years ago, which however turned out not to be true. As a matter of fact, it is natural for China, as a developing country, to have a rising Gini coefficient during the establishment of market economy. Therefore, we need wait patiently before conditions are ripe.

However, I've somewhat changed my mind after having thought it over. I found out that the issue as to whether income gap has reached the limit and the readjustment of the relations between efficiency and equity by attaching further importance to social equity are not on the same level. If income gap reaches the limit someday, it might probably be caused by polarization. However, we hadn't gone that far at that time, so we should neither say that income polarization had emerged (which, Deng Xiaoping said, would lead to the failure of reform), nor state that income gap had already reached the limit. Now, our Gini coefficient is still on the rise. If wed do not act now, polarization would soon emerge and income gap would risk reaching the limit immediately.

Therefore, we must start from now on to attach further importance to social equity and readjust the relations between efficiency and equity. At first, we need slow down the expansion of income gap; and then we should try to reduce the absolute value of Gini coefficient progressively. So, from now on, we can gradually abandon the policy of "giving priority to efficiency with due consideration to equity" and then try to achieve a gradual transition to that of "paying equal attention to equity and efficiency" or "achieving an optimal combination of equity and efficiency".

So, why should it be now?

After two decades' reform and economic development, our economic aggregate and national economic strength have been greatly enhanced. We have already completed the first two tasks, i.e., doubling and quadrupling of per capita GDP, and now are striving to obtain the goal for the third step. So we are fairly strong and capable enough to solve the chronic problem of income inequality gradually; that is to say, time has been basically ripe for the solution of the problem that Deng Xiaoping put forward in terms of income distribution.

Rapid expansion of income gap has become a severe problem affecting social harmony and stability. For over two decades, Gini Coefficient has multiplied by folds, growing at such an unprecedented pace that it has overtaken some capitalist countries (0.3-0.4) such as UK, the United States and France, and some welfare capitalist states (0.2-0.3) such as Norway and Swede. Some organizations and experts from home and abroad warned us that it has already surpassed the international warning line. Whether it is exaggerated or not, we should remain vigilant and pay particular attention to such trend. Moreover, our officially announced Gini Coefficient did not include the unreasonable, abnormal, or illegal income resented by people, because they are very hard to be counted. If included, the Gini Coefficient will grow to 0.5-0.6, which is over 20% higher than the official data. Social inequity leads to many contradictions and social disharmony, which are ready to explode at any time.

At the very beginning of reform, people's lives have generally been improved, and thus they all vigorously embraced the reform. So, till then the whole society hadn't been divided into interest groups yet. However, since the 1990s, different interest groups were formed gradually: some benefited a lot from the reform; some less; and some people's interests were even hurt. That explains why some people's enthusiasm for reform has changed over time. Besides, what people from different classes expect to take from the reform also varies. For example, some people that have benefited a lot from the reform said, "the reform has to be achieved at the expense of interests of a generation, that is, tens of thousands of veteran workers." And then, some people argued back and made a tit-for-tat response, "why has it to be us instead of you?" Therefore, in order to win wider support for the reform, we need to stress social equity and justice to ensure social harmony and stability in a long run.

Factors leading to the rapid expansion of income gap and a surge of problems concerning social distribution are very complicated. A vast number of cadres are quite inexperienced, and some of them even misinterpreted the policy by focusing too much on efficiency and placing equity on a secondary place, which is one of the major causes. However, it does not mean that we shouldn't "give priority to efficiency"; rather, it is very fit for production rather than income distribution. Transformation of development patterns require us to value quality, benefits and efficiency as the most essential factors, and attach due importance to input, quantity and speed, which is in conformity with Deng Xiaoping's tenet that "development is the absolute principle".

Besides, I also think that primary distribution not only involves efficiency but also equity as well. It is primary distribution that gives rise to competition between capital and labor. Besides, income gap between monopoly and non-monopoly enterprises, that between senior executives and common employees, and many irrational, illegal or nonstandard black income and grey income from a dubious source are all formed in primary distribution. Therefore, in order to solve the problem of income inequality, we must trace it from the very source, i.e., primary distribution. It is far from enough to solely rely on redistribution leverage such as taxation to solve inequitable distribution in China.

Some people also worried that such a great emphasis on social equity might steer us back to egalitarianism inherent in the traditional system, but I don't think that will happen. Since our reform has advanced to such a stage, no one will want the old indiscriminate egalitarianism any more. What really irritates people are the grey income "off the books", illegal (black) income and exorbitant pay resulting from an unsound legal system and imperfect policies. What people want is no more than the adjustment and correction of inequitable distribution and improvement of redistribution leverage to narrow moderately the gap between the rich and the poor rather than jeopardize those rational and legal high pay. Currently, the vestiges of egalitarianism have been increasingly reduced and confined to a very small number of state-owned organizations and industrial sectors, and even within state-owned sectors, a large gap has already emerged among different units. We still need to remove the last vestiges of egalitarianism, but more priority should be given to the problem of social inequalities, which is on the other side of the balance of distribution.

But I do have another concern. If socialism and its ultimate goal of "common prosperity" are neglected, China's market economy under both the rule of law and the rule of man would surely lead to the so-called “bad market economy”, “crony market economy” or “polarization-bound market economy”. According to Deng Xiaoping, if things develop like this, the reform would end up with a failure. We must and will surely prevent this from happening. There’s only one solution, that is, to attach more importance to social equity.

Out of these considerations, I published an article entitled “Attaching Further Importance to Social Equity” in 2005. Afterwards, I also wrote another article titled “Applying the Principle of ‘Giving Priority to Efficiency’ to Wherever It Is Needed”, proposing that we should gradually abandon the policy of “giving priority to efficiency with due consideration to equity” and that it is inappropriate to view “equity” secondary to efficiency as it should also be valued in primary distribution.

These articles have caused a great sensation. Most people have given positive comments regarding them; whereas some people attacked me vehemently, criticizing that my ideas were populism. The latter insisted that we should still give priority to efficiency with due consideration to social equity. I believe that the latter are defending for wealth and capital rather than the working class. If we had followed this course, China’s reform would be bound for crony capitalism and end up with failure. Sure, that is only my personal opinion, which is open for discussion.

Since 2005, I, already in my 80’s, seldom participated in social activities and did not take part in the drafting of any central documents any longer, but I still submitted these articles to the Central Committee. Luckily, it was very much valued by the Central Committee and then recommended to the drafting panel of the Fifth Plenary Session of the 16th Central Committee. However, words like “giving priority to efficiency with due attention to equity” and “attaching more importance to efficiency in primary distribution and equity in redistribution” appeared again in the exposure draft of the Fifth Plenary Session of the 16th Central Committee report, which incurred disapproval from many people. I also voiced my disagreement in CASS. However, these words were eventually crossed out and the policy of "attaching further importance to social equity" was more highlighted. As far as I know, this is the first time that central documents ever proposed "to attach further importance to social equity". No doubt, it is in conformity with the tendency of reform and the will of the people as well as conducive to the mobilization of most people's enthusiasm, which is definitely a major step forward for our policies and theory-building in terms of income distribution.

Major steps to achieve equitable distribution of income

The Fifth Plenary Session of the 16th Central Committee is a great turning point. The policy of "attaching further importance to social equity" marks the Central Committee's shift of focus from efficiency to both efficiency and equity, but social equity is relatively more emphasized. In 2006, the Political Bureau of the Central Committee held special conferences to study how to solve income inequality. The policy of "attaching further importance to social equity" was emphasized again in the Sixth Plenary Session of the 16th Central Committee. In 2007, the 17th National Congress report proposed, "Equitable income distribution is an important indication of social equity "; besides, it also added that social equity should be ensured in primary distribution as well. In recent years, top leaders have expressed their determination of "adjusting the income distribution structure" many times.

Since 2010, the phrase of "adjusting income distribution" has been used in official documents unprecedentedly. During their on-line conversations with netizens, chief government leaders also pledged that the government is not only responsible for "baking a big cake" but has the "conscience" to "divide the cake equitably". These are all signals for the deepening of our reform sent by top leaders who are greatly concerned about inequitable distribution and the widening gap between the rich and the poor. They have gained great popularity among the people who expect to share the fruits of reform and development.

Currently, the government is studying how to narrow the gap between the rich and the poor and to ensure equitable distribution. On February 4th this year,

Premier Wen Jiabao summed up the reform of distribution system and gradual steps to reverse the growing income disparity in a panel discussion among chief provincial leaders held by the Central Committee and boiled them down into the following three points. First, we should step up efforts to adjust the structure of income distribution and increase gradually the share of personal income in the national income and that of work remuneration in primary distribution; second, we should strengthen the regulatory role of taxation in income distribution; Third, we should attend more to the needs of those low-income people both in rural and urban areas.

On March, 5th, Premier wen delivered his government's annual work report, making a summary of the reform of income distribution system and measures to divide the cake equitably. There are also three points. First, we should step up efforts to formulate policies concerning the adjustment of the structure of income distribution; second, we should deepen the reform of income distribution system in monopoly industries; Third, we should continue to overhaul income distribution practices.

Premier Wen's wordings are slightly different and serve as supplement to each other. Both of them meet the requirements of our reform of income distribution system and help curb the widening of the gap between the rich and the poor. Therefore, it is urgent that we work out some practical solutions and try to implement them.

I think that the solution of inequitable distribution, involving many aspects, would be very complicated. We should at first slow down the expansion of income gap, try to reverse the widening and then narrow it to the extent that income can be distributed properly and rationally. Therefore, we need to study deeply the theory behind income distribution and choose the right course for the reform of income distribution system so as to achieve common prosperity as expected. Among many complex distribution relations, I believe the most important one is the relations between distribution system and ownership. I analyzed this issue in my article entitled "Reflections on several issues concerning the relations between distribution and ownership"[1], which might serve as a reference for the current reform of income distribution system. The summary is mainly as follows:

Ownership and distribution both fall into the category of relations of production. According to Marxism, ownership determines distribution, which people tend to neglect. People made a long list of reasons for the widening of the gap between the rich and the poor, such as the expansion of urban-rural disparity, regional imbalances, industry monopoly, corruption, uneven supply of public goods, and inadequate redistribution etc., to name but a few. All these reasons make sense, but neither of them is the most fundamental one. The rooted cause of inequitable distribution has been ignored.

Inequitable distribution of income is formed in primary distribution, and the core issue that influences primary distribution the most is the relations between labor and capital, which is closely linked with the basic relations of production or property relations. Property ownership tends to affect income gap the most. However, some people tend to overlook these and talk with relish that individuals varying in capabilities would make different contributions. The more contribution, the higher pay; the less contribution, the lower pay. It seems to them that personal income is just determined by capabilities, knowledge and contributions.

As a matter of fact, Marxism does not deny the influence of individual capabilities on personal income (complex labor). Even Paul Anthony Samuelson[2], an American bourgeois economist, had to acknowledge that wealth determines income inequality the most, whereas individual capabilities do not make any big difference. He also said that property ownership is the number one factor determining income gap, with individual capabilities, education, training, opportunities and health coming next to it one by one.

1 *HongQi WenGao* (Red Flag Manuscript), 2007, No. 24.

2 Samuelson, Paul A. *Economics: An Introductory Analysis, 1948.*

Aside from the abovementioned reasons, the change of ownership structure, i.e., the decline in the proportion of the public sector and the rise in that of the private sector and the process of privatization is also another major cause for the widening of the gap between the rich and the poor over more than three decades since the reform and opening-up.

We believe that such argument made by this distinguished western economist is fair and scientific, but such point will be even clearer if we explain it with Marxist political economics. According to Marxism, production determines distribution and distribution of any consumer goods is determined by allocation of production conditions, which reflects the nature of the mode and the relations of production. Varying relations of production lead to different distribution relations and modes. Therefore, what fits capitalist private ownership is distribution according to factors of production (mainly capital and the price of labor), and what suits socialist public ownership is distribution according to work. However, in the primary stage of socialism, we have to allow factors of production to have a share of gains while holding distribution according to work as the dominant mode of production, that is to say, with distribution according to capital and other factors of production as a secondary mode of distribution.

When it comes to adjusting income distribution relations and narrowing the gap between the rich and the poor, people tend to check the system of distribution first, especially means of redistribution such as taxation and transfer payment so as to enhance social security and public welfare, and improve the livelihood of low-income people. These measures are absolutely necessary and we've already begun to take them. However, all these measures are still far from enough, we still need further step up efforts to implement them, such as to adjust the personal income tax threshold and progressive tax and to levy property tax, inheritance tax, and luxury consumption tax. Our government should use these new tax revenues to increase spending on social security and public welfare, to fund the reform of health care, education, and housing (the so-called "three new big mountains" in China) and to improve the low-income people's livelihood.

As a matter of fact, it is impossible to reverse the widening of the gap between the rich and the poor by just focusing on distribution and redistribution. Besides, we also need check our ownership structure and property relations. That is to say, we need consolidate the basic economic system in the primary stage of socialism, consolidate the mainstay status of public ownership, and weaken the trend of privatization. Only in this way can we possibly prevent income gap from further widening, guard against any worsening of the polarization trend and finally achieve common prosperity.

Just as Deng Xiaoping ever noted, "so long as public ownership remains the mainstay of the economy, polarization will be avoided". "If basic means of production is owned by the state or the collective, i.e., public-owned, a new bourgeoisie would not emerge," he added. Such inference is so profound that textbooks on political economics cannot afford to abandon it. It pointed out that in the primary stage of socialism, only if public ownership is the mainstay of the economy and distribution according to work constitutes the major mode of distribution, private property rights and distribution according to non-labor factors (mainly capital) would be both tolerated, and the gap between the rich and the poor would never reach the limit, i.e., polarization. Only in this way, income gap would be well controlled within proper bounds and common prosperity would be eventfully achieved. Otherwise, polarization and social split will inevitably happen.

Therefore, the reform of distribution system and the reversal in the widening of the gap between the rich and the poor should be viewed from the perspective of the Constitution of PRC. We must take necessary measures or policies to implement the two constitutional principles, i.e., public ownership as the mainstay of the economy and the dominant position of distribution according to work among all distribution modes.

(This article was published in *Bai Nian Chao Journal* (Hundred-Year Tide), 2010, No. 4)

Appendix

On the Relations between Planning and Market in Socialist Economy

In theory, economic restructuring in the socialist country often starts from an exploration of the relations between planning and market. This article, written at a time when the Third Plenary Session of the 11th Central Committee of the CPC uncovered a new historical page, i.e., the era of economic reform, raised very earlier the necessity of introduction of market to combine with planning as another means of economic management. It attracted a lot of attention from both home and abroad and triggered a wide discussion. Hu Yaobang, then General Secretary of the Central Committee of the CPC, commented on this article, "This original article aiming to study new problems has set good examples for other theoretical researchers. In theoretical studies, we must strongly encourage such spirit before most theoretical researchers haven't been determined enough to study these new problems." And then, this full article was published in restricted periodicals of Party School of the Central Committee of the CPC, State Development Planning Commission (SDPC) and Chinese Academy of Social Sciences (CASS) etc.

Besides, the revised version of this article was also submitted to the annual meeting of the International Atlantic Economic Association (IAES) held in Australia in May 1979. Helmont Shuster, then executive President of IAES told

Hu Qiaomu, then president of CASS, in the telegram that this article has "won great applause" in the annual meeting and that it was believed to "have great significance in the academic research". He also said that they have decided to publish the full article of this paper along with the one by James Edward Meade, the Nobel laureate, in the *Atlantic Economic Journal*, December, 1979.

Currently, the focus of the whole party is being shifted onto the socialist modernization drive. In order to accommodate to such change and guarantee the sound economic development, we must draw lessons from prior experiences over the three decades and reform the system of economic management and its approaches meticulously. It is urgent that we should study and solve in both theory and practice many major problems as to how to complete such an overwhelming task of reform. One of these issues concerning the overall situation of socialist economic management is how to deal with the relationship between planning and market properly. The "planning" this article mentioned is not an ideological concept, but an objective process in which people consciously adjust and control social and economic development, which used to be summarized as "planifying". Besides, any plans that were not specifically marked as "plans of enterprises" in this article are all state plans or social plans, which are the very issue that this article attempts to study.

1. The necessity of a combination between planning and market in socialist economy

Over a long period of time, there has been such a point of view in socialist political economics to the effect that since socialist economy is planned economy and capitalist economy market economy, socialist economy is incompatible with market, and therefore, it was easily concluded that socialist planned economy shouldn't tolerate any use of market, which is however too absolute. Even though the existence of commodity production and the law of value in socialist economy were gradually recognized, people still tended to consider commodity production, the law of value, and market mechanism as the antithesis of planning. It seems that once planning works, market mechanism shouldn't be used; and market mechanism would only be used when planning doesn't work. According to this logic, the superiority of socialism should never manifest itself in any use of market, but instead, just in its restriction or rejection of market. It seems that the larger part planning plays and the smaller part market does, the more likely the superiority of socialism is to be seen. Such a view regarding market totally incompatible with the nature of socialist economy has in fact brought about a series of negative consequences to our economic life. Here, I would like to list some.

First, it has led to separation of production from demand. Due to partial emphasis on the role of planning and the neglect of market, what products and how many items the enterprise will manufacture are mainly up to the quota set by mandatory planning in a top-down way, and therefore it is hardly possible for enterprises to manufacture goods to suite real needs of the society. In principle, plan-based production should correspond with demand-based production. However, in socialist conditions, without the market mechanism, central planning cannot reflect the changing needs for tens of millions of products. In this way, the goods manufactured according to the quota set by central planning often turned out to be unwanted ones and just added to the stock of piles, which often resulted in the society running low on the goods in great need.

Besides, the state imposed monopoly on purchase and sale of most products manufactured by factories; most of the means of production that enterprises needed were allocated by the state according to the plans. So, there is almost no horizontal connection between manufacturing enterprises and consumers, i.e., no face to face communication. As a result, manufacturers do not know the real needs of consumers; consumers can hardly exert any influence on production; the mismatch between planned quotas and real needs cannot be reflected flexibly through the market mechanism and thus cannot be promptly rectified; and the imbalance between production, supply and sale remained unsolved for long.

Second, planned prices have been divorced from real values. Due to the neglect of objective requirements of the law of value while setting prices, planned prices of many commodities have deviated dramatically from real values in the long run. Due to unreasonable pricing policies, neither output values nor profits, neither deficit nor surplus can reflect the real performances of enterprises. Planned prices tended to be fixed for a long period of time as they seldom took into consideration changes in supply and demand. When the supply of a commodity fell short of demand, the government seldom adjusted prices to increase supply and control demand, but instead usually issued a limited quantity of tickets. In this way, those tickets served as a supplement to the currencies, resulting in the diversification of measures of value.

Marx ever pointed out, "the duality of measure of value often conflicts with its functions", "when two commodities are both the measures of value pursuant to the law, it often turns out that only one commodity can preserve this property."[1] Many of the tickets without value issued in China have de facto had value. The issuance of limited tickets was called "planned supply" and naively considered as something associated with the nature of socialist planned economy. As a matter of fact, almost any commander of city defense would come up with such an idea while being surrounded by their enemies, and therefore it has nothing to do with the nature of socialist planned economy.

However, it does not mean that under socialist planned economy goods shouldn't be supplied with quotas and fixed prices in given conditions within a particular period of time. As a matter of fact, such means failed to encourage any increase in the production of goods in short supply and even tended to throw their producers into a even more disadvantageous position so that their production and supply reduced. In consequence, it not only failed to solve the contradiction between supply and demand at its source but also complicated the matter.

Third, even fund allocation was subject to the supply system. We used to overlook the role of market in not only production and exchange of products, but

1 *Marx and Engels Collected Works*, vol. 23, Beijing: People's Publishing House, 1972, p.114.

in fund-raising and fund allocation, which can be reflected in the unified state control on income and expenditure. In the past, enterprises were required to turn over most or all of their incomes, including net income and basic depreciation fund, to the state; as for funds for expansion of production and improvement of welfare etc., enterprises would ask for money from the state. The state provided enterprises with all fixed assets and most circulating capital for no returns, and enterprises need not be accountable for the good or ill use of such fund. No matter what outcome enterprises produce, good or bad, gain or loss, they and their employees still enjoy the same amount of fund and salary. In other words, due to the policy of indiscriminate egalitarianism, the enterprise got the same reward regardless of its performance and its employees held secure jobs.

Because material gains were detached from operating results, economic calculation became a mere formality, that is to say, it was just regarded as a way of bookkeeping rather than a means to link material interests of all employees with operational results of enterprises so as to promote production. Therefore, regardless of many administrative orders and political slogans, enterprises and their employees still cannot be strongly or permanently motivated to reduce consumption, to improve product quality, to increase the variety of goods to suite the needs of consumers and market. As a result, all sorts of delays and waste began to develop, which were rather stubborn to overcome in the long run.

Fourth, it has given rise to a surge of self-sufficient enterprises. Socialist economy is based on socialized mass production, which is characterized by both specialization and collaboration between enterprises, regions or sectors. Especially with scientific and technological advancement, specialization of production and collaboration are supposed to be even more developed. However, due to the neglect of market relations and the application of small-scale production management methods to socialist mass production, many Chinese enterprises tended to be more self-sufficient and self-reliant. For example, a lot of industrial enterprises, big or small, have developed into comprehensive plants and even mini-societies. Surely, we should not ascribe all these problems to enterprises. Imbalance between production, supply and sale, breach of contracts by cooperative units, and lack of guarantee in production of collaborative pieces etc. are also their causes.

However, to view it in a larger picture, all these problems are related to the denial of market relations. It shows that neglect of commodity production, the law of value and the market mechanism is actually not conducive to the development of socialist planned economy at all. One essential characteristic of socialist planned economy is the balanced, proportionate development of the national economy, which helps to strike a balance between production and demand. Vladimir Lenin ever said, "Conscious and regular efforts to maintain an economic balance is indeed a planning."[1] However, exclusion of the market mechanism from socialist economy will more often than not cause an imbalance between production, supply and sale and thus make it hard to strike a balance between production and demand; if planned prices of various products have contravened the law of value for long, or price relations are not reasonable enough, the balanced proportionate development as required by objective laws would not be guaranteed.

Another important characteristic of socialist planned economy is less consumption of living labor and materialized labor. Surely, the economy of time is linked with distribution of labor time in definite proportions. As what Karl Marx pointed out, "The economy of time, along with the planned distribution of labor time among the various branches of production, remains the first economic law on the basis of communal production, and even a very advanced law as well."[2] However, if we deny commodity-money relations, disregard the law of value and abandon economic calculation in socialist conditions, our economic development will surely end up with high consumption, low quality and low efficiency, that is to say, we would fail to gain the maximum effect with the minimum consumption

1 *the Collected works of Lenin*, Vol. 3, Beijing: People's Publishing House, 1959, P.566.
2 *Grundrisse*, vol.1, Beijing: People's Publishing House, 1975, p.112.

of labor as required by the the nature of socialist planned economy.

In practice, whether to recognize the existence of market and make full use of it to serve planned economy has a great bearing on the development of socialist economy. The past three decades witnessed two periods of rapid economic growth in building socialism: the period of the First Five-Year Plan and the three-year-adjustment period. These two periods had something in common: the law of value and market were both made good use of in both periods, which turned out to have some positive effects. For instance, urban and rural areas collaborated with each other fairly well; some balance has been achieved between agriculture, light industry and heavy industry; people began to value economic calculation and economic benefits, too. However, China's economy also experienced two major setbacks during the past three decades. The first one happened in the period of the Second Five-Year Plan and the second one occurred in the period from the mid 1960s to the mid 1970s. In political sense, Lin Biao, Chen Boda and the Gang of Four who deliberately sabotaged the cultural revolution are mainly to blame; in theory, it also has something to do with their denial of the market's role and malicious creation of confusions about commodity, currency and the law of value. It should be noted that the very idea denying the positive role of commodity-money relations in the socialist society and viewing market as an antithesis of planning was not only very harmful in practice, but very lame in theory.

Socialist economy based on public ownership of the means of production is a planned economy. Rather than an antithesis of market economy, planning is opposite to spontaneity or anarchy of production, a basic economic feature of all societies based on private ownership. However, market economy is not exclusive to such society. Natural economy instead of planned economy is opposite to market economy. Natural economy does not involve commodity-money relations but only relations of physical distribution, which is one of the basic features of self-reliant and isolated social economies. In contrast, relations of market economy are based on social division of labor and collaboration. Market economy is not necessarily the synonym of spontaneity or anarchy; it all depends on ownership. For example, under socialist public ownership, the relations of market economy can be put under good control by the state so that they could work for the benefit of socialist planned economy. Since the relations of market economy are materially conditioned by social division of labor and socialized production, they are not incompatible with socialist planned economy based on socialized mass production. To summarize, socialist planned economy, a planned economy conditioned by commodity-money relations, is just opposite to a spontaneous market economy or natural economy rather than the market economy subject to state control.

For long, people have been laying one-sided emphasis on planning and neglecting the role of market. Actually, they were mainly influenced by these two traditional notions: the first one regarded spontaneity and especially anarchy of capitalist market economy as the synonym of market; the other one mixed up planned economy with natural economy. Those who opposed market often used the first idea as their weapon to attack whoever advocated the use of market and thus labelled them as "advocates of capitalism". Those who passed natural economy off as socialist planned economy often referred to the second notion.

Justified by the two interconnected traditional notions, some people kept chanting the slogan of "supporting socialist planned economy and opposing capitalist market economy", which has however become a hotbed of ills affecting socialist economic development. For example, economic means have been replaced by administrative means so as to manage the economy; people tend to act according to "will of superiors" rather than the law of economy; the patriarchal system has replaced the ruling system in which the people serve as masters of the country; feudal bureaucratic management peculiar to the natural economy has taken the place of the scientific approach for socialized mass production, etc.

However, all these traditional notions and practices are deep-seated in our society, which used to be an undeveloped commodity economy and is now still mainly made up of semi self-sufficient farmers (80%). Under the circumstances, our current task is to develop commodity economy practically in accordance with objective economic laws in an effort to achieve the "four modernizations". In order to break with these traditional notions, we must make good use of the commodity-money relations, deal with the relations between planning and market properly, and reform various management regulations inconsistent with the objective laws of socialist economy.

Therefore, we need further explore the reasons why the commodity-money relations and market should exist in socialist conditions. Quite many economists explained it with the co-existence of collective ownership and the ownership by the whole people under socialism. We do believe that the commodity-money relations under the two types of socialist ownership are crucial to socialist economic development. Especially when farmers still account for an overwhelming majority of the population and collective ownership is still playing an indispensable role in agricultural production, we must attach more importance to the commodity relations between the two types of public ownership and respect the decision-making power of collective entities as commodity manufacturers.

However, such explanation fails to touch upon the core issues, because in effect it still holds that commodity-market relations are incompatible with the ownership by the whole people, the key component of socialist public ownership. In view of that, it can only explain the existence of commodity-market relations with external factors, i.e., influences beyond the ownership by the whole people, rather than internal influences. As a matter of fact, many current prevailing models are just derived from the theory of "external causes". For example, some people believed that the means of production allocated within the system of ownership by the whole people are just the shells of commodities (it is called the "shell model"); some people thought that the law of value has been replaced by the the economic law of balanced, proportionate development of the national economy (it is called the "replacement model"); Some people even dismissed the objective law of value and other value categories such as price, profit, cost and interest rates as optional accounting tools (it is called the "pragmatic tool model") etc. It should be noted that some opinions which are said to be based on experiences from almost all socialist countries are not good for all. Therefore, if they still stubbornly persist with these ideas, bad consequences would be foreseeable.

We believe that the existence of commodity-market relations under socialist ownership by the whole people is determined by material interest relations peculiar to the stage of socialism., Although exploitation characterized by antagonism between classes in material interests has been wiped out under public ownership and labor is expected to be the first need for the people in the stage of communism, labor is still a means of subsistence and material interests still vary in the stage of socialism due to differences in individual capabilities and contributions. Besides, material interests also vary among enterprises owned by the whole people. Operational results of the enterprise must be linked with material interests of its employees, otherwise it would hinder the economic development.

Therefore, all enterprises (entities with relative independence in accounting) under socialist ownership by the whole people must obey the principles of equivalent exchange and equal compensation while interacting with each other. Disregard for these principles means no recognition of any material interest differences, and people's material interest relations would thereby be disarranged. Therefore, such material interest relations peculiar to socialist conditions are the direct cause of existence of commodity-market relations in socialist conditions (division of labor and socialized production are material conditions). Economic categories reflecting such relations are absolutely neither optional tools nor just shells of commodities, but an objective and substantial economic mechanism instead.

It should also be noted that labor under socialist public ownership is called direct social labor, just because under public ownership there would be no spontaneous market based on private ownership and connections between individual labor and social labor would not be thus affected. As a matter of fact, in the stage of socialism, workers has to make a living by selling their labor, because only in this way can they combine their labor with the means of production owned by the society. So, both individuals and enterprises have to follow the principle of equivalent exchange, and direct social labor has to be realized by a planned market. That is to say, planned distribution and the economy of social labor have to be realized by the market mechanism which is capable of reflecting material interest relations peculiar to the stage of socialism.

It follows that planning and market in socialist economy are neither mutually exclusive nor combined just for expediency, but instead they were integrated with each other and formed an organic unity, which was determined by the nature of socialist economy. If the same fundamental interests among the people under socialist public ownership ensure planning in the socialist economy, people's material interests differences mentioned above should be the direct cause of the existence of market in the socialist economy. These same fundamental interests and different material interests constitute exactly the objective basis for the unity of contradiction between planning and market in the socialist economy.

It has been proved that if we just attach one-sided importance to planning and neglect market, we tend to just see the same fundamental interests of the people and overlook their different interests, that is to say, we tend to just see the overall interests while neglect individual or local interests. In this way, enterprises and their employees' enthusiasm would be dampened. Just to the opposite, if we just attach one-sided importance to market and neglect the role of planning, the effect would be reversed, and hence enthusiasm of grassroots and the masses would run so wild that the society would be driven into an anarchic state of chaos. Therefore, in order to handle all material interest relations in socialist economy correctly and mobilize all positive factors to accelerate socialist economic development, we must try to combine planning with market both in theory and practice.

2. How to make use of market in socialist planned economy

From the above analysis, we learn that planning and market do not conflict with each other in the socialist system, but instead they must be combined so that the superiority of socialism will be fully demonstrated. While studying the relations between planning and market, we can not focus exclusively on either of them.

So far, we still tend to overemphasize planning and neglect market. Therefore, first and foremost, we need solve the problem as to how to develop commodity economy and make use of the market mechanism in socialist economy.

The development of commodity economy and the role of market mechanism cannot do without economic activities of commodity producers in the market. Aside from those enterprises owned by the collective, the major players of the socialist market are mostly enterprises owned by the whole people (in some countries, they are enterprises owned by the society). These enterprises not only produce various consumer goods and means of production, but purchase means of production from the market. If the role of market is to be brought into full play, these enterprises owned by the whole people must be given some economic autonomy and treated as relatively independent commodity manufacturers. If these enterprises are always so tied down that they have neither power nor responsibilities, the so-called use of market is nothing but empty talk. In this sense, the use of market is also closely linked with the expansion of decision-making power of enterprises.

In order to make full use of market in planned economy, we must in the meantime manipulate economic levers and economic mechanism (such as supply and demand, price, cost, profit, credit, interest, and tax etc.) to link operational results of every manufacturing enterprise with material interests of their workers, which constitutes the very essence of "management of economy through economic means". If we overlook economic levers or mechanism, disregard economic interests of enterprises and individuals, and just adopt administrative means to manage economy, the use of market will just be empty talk. In this sense, the use of market in socialist planned economy is also closely linked with "management of economy through economic means".

To summarize, the use of market in planned economy is closely linked with both the expansion of decision-making power of enterprises and the full use of economic means to manage the economy. All these are done to ensure reasonable distribution and economical use of material, financial and human resources based on social needs. So, how to closely link the devolution of administrative power with the use of economic means so as to make better use of the market mechanism?

First, it concerns how to arrange the use of material resources, which mainly involves production, supply and sale of commodities. In order to strengthen the role of market mechanism, we need to base production on demand and supply on production with a view to linking production with demand.

What products and how many items will an enterprise produce? Why has it to be this way? In what ways should these products be sold? How will an enterprise be supplied with the means of production needed by production? Currently, enterprises mainly manufactured products according to the quotas set by mandatory planning in a top-down way; purchase and sale of these products are mainly monopolized by the state; the means of production are mainly allocated by the state according to plans. These policies tend to result in separation of production from demand, so that the goal of socialist production couldn't be achieved very effectively.

As we all know, socialist production aims to satisfy the needs of the society, and therefore, we should base our production on these social needs, which is a fundamental principle of socialist economy. In principle, production based on state plans and production based on social needs should be the same, but in reality there is a discrepancy between them. State planning mainly focusing on the needs of the country can only reflect the general need of the society as a whole; it is impossible to reflect the changing needs in every aspect of economic life precisely and flexibly or to consider every enterprise's specific conditions in terms of production and technology.

In order to overcome this problem, we must make sure socialist production meet the needs of the society in terms of their products' quantity, variety and quality. That is to say, enterprise production should not be dictated by mandatory quotas set by higher authority, but instead these enterprises should manufacture products according to the specific needs of the market and their own circumstances under the guidance of state planning. Accordingly, with regard to the circulation of both means of subsistence and means of production, monopoly of purchase and marketing imposed by state-owned enterprises or state materials sectors disregarding any market demand should be abandoned. All supplies should be purchased and sold through the market except for the goods in short supply that cannot be guaranteed in the short run.

As far as the circulation of means of subsistence is concerned, we need to progressively combine the methods of selective purchasing and self-marketing within the industry to cater for the needs of consumers; as regards to the circulation of means of production, we should also try to commercialize it gradually by establishing a direct link-up between manufacturers and distributors or selling products through wholesale enterprises so as to suite the needs of manufacturers and ensure that supply is based on production. As for supplies in short demand, enterprises can expand their production to satisfy social needs through joint or exclusive investment. In order to overcome the imbalance between production, supply and sale, it is very necessary to adopt these methods to strengthen the role of market mechanism, which helps to close the gap between production and demand, to overcome factory overstock and shortage of some products, to improve the quality of products, reduce their costs, increase the variety of goods, benefit the interests of producers, and to protect the rights of consumers etc.[1]

In order to gear production to social needs or to balance production and demand, we need to reinforce the contract system, which is a matter of extreme importance. A contract is usually made by and between the buyer and the seller, who know and care for their own economic interests very much so that terms and measures they come up with tend to be fairly practical and reasonable. Besides,

1 Huang Fanzhang, "My Perspective on Consumer Rights", *Economic Management Journal*, 1979. No.2.

the variety, specifications, quantity and quality of products stipulated by contracts take the needs and capacity of both parties into consideration. In this sense, a contract serves as a very good tool to achieve the balance between production, supply and sale as well as a reliable reference for plan-making. If any party breaches the contract, they must undertake necessary financial responsibilities. If both parties fulfill contracts, they will not only satisfy the needs of the market but also accomplish the planned tasks stipulated by contracts.

Surely, by emphasizing the necessity of reflecting the needs of the market in production and more use of market in supply and marketing, we do not mean to abolish state planning. Due to various reasons, the choices of some consumers and enterprises are not necessarily in the interests of the whole society. Besides, the needs of consumers keep changing, and production more often than not creates more needs rather than just passively reflect the needs of consumption. Therefore, the society can influence the change of needs by regulating production and distribution. All these factors along with other reasons have determined that regulation by market forces must be carried out under the guidance of state planning in order to strike a balance between production, supply and sale. The abovementioned contracts for manufacture & sale of goods and purchase & sale agreements cannot do without the guidance of planning either, though they have succeeded in reflecting the needs of the market. Such a balance between production, supply and sale achieved through these contracts or agreements is a necessary condition for the success of socialist planned reproduction.

Second, it concerns how to allocate and use financial resources, which involves financial management and funds management. In this regard, we must strengthen the role of market mechanism. Therefore, enterprises need to be financially independent, assume sole responsibility for their profits or losses; any use of state-owned assets should be compensated; the investment should be based on its effects. So far, in terms of financial management, we have been adopting the policy of unified state control over income and expenditure; in terms of infrastructure investment and allocation of some circulating capital, funds were appropriated for no compensation under supply system.

These policies have caused a disconnection of operational results from the collective interests of enterprises and individual interests of employees, and hence these enterprises can't feel obligated or be motivated to use state funds effectively and rationally. Moreover, they even became more apt to bargain for more investment, more allocation of materials, and more foreign exchanges, etc. while making plans. All in all, the pure administrative method in financial and capital management neither helps to increase investment returns nor encourages enterprises to budget carefully. In order to correct this trend, we need also strengthen the role of market mechanism under the guidance of state planning. Most importantly, we need abandon the previous policy of unified state control over income and expenditure and encourage the enterprises to be more financially independent and assume sole responsibility for their profits and losses. Besides, we should also strengthen the role of credit issued by banks.

The most effective way is that enterprises should be just required to pay taxes, necessary expenses, and loan principal and interest pursuant to laws and regulations, and needn't turn in profits any more. Besides, they should decide on the specific use of the remaining income, such as to expand reproduction, to raise payroll and improve the collective well-fare of employees. In order to ensure a smooth transition, enterprises are encouraged to use a given proportion of funds to cover both bonuses and collective welfare of their employees, and use basic depreciation fund retention and fund for major overhaul to tap more potentials of enterprises, bring about more technical innovations or upgrade their equipment etc. to meet their needs of production.

In order to put an end to the way enterprises used to be funded, that is, from use of funds without compensation to with compensation, we need at first levy occupancy tax on fixed assets, which used to be established by state finance, in proportion to the appropriation so as to support the new policy of compensation for the use of funds. Such measure, combined with the policy of enterprise profit retention, will make those enterprises capable of using funds more effectively and yielding good results retain more of their profits and material gains. But less capable enterprises will get less or even no material gains. Therefore, the system of compensation for use of funds spurs enterprises and their employees on to bring all their potentials into full play by making effective and economic use of the funds.

After enterprises having gained total financial independence, the state should gradually stop funding all capital construction and some circulating capital would not be financed by the state any more. That is to say, enterprises should use some net income or profit retention to fund production and development, apply for bank loans to fund capital construction and credit to cover all circulating funds. However, while issuing these loans, banks should be guided by state planning, and at the same time, they should also issue loans selectively based on investment returns from all sectors or projects.

If enterprises have to assume sole responsibility for their profits and losses and use their profits and bank loans (both principal and interest must be paid off) to fund their production, they would naturally stop acting indifferently or irresponsibly like before when the funds were allocated and used without compensation; but instead, they would have no choice but budget carefully and run their own business conscientiously. Besides, we should also increase the use of interest as an economic lever to mobilize temporary idle monetary resources, to control the investment in credit funds, and to urge enterprises to improve economic calculation, speed up the turnover of capital, and attach more importance to the effects of investment. Therefore, we need ensure that changes in fund supply and demand benefit commodity production and circulation, adopt a differentiated interest rate policy, adjust interest rates flexibly in good time, and abandon the policy of a fixed interest rate or just one-way change, i.e., going upward.

Third, it concerns the allocation and use of labor. In this respect, we also need to reinforce the role of market mechanism. In order to achieve that, we should use selective hiring and respect people's free choice, and adjust supply and demand of labor through economic means.

In the past, administrative means were exclusively adopted in regulating allocation of personnel, financial and material resources, among which allocation of labor was almost irrelevant to the market mechanism. Actually, labor was allocated according to planned quotas by labor departments. In this way, it did to some extent satisfy some sectors' need for labor and in the meantime help some workers find their jobs. However, such way of allocation of personnel has resulted in many problems. For example, enterprises couldn't hire or dismiss workers according to their own needs; individuals couldn't choose professions according to their interests or strengths, but instead they had to obey orders issued by higher authority with the result that personnel were placed inappropriately or mistakenly. This was obviously not conducive to the rational use of labor force and thus dampened people's enthusiasm; it also did no good to economic calculation and thus hampered the improvement of economic benefits. As a result, some people did jobs they were ill-suited for; some workers had suffered from long-distance marriages for long; and a good number of workers were still being unemployed, etc. Though the ultra-left trend of thought led by the "Gang of Four" and Lin Biao ate mainly to blame for, they were also closely connected to the absence of market mechanism in allocation of labor. Malpractices such as pulling strings or nepotism in allocation and use of labor are not only incompatible with the nature of socialist economic system, but so feudal and backward that they were even rarely seen in capitalist commodity economy.

In order to solve these problems in allocation and use of labor and try to bring out the best in people, we should use selective hiring and allow people to choose occupations of one's own accord under the guidance of state planning. Enterprises are empowered to hire people selectively through labor departments according to their own needs in production and technology under the guidance of state planning and pursuant to national laws. They should also have the right to lay off redundant workers, who would be transferred to labor departments for redistribution or vocational training for the sake of future job placement. Those unemployed workers' living expenses during their job displacement should be covered by social security funds. Individuals do need consider the overall needs of society, in the meanwhile they should also be fairly free to choose occupations. It should be noted that freedom to choose occupations is an important and integral part of every individual's free development, which makes all types of free development possible just like what founders of scientific theory of communism ever put.

In the stage of socialism, especially in the current period when our productive forces are so underdeveloped, it is almost impossible to let workers choose their occupations as freely as their equivalents in the stage of communism. However, socialism still tacitly acknowledges everyone's labor power as their natural right, and that under the policy of distribution according to work, the costs of simple reproduction and even expanded reproduction of labor power (including upbringing, training and further education etc.) still need to be paid by workers and their families. Therefore, we have to admit that each worker does own their labor power to some extent, and thus people are allowed to choose their work freely in this sense, which will not only help better fulfill the principle of distribution according to work and ability but also encourage people to bring their talents into full play and even benefit the development of the whole society.

Surely, some degree of freedom to choose occupations does not mean tolerance of free flow of labor force between enterprises, sectors, regions, or between urban and rural areas. We should adopt economic means instead of administrative or legal ones to control the flow of labor force. For example, workers should be given grants for long uninterrupted service to improve retention; In order to make workers who work in remote areas hold on to their jobs, we should take some measures to differentiate wages and to improve their living conditions. Besides, given an abundant labor force and lower labor costs in our country, we can also be flexible in creating more job opportunities to suite the needs of market both at home and abroad, such as expanding the service sector and increasing various export of labor services etc., which will not only place those unemployed, but also improve the supply side, increase foreign exchange earnings and upgrade our technologies.

In the above section, we have already discussed how to use the market mechanism in socialist planned economy to strike a balance between production, supply and sale of commodities and realize better allocation and use of manpower, financial and material resources. There are two comprehensive issues deserving our particular attention, i.e., price and competition. In the following part, I would like to make a brief and general analysis of them.

The first issue is price. In China, the regulatory role of the law of value in socialist production had long been denied and any economic categories related to the law of value were reduced to unimportant tools or means of accounting. It was believed that the price should be fixed for long and therefore the policy of a relatively fixed planned price was turned into a long-term price freeze. However, as our economic life and objective factors affecting pricing decisions keep changing, prices would inevitably change too. As a result, the policy of price freeze will lead to gradual deviations of fixed prices from real values of commodities and thus objective laws would be violated.

For example, changes in productivity tend to cause product value to rise or decline, which is a fundamental cause of price fluctuation. As we all know, productivity growth varies from sector to sector. Currently, our industrial productivity grows faster than agricultural one. However, due to long-term fixed prices, price relations failed to reflect any real changes in productivity growth as well as product value. Our current price scissors between industrial products and agricultural produce are not completely due to historical reasons. If industrial productivity grows faster than agricultural one, price freeze would surely lead to the widening of price scissors, because price relations between industrial products and agricultural produce are relative.

Besides, supply-demand relations are another major factor affecting prices. But fixed prices can reflect no changes in supply and demand, which helps to explain why the problem of supply-demand imbalance of many products remained unsolved for long. In order to maintain the prices of products unchanged, our government has subsidized some enterprises to compensate them for their losses caused by extremely low prices. Even though it did help to maintain production and bring stability to people's life for some time, it was just a stopgap which would in the long run hamper the improvement of business operation and management and the development of production.

Therefore, we need develop production and increase the supply of goods with a view to solving the problem of supply falling short of demand at its source. In the past, we had paid a very high price to keep the price unchanged. For instance, massive tickets and queuing policies ended up with even distribution and poverty, rather than a rapid growth in production or supply. And what's more, it tended to cause a vicious cycle: whatever goods were supplied with restricted quantity and fixed prices would be less produced due to no necessary incentives, and hence such goods would be even harder to get than before. Although the government had repeatedly issued planned targets, they still made no big difference. Many facts have proved that planned targets would be hard to achieve if prices are not reasonable enough. The widening gap between prices and real values of many products has already hindered the development of some industries especially agriculture, raw materials and fuel industries as well as the balance between agriculture, light industry and heavy industry.

In order to improve such situation, we should act in the spirit of the Third Plenary Session of the 11th Central Committee to reduce price scissors between industrial products and farm produce through continued efforts to adjust price relations between products from major economic sectors; besides, planned prices should be allowed to fluctuate within a certain range, which is actually a matter as to whether prices will be recognized as part of the market mechanism. Price fluctuations within a range is conducive to the adjustment of supply-demand relations and promotion of development, which is one of the ways to make good use of the market mechanism under the guidance of state planning. Surely, it does not mean a total abandonment of price control. Rather, whatever ranges prices are allowed to float within must be guided by planning. It is more necessary for the state to set and control, on the uniform basis, the prices of major consumer goods closely linked with people's lives and key means of production having a great bearing on the cost of production in a particular period of time.

Besides, we are supposed to figure out how prices are made in order to know economic performances of every sector. Here, it would not be discussed in great detail. It has been agreed upon that profit rate can be used to evaluate performances of an enterprise or sector, but every product must have a price that can be compared with each other. And such price is based on production price. Only in this way can we adopt a unified standard for sectors and enterprises varying in technology, equipment and the amount of capital to reflect in an all-round way their economic performances through different real profit rates. Besides, only in this way can we determine where to invest and how to allocate social labor rationally so as to create more favorable conditions for the development of socialist economy.

The second issue concerns competition. So long as commodity economy exists, there will be a competition. A certain degree of competition and price fluctuations within a certain range are interconnected and mutually conditioned, which are both part and parcel of the market mechanism. Without price fluctuations or differences, there will be no competition. And in reverse order, if there is no competition, floating prices and differentiated prices would not be truly guaranteed, and hence the law of market supply and demand will not function normally, and the law of value can not be truly fulfilled, either. Friedrich Engels said, "Only if through competition-driven price fluctuations can the law of value be fulfilled and thus commodity values will be truly determined by socially necessary labor time. [1]

In socialist planned economy, we have to introduce some degree of competition if we want to use the market mechanism to regulate the allocation of material, financial and manpower resources. All in all, production, supply and sale of

1 *Marx and Engels Collected Works*, vol. 21, Beijing: People's Publishing House, 1965, p.215.

products according to the needs of market, investment based on effects, allocation of labor based on the principle of selective hiring, tolerance of price fluctuation within a target range according to market supply and demand cannot do without competition.

When it comes to competition, people tend to associate competition with capitalism, especially those bad consequences brought about by capitalism. In effect, competition is not exclusive to capitalism, but an economic category of commodity economy. As early as in the slave society and feudal society, competition had already emerged along with the development of commodity production and exchanges. For example, the handcraft guild system in the feudal society was partly designed to restrain competition. If there was no competition at that time, how come people designed a way to restrain it? Later, guilds disappeared gradually with the development of capitalism, which suggests in a sense that capitalism is a process of popularizing competition with the prevalence of commodity relations. Besides, from a historical perspective, competition in capitalist commodity economy also had positive effects, for example, it did ever promote huge developments of capitalist productive forces. Since in the socialist system, it is necessary to have commodity production and exchanges, we should not deny the role of competition; otherwise, it would mean to deny the objective existence of commodity economy and the significance of the law of value. In the socialist society, enterprises emerged as commodity producers and are also regarded in this way. The issues as to whether the quality and variety of commodities are popular among consumers, whether individual labor time is more than socially necessary labor time, and how large the gap is, etc. all affect material interests of enterprises and employees. Competition among enterprises is conducive to upgrading technologies, enhancing operational management, reducing consumption, raising productivity, improving quality and variety of products.

Due to competition, the operational results of enterprises can be tested by market, the needs of consumers for cheap and a variety of commodities have been satisfied, and the development of social productive forces have been promoted. If we call efforts to seek more material interests an internal motivation, competition between enterprises would be an external one for their development. If no competition is allowed, all the business of the same kind would be monopolized by just one enterprise. As a result, commodities will surely decline in both variety and quality, and the waste in both production and circulation will keep increasing. To sum up, competition induces progress and monopoly leads to stagnation and recession, which in some sense also applies to socialism. Competition is allowed among enterprises owned by the whole people; besides, it is even more necessary for competition to take place among collective-owned enterprises, and even between collective-owned enterprises and those owned by the whole people. Besides, it should also be allowed in open markets within legal framework. Such competition not only helps to increase the supply of goods attractive in both price and quality in the market and the income of farmers, but benefits enterprises owned by the whole people a lot by urging them to improve management and service quality.

Surely there are fundamental differences between competition in the socialist market and that in the capitalist market, among which the most basic one is that competition under socialist public ownership is based on the same fundamental interests, whereas that under capitalist private ownership is a zero-sum game between parties with opposing fundamental interests. Rather than resist any cooperation, competition in the socialist market is based on and combined with cooperation. Therefore, it must be carried out according to socialist laws and under the guidance of state planning. Only in this way can those at the rear be encouraged to catch up with the front runners and the latter's edge be even more sharpened in the socialist society; moreover, only in this way can socialist countries guard against any bad consequences caused by capitalist competitions such as anarchy, income polarization and unemployment etc.

Competition in the socialist society and socialist emulation have both similarities and differences. They both are means to urge those at the rear to catch up with the front runners and make the latter's edge even more sharpened than before. However, socialist emulation is not necessarily linked with material interests of participants, and therefore will not lead to any elimination of outdated capacity. In sharp contrast, competition in the socialist society is inevitably linked with competitors' material interests, which might result in some outdated capacity being eliminated. Those loss-making enterprises that failed to maintain simple reproduction in the long run due to non-objective reasons and proved to be ill-suited to the needs of the market in competition have to be knocked out, that is to say, they should be either closed, transferred or merged; besides, negligent personnel must be held accountable for material losses. Employees from these enterprises would be offered other jobs through state labor departments, and would not be unemployed just like workers from bankrupt enterprises in capitalist states. However, before they are re-employed, their income cannot rival that of employees from enterprises which function normally, because the former's material interests will have to be affected by the outcome of their original enterprises. Therefore, this is also a strong economic means to encourage all personnel to be more concerned about the fate of their enterprises. However, in order to make employees bear economic responsibilities for any economic consequences, employees should be empowered with real democratic rights in management of enterprises.

In consequence, the market can play a constructive role in many fields in the socialist planned economy. For instance, the market mechanism can be fully used to benefit socialist development in terms of production, supply and sale of goods, management of funds, and allocation of labor, etc. It is very necessary to allow for price fluctuations within a range and some degree of competition. Proper use of the market mechanism will help us achieve the planned targets, utilize all kinds of social resources effectively and reasonably and satisfy various social needs.

3. On intensifying economic planning while using the market mechanism

Due to the ill influence of the ultra-left trend, people had been overlooking for long the role of market in socialist economic development and refusing to use the market mechanism to serve socialist planned economy, which was the wrong tendency prevalent in the past. We must strongly fight against such ill tendency, otherwise the positive role of market will not be brought into full play, and thus planning and market will not be combined in a better way. However, in order to deal with the relations between planning and market correctly, we must guard against and oppose another tendency, that is, over-exaggeration of the market's role and neglect or even denial of the role of planning. It should be noted that such tendency did ever exist both at home and abroad. For example, some people ever oversimplified planned economy as bureaucratic economy, believing that people have to choose one: either market or bureaucracy; some people mistakenly regarded planned management as exclusively administrative management, etc. All in all, they all regarded planned economy as something bad.

To sum up, those who opposed planning to market and denied the necessity of their combination are based on two extreme grounds. In one extreme, some people favored one-sidedly planning and denied the role of market, believing that everything should be planned by higher authority and this is socialist economy. In another extreme, some people favored one-sidedly market and denied the role of planning, believing that social needs can only be reflected through market needs, and that planning is the tool of bureaucracy hindering the satisfaction of market needs. Obviously, the second view is also not right. We believe that planning must be valued in socialist economy; especially when we reinterpret the role of market in socialist economy, we cannot afford to overlook the guiding role of state or social planning. Planning whose role cannot be ignored during the use of market mechanism has nothing in common with bureaucracy. Only the so-called "planned management" dictated by administrative orders or "will of superiors" is bureaucracy. Since the planned management we're discussing here is the one combined with the use of market mechanism, it surely can't be mixed up with bureaucracy at all.

Why should we intensify the guiding role of state planning while using the market? Because the market under socialist public ownership is fundamentally different from the one under capitalist private ownership. The latter functions spontaneously and blindly in the anarchy of capitalist production. Marx pointed out, "The essence of bourgeois society consists precisely in this, that *a priori* there is no conscious social regulation of production. The rational and naturally necessary asserts itself only as a blindly working average."[1] Even though market exists in the socialist economy, the essential nature of socialist economy is not anarchy, but the conscious social regulation of reproduction, i.e., planned regulation. Just like what Friedrich Engels pointed out, "With this recognition, at last, of the real nature of the productive forces of today, the social anarchy of production gives place to a social regulation of production upon a definite plan, according to the needs of the community and of each individual." [2]

Seen from the practice of socialist development, such planned regulation also applies to the market under the socialist system. Therefore, the market in the socialist economy can not function spontaneously without the guidance of state planning or regulation by planning. Even though we should strive to develop socialist commodity production and make better use of market to work for the socialist cause, we, no laissez-fairism at all, would not allow "the invisible hand", proposed by Adam Smith, to dictate our economy, because it was designed to benefit the interests of the bourgeoisie; whereas material interest relations in the socialist economy are characterized by the combination between individual/local interests and overall interests, with the former being subordinate to the latter. These relations can only be dealt with properly through regulation by state or social planning. Consequently, socialist economic development cannot do without the guidance of state planning.

As mentioned before, buyers as major agents tend to make choices based on their own preferences; production units tend to make decisions based on their own

1 *Marx to Kugelmann In Hanover*, London, July 11, 1868; *Marx and Engels Collected Works*, vol. 4, Beijing: People's Publishing House, 1972, p.369.

2 *Marx and Engels Collected Works*, vol. 3, Beijing: People's Publishing House, 1972, p.319.

interests; however, all these decisions are not necessarily in the interests of the society as a whole. Accordingly, allocation and use of manpower, financial and material resources based on their own free choices are not necessarily rational, economical or in line with the requirement of social development. In order to speed up the realization of socialist industrialization and modernization, social industrial structure and distribution of productive forces need to be radically changed in a short period of time. However, the need of such rapid changes in both industrial structure and distribution of productive forces would probably not be satisfied if every economic agent is so free to make their own choices. For instance, problems concerning the overall situation of socialist economic development cannot be solved by the market mechanism alone, but in the meantime state or social planning must also be needed. Just imagine how hard and slow it would be to rationalize the distribution of productive forces, especially in the remote and backward areas, if there is no state planning and economy is totally dictated by the market!

Besides, in socialist economy, differences in objective conditions such as natural conditions, market conditions, equipment etc. tend to give rise to income differences. If such income differential is totally regulated and distributed by market forces without any guidance from state planning, the material interest gap between production units would be expanded irrationally and thus the socialist principle of distribution would be thus violated. In a broader sense, neither too large income gap nor egalitarianism should be tolerated in socialism; besides, in order to prevent indiscriminate egalitarianism from happening again, we need carry out differentiating policies by encouraging some people to get rich first and then to help others to catch up so that the ultimate goal of common prosperity would be achieved, which is a way to encourage everyone to move forward rather than draw back. That is to say, in some circumstances material interest gap needs to be widened, whereas sometimes narrowed (as far as the whole stage of socialism is concerned, the gap should be narrowed). However, it is obvious to all that market alone cannot succeed in making such due adjustments.

Both economic behaviors beneficial to local interests but detrimental to the overall interests, and economic behaviors damaging local interests but beneficial to the overall interests must be regulated by social planning. For example, as for some production units, efforts to protect the environment and find solutions to pollution nuisance might increase their expense and reduce their income. And it would be very hard for the market alone to deal with these problems very well. Let me take another example, standardization of products will undoubtedly be conducive to promoting specialization of production, improving productivity and using resources rationally, but some producers might deliberately hinder the realization of standardization in order to gain advantageous positions technically in a competition-friendly social climate. Even if competition among syndicalist cooperative enterprises is carried out under socialist public ownership, it would still possibly lead to anarchy and other bad consequences, because it is not under unified control of the society. Therefore, while trying to bring the constructive role of competition into play, we must have unified social planning to guard against any possible negative consequences competition might bring about.

All in all, in order to keep our economic development in the right socialist direction, to guarantee coordinated development of all economic sectors and regions, to safeguard public interests of the whole society and to deal with material interest relations concerning all aspects correctly, we must strengthen the regulatory role of state planning while using the market mechanism. Some people ever vividly described relations between planning and market in this way: as far as decision-making is concerned, state planning can be compared to a person standing on the top of the mountain, who fails to see everything clearly but get a bird's view; whereas market can be compared to another person standing inside the valley, who fails to get the whole picture but see very clearly things in its vicinity including itself. In a sense, this analogy does make sense: leading organs of social and economic planning tend to consider the overall interests, whereas commodity producers and consumers mainly focus on individual, partial and local interests. The principle of socialist countries in dealing with the relationship between the country, collective and individuals is to make overall consideration of every party concerned duly and avoid taking sides. Therefore, we need attach great importance to both market mechanism and unified planning and never take sides; the guiding role of planning should never be neglected while planning is being combined with market.

So, what should we do to intensify planned management of the national economy and bring the guiding role of unified planning into full play? The answer to this question is closely connected with people's understanding of planned economy. For rather long in the past, it had been believed that only a top-down planning system in which mandatory planned targets were issued by the state can be called socialist planned economy. Besides, it was often held that the more inclusive mandatory plans were and the more targets the state issued, the larger role state planning would play in economic management. As a result, when it comes to strengthening the role of unified planning or centralized leadership, people tended to associate that with the tightening of state control on the management of enterprises as well as property rights and human rights. Accordingly, economic leading organs overstepped their own position and began to take charge of things that were supposed to be done by local governments or enterprises, only to leave grass-root units and enterprises no leeway to make their own decisions, which would obviously not benefit the socialist economic development. In response to this, the resolution adopted in the Third Plenary Session of the 11th Central Committee had already criticized the problem of over-centralization. Actually, such traditional perception of planned economy is closely linked with the idea of opposing the use of market mechanism. So, what should we do to strengthen the guiding role of planning since we've realized the great necessity of combining planning with market and decided to make good use of the market mechanism to benefit socialist development?

First of all, the focus of planning should be shifted onto long-term plans especially five-year plans so as to solve strategic economic problems and set major targets or key proportions crucial to our national economic development, such as the proportion of accumulation to consumption in national income, the scale of capital construction, the direction of investment, key construction projects, the technological level for key industrial products and agricultural produce, and the extent of improvement of people's living standard etc. Besides, the Five-Year Plan should also list annual targets, which can be adapted into annual plans with slight changes, but it should mainly concentrate on policies and measures to fulfill these plans.

State plans should improve the scientific forecasting of national economic development, provide more information, and strengthen the guidance of planning for enterprises and local economic activities. Based on market conditions, each enterprise should tap into their full potentials and make their own plans autonomously in accordance with state plans. But the guiding role of state planning mustn't be underestimated, as each enterprise cannot see clearly the whole picture of national economic development as well as its major direction, which however have a great bearing on market, the very thing that these enterprises rely on to make their own development plans.

Therefore, in order to judge the situation of market as precisely as possible, the enterprises must also rely on the information or guidance from state planning. The more rational and practical state plans are, the more reliable these plans would be in guiding the economic decision-making and behaviors of enterprises, and the more willingly these enterprises would base their economic decisions and behaviors on state plans. In this way, the authority of state plans would be improved as well. In contrast, he who has any senses can see very clearly that subjective plans made by the superiors on impulse are missions impossible. No matter how "solemn" or "mandatory" these orders seem to be, they are just lacking in any real authority. Aren't our lessons in this aspect bitter enough? Therefore, as for leading organs in economic planning, they bear even more responsibilities than before to work out rational national economic plans to offer reliable guidance for economic activities of enterprises.

In order to improve the real authority of state plans and to combine them with grassroots enterprise plans in a better way, the state should at first allow enterprises enough leeway to make their own development plans and then try to make state plans through coordination at different levels. If imbalance between production and sale or the problem concerning joint capital or labor collaboration could be solved through horizontal cooperation agreements between enterprises or firms in the market, they needn't be submitted to higher authority for solutions. Only those problems that cannot be solved by enterprises or firms alone or collaboratively should be submitted to higher authority and finally to the top one for solution after having gone all the way through the hierarchy. So, on the part of grassroots enterprises, they would get away from tedious administrative formalities; and leading state organs wouldn't bother to attend to unnecessary administrative matters any more. Such way would spare the latter a lot of time and energy so that they could be more committed to studying and making policies and major development plans concerning the overall situation of the national economy.

In order to ensure the coordinated development of social production and the achievement of goals set by state plans, one crucial issue is that we should fully implement each economic policy to guide economic activities. Those policies include pricing policies, taxation policies, tariff policies, credit policies, investment policies, income distribution policies and foreign trade and exchange policies etc. The state should use such economic policies to encourage production or construction necessary for the society and place restrictions on those that the society doesn't need that much or not at all with a view to facilitating those enterprises' fulfillment of tasks prescribed in state plans.

For instance, in order to overcome the current situation of raw material and fuel industries lagging behind the processing industry and speed up the development of the former, the state must give green lights to these industries in the implementation of economic policies, such as granting them preferential loans, adjusting prices and reducing taxes etc. to make them have good prospects of gain. In contrast, in order to restrain common machine tool industries from expanding, the state could set a credit limit, charge high interests, levy high taxes and reduce the prices of products etc. Therefore, regulation through economic policies will encourage those enterprises to take not only their own economic interests but the requirements of state plans into consideration while arranging their economic activities.

Consequently, the guidance of economic policies for economic development and the achievement of goals set by state plans through economic means is closely related to the use of market mechanism. In some sense, economic polices serve as a bridge between state planning and market mechanism.

Some people often worried about the use of market mechanism in socialism, fearing that various choices made by tens of millions of commodity manufacturers and consumers as well as their varying economic behaviors can not be put well under control so that they would deviate from the socialist road and undermine the coordinated development of national economy. But such doubts could be removed by the aforementioned guidance from planning or policies, planned coordination and some restrictions on the use of market mechanism. Besides, the state should improve the legal system especially economic legislation and establish a supervision system in which all forms of supervision by the masses and society are to be widely encouraged so as to coordinate market relations and guide the development of national economy as a whole. It would not be discussed in great detail here; rather, this paper would just analyze briefly the supervision on bank bookkeeping, an important tool of planned management, which was ever repeatedly mentioned by Karl Marx and Friedrich Engels.

Karl Marx said, "After the abolition of the capitalist mode of production, but still retaining social production, the determination of value continues to prevail in the sense that the regulation of labor-time and the distribution of social labor among the various production groups, ultimately the book-keeping encompassing all this, become more essential than ever."[1] Vladimir Lenin ever said, "A single

1 *Marx and Engels: Collected Works*, vol. 25, Beijing: People's Publishing House, 1974, p.963.

State Bank, the biggest one, with branches in every rural district, in every factory, will constitute as much as nine-tenths of the *socialist* apparatus. This will be country wide *book-keeping*, country-wide *accounting* of the production and distribution of goods, this will be, so to speak, some thing in the nature of the *skeleton* of socialist society."[1] In a commodity economy, strict and sensitive supervision on bank book-keeping will be needed more than ever, so that the society could keep up with each relatively independent commodity manufacturer's economic behaviors and put them under control, and take measures to stop them from deviating from the socialist road and state plans. We should establish a bookkeeping supervision system based on our national conditions in the future economic restructuring as what Karl Marx suggested in an effort to promote a more effective combination between market and planning in socialist development.

Even though the socialist economic management system is not all about the relations between planning and market, the latter is indeed a crucial issue concerning the overall situation of the national economy which involves almost every aspect of socialist economic management and many fundamental theoretical issues of socialism in political economics. Currently the academic world of economics is mainly focused on defining some relevant concepts and elaborating on the necessity of combining planning with market, which are no doubt very important. However, our studies and discussions are still lagged far behind practical needs. Both our party's shift of working focus and major tasks of economic restructuring call on us to act urgently to further explore ways in both theory and practice to deal with the relations between planning and market properly in the right direction of socialism. Given its extreme complexity, the problem cannot be solved overnight; but instead, it needs to be fixed step by step in certain conditions. For starters, we need straighten out the economic order

1 Vladimir Lenin, *Lenin's Collected Works,* vol. 26, Beijing: People's Publishing House, 1959, p.87.

and then make plans for key proportions gradually. We should keep making adjustments while moving forward in an effort to make further progress and even more adjustments, find ways to carry out reform and prepare well for a comprehensive reform in the future. Only after we have undergone the whole process of adjustment, rectification and reform can we succeed in handling the relations between planning and market properly.

(This article was co-written with Zhao Renwei and the abstract was ever published in *Economic Research Journal*, No. 5, 1979.)

A Further Study on the Relations between Planning and Market

Regulation by market forces is not for expediency

Since the Third Plenary Session of the 11th Central Committee of the CPC, many local governments and departments, upon the Central Committee's instruction of acting according to the economic law, have initially reformed the economic system in the current phase. One of the major reforms is that production and circulation of some products should be regulated by market forces in the condition of socialist planned economy. This reform, along with other reforms such as the expansion of the decision-making power of the enterprise, has already had a huge impact on the invigoration of economy.

Actually, market is not new at all. As state plans cannot cover everything, there will always be some products whose production and circulation are not included in state plans. Instead, production and circulation of these products are fulfilled by enterprises through purchases and sales in the market. However, due to ideological and theoretical limitations at that time, regulation by market forces was not legitimized in the socialist economy, for our economy as a whole was still exclusively regulated by planning. As a result, bureaucracy in economic life kept increasing and the economic structure got even more rigid, with everything lacking in vitality and vigor. Last spring (1979), economic theoretical circles made the first step to break these traditional chains; at the same time some progress was also made in practical work: it was proposed that in practical work we should combine planning with market to regulate economy by mainly relying on planning and giving full play to the role of market. Since then, market began to play a part in economic regulation. Within more than one year, we've managed to crack a hole in the system of planned distribution (of means of production) and state monopoly on purchase and sale (of means of subsistence), and begun to take advantage of the market mechanism to regulate production and circulation of products.

The use of market forces as a means of regulating economy has benefited our economy in the following ways. First, it has made up for the deficiency of planning in the era of national economic adjustment; second, the most important of all, some progress has been made in overcoming the chronic problem of separation of production from demand. Since then, some improvements have been made in this regard. Third, it has given rise to competition and the expansion of the decision-making power of the enterprise and thus provided these enterprises with both internal and external incentives to improve their operation, management and product quality, increase the variety of goods, reduce the cost, and improve customer service. As a result, much gratifying progress has been made in these aspects and the past time when enterprises would only act with much prodding or even indifferently will never return. Such favorable turn has just started and later on the impact will be felt even more as market plays an increasingly large part in economic regulation.

After many years of confinement, market has finally been legitimately acknowledged in our economic arena, but it is still quite new. Instead of being fully embraced, it was still questioned or not taken readily by some people. For example, those who have been used to taking orders from higher authority tended to feel ill at ease once enterprises are given no planned tasks and encouraged to seek business opportunities in the market on their own. "Having worked in the factory for 30 years, we have never heard of letting the factory earn its own bread," grumbled they. Some people, who believed that regulation by market forces was just an expedient measure so as to make up for the deficiency of planning in the period of national economic adjustment, are still dreaming of the day when the period of economic adjustment comes to an end three or five years later, planning will be good and mature enough so that any regulation by market forces would be abolished! Some people thought that regulation by market forces and especially competition are the very reasons that "lead to waste and anarchy", and therefore they suggested that regulation by market forces had better be abolished as soon as possible. Their partial opinions were mainly based on the following ill trends after market and competition mechanism was introduced: an excessively large gap of profit retention has emerged between industries and enterprises; some regions and sectors have begun to make some protective measures for their own benefits; unnecessary repetitive production or construction has increased; some enterprises tended to block the access of others to their technology in order to keep their edge etc.

We have to admit that these phenomena did exist during economic regulation by market forces, but they were not necessarily caused by the introduction of market. Rather, many of them had already existed before that. These problems were largely attributed to old administrative management system in some regions or sectors and especially the unreasonable price system that failed to be radically changed in the new reform. Besides, we still lack in specific guidance as to how to carry out a reform. All these problems arose while we were moving forward. If we carry forward the reform step by step, keep drawing lessons and provide more guidance, these problems will be solved.

Therefore, it is unnecessary to have misgivings about regulation by market forces. Initial practice of reform has proved that regulation by market forces under the guidance of planning is obviously more superior to regulation by mandatory planning. Take production and circulation of mechanical and electronic products as an example. As for those regulated by market forces, there were almost no unsalable products and thus no factory overstock (just to the opposite, it helps to reduce overstock caused by regulation by mandatory planning), and supply contracts were fulfilled fairly well thanks to a rather good balance between production and demand; in sharp contrast, as far as products whose production and distribution are still planned by the state are concerned, their overstock got even worse and their supply contracts were not fulfilled as well as those through self-marketing strategies. If we abolish regulation by market forces and revert to the old path of regulation by planning, problems like separation of production from demand, low efficiency and a huge waste of financial, material and human resources etc. would remain unsolved for long and thus hinder severely our modernization drive. To summarize, regulation by market forces under the guidance of state planning was absolutely not an expedient policy in the period of economic adjustment, but an integral part of our future economic restructuring instead. We must persist with regulation by market forces, because socialist economy in the current phase is not only a planned economy, but has properties of commodity economy.

A buyer's market should be formed

What should we do to make the market mechanism and regulation by market forces continue to work for a rather long period of time extending from the period of readjustment and become an integral part of a new planned economic system? Seen from experience of initial reform, the use of market mechanism and market forces as a means of economic regulation needs to satisfy certain ideological and material conditions. If we cannot abandon a series of traditional ideas (e.g., means of production are not commodities, the law of value cannot regulate the economy, planning conflicts with market etc.), regulation by market forces cannot be carried out smoothly. In order to remove all kinds of doubts and further implement regulation by market forces under the guidance of planning, we need, on the one hand, hold more in-depth discussions on theoretical issues concerning planning and market in socialist economy, trying to integrate its theoretical results with practice of reform success and make it publicized through wider educational campaigns. On the other hand, we've learned from over one year's reform experience that if overall equilibrium is not valued, if plans allow for no leeway, and if commodities are still in short supply, it would still be very hard for market to play a regulatory role. Now let's check it out.

Why did some enterprises in certain industries resort to market to regulate economic activities during this period of time? To put it simply, because enterprises were assigned less tasks according to state plans in the period of readjustment. Let's still take the mechanical and electronic industry as an example. Due to the policy of economic readjustment, in 1979, state plans were drastically reduced and refund increased sharply accordingly; enterprises can hardly feed on tasks planned by the state, and therefore, they had to resort to market for more opportunities. Unexpectedly, a number of unsalable products were thereafter sold out and enterprises didn't operate under capacity any more. In this way, many enterprises' production picked up very soon after they linked production with demand.

Take Ningjiang Machine Tools Plant in Sichuan Province as an example, it is capable of manufacturing 500-meter machine tools annually, however, targets are just set for 260 by state plans. Given the circumstances, this plant emancipated their mind by carrying out boldly marketing campaigns, with the result that its annual capacity was increased to over 600. Mechanical and electronic industry was not the only one to benefit from such transformation. Many enterprises began to do their business through purchase and sale in the market. Take textile industry as another example. In early 1979, many textile enterprises suffered from factory overstock, with a decrease in purchase and shortage of funds; some were forced to cut or even suspend production resulting in an inevitable decrease in output. These problems were not mitigated until market began to play a regulatory role in economic management. Take the metallurgical industry as a third example, a portion of steel products whose purchases and sales used to be monopolized by the state have also begun to be regulated by market forces. As planning failed to distribute some steel products and material supply departments refused to purchase them, these enterprises had no alternative choices but resort to market. In this way, the monopoly of material supply departments on steel products was broken, and some steel products were thereby great in both demand and supply.

These cases have one thing in common, that is, these enterprises all began to carry out regulation by market forces after having been cornered by the policy of economic readjustment, which aimed mainly to overcome a serious imbalance between supply and demand. Accordingly, some impractically high speed must be slowed and social demand mainly propelled by capital construction investment must be reduced. As a result, products would be in excess supply and excess production capacity would be formed. Therefore, these enterprises had to resort to market to seek more business opportunities; otherwise, their profit retention will be affected and thus even salaries of their employees would not be guaranteed, so much so that the expansion of decision-making power of pilot enterprises would end up with failure.

In this sense, such policy of economic readjustment has just created a very favorable condition for regulation by market forces. It reveals to us that we should continue to use market forces as a means of regulating economy. Not only in the period of economic readjustment, but also for rather long we must avoid setting impractically high targets, which would lead to many shortfalls in the national economy and a tight economy; rather, we should make practical plans, leave more leeway, and allow for rational overcapacity so as to make our national economy advance with ease in a steady pace.

Not long ago, a foreign economist studying economic reforms of East Europe proposed during his visit in China that decentralization is incompatible with tight economy. That is to say, in the economic restructuring, decentralization is unlikely to be achieved in a tight economy. A tight economy tends to expose the weakness of national economy, and thus the country would have to employ administrative means to intervene in the economy to help solve these problems. If so, the reform would go in the opposite direction and a vicious cycle would be thus formed. I think that this analysis makes some sense. With the economy exclusively regulated by planning, almost every economic decision was made by the state; after the introduction of market mechanism and the use of market forces as a means of regulating economy, the economic decision-making power has to be duly relegated to enterprises and individual laborers. However, it is hard to achieve in an imbalanced economy or in a situation when supply of all products falls short of demand. In that circumstance, the country needs to invest limited funds and materials in key sectors or projects (weak links), and set quotas in the order of importance and urgency. In this way, the state will neither possibly relax its grip on mandatory production, monopoly of purchase and sale of products, and planned allocation etc., nor probably loosen its control on the prices of means of subsistence and means of production, and therefore enterprises and individuals would not make their own choices based on market changes. As a result, the market mechanism would be severely restrained and thus the regulatory role of market forces would be drastically reduced.

At the same time, in the tight economy with supply falling short of demand, market relations are usually dominated by suppliers or sellers, whereas consumers or buyers do not have the say and usually have to be dictated by suppliers or sellers. Given the circumstance, suppliers tend to neglect the needs of consumers and thus pay no particular attention to the quality or variety of products and customer service, just like what an old proverb says, "the emperor's daughter need never fret about finding a husband". That is to say, shops with a variety of goods never lack customers. So, in such circumstance there is no competition between sellers, which however is a necessary condition for regulation by market forces. It would be possible for sellers to compete with each other only if supply exceeds demand, when the market is no longer dominated by sellers and when buyers can enjoy deservedly their consumer rights.

It shows that if social production exceeds direct demand, and supply exceeds purchasing power, a buyer's or consumer's market will be established and thus regulation by market forces will possibly be carried out normally. Surely, just like everything else, there is also a limit on the buyer's market, that is, as for how much production exceeds direct social demand and how much supply exceeds demand, there should be a limit, which ensures necessary competition between sellers and rational overcapacity. If the limit is overstepped, overproduction would lead to a waste too. So, production exceeding slightly direct need is fundamentally different from overproduction in the capitalist economy due to insufficient purchasing power. The principle of production exceeding slightly direct need and supply demand is not only necessary for regulation of production and circulation of some particular products by market forces, but even more necessary for the national economy as a whole.

Only if aggregate supply exceeds slightly aggregate demand, we would possibly have a restricted buyer's market in the national economy and provide a favorable condition for the combination of planning and market. In order to achieve this, we have to keep purchasing power slightly lower than national income, which is exactly the primary issue that the state aims to solve while making macroeconomic policies and striving to achieve an overall equilibrium through planning. If we continue to maintain excessively large investment in capital construction and overextend the national economy, it would produce chain reaction and thus make aggregate demand expand so rapidly that it would far exceed aggregate supply, with the result that a very big gap would be formed between production and use of national income. If so, the restricted buyer's market would not appear and regulation by market forces cannot function normally either.

Therefore, we should leave some leeway for national economic growth and have alternative plans for national economic development, which is crucial to regulation by market forces and invigoration of economy. To sum up, regulation by market forces in the socialist economy will not function without the guidance of state macroeconomic plans, and what's more, it should be based on correct macroeconomic policies and overall economic equilibrium through planning.

Plates? Penetration? Colloid?

In 1979, a great breakthrough was made while the academic world of economics held discussions about the law of value. Having abandoned the old conception that planning is incompatible with market, the academic world reached a consensus that planning and market can be combined in the socialist economy. However, as for how to combine them, opinions were quite divided. Should they be joined together like two plates? Should they penetrate into each other so that there is something of each in the other? After heated discussions, many people were persuaded into accepting the latter. I was also one of them. However, in the following two circumstances, inter-penetration also differs slightly. In the first circumstance, the overall national economy falls into two parts, regulation by planning and regulation by market forces, but their boundaries are quite blurred. That is to say, there is something of each in the other; In the second circumstance, the national economy does not fall into two parts any more, but instead planning and market are already merged into a colloid. That is to say, the market mechanism will function under the guidance of unified state planning. So, which one should we adopt?

Our practice of structural reform in recent two years has shown that at the very beginning, market was usually introduced as another means of economic regulation aside from mandatory planning which used to be exclusively adopted to regulate economy. Therefore, planning and market are still combined like two plates joining together so far, which is still necessary given the current circumstance; besides, it is already a big step forward compared with the past when planning was exclusively adopted to regulate economic activities. For example, over one year later, means of production have begun to be regarded as a type of commodity and gradually entered the market, which is one of the significant progress.

When enterprises produce and sell products according to market needs, such economic activities are called “regulation by market forces”; when production, purchase and distribution of some products are determined by state mandatory planning, it is called “regulation by planning”. Percentage is usually used to reflect their ratio in the combination. For instance, in the gross value of industrial output in Jiangsu Province in 1979, regulation by market forces accounted for 40%, and regulation by planning 60%. Here, the “regulation by market forces” refers to the purchase and sale of products based on self-marketing strategies, whereas “regulation by planning” refers to the fulfillment of economic tasks assigned by state mandatory planning. This is a typical example of plate-joining model.

The plate-joining model refers to a combination in which planning and market exist side by side, and it will continue to be used for rather long. However, it is far from enough to just have the plate-joining combination; rather, we should also try to combine them from within, namely, to make them penetrate into each other. On the one hand, when blind regulation occurs due to limitations of market, the state should intensify the guidance of planning and consciously use economic and administrative means to regulate the economy. That is to say, we should make planning penetrate into wherever regulation by market forces works, trying to make the latter meet the requirements of sate macroeconomic planning. On the other hand, we should also strengthen economic levers such as price, taxation, and credit etc. to help solve problems caused by mandatory planning such as separation of production from sale etc. In other words, we should intensify the use of market mechanism, and at the same time expand the role of guidance planning gradually while preserving necessary mandatory planning. With the narrowing of mandatory planning, expansion of guidance planning and the wider use of economic levers, we would manage to make full use of the market mechanism under the guidance of unified state planning, integrating planning with market to form a colloid-like unity.

In principle, we should bring the market mechanism into full play under the guidance of centralized state planning so as to regulate the national economy as a whole. However, the system of economic regulation which the structural reform is to establish will surely be far complicated than that. On the one hand, it would not be wise to abolish mandatory planning on key products concerning the national economy and people's livelihood, whose shortage of supply cannot be overcome in the short run. Even after the completion of the comprehensive reform, we still need to preserve mandatory planning to regulate directly production and circulation of some key products so as to satisfy some special key needs. Especially in crises, direct regulation through mandatory planning tends to produce more rapid effects and be more easily controlled than the market mechanism, and therefore such compulsory means cannot be totally abandoned. On the other hand, we should allow for free production and circulation of some products aside from planned tasks, namely, regulation by free market forces.

It seems that in the comprehensive reform three types of regulation could possibly be carried out: the first type is regulation by mandatory planning, which would be carried out in few but crucial circumstances; the second type is regulation by free market forces, which would be used as a rare supplement, if at all; the third one is regulation by guidance planning or regulation by market forces under the guidance of state planning, whose role would be expanded as reform deepens. Among these three types of regulation, some people believed that the decisive factor differentiating one from another is whether the law of value and economic levers concerning the value category would be made good use of. They held that only regulation through the market mechanism under the guidance of planning involves the conscious use of the law of value, but regulation by mandatory planning and regulation by free market forces don't.

However, it is imprecise to say so. First, even if we will possibly use mandatory planning in some circumstances, we still cannot afford to overlook the law of value or neglect these economic levers such as price, taxation and credit etc. Second, even though it is called free market, it still cannot be totally free from the influence of national economic policies and state planning. In the socialist economy, a totally free market does not exist at all.

I believe that the decisive factor that sets one type of regulation apart from another is the way regulation is organized. Aside from the conscious use of the law of value and economic levers concerning the value category, the third type of regulation also needs to be carried out through planned coordination and consultation in accordance with state macro-economic plans. Such coordination or consultation needs to be carried out in a bottom-up approach by economic management establishment and social coordination organizations at all levels, economic associations in various forms and grassroots economic units, with needs of different levels being taken into consideration so that balance would be achieved one level after another. In contrast, the first type of regulation, namely, direct regulation by mandatory planning, does not necessarily undergo such planned coordination and consultation, although the economic means is also used as a supplementary way to regulate economy aside from the assignment of mandatory tasks through administrative orders. Not to mention the second type of regulation, i.e., regulation by free market!

Whether to lay emphasis on regulation by planning

Should we lay emphasis on regulation by planning while combining planning and market to regulate economy? Some people don't think it advisable. In my opinion, it is just a reflection of the reality and objective needs of the current structural reform. So far, production and circulation of quite many key products still need to be directly controlled by the state through planning, and accordingly, only a small proportion of social production was regulated by market forces (that is, enterprises products and sell products according to demand).

It was estimated that in the first half of 1980, products regulated by market forces accounted for just 15% of the gross industrial output, that is to say, more than four fifths of industrial output were produced under the guidance of state planning. So, "emphasis on regulation by planning" is just the current reality. Even though the share of mandatory planning might gradually reduce, say, to below 50% of GDP in the future, it will still dominate production and circulation of the most key products concerning the national economy and the people's livelihood and thus would influence greatly the development of the national economy. Therefore, regulation by planning will still play a dominant role in the national economy as a whole.

But what if planning and market turned out to be not combined like two plates joining with each other, but so integrated that a colloid-like unity has been formed instead? Should we still lay emphasis on regulation by planning? In 1979, we ever made a brief analysis of such issue in an article, to the effect that both regulation by planning and regulation by market forces, in conformity with objective laws in the socialist economy, are required to rebalance production and demand so as to make social labor (living labor and materialized labor) utilized effectively and reasonably in proportions needed by the society. In this sense, regulation by market forces and regulation by planning in the socialist economy aim to achieve a fundamentally same end. However, these two means of regulation are also contradictory due to different objective bases. In essence, the unity of opposites between these two means of regulation is also indicative of that between partial interests of enterprises and individuals and overall interests of the state and society in the socialist economy. While these two interests are in conflict, local and short-term interests must be subordinate to the overall and long-term interests. Likewise, regulation by market forces must be subordinate to regulation by planning. Therefore, in this sense, we need lay emphasis on regulation by planning and make full use of the market mechanism while combining planning with market.

Those who opposed "laying emphasis on regulation by planning", on the one hand, failed to realize that transition from plate-joining combination to the colloid-like unity is an inevitable reality, and on the other hand, failed to notice any contradictions but just consistency between these two means of regulation. This is closely related to their understanding of socialist economy and the nature of economic laws. Some people holding such view just acknowledged that socialist economy is a commodity economy but refused to admit that it is in the first place a planned economy, or dismissed "planned development" as just a property of socialist commodity economy; some people treated regulation by planning with regulation by market forces alike, oversimplifying them as both means of regulation by the law of value.

But in my point of view, whether socialist economy is a planned economy or not is a matter of principle that can never be evaded. There is no denying that planned economy (though imperfect) based on the same fundamental interests under socialist public ownership is the basic feature that sets socialist economy apart from capitalist economy. On the other hand, we cannot oversimplify regulation by planning as a means of regulation through the law of value (even if words like "the conscious use of the law of value by the state" were added). As we know, regulation by market forces is indeed a type of regulation through the law of value. When economy is totally regulated by the law of value, manufacturers and consumers tend to make choices based on their own interests and needs, regardless of any effects on the overall and long-term interests. I believe nobody in our country would openly agree to leave these overall and long-term interests to the "invisible hand". Likewise, while carrying out regulation by planning, the state and the society must not simply "imitate" the "invisible hand", or just rely the law of value, but instead it should also take into account the basic socialist economic law and other objective laws and try to put our economic development on the right track of socialism. It should be noted that even though the law of value is an extremely important law that we should attach particular importance to, it is not the only way to regulate the socialist economic development, which alone cannot guarantee our development in the right direction or on the right track of socialism.

How to link macroeconomic policies with micro-economic activities

Planned management by the state is mainly focused on macroeconomic matters, tending to consider the overall interests of the national economy; whereas enterprises and laborers tend to base their choices on their partial interests while making plans according to changes in the market and supply-demand relations. How should we incorporate macroeconomic policies reflected in the long-term and medium plans into micro-economic activities of enterprises and individual laborers? What should we do to test its effectiveness? This is the very core issue as to how to combine planning with market.

In the current discussion, some people gave a long list of ways to link macroeconomic policies with micro-economic activities, ranging from controlling the scale of capital construction, major projects and major supplies to the use of economic levers such as price, taxation and credit etc., from the establishment of information and forecast system to economic legislation, judicial system and social supervision system, and so forth. All these are surely very important, but they failed to point out which one is the most important of all. Some people summarized the combination between planning and market as the conscious use of the law of value to regulate economy. In other words, they regarded the conscious use of economic levers concerning the value category (such as price, taxation, credit, wage etc.) as the most important way to link macroeconomic policies with micro-economic activities. Such view deserves our attention because the conscious use of the law of value by the state to regulate economy embodies both regulation by planning (conscious efforts) and regulation by market forces (regulation by the law of value).

However, I still think that something is wrong with such view, that is, the way how regulation is organized, an important aspect of socialist economic regulation, has been neglected. As I mentioned earlier in this article, as far as three types of regulation are concerned, what sets one apart from another is that the type of regulation by combing planning with market is carried out through well-organized and planned coordination, which does not necessarily happen in the other two types of regulation. It seems that well-organized and planned coordination as well as the conscious use of value levers should be the two major ways to link state macroeconomic policies reflected in long-term and medium plans and micro-economic activities of enterprises and laborers in the market, because they would succeed in incorporating state macroeconomic policies into microeconomic activities of enterprises and laborers, and having the former tested and corrected by the latter.

As mentioned before, such planned coordination should be carried out in a bottom-up approach and the needs of different levels should be also taken into consideration so that the balance would be achieved in one level after another. If imbalance between production and sale or the problem concerning joint capital or labor collaboration could be solved through horizontal cooperation agreements between enterprises, between members of each economic alliance, or between different economic alliances in all forms without hampering the implementation of macroeconomic policies, they needn't be submitted to higher authority for solutions. Only those problems that cannot be solved by these enterprises or economic alliances alone or collaboratively should be submitted to economic management establishment or social coordination organizations for solution one lever after another.

Surely, some key development tasks and projects concerning the overall situation of national economic development prescribed in long-term and medium plans should also be fulfilled through administrative coordination and consultation with a bottom-up approach. So, on the part of grassroots enterprises, they would get away from tedious administrative formalities; and leading state organs wouldn't bother to attend to unnecessary administrative matters. Such way would spare the latter a lot of time and energy so that they could be more committed to studying and making policies and major development plans concerning the overall situation of the national economy.

The conscious use of various value levers while carrying out planned coordination is also another extremely important way to link state macroeconomic planned targets with micro-economic activities of enterprises and individual laborers. On the one hand, the state needs maintain a flexible and effective control over price, wage, taxation and interest rate etc. and thus use these "parameters" to influence economic activities of enterprises and individual laborers so as to make them conform with state macroeconomic planning. Especially in the process of planned coordination when a bottom-up approach is adopted to achieve a balance at all levels and a top-down method is employed to ensure its implementation at each level, it is even more necessary to change these parameters or adjust interest relations to achieve coordination, or to reset state macroeconomic planned targets to make them more practical if they are in great conflict with economic decisions made by grass-root units and individual laborers.

However, if value levers are not used and various interest relations cannot be rebalanced, planned coordination would be empty talk. On the other hand, without well-organized planned coordination, any control on economic parameters alone would be nothing different from economic interventions by capitalist states or regulation by free market forces (as the free market is also affected by economic policies of the state, but involving no well-organized planned coordination).

Therefore, both well-organized planned coordination and the conscious use of value levers are of critical importance for linking state macroeconomic policies with micro-economic activities by enterprises and individual laborers and combining planning with market in economic regulation. Surely, it does not mean that other means are not important. Rather, we should improve, in the meanwhile, economic legislation, judicial system, information forecast system, and social supervision system etc. to support and complement such measures. Only in this way can our economic restructuring achieve remarkable success.

Planned coordination and the use of economic levers involve a lot of work. First of all, we should formulate a medium-to-long term plan allowing for some leeway after having weighed up things in a scientific way. Besides, the state should not and cannot attend to all matters indiscriminately; rather, it should focus mainly on macroeconomic issues included in state medium-to-long term plans, such as the direction of national economic development, growth rate, distribution of national income between accumulation and consumption, the scale and direction of investment, major industrial structure, income structure, etc. If medium-to-long term plans lack in scientific soundness, macroeconomic policies have no consistency, and the national economy fails to achieve an overall equilibrium, any solutions or means based on local and partial interests would be of no avail, be it planned coordination, value levers or other market means.

However, if an overall equilibrium is achieved under the guidance of macroeconomic planning, whatever initiatives are taken just for the benefit of local and partial interests would hardly do any harm. Moreover, if we can achieve planned coordination and make better use of economic levers, our economy would be vigorous, well controlled and in good order. The secret is that we need plan the scale and proportion of accumulation and consumption beforehand, control the growth of purchasing power in both investment and consumption slightly below that of national income, and maintain a balance in terms of finance, credit, material supply and foreign exchange so that there is always a consumer's market or a restricted buyer's market as I mentioned earlier. And then, everything will be under control no matter what initiatives enterprises or individual laborers take.

Surely, it is a very complicated issue as to how to arrange the scale and proportion of accumulation and consumption properly and put the growth of purchasing power in both consumption and investment well under control. Some economic scholars ever pointed out that a highly centralized economic system tends to result in excessively high accumulation and investment, and many bad consequences on their heels. But it turned out that even though some countries had completed economic restructuring and adopted decentralization in management of enterprises, they still failed to solve such problems thoroughly. Therefore, we need combine theory with practice to study conscientiously these problems and try to find solutions.

(The original title of this article is "A Brief Analysis of Several Issues Concerning Regulation by Planning and Regulation by Market Forces", which was published in *Economic Research Journal*, 1980, No. 11)

Macroeconomic Regulation and Economic Equilibrium through Planning

In recent years our economic development and economic reform have given rise to many new words in economics articles, among which some are coined words and some are loan words. These loanwords were borrowed from both the West and the Orient. People tended to use words or ideas borrowed from western economics very cautiously. For example, concepts like "macroeconomic" and "micro-economic" were quite doubted by some people when they were first introduced to China to analyze our economic problems. Actually, these two concepts were not exclusive to western economics, which had originally existed in the natural science. It is not until the 1930s or 1940s that they began to gain popularity in western economics. In the 1960s, eastern economics scholars begun to use this pair of concepts more frequently. In late 1970s and early 1980s, these concepts began to be used in China. A rather late use of these words also reflected the real situation of our economics at that time.

In China, economic issues were firstly divided into macroeconomic and microeconomic issues when discussions about the structure of economic decision-making power were being held. Chinese economic scholars, who had realized that overconcentration of economic decision-making power in the hands of the state administrative body had dampened the enthusiasm of grassroots economic units and producers, proposed hereby to change such unitary decision-making structure to a multi-level economic decision-making one. To put it more specifically, state organs would mainly attend to macroeconomic matters and enterprises would be mainly responsible for microeconomic activities such as production, supply and sale of products.

Generally speaking, our economic reform did follow this course over these years. With the implementation of measures to streamline administration and decentralize as well as the increasing role of market mechanism, the vigor and vitality of enterprises has been gradually brought into full play in microeconomic activities. However, macroeconomic management failed to keep up with these measures, with the result that macroeconomic situation was somewhat out of control. In response to that, the state proposed that macroeconomic control should be strengthened. Accordingly, many academic articles began to study how to strengthen such control, which is a very favorable turn. It indicates that our economic restructuring is now entering a new phase.

Even though concepts like "macroeconomic management" and "macroeconomic control" emerged as the economic restructuring demanded a couple of years ago, it does not mean that we didn't have such ideas in the past. Macroeconomic issues concern the overall situation of the national economy. Accordingly, macroeconomic management refers to the management of the national economy as a whole. To correspond with the word "macroeconomic management", we had been using the term of "planned management of the national economy"; To correspond with the concept of "macroeconomic control", we had been using the term of "overall equilibrium of the national economy".

Since we had been long since practicing the "planned management of the national economy", and that nobody has ever openly proposed to disregard "overall equilibrium in national economy", why should we bother to replace them with new concepts, namely, "macroeconomic management" and "macroeconomic control"?

The crux of the matter is that traditional planned management of the national economy not only attended to the matters concerning the overall situation of the national economy, but microeconomic activities such as production, supply and marketing of grassroots enterprises, job placement and distribution of key consumer goods. That is to say, it includes both macroeconomic and microeconomic management. However, the reform requires the state to gradually relegate the decision-making power in terms of micro-economic activities to lower levels and narrow its direct control over micro-economic activities. As a result, it is very necessary to separate macroeconomic matters from microeconomic ones in the planned management of the national economy and prioritize the former.

The traditional "overall equilibrium of the national economy" also involves many aspects, including production and distribution of aggregate social product and national income, finance, credit, material supply as well as many physical products, with distribution of physical products usually being the first priority of the state while striving to maintain an overall equilibrium. In the reform, with the narrowing of mandatory planning on production and distribution of material goods and the expansion of the role of market mechanism, it is even more necessary to emphasize the equilibrium in terms of gross value and value composition, especially the balance between aggregate demand and aggregate supply and that between their components, that is to say, overall equilibrium of the national economy would be mainly reflected in the outcome of macroeconomic control on social gross value.

Therefore, in order to reform traditional planned management and improve ways to achieve overall equilibrium, it is very necessary and beneficial to highlight the macroeconomic aspect and propose the new concepts of macroeconomic management and macroeconomic control. Rather than deny the previous work concerning the overall equilibrium through planning, such reform aims to make it more scientific, modernized and suited to the needs of our economic reform and development. As a result, we should study the issue as to how to strengthen macroeconomic management and macroeconomic control in a larger picture, i.e., how to reform planning to achieve the overall equilibrium in a better way. That is to say, planned management of the national economy cannot be abandoned.

However, western economics (macroeconomics) is different. When it comes to the goals for macroeconomic management and control, western macroeconomics mainly aims to achieve a balance between aggregate demand and aggregate supply, seldom proposing to achieve any planned targets; rather, it pays more attention to economic means such as fiscal and monetary policies etc., rarely mentioning planning as a means of regulation. But it is not at all surprising, for western countries are market economies, which do not usually make plans, except a few countries such as Japan, France, etc. Along with the spontaneous regulation of the economy by the market mechanism, most western market economies usually use indirect policies to exert macroeconomic control with a view to realizing a balance between aggregate supply and aggregate demand. However, such balance is often very hard to achieve in market economy based on capitalist private ownership.

The direction of economic development and structural change does not necessarily need guidance from planning. However, as for socialist China, whose reform aims to establish a planned commodity economy, its macroeconomic control on the supply and demand of the market must be guided by state planning. We should be aware that to achieve a macroeconomic equilibrium is not the end, but just a means to achieve the strategic goal of state planning. Therefore, we should carry out macroeconomic control in accordance with state planning to help achieve overall equilibrium.

Chen Yun pointed out recently, "planning is the fundamental basis for macroeconomic control", which is an important principle for the macroeconomic management in socialist countries. Surely, the planning mentioned here does not mainly refer to those traditional short-term, mandatory, tactical development plans any more, but mostly innovative, medium-to-long term, guidance, strategic ones instead. Such medium-to-long term plans play a very decisive role in changes in aggregate supply and its components; whilst macroeconomic control focuses mainly on the short-term adjustment of aggregate demand and its components so as to make it more suited to changes in the aggregate supply. In this sense, it is even more necessary for macroeconomic control to be put under the guidance of state planning so as to rationalize resource allocation, satisfy effective demand and thus strike an overall equilibrium.

Currently a core issue of our macroeconomic management reform is that state control and regulation over the national economy should undergo a gradual transition from direct control to indirect control, corresponding to the gradual transition from mandatory planning to guidance planning in the reform of planned economy. Some people suggested that since a gradual change to indirect control is needed, we should abandon direct administrative means peculiar to the old system and employ indirect economic means required by the reform and new economic system so that the economy would be stabilized. However, we should also be aware that administrative means is still needed even in the new system; moreover, they might even need to be strengthened in some special occasions. Especially in the transitional period when both old and new systems coexist, the market mechanism is still far from being complete, and enterprise are still not very sensitive to any changes in economic parameters (such as profit and price etc.), it is even more necessary to do so. But we should also bear in mind that we are doing so to create a more favorable economic environment for the reform rather than revert to the old system. Therefore, transition to an indirect control should be achieved soon after conditions permit.

While striving to achieve an overall economic equilibrium, the state should pay attention to the combined use of fiscal and monetary policies, which is a very crucial issue. There are roughly four types of combination between fiscal and monetary policies. The first type is a combined use of loose fiscal policies and loose monetary policies, which aims to stimulate economic growth and increase employment, often resulting in inflation. The second one is a combined use of tight fiscal policies and tight monetary policies, which is an effective means to fight against inflation. It is also called contractionary policies. The third type is a combined use of tight fiscal policies and loose monetary policies. And the last one is the combined use of loose fiscal policies and tight monetary policies. The latter two both aim to strike a balance between aggregate supply and aggregate demand, and to adjust the structure of demand and production.

Which one should China choose? On the one hand, "desire for expansion" and "hunger for investment" inherent in the old system still exist; on the other, enterprises and employees tend to seek short-term interests after the state loosens its control on microeconomic activities, resulting in "hunger for consumption". As a result, aggregate demand expands more than it should. Given such circumstance, we need combine tight fiscal polices and tight monetary polices, that is to say, we should strive to achieve a fiscal equilibrium as well as an overall equilibrium between finance and credit so as to curb excessive demand and make supply slightly exceed demand, which would create favorable economic conditions for the reform.

Besides, it would also benefit sustained, steady and coordinated economic growth. Some economics scholars think that in the long run China should combine tight fiscal polices with loose monetary policies, because tight fiscal policies could restrict public and individual consumption and loose monetary policies could encourage investment, which are both conducive to economic growth. As we know, western developed countries usually increase the supply of money to stimulate its economy due to its insufficient demand; some socialist developing countries also need inflation to lift its economy out of stagnation. However, China, due to its hyperactive economy, doesn't need anything like that. But instead, what deserves China's constant attention is its aggregate demand including consumption demand especially investment demand, which should be put under control. Even if it is viewed in the long run, it is still questionable to use a loose monetary policy to stimulate investment. Surely, China does need flexible monetary policies and interest levers as well as capital market to improve the mechanism of macroeconomic control. All these need to be settled gradually in the process of reform.

Finally, I would like to discuss briefly the theoretical foundation of macroeconomic management, i.e., macroeconomics. Some people think that macroeconomics is exclusive to western economics and thus it is not included in Marxist economics, which is at least a misunderstanding of the latter. Surely, the term "macroeconomic" was never used in Marxist classic works, because they hadn't been invented at that time. However, in *Das Kapital,* theories concerning the reproduction of aggregate social capital, conditions for equilibrium of total social product, market realization conditions, and the total process of social production all study the capitalist economy as a whole, that is to say, it is also a theory focusing on macroeconomic matters.

Marx has ever said some words to the effect that "overproduction" caused by production exceeding direct need and supply exceeding direct demand is a type of anarchy, the very "villain" leading to a crisis in the capitalist system; in sharp contrast, it is a "benefit" for socialist planned economy, conducive to controlling and adjusting any imbalances in the process of social reproduction. It couldn't be more apt for our current equilibrium through planning and macroeconomic control! Surely, we shouldn't oppose any useful macroeconomic approaches in western economics. However, we should, on the basis of Marxism, tap as many valuable things as possible from Marxism and try to combine them with the practice of our reform and development in an effort to create Marxist macroeconomics with Chinese characteristics, which requires joint efforts from our academic world of economics!

(This article was published in *Finance & Trade Economics*, 1986, No.1)

Several Thoughts on Planning and Market

1. Attaching more weight to the reform

Both *Recommendations for the Ten-Year plan and the Eight Five-Year Plan for economic and social development* (*Recommendations* for short) adopted in the seventh Plenary Session of the 13th Central Committee of the CPC and *the Outline of the ten-year plan and the eighth five-year plan for national economic and social development of the PRC* (*the Outline* for short) adopted at the Fourth Session of the Seventh National People's Congress of the People's Republic of China proposed that the establishment of a new planned commodity economy and combination between planned economy and regulation by market forces should be set as a basic requirement of our economic development for the next ten years. The document of the national working conference on economic structure held not long ago pointed out that we should seize the opportunity, allow things to take their course a positive way, intensify supervision over reform, and give more weight to the reform.

"To give more weight to reform" is sometimes called "to strengthen reforms", or "to further speed up the reform", but they all mean the same thing. Now, the whole nation has reached a consensus on this. It is the inevitable result of our efforts in carrying out the economic rectification campaign in the recent couple of years; besides, it is also the objective requirement of further economic rectification as well as economic development for the next ten years. Although it is proposed that we should give more weight to the reform, it surely does not and shouldn't mean that we are to underestimate the positive role and the significance of economic rectification campaign.

During the economic rectification campaign, we persisted in carrying out the reform, so that many reform measures remained constant and consistent; and what's more, many prominent reform measures to rationalize prices have been officially made. Thanks to economic rectification campaign, imbalance between aggregate demand and aggregate supply has been somewhat improved and the national economy has in general changed for the better. If it is true that we must rely more on administrative means and centralized decision-making to cool down the overheated economy rapidly in the initial phase of economic rectification campaign, it will be more necessary for us to use more economic means and reform the economic structure and mechanism more radically so that deeper problems with the economic structure would be solved in the later phase. Therefore, we need give more weight to reform in due time.

To give more weight to reform is not only a key step to achieve economic rectification, but the only way to realize the strategic goal of our economic and social development in the 1990s. In the period of the Eighth Five-Year Plan and the whole 1990s, we aimed mainly to achieve the following economic goals. First, we aimed to achieve a balance between aggregate supply and aggregate demand and a sustained and steady economic growth; Second, we aimed to achieve structural coordination, rationalization and modernization in the economic development; Third, we aimed to improve the quality of national economy as a whole while increasing economic benefits. Though differing in goals, they all have one thing in common, that is, economic mechanism counts. If we fail to straighten out the economic mechanism, the aforementioned tasks in the 1990s would be hard to complete. In view of this, we should be more dedicated to strengthening the reform and transforming the economic mechanism. The economic rectification campaign has given rise to a relatively tolerant economic environment and thus created favorable conditions for the strengthening of reform. We should seize the current opportunity and try to maintain and consolidate the hard-earned, relatively tolerant economic environment while setting targets for the growth rate and the scale of construction in the Eighth Five-Year Plan period and the next ten years, so that we could transform our economic mechanism as soon as possible into a planned commodity economy.

During the formulation of *Recommendations* and *the Outline,* valuable advice from all sides had been taken, including the suggestion of attaching more weight to the reform. Compared with the period when the Eighth Five-Year Plan and Ten-Year Development Plan were being formulated and the initial phase of economic rectification, more emphasis has now been laid on the reform in the official document of *Recommendations* and *the Outline*, which would be mainly reflected in the content rather than word count. Now I would like to list some ideas clarified in *Recommendations* and *the Outline*, which however used to be very ambiguous.

First, *Recommendations* and *the Outline* proposed very clearly, "we should establish a new planned commodity economy in the next ten years". As a matter of fact, in recommendations for the seventh Five-Year plan, the central committee had ever come up with the policy that we should establish a new economy with Chinese characteristics in the near future. It said, "we would strive to establish a new economy within 5 years or longer". But as for how much longer, it was not made clear. As we all know, the reform met up with some setbacks later on, and people were not sure when the new economic system would be established. Now, *Recommendations* and *the Outline* have made it very clear that we should establish a new economic system and operational mechanism in the next ten years, i.e., before the 21st Century, which is very heartening.

Second, with regard to the relations between planned economy and regulation by market forces, *Recommendations* and *the Outline* reiterated that we should narrow the scope of mandatory planning, expand the role of guidance planning and increase regulation by market forces. As a matter of fact, these polices were ever proposed to deal with the relations between mandatory planning, guidance planning and regulation by market forces properly. However, such policy hasn't been mentioned for a period of time, during which it was just suggested that we should make due adjustments in varying circumstances. Now, people's doubts have been removed.

Third, consistent with changes in the above relations and policies, *Recommendations* and *the Outline* re-emphasized that price reform aims not only to rationalize unreasonable prices, but more importantly, to establish a reasonable price formation mechanism. That is to say, prices of many common goods and services should be regulated by market forces except for very few key products whose prices should be controlled by the state.

Fourth, with regard to the market, it was ever emphasized that the state should control more material resources. Now it was restated that the state should expand the market of means of production; besides, it was even further clarified that we should develop the factor market including capital, technology, information, and real estate so as to keep up with the development of commodity market.

Fifth, with regard to enterprise reform, it was restated that we should regard "separation of government administration from enterprise management and separation of ownership and management" as the direction of enterprise reform, which is a fundamental issue, although we should still continue to improve the household-responsibility system. Whether we will succeed in separating government administration from enterprise management and handling ownership organization and operational mechanism properly concerns the outcome of enterprise reform and even that of the economic restructuring as a whole. Therefore, it is very necessary to re-clarify the direction of enterprise reform.

Sixth, with regard to macroeconomic management, it has been quite long that the government did not mention the policy of a gradual transition from direct control to indirect control, which used to be proposed in the Recommendations for the Seventh Five-year Plan. Now, *the Outline* restated that direct management should be combined with indirect management, with more emphasis being laid on the latter. The National Working Conference on Structural Reform held not long ago further clarified the direction of macroeconomic management reform, i.e., a gradual transition to indirect management.

Finally, to complement with every other reform, reforms of social welfare and social security system including the commercialization of housing were also highlighted.

To sum up, we can see very clearly the determination of the central committee to strengthen the reform from *Recommendations*, *the Outline* and documents of the National Working Conference on Structural Reform. It has removed people's doubts about the reform and enhanced people's confidence in it. Policies and measures to speed up the reform listed above or even not listed have been sufficient enough to prove the central committee's determination to strengthen the reform. All in all, the spirit of all these polices and measures is that we should increase the use of market mechanism, expand the role of market forces in economic regulation, and carry out macroeconomic management mainly through indirect control in accordance with the requirements of socialist planned commodity economy while adhering to planned economy.

2. the market orientation of the reform

The aforementioned efforts to expand the role of market mechanism were called by many economic scholars a market-oriented reform. The reform aimed to bring about some radical changes in the economic structure. We used to practice a centralized planned economy that evolved from natural economy and product economy and opposed market; now, we are trying to establish a new planned commodity economy characterized by combination between planning and market. In a sense, it can be called a market-oriented reform. The fruits of reform were firstly seen from its market orientation. As we all know, before the reform, we just had an exclusive public sector. Therefore, it was widely held then that large public-owned people's communes and a unitary public sector were believed to be the best forms of socialism. At that time, we used to manage economy through mandatory planning and direct administrative control, which is in nature opposed to market and market mechanism. Since the reform, many types of ownership began to develop side by side while public ownership remained the mainstay of the economy and the decision-making power of enterprises were expanded, which thus made it possible for them to act according to the law of the market.

At the same time, market system and market mechanism also started to grow up; and focus of macroeconomic management has gradually been shifted onto indirect management, a type of economic management through market means and value levers. All these changes have shown one thing, that is, the reform is a process in which market orientation keeps expanding and deepening. Surely, the "market orientation" discussed here is public ownership-based rather than private ownership-based; it is not oriented towards a blind and anarchic market but a market under the guidance of planning and subject to macro-control. Some people viewed the concept of "market-oriented" as the antithesis of "planning-oriented", reducing the former to "anti-planning", which is at least an imprecise understanding.

Which has brought about all these achievements in our reform in more than a decade, the expansion of administrative and mandatory planning or the expansion of the role of market? It seems that the latter is preferred, which can also prove to be a more satisfying answer through comparison. Let's compare China's reform with the reforms carried out in the Soviet Union and Eastern Europe in the past. Why has China's economy been greatly invigorated with an abundance of commodities and people getting real benefit from the reform whereas the Soviet Union and Eastern Europe haven't? Currently, the Soviet Union and some countries from the Eastern Europe are very poor, with a severe shortage of commodities. Why is there such a huge difference?

With other political and economic factors being put aside, what makes a big difference is the fact that China has conscientiously carried out a market-oriented reform and made real and practical progress despite many difficulties or problems. In sharp contrast, the Soviet Union didn't take the market-oriented reform seriously even though they kept chanting many slogans as to how to carry out the reform several years ago. Recently, some Soviet Union scholars made a U turn, proposing to realize market economy within as short as 300 or 500 days, which seemed to have failed after severe setbacks.

In China, it has been proved that the more market-oriented the region, sector or enterprise is, the more vigorous the economy has been. The map of economic upturn is also highly related to this tendency. The provinces, sectors or districts whose economy picked up very soon proved to be closely linked with the market, whereas those provinces, sectors or districts having little to do with or failing to make good use of market tended to recover very slowly. All these are so self-evident that we cannot evade. It seems that the reform in the next ten years should continue to follow the same course that China took 11 or 12 years ago, that is to say, we should continue to carry out the market-oriented reform under the guidance of planning and subject to macroeconomic control, and strive to make more progress based on all achievements in the past reform so as to push the reform further forward.

Before the reform, almost everything in economic life was under the control of administrative planning, and market just survived in the margin of unified planned management. After more than a decade's reform, products regulated by market forces and products regulated by planning have been half and half, and some people even said that products regulated by market forces had already accounted for more than 50%. Surely, it varies from field to field. In industrial products and farmer produce, subsidiary agricultural products regulated by market forces rank the first, and the next come industrial consumer goods, and then industrial means of production.

Now the circumstances are still changing in different regions. A few days ago, it was reported in the newspaper that during the circulation of means of production in Shanghai, the largest industrial city of China, products regulated by market forces accounted for 70% whereas products regulated by planning just 30%. And then, such a question might be asked: what will the ratio of planning to market be like after the completion of the Eighth Five-Year Plan and the Ninth Five-Year Plan, i.e., 5 or 10 years later? This is also an important issue that we can not evade. In fact, *Recommendations* and *the Outline* have already given the answer, that is, the share of regulation by market forces (and that of guidance planning closely linked with the market) would be further expanded. That is to say, it would increase during the Eighth Five-Year Plan period and continue to rise after the completion of the Ninth Five-year Plan in 2000. Even though it is hard to tell specifically to what extent it will reach, the general trend is already very clear.

In my point of view, even if we will have established a new planned commodity economy by the end of the next decade, macroeconomic matters cannot be said to be state planning's natural and permanent sphere of influence; likewise, market forces cannot and should not dictate microeconomic activities 100%. In the new economic system, macroeconomic management will be *mainly* carried out through indirect means, but "mainly" does not mean "totally"; Rather, some key parts or links of the national economy, natural monopolies, and some key products and services with little supply and demand elasticity still need be under the state's direct management and control. As for the degree of marketization, we know for sure that it varies from region to region, sector to sector, product to product, and therefore, different plans and arrangements would be made according to different circumstances.

3. Adhering to market orientation but no blind faith in market; adhering to planned economy but no blind faith in planning

By establishing a new planned commodity economy and an economic operational mechanism characterized by combination between planned economy and regulation by market forces, we mean to make full use of the advantages of both planning and market, just like what the document of the Seventh Plenary Session of the 13th Central Committee of the CPC emphasized. The merits of planning lie in its capability of gathering necessary financial, material and manpower resources to accomplish great things, adjusting the distribution of income and ensuring social equity. The merits of market lie in its capacity of promoting progress in technology and management and thus linking production with demand through the mechanism of competition and the law of "survival of the fittest".

In theory, we can bring all merits into full play and therefore benefit from such combination. However, in reality, they usually failed to be combined very effectively: instead of combining their merits as expected, we often ended up with the combination of their demerits; we had intended to combine planning with market very well, but often ended up having neither planning (or unrealistic plans) nor market mechanism to ensure the functioning of the competition mechanism through the law of survival of the fittest. So, I would like to offer two suggestions, while the issue as to how to combine planned economy with regulation by market forces is being discussed. On the one hand, we should continue to practice planned economy but avoid any blind faith in planning; on the other hand, we should carry on the market-oriented reform but avoid any blind faith in market. In a nutshell, we need banish two types of blind faith.

First of all, I would like to explain why we shouldn't have any blind faith in market.

The so-called regulation by market forces refers to the invisible hand at work, that is, the spontaneous regulation by the law of value. We should respect the law of value, but it does not mean that the law of value alone can achieve everything so that we should leave all matters to it. In my opinion, at least the following major tasks should not be left to the law of value alone. The first one concerns the balance between aggregate supply and aggregate demand. If we leave this totally to the market and the law of value, our economy would end up with cyclical fluctuations and frequent economic crises. The second one concerns major structural changes in the economy. We hope that within a rather short period of time, say, one, two, or three decades, industrial modernization and structure supererogation would be achieved at very little cost. It is not impossible for the market mechanism to achieve that through spontaneous allocation of resources, but our economy might undergo many severe repetitions and crises and pay very dear prices before it is finally achieved. We cannot afford the time.

The third task involves fair competition. The belief that market can assure perfect competition is just a fantasy, which cannot be accomplished even in the period of laissez-faire capitalism. The rule of the market is that the strong bullies the weak, which will inevitably lead to monopoly and unfair competition. In response to this, even governments of western capitalist countries had to make anti-monopoly laws and laws to protect fair competition etc.

The fourth one concerns the issues of ecological balance, environmental protection, and "external diseconomies". The market mechanism is incapable of addressing these issues and would even probably make the situation worse. So if the market does the job alone, social interests and even the interests of our future generations would be jeopardized.

The last one concerns the relations between equity and efficiency. Unable to guarantee real social equity, market can only ensure equivalent exchange and a certain degree of fair competition, which does help to improve efficiency.

However, the spontaneity of market is bound for polarization and a vast gap between the rich and the poor. Such trend has already somewhat developed in the process of market-oriented reform, which has caused anxiety among people and thus dampened their enthusiasm. Therefore, the government must pay attention to such trend and take efficient measures to prevent it from getting worse.

As we can see, at least the five aforementioned tasks cannot be assigned to the invisible hand alone, in the meanwhile, the visible hand, namely, state planning and government management, must be also used. The so-called complete and pure market economy is not what our market-oriented reform aims to achieve. Even in western capitalist countries, market economy has become less pure and typical due to government interventions through policies or planning. To put aside ideological factors, pure marketization in China will be just wishful thinking. As we are practicing a socialist planned commodity economy, we have better reason to emphasize the guiding role of state planning and macroeconomic regulation and avoid any bind faith in the market while carrying out the market-oriented reform, that is to say, we should value the important role of "cage", a concept invented by Chen Yun.

In summer of 1990, I made a speech in a seminar and talked about Chen Yun's economic thoughts. I mentioned that Chen Yun ever compared the relationship between planning and market to that between the cage and birds, which had aroused great interest of people both at home and abroad. Later, my speech was published in *People's Daily* and severely criticized by many overseas newspapers, which dubbed Chen Yun's such economic thought as "birdcage economy". Afterward, some foreigners came to me and inquired about my opinions. I responded that they needn't make a fuss about it, because every country needs a cage in terms of economic management. State budget is indeed a very strongly-built one. For example, in early October of 1990, U.S. state parks and the bureau in charge of pension management were almost closed as people were not so sure whether the U.S. Government could still pay the working staff there after the Congress and the President of the Untied States failed to reach a consensus on budget after several months' negotiations. Due to the same reason, the Statue of Liberty in the port of New York city had to be closed from tourists for two days, and San Francisco airport was almost closed, too. At that time, I was visiting San Francisco with a delegation from CAAS, and almost couldn't fly back to China as scheduled because of this. I told these foreigners that monetary and fiscal policies employed by western countries were also sort of "birdcages". When interest rate is raised by the Federal Reserve, the cost of investment will increase, and the economic birdcage will become smaller; when interest rate is reduced, the supply of money will increase and the economic cage will thus become bigger.

As for the size of the cage of planning, it all depends, varying from sector to sector and from product to product. Besides, the cage can be made of different materials. For example, it can be rigid just like the cage made of iron or steel; it can also be elastic just like the cage made of plastic or rubber. Mandatory planning is rigid, whereas guidance and policy planning is more elastic and flexible. During my stay in the United States, I found that its cage of economic management employed by the government is sometimes even sturdier than planned economies. For example, in order to curb "urban expansion", the U.S. state government drew a circle on the city map to exert control on any construction beyond the circle through levy of extremely high prohibitive taxes. Oregon did this way. This circle in such case is indeed a cage.

Now let's get back to the previous topic—we should neither have any blind faith in market nor neglect any necessary guidance from planning or government management in the market-oriented reform, that is to say, we shouldn't overlook the necessary role of the "cage". Therefore, in order to carry out the market-oriented reform, the reform of planned economy rightfully included, we must strengthen planned management more effectively.

On the other hand, we shouldn't have blind faith in planning while practicing planned economy, because it would also lead to mistakes and bad consequences. Planned economy based on public ownership just makes proportional economic development possible, but it is not sure to happen. If planning fails to consider market supply and demand and the law of value, the economy will also be out of control or end up with severe mistakes. We've already made a lot of mistakes of such kind. In the era of planned economy, our economy has witnessed many major imbalances and has been very up and down. Even during reform, our macroeconomic situation also ever went out of control.

Planning commissions of all local governments above the county level had the final say on the approval of fixed assets investment projects. Now we have already had over 160 color TV production lines, more than 90 refrigerator production lines and many latex gloves or beer production lines etc. Many of them are homogeneous and redundant. It shows that the situation still got out of control even though these projects are all examined and approved by planning sectors of governments at all levels. Humans do err, so planning will inevitably have limitations and thus lead to many contradictions hard to overcome, such as the contradiction between subjectivity and objectivity, one of the major problems in planning.

First, man have limitations in knowing and understanding the world, including real situations and objective laws. We ever made many mistakes in planning such as disregarding national conditions, going beyond the limits of national strength, and rushing for quick results.

Second, man have limitations in collecting and transmitting information. Planning needs information, but collection and transmission of information will never end and thus will never be complete. No matter how many times computers are updated, how advanced technology is, how widely it is used, it will still be impossible for man to collect and process all the economic data in time.

Third, men are also bounded by their interest relations, positions and perspectives. Each planning commission or macroeconomic management organ is affiliated to a certain department, falls to a certain region, has a certain position or perspective, stands for different interests, and is thus bounded by certain interest relations. Besides, government leaders and planning personnel are all humans: man is not the almighty God; humans do err. All these limitations might lead to deviations of their work from real situations and objective laws, and thus result in major mistakes in planning and macroeconomic management.

Therefore, we should keep increasing our knowledge, raising our awareness, and improving our planning so as to make our work conform with the requirement of objective laws and real situations, especially market supply and demand and the law of value as well.

All in all, we should continue to practice planned economy but avoid any blind faith in planning; we should carry out the market-oriented reform but avoid any blind faith in market. We should not only bring their merits into full play, but overcome their demerits and flaws while combining planning with market. This complicated task needs to be carefully studied, requiring joint efforts from many sectors such as the planning body, financial sector, banks, marketing departments, commercial sector, and material supply departments etc. for gradual solution.

4. Some theoretical concepts

The issue of relations between planning and market is not new. Since the Third Plenary Session of the 11th Central Committee of the CPC, we have been discussing this issue for 12 years. It should be dated back to the year of 1956 when our socialist transformation was almost completed. It was Chen Yun that put forward this issue firstly at that time. Besides, as early as in 1920s when the Soviet Union adopted the New Economic Policy, they were also bothered by such problem. Since we carried out the reform, many proposals as to how to deal with the relations between planning and market have been made in some major conferences, speeches and articles by economists. For example, some suggested "combining regulation by planning with regulation by market forces"; some proposed "to combine planned mechanism with market mechanism"; some advised "to combine planned economy with market economy" etc. Many people called them collectively as "to combine planning with market". since June 19th, 1989, it was officially finalized as "to combine planned economy with regulation by market forces". The document of the Seventh Plenary Session of the 13th Central Committee of the CPC said that we must and can combine planned economy with regulation by market forces, and that we shouldn't hesitate to formulate and implement any policies concerning such combination; besides, it also suggested that academic scholars and experts who disagree can reserve their opinions. This is a very good suggestion, and I cannot agree with it any more.

I ever wrote an article in 1983, arguing that the relations between planning and market is a universal issue that needs to be further discussed. As for how to define and deal with it, we needn't rush to a conclusion and have both current and future generations tied down by it to keep them from making bold theoretical explorations. Rather, we just need further explore and strive to find specific solutions good for the specific period of time. For instance, the solution fit for the period of economic rectification will be different from the one good for the normal period of economic development. Given that human history hasn't reached an advanced stage, no reformist or theorist so far dare say that they have already solved the issue perfectly well once and for all. But we still need a standard or norm to refer to in practical work, so it is still necessary for us to accept the version proposed by the Central Committee and persist with such policies unswervingly. It would neither violate the principle of "no rushing to conclusions in theoretical study" nor go against the spirit of contention and competition among a great many academic schools.

For example, even though the controversial issue as to whether our economy can be called a "socialist market economy" is rather sensitive, I don't think it should be barred from further discussion. Is market economy a concept exclusive to capitalist societies or shared by all socialized production and commodity economies? Now let's look back on the past days when Sun Yefang proposed the concept of "socialist profit". It did then spark a very heated debate, but it managed to survive and was later widely accepted. Besides, in the initial period of the reform, people were even prohibited from mentioning "commodity economy" and only allowed to talk about "commodity production and commodity exchanges" while discussing the socialist economy. What a heated debate again! But the concept of "commodity economy" was later widely accepted, too.

Back to the current issue, will the concept of "market economy" be finally admitted to the big family of socialist political economics? Or will it be excluded and labeled as the stubbornly biased opinions held by very few economists? It will be not so hard to tell. However, we have to admit that it will be hard to be accepted widely soon after a new concept is put forward. History often repeats. For example, at the very beginning when they were proposed, the concepts of "socialist commodity economy" and "regulation by market forces" could hardly gain a strong footing in the socialist political economics. Not to mention the concept of socialist market economy! However, with constant update on our theoretical knowledge and enrichment of socialist political economics in the process of reform, people gradually came to understand that socialist economy is a planned commodity economy based on public ownership and that it is necessary to carry out regulation by market forces and combine market with planning. As a result, many proposals on how to deal with the relations between planning and market were made.

Now the level of our discussions over the relationship between planning and market is far higher than 11 or 12 years ago! At that time when the reform was initially carried out, we still needed to start from ABC, i.e., the basic concepts of planning and market; but after 11 or 12 years of explorations, we needn't study these concepts this way any longer. Moreover, both their denotations and connotations have changed a lot, and their contents are also enriched. Take the concept of planning as an example. In the past, planning was understood in the following ways. First, planning used to be exclusively mandatory planning. Joseph Stalin ever said that planning was not forecast but orders, which therefore must be obeyed. Second, planning used to cover everything, ranging from macroeconomic issues to micro-economic activities, from human, financial and material resources to production, supply and sale of products. Third, planning used to be indicator management, especially physical indicators, such as production indicators as to how many products should be manufactured, allocation indicators as to how many products should be distributed. These physical indicators are the embodiment of requirements from plans.

Now, the concept of planning has changed a lot in the following ways. First, planning not only includes mandatory planning, but guidance planning and policy planning, for example, industrial policies are also a type of planning. Second, planning is not that inclusive any more, which currently just attends to macroeconomic matters; micro-economic activities and enterprise affairs have already been left mainly to market forces and enterprises. Third, planning is not mainly or totally indicator management. These indicators, if at all, are mainly value indicators rather than physical ones, though a few key sectors or enterprises still need the latter. State planning aims to control aggregate economy or the major structure, such as to maintain a balance between aggregate supply and aggregate demand and structural balance between agriculture, low industry and heavy industry. Besides, investment and consumption etc. all need value indicators. At the same time, in order to control the aggregate amount and adjust major structures, we also need value levers such as price, interest rate, exchange rate and tax rate etc. to make planning rely more on value indicators rather than physical ones. In this way, the concept of planning has dramatically changed.

Similarly, our current understanding of market is also different from 11 or 12 years ago. First, we used to believe that market was incompatible with public ownership and thus can only be based on private ownership. Currently, we realize that market is not exclusive to private ownership or capitalism and the economy based on public ownership can also have and need a market. Therefore, market is not incompatible with public ownership and thus they can be combined. Market, market mechanism, and regulation by market forces are all results of socialized production and commodity economy. These pairs of concepts—market VS planning, market mechanism VS planned mechanism, regulation by planning VS regulation by market forces—are all different means of regulating resource allocation rather than essential features of socialism or capitalism. What really sets socialism apart from capitalism is the two principles proposed by Deng Xiaoping, i.e., public ownership as the mainstay of the economy and common prosperity.

Second, in the past people tended to associate market with anarchy and spontaneity, viewing market as an antithesis to and incompatible with planning. They were considered to be in a zero-sum game, that is, if planning is to be strengthened, market will be weakened; if market is to be expanded, planning will surely be reduced. Currently, we have come to realize that market does not necessarily lead to anarchy or spontaneity, which can also be guided by planning and subject to macroeconomic regulation, and therefore planning and market can be combined.

Third, we used to think that market just needed to serve as a supplement to planned economy so that it would suffice to account for a very tiny part in circulation of goods; the large bulk of consumer goods were rationed according to tickets, which were not commodities in a real sense and thus did not enter the market in a real sense, either. But now the circulation of all consumer goods has been marketized with only a few exceptions. Means of production used to be excluded from commodities, but now the circulation of means of production has been more and more commercialized.

Fourth, in the past, we had never dreamed that socialist economy would have any factor market, for land, capital and labor were never regarded as commodities. So, how come there would be a factor market? However, the concept of factor market has been gradually formed with the deepening of reform. Now it includes capital market, labor market, real estate market, information market, and technology market etc., which was too hard to imagine 11 or 12 years ago. Surely, such market mechanism is still far from complete in both theory and practice, and the new socialist market system is still in the making.

All in all, our understanding of the concepts of planning and market has been deepened greatly after 11 or 12 years' practice and theoretical explorations in the process of reform. Therefore, we shouldn't be too obsessed with the wording just like what we did in the past. For example, some people kept arguing with each other about the "best" wording. Should it be "a combination between regulation by planning and regulation by market forces"? or "a combination between planned economy and market economy"? or "a combination between planned mechanism and market mechanism"? or the current official version, namely, "a combination between planned economy and regulation by market forces"? Some people argued that since planned economy, which refers to an economic system, and regulation by market forces, which refers to a means of regulation, are not of the same kind or not on the same level, they should not be combined at all. However, I personally think that it is senseless to argue about the wording. What really counts is that we should draw lessons from the past and find out specific and practical ways to combine planning and market. We should thrust our major efforts at these issues.

There used to be a lot of proposals on how to combine planning with market. Some focused on theoretical models, while some operations. For example, it was ever proposed that planning and market could be combined in the following three ways: mandatory planning, guidance planning and regulation by market forces. That is to say, there are three types of micro-economic management, among which mandatory planning is direct management and guidance planning is indirect management; as for regulation by market forces, though it does not belong to planned management in name, it is in reality also part of macroeconomic planned regulation and under indirect control of macroeconomic overall equilibrium planning in the whole society. Besides, it has been very obvious that the role of mandatory planning is to be further narrowed, the role of guidance planning and regulation by market forces would be further expanded. In macroeconomic management terms, overall-equilibrium planning and aggregate control in the whole society is usually equivalent to guidance planning.

After the traditional thinking that market is the antithesis of planning and that market cannot be used in planned economy was abandoned, economic theoreticians came up with many theoretical models as to how to combine planning with market, such as "plate-joining combination", "inter-penetration combination", "colloid combination", "organic unity combination", "superimposition", and "double-coverage combination" etc. (colloid combination, superimposition and double-coverage combination mean almost the same, that is, planning and market are formed into an organic unity). In the so-called model of "plate-joining combination", planning (mostly mandatory planning) and market are just glued to each other, with very distinctive boundaries between them. Market factors were not or seldom considered in traditional planning. For example, many planned prices fixed for long were too much deviated from real supply and demand relations. Whereas market just served as a supplement to planning and thus was not under the control of planning.

In the so-called model of "inter-penetration combination", though planning and market are still not integrated into a whole, their boundaries are already somewhat blurred. The supply and demand relations would be taken into consideration while plans were made; the market would be guided by economic policies and macroeconomic planning. In such way of combination, the boundary between them is not so distinct as in plate-joining combination, and there is already something of each in the other. In the organic unity combination (or colloid combination, superimposition combination etc.), planning and market, rather than exist side by side, will have been integrated into a whole and both used everywhere in every corner of the society and every sector of the national economy. Inspired by this model, a formula of "the market being regulated by the state and the enterprise being guided by market forces" was written into the document of the 13th National Congress of the CPC. In this way, planning, market and enterprise were indeed integrated into a whole. Such combination was also called an "intrinsic combination".

At that time, there was also another opinion to the effect that, from the perspective of the relations between planning and market, economic restructuring would in general undergo the following phases: before the reform, economic management was exclusively relied on planning; in the initial period of reform, market emerged as a supplement to planning; later, planning and market joined with each other like two plates and existed side by side; and then, they gradually penetrated into each other; finally, planning and market are to be integrated into a colloid. However, looking back on this, we will now find out that though the general trend is quite right, the process of economic restructuring shouldn't be divided mechanically into several phases with clearly cut boundaries. For example, we shouldn't conclude that in the final stage a colloid combination will cover the whole society, and that plate-joining combination and inter-penetration combination would disappear completely. Rather, the latter two would exist for long within a certain scope.

As mentioned before, even by the time the focus of macroeconomic management has already been shifted onto indirect regulation, direct management will still be necessary in some fields, such as natural monopolies, goods or services with little elasticity in supply and demand, and public goods or services, etc. Even western market economies also put public services and issues concerning the protection of ecological environment etc. under direct control of the government. Notwithstanding these, China currently still need reduce gradually direct management, and strive to increase indirect management with the deepening of reform and the improvement of management.

We should also observe objective laws while implementing direct administrative management. Now even mandatory planning is required to reflect the needs of the law of value. That is to say, the supply and demand relations and the needs of the law of the value should be also taken into consideration while direct management through planning is being carried out. In this sense, plate-joining combination and inter-penetration combination are inseparable. Pure plate-joining combination characterized by distinct boundaries between planning and market did ever exist in the traditional planned economy, but it has disappeared ever since the reform. Besides, it should be noted that it is too ideal to have the law of the value fully obeyed during direct planned management, i.e., mandatory planning. If we can totally rely on the law of value to solve all problems, there would be no need to keep any direct mandatory planning, but instead our economy would be managed totally through indirect regulation. The very reason why we must have administrative intervention and direct mandatory planning is that market is not almighty and the market mechanism has many flaws as discussed before. We can not totally do as the supply and demand relations or the law of value require(s) while attending to issues concerning the overall situation or interests in the long run. That is to say, the state must step in, otherwise it would do great harm to social interests.

Therefore, with regard to direct management through state planning, the formula of "the state being regulated by the state and the enterprise being guided by the market" would not apply because the state needs to manage enterprises directly rather than indirectly through market. Surely, in this case, the state still needs to take the law of the value into consideration though we can't totally conform with it. In other words, the state needs to consider market factors, which however does not mean that the state would rely on market to manage economy. In this sense, the formula of "the state being regulated by the state and the enterprise being guided by the market" fails to cover the whole society. However, within the sphere of indirect regulation, which is to dominate macroeconomic management, market is always used to regulate the economy and thus guide the development of enterprises, whether the formula is mentioned or not. In this sense, this formula cannot be evaded, whose important role in the new economic operational mechanism characterized by a combination between planned economy and regulation by market forces can not be neglected.

(This article, written on May 4th, 1991, is the transcript of my speech in the second convention of the National Planning Association, which was incorporated into the collected works entitled *Explorations of Combination between Planned Economy and Market Economy*, compiled by Fang Weizhong, Beijing: China Planning Press, 1991.)

Q & A Concerning the Market-Oriented Reform

—An Interview of Liu Guoguang by *Southwest Materials Business Newspaper*

Journalist (Shi Ye): People are quite divided on the orientation of our economic restructuring. Some people ever classified these opinions into three types: planning-oriented, market-oriented and a combination between planning and market. Now, it seems that such classification has already been accepted by many people. How do you like it?

Liu Guoguang: Though such categorization seems to be very succinct and lucid, it is far from precise because it fails to reflect real divisions in theoretical circles. According to this classification, it seems that only the third type agrees that planning and market should be combined while the first two types goes against it. Actually, economics theorists all agreed (at least verbally) that planning should be and can be combined with market. Besides, the concept of market-oriented reform proposed by economics theorists can be frequently seen in print, but so far I haven't seen any idea of "planning-oriented reform", though I did ever hear or see somebody say that planning should be attached more importance. Therefore, in a strict sense, I don't approve of such categorization.

Journalist: But before that, we need to figure out the real meaning of this concept, i.e., the orientation of reform. What is the orientation of reform? Or in what way should the orientation of reform be interpreted?

Liu Guoguang: I guess, the person who made such classification might have his or her own way of interpreting the orientation of reform. What matters, according to him, might be which one, planning or market, should be attached more importance during their combination in the reform target. If the emphasis is laid on planning, the reform is market-oriented; if planning and market gain an equal footing, the reform will be a combination between them. But I disagreed with him. I believe that the orientation of reform should be the tendency of reform, in which direction transformation of economic structure is to be steered.

In the past, on the basis of natural economy and product economy was established an centrally planned economy, in which the use of market was denied. Since the reform, we began to introduce the market mechanism and tried to make economic activities conform to market laws of commodity economy so as to establish a planned commodity economy. On the one hand, we should introduce commodity economy and expand the role of market in economic regulation. On the other, we should adjust the reform of traditional planned economy to the needs of commodity economy and market laws so as to gradually establish a planned commodity economy characterized by a combination between planning and market. To put it simply, the role of market mechanism would undergo a radical change in the process of reform, from being denied or restricted to being used and even intensified. Therefore, I don't think it is implausible to call it a "market-oriented reform".

Journalist: Now more and more people have begun to use the term "market-oriented reform", but it has been interpreted rather differently. Some scholars who maintained that the reform just aimed to practice a market economy also used this term. What do you think of this?

Liu Guoguang: The meaning of the "market-oriented reform" has been discussed before. Here, I want to highlight that the market-oriented reform is not based on private ownership but public ownership instead; it does not mean to be oriented towards a spontaneous and anarchic market, but a market characterized by macro-control and planned management. It would be incorrect to interpret market orientation as anti-planning. The market-oriented reform aims to bring into full play the market mechanism and the positive role of market in economic regulation under the guidance of planning and subject to macro-control.

Journalist: You proposed to carry out the "market-oriented reform" very early. Could you please tell us why China's economic restructuring has to be "market-oriented"?

Liu Guoguang: It is not very hard to understand. Our economic restructuring aims to expand the commodity-money relations, develop market relations, and bring the role of market mechanism into full play. The fundamental difference between the new economic structure and the old one lies in how commodity-market relations are viewed and dealt with. In the past, we relied on mandatory planning and administrative orders to manage the economy, refusing to use market and market mechanism. Such economic structure was rather necessary in the period when China was very poor with just a unitary public sector and needed to concentrate on accomplishing great things. However, with the rapid growth of economy, pluralization of economic structure and diversification of economic tasks, it has become more and more ill-suited to the needs of resource allocation, and thus affected economic benefits and the development of social productive forces.

The only way to break with the rigid or semi-rigid traditional system and to invigorate the economy is to develop market relations and to rely on market to increase pressures on enterprises, so that market forces would replace administrative orders as the major means of regulating our economy especially micro-economic activities and thus the role of market would be expanded in economic regulation. As the market mechanism is intrinsic to commodity economy and market forces are the major means of regulating commodity economy, it goes without saying that we must bring the market mechanism into full play in order to develop commodity economy. That's why I believe that the "market-oriented reform" is the only right choice for China.

Journalist: Since the Third Plenary Session of the 11th Central Committee of the CPC, more than 10 years have passed, during which China has made a remarkable journey in economic restructuring. How do you view this reform?

Liu Guoguang: Despite many mistakes and setbacks in the process of our economic restructuring over these years, we must acknowledge that the direction of economic restructuring is absolutely right. Since the reform, our economic operational mechanism has changed a lot, and the role of market has also become more and more prominent in economic regulation. For example, 50% prices are now set by market; 60% to 70% raw materials needed by enterprises are supplied through market; management of enterprises by the government is undergoing a transition from direct management to indirect management, with the latter being achieved mainly through tax rate, exchange rate, and interest rate etc.; the number of mandatory plans made by State Development Planning Commission has reduced from 120 to 60; the percentage of products manufactured according to mandatory plans in gross industrial output has reduced to 16.2% from over 80% in

1984, etc. Obviously, all these changes have one thing in common, that is, they all proved that the reform is a process in which marketization keeps expanding and deepening.

Thanks to the market-oriented reform within more than a decade, China's economy has made a lot of rapid, remarkable progress: national economy is growing by 9% annually; the rural areas which used to be poor and backward have now changed for the better economically; the lackluster market with shortage economy has now been full of vigor and vitality with a great variety of goods available; the lives of both urban and rural residents have been improved a lot since the founding of new China. Every witness of our economic reform can feel and see these changes. More specifically, the more marketized or the more closely linked with market a region, sector, or enterprise is, the more invigorated its economy would be and the more economic progress it will make. On the contrary, economic sectors or regions which are rather irrelevant to market or less penetrated by the market, or those using the market less effectively tend to make little or no economic progress, which is all there to be seen.

Journalist: But it was also said that all current economic problems and loss of macroeconomic control a few years ago had something to do with the increased role of market, directly or indirectly. And what is more, it was even believed that these consequences were the inevitable result of the market-oriented reform. What's your opinion?

Liu Guoguang: Since the reform, China has gradually broken with the old, traditional economic structure, and the new economic system is now still in the making, which will inevitably give rise to contradictions, disputes, and thus various economic problems. But the market-oriented reform shouldn't be to blame. Rather than the result of introduction of too much market, these problems are, on the contrary, due to the inadequacy of market mechanism. That is to say, our market mechanism is still far from complete; our market-oriented reform is still not that deep, radical or systematic. Therefore, the key solution to various economic problems is that we should still carry the market-oriented reform forward and strive to establish a planned commodity economy characterized by the combination between planned economy and regulation by market forces.

Journalist: I still have another question. why must market orientation be guided by planning and subject to macro-control?

Liu Guoguang: The market-oriented reform aims to bring the market mechanism into full play to regulate our economy, but regulation by market forces, i.e., by the law of value, has its own limitations and flaws, such as spontaneity, blindness, speculation, and arbitrariness etc. Therefore, we should respect the law of value but avoid any blind faith in it in the meantime. We shouldn't fondly believe that the law of value is almighty and thus leave all economic matters to it. I think that at least the following matters shouldn't be left to the law of value alone, but instead they should be guided by planning and subject to macroeconomic control. The first matter is the overall economic equilibrium—regulation over aggregate supply and aggregate demand. If it is left to the law of value alone, our economy would end up with cyclical fluctuations and frequent economic crises. The second matter involves adjustment of major structures, including the balance between agriculture and industry, that between heavy industry and light industry, that between the primary, secondary and tertiary industries, that between accumulation and consumption, that between process industry and basic industry etc. The third matter concerns fair competition. The notion that market can guarantee a 100% fair competition is impractical. The fourth matter involves the issues concerning ecological balance, environmental protection and the "external diseconomy". The fifth matter is the relations between equity and efficiency. All these matters should not be left to the market alone, i.e., the "invisible hand", but in the meantime, the visible hand, i.e., state or government intervention, should also play a necessary role in economic regulation.

All in all, in order to carry out the market-oriented reform, we shouldn't have any blind faith in market while practicing a planned commodity economy, but attach importance to state planning and macroeconomic regulation instead, that is to say, we should value the role of "birdcage". Surely, the size of "birdcage" varies from sector to sector, and from product to product. Here, it is necessary to highlight that the reform of planned economy should be adjusted to the needs of commodity economy. If economic development strategies are plausible, macroeconomic policies are appropriate, and the development of the national economy is proportionate, economic liberalization and privatization would not occur in the process of market-oriented reform; but instead it will stimulate the national economy to grow even more steadily and vigorously.

Journalist: After three years' efforts in economic rectification, our macroeconomic climate has improved a lot and our economic restructuring has entered a new golden era. So, could you please talk about the orientation of our economic restructuring in the 1990s and its major steps?

Liu Guoguang: Practices have proved that the orientation of our economic restructuring since the Third Plenary Session of the 11th Central Committee of the CPC is totally right. So we still need to carry out the reform forward in the same direction that we used to take more than a decade ago, that is, a market-oriented reform guided by state planning and subject to macroeconomic regulation. Though we've made a lot of progress thanks to the reform, we should continue to carry the market-oriented reform forward by further expanding the role of market mechanism and reforming planned economy to suit the needs of market in commodity economy. Only in this way can we establish gradually a new planned commodity economy characterized by a combination between planned economy and regulation by market forces.

I believe that along this course, our economic restructuring in the 1990s should be carried out in the following ways: First, we need to gradually establish an effective and practical macroeconomic regulation mechanism to suite the needs of combination between planned economy and regulation by market forces. In order to achieve this, we need carry forward reforms of fiscal, financial and income distribution systems and improve fiscal, monetary and income distribution policies etc. Second, we should establish gradually a responsive market mechanism, which requires us to narrow the scope of mandatory planning, establish and improve various market rules and mechanisms, maintain the market order, speed up the formation of a unified national market, accelerate the pricing reform, straighten out price relations, and establish a market signaling system that could reflect market changes promptly, precisely and responsively. Third, we should ensure micro-economic activities full of vigor and vitality. In order to achieve this, we need transform the operational mechanism of enterprises by forcing them to enter the market and strive to forge them into competitive market players as both manufactures and operators responsible for their own decisions concerning their operation and development and accountable for their own profits and losses.

I firmly believe that China's hopes lie in the deepening of reform and opening-up, and the key to its success will be its great determination in carrying out the market-oriented reform.

(This article was published in *Southwest Materials Business Newspaper*, February 11th, 1992)

A Marxist Philosophical Approach to Sum up China's Reform and Opening-up

A nation that never reflects on its past will not become a great one. The greatness of a nation is closely related to its relentless spirit. China's thirty years' reform and opening-up is such a great campaign concerning the well-being of the whole nation that we must, more than ever, reflect on it in an all-round way. Reflection means to sum up and learn from the past experiences. However, people might vary in positions, views and approaches while summing up experiences.

Marxists never conceal their positions, views and approaches. It is our communist party's consistent way and tradition to adopt a Marxist approach to analyze problems. Since the reform and opening-up is the result of Chinese people's explorations under the guidance of universal Marxist principles, and that the system of socialism with Chinese characteristics is the result of integration of Marxist basic tenets with China's concrete practice of reform and opening-up, we surely can use Marxist philosophy to sum up China's three decades' reform and opening-up. Here, I would like to use some Marxist methodologies to make a summary of China's reform and opening-up within the three decades.

A dialectical analysis of the reform and opening-up within the three decades

The law of unity of opposites reveals that everything, including all matters, phenomena and processes, is a unity of opposites. "There are two sides to everything", which is a brief scientific summary of the law of unity of opposites, the basic law of materialist dialectics, by Mao Zedong.

The People's Republic of China has witnessed an extraordinary course of development since its founding nearly 60 years ago. It is true that China has met with many setbacks and made some detours as well during the first half of the six decades. But our remarkable achievements should be neither overshadowed by these problems nor be erased from the course of history just like what some people did. In the second half of the six decades, i.e., the period of reform and opening-up, China has achieved more accomplishments than what it did in the first half, which is a fact that is obvious to all. During the second half period of time, China has witnessed a steady and fast economic growth, a rapid increase in the economic aggregate, a marked growth in fiscal revenue for many consecutive years, and the growth of national economic strength by a large margin. By the end of 1999, China had come up to the seventh place in the world in terms of economic aggregate. Afterwards, China has overtaken that of Italy, France and the UK. At present, China has already surpassed Germany in terms of economic aggregate. If we can keep the momentum, it is highly possible that we would surpass Japan within five years. In terms of purchasing power parity (PPP), we've already become the second largest economy in the world, next to the United States. In China, the value of imports and exports has increased very rapidly, and China's share in global trade volume is also on a steady rise. China has now grown into a force to be reckoned with in the world economic arena. In terms of trade voluem, China has now vaulted into the third place from the sixth one in 2001, having surpassed the UK, France and Japan. In the period of rapid economic growth, incomes of both urban and rural residents have increased markedly and people's well-being has been improved a lot. All in all, both our reform and opening-up and the campaign of building a moderately prosperous society in all respects have yielded a lot of good results.

In comparison with the past one, the current economic structure has become more flexible. Currently, we have initially established the system of socialist market economy, in which market forces, subject to macroeconomic regulation by the state, serve as the basic means of regulating resource allocation, and thus have overcome many negative effects caused by the traditional rigid economic system. Transformation of enterprise operational mechanism has vigorously promoted the upgrading of traditional industries, enhanced these enterprises' capacity of linking production and operation with market demand, accelerated the transition of economic growth pattern from the extensive one to an intensive one, and improved both quality and benefits of our economy.

Therefore, we should affirm these gratifying achievements over the past three decades, but at the same time, we should not overlook many problems and potential risks, either. This is exactly what the saying "there are two sides to everything" means.

Over the past three decades, especially in the recent period, our society and economy are faced with profound changes, with many deep contradictions having surfaced. Even though we used to have some problems of this kind, they were just minor ones. But now, they have already stood out as major ones. Here, I would like to list some of them. First, income inequality keeps worsening. The Gini Coefficient, though not valid enough to give the whole picture, has grown very rapidly in recent years. At the beginning of the reform and opening-up, the Gini coefficient was less than 0.3; now it has risen to nearly 0.5, which is rarely high even in the world. Now, our problem of income inequality is almost on the top list in the world. Second, corruption is so rampant that economic crimes keep increasing and even worsening. Third, the society is suffering from moral decline, so much so that things are done usually for the sake of expediency rather than morality. lastly, the environment has been severely damaged and the shortage of resources is getting worse.

People are all very much concerned about these problems, worrying that they would lead to great disasters if they keep growing unchecked. Thanks to the reform, the productive forces might be more developed, and national economic strength might be improved as well. However, the reform could not be called a socialist success if the wealth is more and more concentrated in the hands of very few people; rather, it will be at most a capitalist one. If we cannot keep the reform on the right track, such scenario is not impossible, and that possibility cannot be totally ruled out.

Does it mean that just like what some people claimed, Deng Xiaoping's repeated warning that "the reform would end up with failure if our policies lead to polarization"[1] has already come true? I answered this in my article entitled "Reflections on several issues concerning the relations between distribution and ownership"[2]. I argued that though income inequality was already very serious in China, the society had by then neither been polarized nor reached an unbearable limit. Here I want to emphasize that our party and government are making hundredfold efforts to find solutions to the widening of income gap and other problems concerning people's livelihood very conscientiously.

In short, the reform is in general very successful. We should view it dialectically by dividing it into two sides. Despite many flaws and mistakes, we should neither dismiss all achievements we've made in the reform, nor call it a failure. Our reform tolerates no retrogression or total denial.

Negation of negation—reform as a higher-level synthesis

The law of negation of negation is also a universal dialectical law. To put it simply, it undergoes three phases: thesis, antithesis, and synthesis. Contradiction

1 See: Deng Xiaoping, *Selected Works of Deng Xiaoping* vol. 3, Beijing: People's Publishing House, 1993: 111.

2 Liu Guoguang, "Reflections on Several Issues Concerning the Relations between Ownership and Distribution", *China Opening Journal*, vol. 5, 2007.

exists in everything and every contradiction tends to undergo two rounds of negation. In the first round of negation, quantitative change evolves into qualitative change; and in the second round, a new quantitative change takes place and develops into a new qualitative change. Therefore, in the course of the development of contradiction, the thing in the previous stage is negated and then develops into a new thing, which is later negated again and develops into another new thing. Negation of negation is not a retrogression, but a synthesis achieved on a higher level. This is why things keep moving upward.

We should view the process of China's reform in a dialectical way, too. If we consider the period before the reform as a "thesis", the period of reform and opening-up will be an "antithesis", and a negation is thus formed. Here, the so-called "thesis" and "antithesis" are purely methodological or logic terms, rather than value judgments. Therefore, it does not mean to deny the value of reform and opening-up at all.

"Thesis" and "antithesis" before and after the reform and opening-up respectively have clearly manifested themselves in every aspect and level of social and economic life. They are mainly as follows: First, the economic mechanism has changed from socialist planned economy to socialist market economy. Having taken the place of planning, market forces have begun to serve as the basic means of regulating economic activities. Second, in terms of ownership structure, we used to have an exclusive public sector, believing that it is the best ownership structure for socialism and that everything should be owned by the state. Since the reform and opening-up, many types of ownership have unprecedentedly begun to develop side by side, including individual economy, private sector, foreign sector, and mixed ownership economy, etc. Third, in terms of distribution system, distribution according to work just existed in name before the reform. Indiscriminate egalitarianism used to be practiced only to dampen most people's enthusiasm and passion for work. Since the reform, some people were encouraged to get rich first and such policy did prove to be successful. Just as Deng Xiaoping expected, some people did get rich first and the income gap was indeed created, too. All these are good results of the reform and opening-up, having benefited social progress and economic development a lot.

Only by thesis and antithesis within the three decades could we make so much progress, but in the meantime, it also gave rise to many new contradictions. Three decades later, we are now entering a new phase, in which we must apply new thesis and antithesis to these new contradictions so as to achieve a new synthesis on a higher level.

In terms of operational mechanism, re-emphasis should be laid on state macroeconomic regulation by planning while the market-oriented reform is to be carried forward

Since the reform, our economy has witnessed a gradual change from traditional planned economy to socialist market economy. With the expansion of its role, market has gradually gain an upper hand and thus given a huge boost to our economic growth. In the circulation of all commodities, over 90% products are regulated by market forces. Several years ago, it was estimated that 70% of China's economy had been marketized. In this sense, we can say that socialist market economy has been initially established.

Currently, socialist market economy is still far from being complete and perfect. Market economy has not developed enough in some aspects, such as resource factor market, capital and financial market, etc., which still need further improvement. However, due to lack of experience and "market infantilism", over-marketization occurred in some fields such as education, medical care and housing etc., where marketization was not supposed to occur at all. Market was so blindly worshiped that a series of bad consequences had already been brought about.

Since the initial establishment of market economy, both positive and negative aspects of market have been fully exposed. Three decades later, inherent flaws of market economy have gradually come to the surface despite its strengths in stimulating competition and optimizing resource allocation. For example, something has gone wrong with the balance between aggregate demand and aggregate supply, resource conservation, environmental protection, and income distribution. These problems cannot be solved by market alone.

To sum up, due to the three-decade reform and opening-up, a lot of achievements have been made, but in the meanwhile many new contradictions also emerged, especially in resource conservation, environmental protection, distribution of income and wealth and people's livelihood, etc. It has something to do with the failure of state macroeconomic regulation by planning to keep up with the process of marketization.

The market economy we aim to establish is a market economy subject to state macroeconomic control, which has been written into the document of the 14th National Congress of the CPC.[1] Over these years, China kept improving state macroeconomic regulation and a lot of progress has been made. We have managed to control inflation and deflation successively while striving to mitigate short-term economic fluctuations. However, the guidance of state planning for short-term and long–term macroeconomic development has drastically declined; plans mostly involved compilation of polices but seldom included any tasks with accountability or binding quotas; a huge mismatch existed between plans and real work; state planning failed to control the local blind pursuit of GDP growth. As a result, state planning has been rather weak and even dispensable. All these facts have undermined the effectiveness of macroeconomic regulation and control and thus resulted in many imbalances in social and economic development.

Now It's high time for us to give more weight to state planning and reinforce its guiding role in macroeconomic regulation and control while carrying the market-oriented reform further forward. In response to the situation that state macroeconomic planned regulation cannot keep up with the development of market economy, the 17th National Congress of the CPC put forward, "we should give play to the guiding role of national development plans, programs and industrial policies in macroeconomic regulation and combine the use of fiscal and

1 *Documents of the 14th National Congress of the Communist Party of China*. Beijing: People's Publishing House, 1992.

monetary policies to improve macroeconomic regulation."[1] The re-emphasis on the guiding role of state planning, which hasn't been mentioned for years, by the 17th National Congress of the CPC is of great significance.

As we all know, there are several major means of macroeconomic regulation: fiscal policies, monetary policies and planning. Industrial policies are also a means of planning, the same is true with programs. So, means of macroeconomic regulation mainly break into the three types as mentioned before. Only a few market economies set up planned agencies to make predictive plans, but they seldom used planning as a means of regulation. However, it is necessary for socialist China to use planning as a means of macroeconomic regulation. The report of the 14th National Congress of the CPC has stated very clearly, "state planning is one of the important means of macroeconomic regulation."[2] In the triad of fiscal policy, monetary policy and planning, planning should serve as a guide for both fiscal and monetary policies, and fiscal and monetary policies need the guidance of planning as well. State planning is inseparable from macroeconomic regulation, with the former serving as the backbone of the latter.

State planning covers annual plans and medium-to-long term plans such as Five-Year Plans, Ten-Year Development Plans. Annual plans include indicators of economic growth, total investment volume, fiscal budget, credit volume, foreign exchange revenues and expenditures, unemployment rate, the rate of increase in prices and population growth rate etc. They are all set annually by the State Council and approved by the National People's Congress, and therefore they should have both legal and executive force. These medium-to-long programs and annual plans are expected to guide macroeconomic regulation and commit entities to complete their tasks. When it comes to the crunch, some entity should be held accountable and take legal responsibilities. Only in this way can macroeconomic

1 *Documents of the 17th National Congress of the Communist Party of China*. Beijing: People's Publishing House, 2007, p.26.

2 *Documents of the 14th National Congress of the Communist Party of China*. Beijing: People's Publishing House, 1992, p.23.

regulation be guided by state planning.

After the initial establishment of market economy, both positive and negative effects of the market have fully manifested themselves. However, people are now too obsessed with market under the slogan of "market-oriented reform", so much so that planning has almost been regarded as a taboo subject. Given such circumstance, it seems to be very necessary to reemphasize the role of state planning in macroeconomic regulation for a socialist market economy.

The 17th National Congress of the CPC reemphasized the guiding role of state planning in macroeconomic regulation, which is not a retrogression to the traditional planned economy as some people distorted. But instead, we mean to combine planning with market on a higher level, which can be manifested in the following aspects. First, the current state planning is not inclusive, but instead it only attends to macroeconomic activities; as for micro-economic activities, they are mainly regulated by the market forces. Second, market is the current basic means of regulating resource allocation, whilst planning is the necessary means to remedy the defects of market. Third, the current plans do not mainly refer to administrative orders any more, but include guiding, strategic and predictive plans instead. And at the same time, these plans must serve as a guide and commit entities to complete tasks and some entity to take responsibility when necessary.

Macroeconomic regulation under the guidance of state planning is intrinsic to socialist market economy with Chinese characteristics, so planning should never be excluded from the meaning of socialist market economy. On May 9th, 1992, Jiang Zemin, then General Secretary of the Central Committee of the CPC, revealed that the 14th National Congress of the CPC would decide on the version of "socialist market economy", because "planning is intrinsic to socialist market economy".[1] In accordance with this spirit, we should make great efforts to improve state planning and macroeconomic regulation so as to make planning

1 Jiang Zemin, *On Socialist Market Economy*, Beijing: Central Party Literature Press, 2006, p.6.

guide the development of socialist market economy in a real, practical sense and thus achieve a combination between planning and market on a higher level.

In terms of ownership structure: re-emphasis should be laid on the mainstay status of public ownership while other kinds of ownership are encouraged to develop side by side

Having undergone a negation of negation, the reform of ownership has also reached the phase of synthesis. Before the reform, we used to have an exclusive public sector, believing that it is the best ownership structure for socialism, with the result that we just kept improving relations of production in disregard of productive forces. Since the reform, many types of ownership began to develop side by side. Such radical change is a negation. The thesis-antithesis in this negation is reflected in the changing ratio of public sector to private sector, i.e., the decline in the proportion of the public sector and the rise in that of the private sector. Before the reform, there was almost none private sector in China, whilst the public sector took absolute dominance. As a result, the non-public sector has been growing faster than the public sector for fairly long, leading to a dramatic increase in the proportion of the non-public sector. Such change is very reasonable and natural. This negation involving thesis and antithesis has lasted for three decades.

So, are we now moving upward to a new phase? Are we going to re-evaluate the decline in the proportion of the public sector and the rise in that of private sector? Has it reached a critical point so that we need a new negation to achieve a new synthesis?

There are mainly three opinions about the status of public ownership (all these views were well-documented). The first opinion holds that public ownership still remains the mainstay of the economy. However, its method of calculation is quite questionable, for it also takes natural resources and administrative assets into account. Several years ago, someone tried to justify this view by including all resource assets in the calculation of state-owned assets, which would surely lead to a massive increase in public assets and thus the predominance of public ownership, as land itself has already been a large fortune. However, this explanation is far from being satisfactory. As a matter of fact, resource assets are not supposed to be included in state-owned assets, as the latter just include business assets exclusively. The second opinion holds that the mainstay status of public ownership has already been affected, and that in some regions and sectors public ownership is not the mainstay of the economy any longer. According to the third opinion, public ownership has already lost out to private ownership, and it is now an established fact that the latter has already seized the dominant role.

Those who held the third opinion fell into two groups. The first group insisted that we shouldn't leave this unattended, as it might lead to severe consequences. They suggested that the state government should find ways to reverse the situation. The second group who approved of privatization claimed that China shouldn't make a distinction between public ownership and private ownership any more. They believed that it would make no sense to do so since private ownership has already seized the dominant role and the end of privatization has already been achieved. Besides, some theorists even concluded that the economic reform had already been successfully completed, and therefore we should set about carrying out a political reform. Speaking of the "success of economic reform", they meant that privatization has already been completed. Though varying in purpose and position, these two groups both believed that public ownership was not the economic mainstay any more.

However, all these opinions were just based on their own estimates. It is hard to tell precisely China's structure of ownership before general departments and statistics bureaus release any official data concerning the ratio of public sector to private sector.

Notwithstanding these opinions, all our party's documents, from the 14th National Congress of the CPC till now, have been insisting that we should uphold the basic economic system in which public ownership is the mainstay and many kinds of ownership develop side by side, with none of them having ever denied the mainstay status of public ownership. The 17th National Congress of the CPC reiterated the party's position by affirming that we should "uphold and improve the basic economic system in which public ownership is the mainstay and many types of ownership develop side by the side".[1] These are surely no empty words, but instead economic guidelines that we must implement and carry through. In spite of these, people are nowadays still not very confident about the mainstay status of public ownership and do not know exactly the current situation of ownership structure, so such issue is a quite heated topic among the people. A suggestion has now been made to the National People's Congress in the hope that statistics bureaus and other departments concerned would make statistics or relevant documents public, and that People's Congress should exercise supervision over such matter.

Therefore, it's time that we should apply a new synthesis, which means we should unswervingly develop many kinds of ownership side by side while trying unwaveringly to keep public ownership as the mainstay of the economy, rather than lay one-sided emphasis on the development of the public-sector. That is to say, we must first of all ensure public ownership remain the mainstay of the economy, and in the meanwhile the non-public sector must be developed, too.

Some people criticized that the public sector of the economy had low efficiency, labelling it as "crony economy" or "bureaucratic economy"; they also said that public assets are not the wealth owned by the state, but by very few people[2]. I ever commented on this in an article. Public ownership is not equal to low efficiency, which has been proven by the Charter of the Anshan Iron and Steel Company, the embodiment of good experience of China's SOEs in terms of enterprise management. As we all know, many Japanese, U.S. and European enterprises ever drew on management experience from this charter; besides, some capitalist state-owned enterprises did turn out to be highly competitive rather than less efficient.

The so-called low efficiency of the public sector since the reform had something to do with anticipation of privatization. In recent years, the situation

1 *Documents of the 17th National Congress of the Communist Party of China*, p.25.
2 *China Opening Journal*, 2007, No. 5.

has even gone from bad to worse, which is closely linked with many ill tendencies these years, especially privatization. The policy of economic adjustment in previous years has given rise to "Guo tui min jin"(the state retreats whilst the private sector advances); SOE mismanagement has resulted in a huge drain of state-owned assets, some being taken away by coercion or trickery, some being just given another name, etc.; tens of millions of extremely wealthy elites came from nowhere overnight.

Besides, something is also wrong with management within the state sector of the economy. For example, due to poor management, many state-owned assets have been expropriated by very few senior executives; Even if there weren't MBO (management buy-out), some SOE leaders would still get corrupted. For instance, they enjoy an annual salary as high as several million RMB whilst common employees just get several hundred or thousand RMB per month. All these are against the nature of socialist public ownership. Some criticism that the state sector of the economy is not owned by the state any more is not totally groundless, as it did reveal some problems.

Further reforms should be carried out within SOES, as we can neither revert to the previous old indiscriminate egalitarianism, nor get bogged down in a mess just like now. Rather, we should strive to fight against monopoly and corruption and reform the incentive mechanism within enterprises in the socialist conditions so that SOEs can both have an effective incentive mechanism and guarantee social equity within SOEs. Some western countries had ever made such explorations, too. They also have SOEs and government functionaries, but their income gap is not so shockingly large as ours. Actually, SOE leaders and government functionaries both hold public office, who shouldn't be dictated by the rule of the private sector of the economy. Therefore, corruption within SOE management establishment must be cracked down.

The negation of negation that rural ownership has undergone is mainly reflected in the "two leaps" Deng Xiaoping put forward. The first leap is the abolishment of people's commune and the implementation of household-responsibility system, which is the first negation at the beginning of the reform. Due to the household-responsibility system, rural areas have witnessed tremendous changes and an economic boom over the three decades. Now we should set about achieving the second leap, that is, to develop a new collective sector of the economy, which is another form of public ownership. When Deng Xiaoping put forward "the two leaps", he said, "The principle that public ownership is the mainstay of the economy also applies to rural areas".

In July 1992, when Deng Xiaoping reviewed the draft of the report of the 14th National Congress of the CPC, he said, "I ever said that there would be two leaps in agricultural reform and development. The first one is the abolishment of people's commune and the implementation of household-responsibility system; the second is the development of the collective sector of the economy. Since the socialist economy is dominated by public ownership, there will be no exception to agriculture, in which public ownership would eventually be the mainstay of the economy." [1]This is another negation.

Rather than a retrogression to indiscriminate egalitarianism and the old system of people's commune and production team, this negation leads up to a new synthesis in a higher phase, that is, we are expected to create and embrace a new collective sector of the economy including specialized cooperative economy and community cooperative economy, with property rights of farmers and farming households being guaranteed.

The new collective (cooperative) sector has already taken root and begun to thrive on the vast land of China, such as in Huaxi village in Jiangsu province, Nanjie village in Henan province, Huangcheng village in Shanxi province, Nanshan village in Shandong province, etc. Besides, some community joint-stock cooperative enterprises also emerged in some villages in Southern Jiangsu province, Zhejiang, and Guangdong province. These collective cooperative

1 *Chronology of Deng Xiaoping's Career(1975-1997)* II , Beijing: Central Party Literature Press, 2004, p.1349.

organizations have spurred farmers on to take the road of common prosperity and quickened the pace of building a new socialist countryside. However, media and publicity departments haven't so far given due attention to it. If the government and society gave it due care, it could have opened up a bright future for China's rural economy while taking the socialist road.

In terms of distribution relations: a transition should be made from the policy of "encouraging some people to get rich first" to that of "attaching further importance to social equity"

It is absolutely right that we elect to widen income gap and encourage some people to get rich first through honest work rather than pursue indiscriminate egalitarianism. It is the most successful "negation" ever since the reform. However, if an excessively large income gap leads to a rich-poor divide and even polarization, it would be wrong and perilous. In that circumstance, a new round of negation would be needed. That is to say, those who got rich first should help others to catch up so as to reduce the gap between the rich and the poor and finally achieve common prosperity. And then we'll achieve a higher-level synthesis in terms of distribution.

In the initial period of the reform and opening-up, the policy of "giving priority to efficiency with due consideration to equity" did benefit the economy. For example, it has promoted efficiency, production and economic development. However, it would no longer apply to the next phase when the gap between the rich and the poor has been further widened. Otherwise, common prosperity would not be achieved after some people got rich first, and thus social equity cannot be guaranteed, either. At this critical point, we must pay attention to both efficiency and equity and attach further importance to social equity.

I wrote an article in 2003 entitled *A Focus on the Issue of Income Distribution in the study of Macroeconomic Situation*[1], in which I proposed that we should

1 *Collected Works of Liu Guoguang*, vol. 10, Beijing: China Social Sciences Press, 2006, pp.498-513.

"gradually abandon the previous policy of 'giving priority to efficiency with due consideration to equity' so as to achieve a smooth transition to the principle of 'paying attention to both efficiency and equity'". Later, the wording of "giving priority to efficiency with due consideration to equity" did not appear in the official report of the Fourth Plenary Session of the 16th Central Committee of the CPC.

In 2005, I reiterated it in another article entitled "Attaching Further Importance to Social Equity". Besides, I also wrote another article titled "Applying the Principle of 'Giving Priority to Efficiency' to Wherever It Is Needed"[1], which pointed out that it was inappropriate to view "equity" secondary to "efficiency" as the former should be also valued in primary distribution. However, words like "giving priority to efficiency with due consideration to equity" and "attaching more importance to efficiency in primary distribution and equity in redistribution" still appeared in the exposure draft of the document of the Fifth Plenary Session of the 16th Central Committee, which was met with some criticism. At last, these expressions did not appear in the final draft and were replaced by the slogan of "attaching further importance to social equity". Besides, the principle that "social equity should be also valued in primary distribution" was also included in central documents by the 17th National Congress[2]. It proves that my views are all consistent with the spirit of final documents of the Central Committee of the CPC.

Our policy change from "giving priority to efficiency with due consideration to equity" to "attaching further importance to social equity" does not mean a retrogression to the previous principle of indiscriminate egalitarianism; rather, it is a higher-level synthesis. In terms of the policy concerning the relations between equity and efficiency, the transition from indiscriminate egalitarianism to the widening of income gap, to "encouraging those who got rich first to help others to become rich", to "giving priority to efficiency with due consideration to equity",

1 *Collected Works of Liu Guoguang*, vol. 10, Beijing: China Social Sciences Press, 2006, pp. 623-625.
2 *Documents of the 17th National Congress of the Communist Party of China*, p.37.

and then to "paying attention to both efficiency and equity, with more emphasis on equity", and at last to "attaching importance to equity in both primary distribution and redistribution", is a typical process of thesis-antithesis-synthesis.

To sum up, economic operational mechanism, ownership structure and distribution system have all gone through the process of thesis-antithesis-synthesis. Besides, many other things have also undergone these three phases and therefore it can also apply to other cases.

However, as far as this reform is concerned, synthesis has just begun. And now we are at a crucial turn as to whether we could uphold a correct outlook on development and achieve a higher-level synthesis successfully. If we can achieve a better synthesis, socialism would not fail and China's economic development would hence be sustained. Otherwise, no economic progress would be made and socialism would be aborted, too. However, some people still believe that it would make no difference. But I am sure if we cannot uphold socialism, the society would not be stable enough to achieve a healthy and sustained economic development.

The reform and opening-up heading in the direction of socialism with Chinese characteristics has undergone a process of thesis-antithesis-synthesis, which leads to a higher-level synthesis rather than retrogression. Once it retrogresses to an earlier state, there would be no way out or no going back. It will be in the same case if the market-oriented reform is to be abandoned or over-marketization is to be practiced. Full marketization without state macroeconomic planned regulation, full privatization without public ownership serving as the mainstay of the economy, and polarization guaranteeing no social equity do not conform to the essential features of socialism. Deng Xiaoping ever said so. If we did not take the socialist road with Chinese characteristics, the reform and opening-up would end up with failure; on the contrary, if we do take such road, the reform and opening-up would promise a bright future.

In the above part, tenets of dialectical materialism philosophy such as the law of negation of negation and the rule of "everything having two sides" are applied to summarize the reform and opening-up over the three decades. Besides, the law of transformation of quantity into quality and *vice versa,* one of the laws of dialectic materialism, has also been used widely in analyzing the process of reform and opening-up, which can be shown in many examples. However, due to the limit of space, here I would not analyze it specifically. In the next part, I would like to employ several concepts and approaches to analyze some problems with China's reform and opening-up over these three decades.

On the contradiction between productive forces and relations of production

The contradiction between productive forces and relations of production is the fundamental problem that any society would have along its course of development. Productive forces and relations of production form the mode of production of a society. In the process of reform and opening-up, the contradiction between productive forces and relations of production pervaded our society. For instance, socialist market economy involves both productive forces and relations of production. On the one hand, it is a socialist economy; on the other, it is a market economy. These two aspects form a unity of opposites.

"Market economy" mainly focuses on the development of productive forces, so market must play its basic role in regulating resource allocation; otherwise, it would be hard to guarantee efficiency. This conclusion is very right, which has been put to test by practice. By way of contrast, "socialism" aims to emphasize its relations of production. The uniqueness of socialism lies in its essential characteristics embodying the relations of production, such as public ownership and common prosperity etc., without which it would not be socialism in nature.

First, the so-called "development of the productive forces being the essence of socialism" was declared by Deng Xiaoping just to oppose the absurd slogan chanted by the "Gang of Four" —"it is better to be poor under socialism than to be rich under capitalism". Therefore, it is not the definition of socialism in a broad sense. Rather, it is a feature shared by all forms of society, and each society needs to develop productive forces.

Second, socialism aims to realize prosperity for all, rather than polarization. If we just lay one-sided emphasis on productive forces rather than on relations of production or social equity, if the wealth is just concentrated in the hands of very few people rather than shared by most people, our society would end up with polarization and the rise of a new bourgeoisie. In this way, the reform would, according to Deng Xiaoping, be a failure. Deng Xiaoping ever said, "If our policies lead to polarization, our reform would end up with failure; if it gives rise to a new bourgeoisie, we would definitely have fallen into evil ways."[1] The so-called failure of reform does not mean a failure in the development of productive forces, but that in the relations of production. Productive forces might have developed for the time being, but the price is that socialist relations of production might will disappear. From the capitalist perspective, it is a victory of capitalist relations of production or the success of capitalist "reform". Therefore, "socialism" and "market economy" must be viewed as a unity, and neither of them is to be neglected. We must follow such key principle; otherwise our economy would be turned into a capitalist market economy.

Third, not all the things should fall into the dichotomy between capitalism or socialism, for instance, productive forces can't be labeled "capitalist" or "socialist", and the same is true with the generality of production relations. When it comes to making bigger indigenous jetliners, application of information technology and modernization of technology and management, we should not make any distinctions between capitalism and socialism as usual. However, if individuality of the relations of production is concerned, such distinction must be made. As for some capitalist things which do benefit our economic development, such as Sino-foreign joint ventures, Sino-foreign cooperative joint ventures, exclusively foreign-owned enterprises, we should not throw the baby out with the bath water; rather, they should be used to our advantage. But at the same time, those decaying, decadent capitalist things that run counter to human civilization must be criticized

1 See *Selected Works of Deng Xiaoping*, vol.3, p.111.

and abandoned. Therefore, as to whether to make distinctions between capitalism and socialism, we should make a concrete analysis of a concrete problem! It's also the most basic things of Marxism.

Some people who opposed making a distinction between socialism and capitalism disguised themselves as advocates of Deng Xiaoping's idea of "emancipating the mind", distorting the real meaning of Deng Xiaoping by saying that "emancipation of the mind" means to free our mind from any distinctions between capitalism and socialism, which is absolutely wrong. Deng Xiaoping did not mean to make no distinctions between capitalism and socialism in whatever cases, but instead he just suggested it when it comes to the matters of planning and market as both means of regulating economic activities, and the criteria of "Three Favorables". He said, "The proportion of planning to market forces is not the essential difference between socialism and capitalism. A planned economy is not equivalent to socialism, because there is planning under capitalism too; a market economy is not capitalism, because there are markets under socialism too. Planning and market forces are both means of controlling economic activity."[1] That is all. So, he does not mean that such a distinction should be abandoned in all circumstances. As a matter of fact, when Deng Xiaoping talked about the criteria of "three favorables", he pointed out specifically that it should "promote the growth of the productive forces in a socialist society" and "increase the overall strength of the socialist state". It shows that when it comes to matters of principle, Deng Xiaoping did believe that it is necessary to make a distinction between capitalism and socialism. Besides, Deng Xiaoping also said that he opposed bourgeois liberalization most vigorously, who kept emphasizing the necessity of adhering to the fundamental principles of socialism, namely, public ownership as the mainstay of the economy and common prosperity. So the saying that Deng Xiaoping opposes differentiating capitalism from socialism in all circumstances is just a quote out of context and a malicious intention to distort Deng Xiaoping's

1 See: *Selected Works of Deng Xiaoping,* vol. 3, p.373.

fundamental ideas.

The contradiction between the economic base and superstructure

The economic base and superstructure also form a pair of contradiction.

As far as the reform and opening-up is concerned, the contradiction between the economic base and superstructure mainly manifests itself in the contradiction between economic restructuring and political reform. Political reform falls into the category of superstructure. Such contradiction between economic restructuring and political reform has remained a very prominent issue over the three decades. Especially in recent years such an opinion could be heard among the people, to the effect that economic restructuring has already been successfully completed, but something went wrong with political reform, that is to say, superstructure cannot keep up with the economic base any more. In other words, the reform has successfully transformed China's economic system into the one in which private ownership is the mainstay of the economy, however, the political system failed to keep up with such economic system. In this logic, the political system should be adjusted to the need of privatization, that is, the entire political system needs to be westernized and led by the bourgeoisie. Some malicious forces both at home and abroad all supported such "political restructuring", scheming to make us abandon the leadership of the CPC and the socialist system.

In the beginning of the reform and opening-up, the party's work focus has shifted from class struggle to economic development, with more emphasis laid on economic reform, which is very necessary. At the same time, our party has been consistently stressing the necessity of political reform. The 13th National Congress of the CPC put forward the policy of "separating government administration from enterprise management and separating the functions of party and government", but its implementation was rather delayed since 1989 due to some changes in the situation both at home and abroad. In spite of that, reforms in the electoral system, grassroots democracy, and administrative system etc. were still carried forward in a steady pace so that democracy and the rule of law were improved bit by bit. Therefore, we have been making progress in these respects rather than end up making no achievements or having no reform. Since the 16th National Congress of the CPC, the Central Committee kept emphasizing the necessity of political restructuring. In the 17th National Congress of the CPC, it was proposed that we should unswervingly develop socialist democracy. [1]

However, we have to admit that political reform is indeed quite lagging behind the economic one. It has been suggested that we should accelerate the reform in some aspects which are believed to be rather delayed, say, checks and balances. Problems of such kind are still very serious. For example, supervision over power is much needed; major leaders dictate policy; "rule of man" has replaced "rule of law", etc. We surely don't encourage the "universal" model of the "trias politica principle" (separation of powers), but we still need balances and checks. The power with no checks and balances or no restraints is bound for corruption. Guided by this principle, the party proposed, in the 17th National Congress of the CPC, to establish and improve the power structure and operational mechanism in which the power of decision-making, executive power and the power of supervision would be checked and balanced[2]. We should step up our efforts to reform such aspects.

Take the reform of leadership election system as another example. Vladimir Lenin's idea that leaders should be elected from the people and thus be responsible for them need be promoted one level after another in China. Currently, we have lifted control over differential voting and grassroots election; some improvements have been made in the knockout system, electoral system and universal adult suffrage system, but still far from being satisfactory. We need make greater efforts to combine "electoral democracy" with "consultative democracy" in a better way, and to advance these democratic processes more vigorously within the framework of people's congress and political consultative conference in accordance with the principle of socialism and under the leadership of the Communist Party of China.

---

1 See *Documents of the 17th National Congress of the Communist Party of China*, p.27.

2 ibid, p.32.

However, neoliberalism and democratic socialism are two wrong thoughts far away from the right course of reform, both opposing the Four Cardinal Principles and socialism with Chinese characteristics. They both advocate major parties taking turn ruling the country and oppose the exclusive leadership of the communist party.

Deng Xiaoping opposed bourgeois liberalization most vigorously. Deng Xiaoping said then, "In the whole period leading up to the realization of 'Four Modernizations', at least in the remaining years of the 20th Century and the first half of the next century, we would still oppose bourgeois liberalization."[1] Deng Xiaoping emphasized that we should uphold the fundamental principle of socialism and keep public ownership as the mainstay of the economy, and avoid polarization as well. At that time, he just suggested fighting against bourgeois liberalization from the political perspective without mentioning how to solve the issue in the economic field, because such problem in the economic field was then not very acute. However, it does not mean that there was no such trend in the economic field. It actually existed in both political and economic fields. Privatization, full marketization and the idea of "government as the night watchman" are all typical phenomena of bourgeois liberalization in the economic field. To prevent the trend of bourgeois liberalization in the economic field is to protect the economic field from decay. If that happens, the political field would also fall victim to it. This is the basics of Marxism. Therefore, we need to be on high alert for any erosive influence. Some people said that the economic reform (in terms of ownership) has already been "successfully completed", and therefore a constitutional reform closely related to "universal values" should be carried out to keep up with the economic development, which is a strong signal of bourgeois liberalization. So, those who believed that the economic field did not have any ideological problems cannot be more wrong.

---

1 See *Chronology of Deng Xiaoping's Career(1975-1997)* II , Beijing: Central Party Literature Press, 2004, pp.1172-1173.

Deng Xiaoping suggested that we should oppose the "leftist" thinking and guard off the rightist thinking (note that leftist has quotation marks on it). "Leftist" ideology refers to radical left or extreme left that we must fight against. Especially in the period of democratic revolution and socialist revolution, China was severely troubled by extreme "leftist" ideology and thus suffered from a huge loss. So, from that time on, we drew a lesson from that bitter experience and were determined to fight against it. However, it should be also noted that Deng Xiaoping never opposed the leftist ideology (without any quotation marks), because Marxism, Scientific Socialism, communist party and Deng Xiaoping are all to the left. We cannot say that Deng Xiaoping is the right-wing politician or in the middle ground. If left-wing ideologies are to be indiscriminately fought against, there would be no Marxism or leadership of communist party! It would be extremely bizarre if the left is to be avoided like a plague! The communist party should be aware that it is a leftist party and therefore it should maintain a very clear stand. In fact, the communist party has been on the one hand following the center-left line and uniting with the center-rightists, and on the other opposing radical rightist ideologies and guarding off extreme "leftist" ones. If the communist party is not viewed as a left party by its members, it would surely get lost.

At least within a hundred years in the primary stage of socialism, the leadership of the CPC would remain unchanged and "the Four Cardinal Principles" can't be abandoned. So long as the communist party remains as the vanguard of the working class and keeps to the scientist socialism without being assimilated into the socialist democratic party, the basic line of the primary stage of socialism and the socialist road with Chinese characteristics will surely not be abandoned, either. However, such basic line would go nowhere without the leadership of the Communist Party of China. There would be no primary stage of socialism if our country is to be ruled by other parties. As for what is going to be like politically one hundred years later, that is, after the completion of the primary stage of socialism, it all depends. However, within a foreseeable period in the primary stage of socialism, we must continue to embrace the leadership of the

CPC, oppose any form of multi-party system, and adhere to "the Four Cardinal Principles". If many major parties take turns ruling our country, the primary stage of socialism would be put to an end. If our country is ruled by another party, the guideline would be radically changed and thus we will never reach the advanced stage of socialism.

Internal contradictions within the productive forces

There are a lot of internal contradictions within the productive forces, among which the key contradiction vital to the overall situation of the economic development is the relations between intention and extension, and those between extensive development and intensive development. The issue as to which factors we should prioritize among speed, quantity, structure, resource, environment, and quality stands out as a major issue in the development of productive forces.

The change from extensive growth to intensive growth is just one of the "dual patterns of transformation", which includes structural transformation and development pattern transformation. Actually, development pattern transformation involves internal contradictions within the productive forces. Brief though it sounds, it is indeed an essential problem. In the past, speed and quantity took precedence over structure, resource, environment and quality; and such development pattern hasn't been uprooted yet: output and speed still override other factors; especially some local governments are still blindly pursuing GDP growth, seeking to accelerate economic growth in the short run at the expense of the interests of later generations. In fact, these are typical cases of unsustainable development. Such development pattern has been so deep-rooted over the three decades since the reform and opening-up that it will be hard to reverse. Now, we are working hard on it.

In line with the requirement of the Scientific Outlook On Development, it is suggested that some changes should be made in the pattern of economic growth: in the past, economic growth was mainly propelled by investment and export, whereas nowadays consumption, investment and export should be used collaboratively to promote economic growth; in the past, the economic growth was mainly driven by the development of the secondary industry, whereas nowadays the primary, secondary and tertiary industries should be coordinated to spur the economic growth; in the past, the economic growth was mainly fueled by increasing the consumption of material resources, whereas nowadays advanced science and technology, improved personnel and management innovations are the major driving forces. These are the right ways to promote the transformation of economic development pattern from a speed-oriented growth to a comprehensive, coordinated, sustainable growth.

"Dual patterns of transformation" was put forward in the mid-1980s, and was later officially reworded as "two fundamental transformations" in party documents since the Ninth Five-Year Plan. Since the 16th National Congress, it was even more stressed by the party. In the report of the 17th National Congress of the CPC, "growth pattern" was reworded as "development pattern". [1]

Internal contradictions within productive forces are associated with the relations of production and superstructure. 30 years' experience has proved that development pattern transformation would be inhibited by the relations of production and superstructure. An excessive emphasis on GDP growth at the local level has something to do with the financial system and evaluation system etc. For example, county-level cadres were evaluated and awarded bonuses according to GDP growth; some local governments even broke the task of attracting investment into smaller ones and assigned them to every unit. No wonder they laid excessive emphasis on GDP growth! Besides, problems with resources and environment also have something to do with the price mechanism and competition. All these problems need a structural reform.

Internal Contradictions within the Relations of Production

There are also numerous internal contradictions within the relations of production. Here, I would like to only elaborate on the relations between ownership and distribution, which is an important issue in the process of our

1 see *Documents of the 17th National Congress of the Communist Party of China*, p.15.

reform.

Ownership and distribution both fall into the category of relations of production. According to Marxism, ownership determines distribution, which people tend to neglect. People made a long list of reasons for the widening of the gap between the rich and the poor, such as the expansion of urban-rural disparity, regional imbalances, industry monopoly, corruption, uneven supply of public goods, and inadequate redistribution etc., to name but a few. All these reasons make sense, but neither of them is the most fundamental one. The rooted cause of inequitable income distribution has been ignored.

Property ownership tends to affect income gap the most. Even Paul Anthony Samuelson, a western capitalist economist, had to acknowledge that wealth determines income gap the most, whereas individual capabilities do not make any big difference. He said that property ownership is the number one factor determining the income gap, with individual capabilities, education, training, opportunities and health coming next to it one by one.[1] Besides, the widening of the gap between the rich and the poor over the three decades since the reform and opening-up is also closely related to changes in ownership structure, i.e., the decline in the proportion of the public sector and the rise in that of private sector and the spread of privatization. Such connection has however been deliberately avoided by some scholars in their analysis of reasons for the widening of the income gap.

When it comes to adjusting income distribution relations and narrowing the gap between the rich and the poor, people tend to focus on distribution relations and especially redistribution such as taxation and transfer payments so as to enhance social security and improve the livelihood of low-income people. These measures are absolutely necessary and we've already begun to take actions. However, it is far from enough to just focus on distribution and redistribution, as it is impossible to reverse the widening of gap between the rich and the poor at its

1 See Samuelson, Paul A.: *Economics: An Introductory Analysis,* 1948.

source. Rather, we also need to take other perspectives into consideration as well, such as ownership structure and property system etc. Only in this way can we eventually prevent income inequality from widening and the trend of polarization from worsening and thus achieve common prosperity. Just as Deng Xiaoping ever noted, "So long as public ownership is the mainstay of the economy in our economy, polarization will be avoided."[1] The aforementioned new synthesis in terms of distribution is conditioned by the new synthesis in terms of ownership. Therefore, we need keep public ownership as the mainstay of the economy and unswervingly develop both public and private sectors of the economy, rather than lay one-sided emphasis on either of them. Besides, we also need slow down the decline in the proportion of the public sector and the rise in that of the private sector, and strive to prevent private ownership from replacing public ownership and becoming the mainstay of the economy.

The relations between social being and social consciousness

The relationship between ideology and social being is another important issue in historical materialism.

Social being determines social consciousness, and social consciousness would reversely affect social being. Advanced social consciousness promotes social progress, while decadent social consciousness hinders social progress. In this respect, we have gone through a lot over the three decades, especially with regard to the relations between the emancipation of the mind and the reform and opening-up.

Deng Xiaoping handled the relations between them very well. "Emancipating the mind and seeking the truth from facts" has been reestablished as the ideological line, which is closely linked with Deng Xiaoping's idea of reform and opening-up. Deng Xiaoping pointed out, "Only thus (by emancipating our minds) can we, guided as we should be by Marxism-Leninism and Mao Zedong Thought,

1 See *Selected Works of Deng Xiaoping,* Vol. 3, Beijing: People's Publishing House, 1993, p.149.

find correct solutions to the emerging as well as inherited problems, fruitfully reform those aspects of the relations of production and of the superstructure that do not correspond with the rapid development of our productive forces, and chart the specific course and formulate the specific policies, methods and measures needed to achieve the 'four modernizations' under our actual conditions."[1] By emancipating our minds, Deng Xiaoping means that we should understand correctly Marxism, Leninism and Mao Zedong thought so that they would guide us while we're striving to solve a series of problems we might be confronted with on our way forward. They are the very foundation for the emancipation of the mind.

The reason why I repeatedly quoted Deng Xiaoping's words is that some people's so-called emancipation of the mind is already divorced from this very foundation, but they are still "holding high" the banners of Deng Xiaoping thought and using grandiose words to "encourage" people to "further emancipate their minds". They called it a "new emancipation of the mind" or "the third emancipation of the mind", claiming that people are supposed to further emancipate their minds by "breaking with distinctions between socialism and capitalism" and "breaking with distinctions between public ownership and private ownership" . To put it briefly, they encourage people to break away from "ownership worship". The real intention of the so-called "new emancipation of the mind" is to put an end to the mainstay status of public ownership and the basic economic system of socialism and thus end socialism.

Some people misleadingly called the slogan of "emancipating the mind" proposed in the 17th National Congress of the CPC a "new" emancipation of the mind. They purposefully highlighted the ideological debate concerning "socialism VS capitalism" and "public ownership VS private ownership" running through the past three decades' reform and stressed that every major breakthrough in the reform and opening-up was preceded by the emancipation of the mind.

1 *Selected works of Deng Xiaoping*, Vol. 2, People's Publishing House, 1994, p.141.

So what is new in their so-called "new" emancipation of the mind? In their own words, the reason why it is said to be "new" is that people should emancipate their minds by breaking with distinctions between socialism and capitalism, and that socialist concepts shouldn't be used to thwart any efforts to realize capitalism. These people have totally twisted the original intention of Deng Xiaoping. Mr. Deng made it very clear that adherence to socialism is the precondition for the reform and opening-up. He said, "the reform and opening-up concerns how we take the socialist road. In terms of system, socialism is the very foundation we cannot do without in the reform and opening-up, otherwise we will head towards capitalism, say, polarization.[1]

To sum up, there are altogether two types of "emancipation of the mind". The first type is guided by Marxism, Leninism and scientific socialism, steering the reform and opening-up to the self-improvement of socialism. The other one is guided by neoliberalism and democratic socialism, steering our reform and opening-up away from the path our party had planned. So, we should not naively believe that all ways to emancipate the mind would guide and promote our reform and opening-up in the right direction. Rather, we should guard against any attempts to misguide the reform and opening-up under the disguise of the emancipation of the mind.

Surely, it is an inevitable trend that many social thoughts including non-Marxism and anti-socialism will emerge with the pluralization of social being and social interests. We can learn from the history that neither a laissez-faire attitude nor forbidding policies will work. A harmonious society should rightfully embrace all of them, but there should also be a limit. We would not allow some wrong thoughts to confuse and numb people; we would not let disasters in the former Soviet Union resulting from Mikhail Gorbachev's promotion of "pluralism" and "glasnost" repeat in China; we would not allow these wrong thoughts to misguide

1 See *Chronology of Deng Xiaoping's Career(1975-1997)* II, Beijing: Central Party Literature Press, 2004, p.1317.

our reform and development. Therefore, while tolerating the coexistence of non-Marxist and anti-socialist thoughts, we must emphasize the central theme. In other words, we must publicize Marxism more practically rather than merely as a formality; we must publicize scientific socialism and socialism with Chinese characteristics marked by adherence to the Four Cardinal Principles and the reform and opening-up. It is necessary that we should use these thoughts to educate people, unify their thinking, and consolidate the ideological basis for social unity and progress. We should give people more rights to speak to publicize correct thoughts and criticize wrong thoughts. Criticism and anti-criticism has always been the only road to the scientific truth. It is too naïve to believe that the peaceful coexistence of all social thoughts will be conducive to the building of a harmonious society, which turns out to be just the way round. But at the same time, we must prevent anybody from taking advantage of contention and rivalry among many social thoughts to sow discord in the harmonious society.

Now, three decades have passed since the reform and opening-up. We should continue to emancipate our minds and keep pace with the times. But the precondition is that we must be guided by Marxism, Leninism and Mao Zedong thought the way they should. That is to say, we should be guided by the theory of socialism with Chinese characteristics, the result of integration of the basic tenets of Marxism with the practice of contemporary China, trying to find solutions to the inherited and emerging problems and to reform those aspects of the relations of production and of the superstructure that do not conform to the rapid development of the productive forces. We must banish the traditional socialist thoughts that failed to adapt to the self-improvement of socialism so as to establish socialist market economy fit for the primary stage of socialism. For example, people used to believe that commodity/market economy is incompatible with socialism, that there should be just a unitary public sector, and that the non-public sector of the economy would never be tolerated to co-exist with the public sector, etc.

In future, we need make further efforts to remove ideological obstacles hindering the self-improvement of socialism so as to establish new thoughts and concepts promoting social progress. However, we should set a limit for the emancipation of the mind, that is, Marxism and scientific socialism keeping pace with the times. If the line is overstepped and the primary stage of socialism is skipped, it is not the type of "emancipation of the mind" we desire or anticipate to have.

(This article's original title is "A Marxist Philosophical Approach to Sum up China's Reform and Opening-up over the Three Decades", which was published in *Social Sciences in China,* 2008, No. 6)

An Overall Perspective on the History of PRC over the Past Six Decades

—the first half and the second half

This year marks the 60th anniversary of the founding of the People's Republic of China. Under the leadership of the Communist Party of China, China has made remarkable achievements in both the first and second half of the six decades after painstaking efforts of its people in building socialism. It is natural that, based on what China has achieved in the first half of the 60 years, China has achieved more during the second half. But during these two periods we have both made many detours and some mistakes. It is necessary for us to summarize and draw valuable lessons from prior experience so that we can refer to and reconsider them in future explorations.

Last year marked the 30th anniversary of the Third Plenary Session of the 11th Central Committee. At that time, it was very necessary to highlight our achievements over the three decades since the reform and opening-up. And it was also not strange that people tended to make a difference between the first half and the second half, because they wanted to highlight the second one. However, some people took advantage of such occasion to deliberately deny what we have achieved in the first half of the 60 years, to distort the history of our party, to deny the leaders of our party, to erase the period between 1949 and 1978 from history, to "straighten out the history" and to "force it to stand trial".

Under the disguise of academic studies on historical segmentation, some unscrupulous scholars even proposed that there were only two epoch-making events in China's history since the First Opium War, namely, the Revolution of 1911 and the reform and opening-up in 1978. Such malicious intention of denying the symbolic meaning of the founding of the People's Republic of China and all achievements China has made during the first half of the 60 years is all too clear.

In contrast, some people did admit that the founding of the People's Republic of China ushered in a new era of socialism (away from the semi-feudal and semi-colonial society), but in the meanwhile they also believed that the Third Plenary Session of the 11th Central Committee of the CPC was of the same epoch-making significance. It seems that they just elevated the role of the Third Plenary Session of the 11th Central Committee, but in essence the epoch-making significance of the founding of the PRC in bringing about a fundamental change in the social system was thereby unconsciously written off from the modern and contemporary history of China. We have to admit that due to the Third Plenary Session of the 11th Central Committee, China did move upward to a new phase of socialism (i.e., the reform and opening-up), and therefore this session was indeed of great importance in the history of the PRC. However, it did not usher in a new era so that it could not be said to have epoch-making significance.

History is always full of twists and turns. In the first half of the 60 years, China did make some detours and many mistakes, most of which stemmed from a rush for quick results in terms of economic development and social transformation. For instance, we were too eager to succeed in the period of "Great Leap Forward"; class struggles were artificially extended such as the extreme "leftist" thinking in the period of "the Cultural Revolution". However, these mistakes can never overshadow great achievements that China has made in the first half of the 60 years, including the establishment of socialist system putting an end to semi-feudalism and semi-colonialism, the establishment of a rather complete industrial system and national economic system, and its success of gaining an independent footing in the world arena. Mistakes in the first half of the 60 years should be secondary to its achievements in that period. The same holds true with respect to the second half of the 60 years, during which China has made many remarkable accomplishments such as a rapid economic growth, the improvement of people's lives in general, and its entry into the world arena in terms of both economy and politics, etc. However, a lot of regressions also occurred at the same time. Regressions in social relations include "the three big gaps", the widening of income inequality, the decline of morality, etc.; regressions in the relations between society and nature include damages to resources, and deterioration of the ecological environment, etc. The party and government are making great efforts to solve all these problems. However, these flaws can never eclipse immense achievements we've made since the reform and opening up, i.e., in the second half of the 60 years. Likewise, flaws and mistakes in the second half of the six decades are secondary to its remarkable achievements in this period.

On the occasion of celebrating the 60th anniversary of the PRC, we should see both achievements and mistakes in the two halves of the six decades in perspective. We must neither compare mistakes in the first half of the six decades with achievements in the second half, nor depreciate the first half so as to highlight and compliment the second half. It is not fair to do so. It is socialism that united the 60 years since the founding of the PRC into a whole; and the most precious gift the PRC gave to the Chinese people is also socialism. Six decades ago, China ushered in a new era of socialism just like a rising Sun. Over the six decades, new China has undergone two critical phases. In the first phase, i.e., in the first half of the six decades, China established the socialist system and pointed out the basic direction for socialism; in the second phase, i.e., in the second half of the six decades since the Third Plenary Session of the 11th Central Committee, China continued to build socialism on the basis of achievements it has made in the first half of the period. Achievements and mistakes, be it in the first half or in the second half, are both closely linked with socialism like what flesh is to blood. Six decades later, new China is still towering in the east of the world keeping to socialism with Chinese characteristics. Socialist China has never abandoned the socialist road, and its people would never allow it to do so, which is the source of pride for hundreds of millions of Chinese people.

Economic development and class struggle

Since the reform and opening-up, the focus of our party has been shifted from class struggle to economic development. Such shift has vigorously spurred the party and the whole country on to concentrate all their efforts on economic development and thus greatly enhanced our economic strength. At the same time, it also gave rise to such an opinion that only in the second half period did we begin to abandon the class struggle and value economic development so that China was finally built into a strong and prosperous country. However, in the first half of the six decades, they believed, China had been focusing on class struggle at the expense of economic development, resulting in backwardness and isolation. As a matter of fact, such description did not fit the reality of new China's development.

1. Division on the principal contradiction in China's society

Major tasks are usually determined by the principal domestic contradiction. So what is the principal contradiction in socialist China? Is it the contradiction between the proletariat and the bourgeoisie, that between the socialist road and the capitalist road, or that between the ever-growing material and cultural needs of the people and the low level of production? Since the nationwide success of the New-Democratic Revolution in 1949, the whole party has reached a consensus that contradictions between the proletariat and the bourgeoisie, between the socialist road and capitalist road have become the principal contradiction in Chinese society.

However, since the completion of socialist transformation and the establishment of the socialist system, our understanding of the principal contradiction with the society has undergone some twists and turns. In the Eighth National Congress of the CPC it was declared that the principal contradiction has already been the one between the ever-growing material and cultural needs of the people and the low level of production, and that the major task of the party and country has been transformed from liberating the productive forces to protecting and developing the productive forces. That is to say, the focus of our work should be shifted onto economic development. However, given the circumstance after the Anti-rightist struggle in 1957, Mao Zedong reestablished the contradictions between the proletariat and the bourgeoisie, between the socialist road and the capitalist road as the principal contradiction. He further developed and reinforced this notion in the Tenth Plenary Session of the 8th Central Committee of the CPC in 1962. He believed that the struggle between two classes and two roads would continue to exist even in the whole historical period of socialism, which also explained why he proposed the theory of "ongoing revolution under the dictatorship of the proletariat" in the Cultural Revolution. In this way, the class struggle that should have existed within a certain scope has been extended and absolutized, resulting in social unrest and turmoil over a decade.

2. The opinion that China just focused on class struggle disregarding economic development in the first half of the six decades is wrong

Even though we had made some detours by exaggerating and extending the class struggle, it shouldn't be simply said that Mao Zedong and our party were then just focused on the class struggle disregarding economic development. Mao Zedong has long since proposed that the advanced nature of a party lies in its capacity of promoting the development of the productive forces through reforms of the superstructure and the relations of production. In the revolutionary war, Mao Zedong attached great importance to the economy in revolutionary bases so as to guarantee the supply to maintain war efforts. Shortly after the seizure of key cities, the work focus was shifted onto production. In the adjustment and recovery period when a transition was being made to socialism, even the struggle between restrictions and counter-restrictions on private capital and transformation of ownership were also arranged around the central task of socialist industrialization.

The general line for building socialism did reflect the vast people's urgent desire to end economic and cultural backwardness, but such eagerness to succeed has led to premature advances in disregard of objective economic laws, which were later corrected through some readjustment measures in the 1960s. Even though the class struggle was elevated to the unprecedented high position in the Tenth Plenary Session of the 8th Central Committee of the CPC, Mao Zedong still pointed out that we should separate work from class struggle, that is, we should neither allow our work (including the economic work) to be hampered by the class struggle nor let class struggle be superior to our work. It turned out that the reemphasis on class struggle did not affect our economic work too much and the task of economic readjustment and recovery was successfully completed.

Even in the turbulent decade of the "Cultural Revolution", it was still proposed that we should "promote production" aside from the slogan of "emphasizing revolution". Even though the national economy did suffer some losses due to the class struggle, only two years in the decade witnessed economic decline and in the remaining eight years the economy still continued to grow. Besides, some achievements were even made in certain key fields. In the Fourth National People's Congress in 1975, Premier Chou En-lai reiterated the great two-step development strategy for the achievement of "Four Modernizations", which was put forward as early as in the Third National People's Congress in 1965 and later became the guiding principle for our economic development campaign, including the period after the "Cultural Revolution".

Therefore, we mustn't deny any efforts and achievements the Chinese people have made in economic development campaigns under the leadership of Mao Zedong in the first half of the six decades. Otherwise, there would be no "socialist economic base" or "a rather complete industrial and national economic system" we have had today! We have to admit that economic development campaigns were indeed affected by the extended class struggle, such as the economic regression in the era of "Great Leap Forward", some economic losses in the "Cultural Revolution", etc. Without these detours and mistakes, we would have gone even further in terms of economic development.

3. From the reemphasis on economic development as the central task in 1978 to the formation of "Scientific Outlook on Development"

It was proposed in the Third Plenary Session of the 11th Central Committee that the focus of the whole party and country should be shifted back to economic development, which was originally put forward in the resolution of the Eighth National Congress of the CPC. The Eighth National Congress of the CPC believed that the major task should adapt to the change of principal contradiction since the completion of socialist transformation in 1956. Such resolution was preserved intact in official documents of each National Congress successively, but the major task of economic development was not implemented very well because class struggle was viewed as another principal contradiction. Therefore, it was very necessary to reiterate, restore and carry on the major task of economic development after the Cultural Revolution. As mentioned before, such a shift has vigorously spurred all the Chinese people and the whole country to concentrate all their resources and energy on economic development so as to develop the productive forces wholeheartedly, with the result that unprecedentedly huge progress has been made, which is even very rare in the world history.

After the working focus was shifted, "development as the absolute principle" was regarded as the guiding principle for all work, which unfortunately also gave rise to the national trend of blind pursuit of GDP growth. In order to overcome such ill trend, we need further transform our economic development patterns and adopt a comprehensive, coordinated, and sustainable Scientific Outlook on Development that puts people first. Based on "overall consideration and due arrangement" of Mao Zedong thought, we should carry such strategic thought further forward and strive to build the Scientific Outlook on Development into a profound theoretical system to guide our future development.

4. Classes and class struggle mainly exist in the superstructure, but they can also be found in the economic base

Classes and class struggle not only exist in the superstructure, but also can be found in the economic base. The ruling class was already wiped out three decades ago. Since the reform and opening-up, we acknowledged that private enterprises would be allowed to develop in the primary stage of socialism. In 1981, the first private enterprise re-appeared in China and the number has increased to 4.974 million till 2006, over 30 times as large as that in 1956 when the number was still 160,000. Private capital, which has no doubt been of great help to the development of social productive forces, has however two sides, namely, the capacity of promoting the productive forces and the nature of exploitation in pursuit of surplus value. The profit-seeking nature of private capital involving exploitation has given rise to a series of problems for the social and economic life.

So, can this group, which has increased by several ten folds (compared with the national bourgeoisie) since the founding of the PRC, be called a class? Actually, "they are also builders of the socialist undertaking", and therefore they should play an active part in it, too. Besides, this group can only be categorized as the bourgeoisie according to their positions in the relations of production. Now we tend to use "stratum" rather than "class", but such theory of social strata can just replenish rather than replace the Marxist theory of class analysis. Even though Deng Xiaoping did not expect such a new "bourgeoisie" to emerge in China again, it has already occurred and such group has their own economic appeals (such as demands of entering the key monopolized fields concerning the lifeblood of the national economy) and political appeals (e.g., some bourgeoisie deputies to the NPC proposed to maintain an equal footing with the Communist party). So isn't that clear enough?

The issue as to whether structural changes in ownership of the means of production will affect the mainstay status of public ownership has attracted people's attention and thus triggered heated discussions. The decline in the proportion of the public sector and the rise in that of the private sector, the trend of privatization, and corruption resulting from collusion between government officials and businessmen, etc. are major causes of the expansion and worsening of income inequality. The expansion of Gini Coefficient has led to people's insufficient effective demand and overproduction, which is the result of the law of capital accumulation and the gap between the rich and the poor, rather than caused by socialist principal contradiction, i.e., the one between the ever-growing material and cultural needs of the people and the low level of production.

Various problems aforementioned concerning the superstructure and economic base all have something to do with the existence of class, contradiction between classes and class struggle, which we could not turn blind eyes to, downplay or cast aside. Foust Matlock, Jr., who served as U.S. Ambassador to the Soviet Union from 1987 to 1991, commented on the former Soviet Union's abandonment of class struggle theory in his book *Autopsy on an Empire: The American Ambassador's Account of the Collapse of the Soviet Union*. He said that the first radical change should be made to Marxist theory of class struggle. If Soviet leaders could give up such theory in a real sense, he thought, it will make no difference whether their ideology would be called 'Marxism' or not, because it had already been turned into another "Marxism". He believed that such type of socialist system would be readily accepted.

Interpretation of "the reform and opening-up"

Since the Third Plenary Session of the 11th Central Committee in 1978, China embarked on the great journey of reform and opening-up. Deng Xiaoping combined "reform" with "opening-up" and established "the reform and opening-up" as China's national policy in the current phase. From then on, China's economy began to grow in leaps and bounds. This is one of his great achievements.

However, after some research I found out that the phrase "reform and opening-up" proper hadn't appeared yet when the Third Plenary Session of the 11th Central Committee document was finalized; rather, it took some time before it was officially announced and widely used.

1. The formation of the policy of "reform and opening-up"

The ideas concerning "reform" and "opening-up" did ever appear respectively in the communique of the Third Plenary Session of the 11th Central Committee. The two quotes are, "(we should) carefully reform the economic management system and operational mode", and "(we should) seek actively to establish equal and mutually beneficial economic cooperation with countries all over the world".[1] The word "reform" and the expression of "economic cooperation with countries" were mentioned separately in the official document, however they are just the general accounts of guiding principles or policies rather than core tasks. By then, this communique hadn't come up with the boiled-down phrase of "reform and opening-up" yet. At that time, the Central Committee was still advocating people's commune system and hadn't proposed the household-responsibility system yet. In 1982, the reform was, for the first time, officially set as the major task in the second No. 1 Central Committee document.

In his opening remark of the 12th National Congress of the CPC in 1982, Deng Xiaoping firstly called on the whole country to "build socialism with Chinese characteristics".[2] But, in this report, the phrase of "reform and opening-up" did not appear in the section concerning general tasks in the new historical period, either. Rather, in the section concerning the Sixth Five-Year Plan (1981-1985), the "reform" was elevated to an equal status with other constituents of the new guiding line, namely, "adjustment, reform, rectification and improvement".[3] In this report, the word "reform" was mentioned over ten times, including reforms of economic management system, prices, and labor income system, as well as political restructuring and the reform of leadership system etc. The word "opening-up" was mentioned three times in the report, which even stipulated that the policy of "opening-up" would be "our unswerving strategic policy". However, the report of the 12th National Congress of the CPC still did not put "reform" and "opening-up" together into one phrase, which did not occur until the 13th National Congress of the CPC in 1987.

1 *Collection of Selected Major Documents Over the Three Decades Since the Reform and Opening up* I, p.16.

2 *Collection of Selected Major Documents Over the Three Decades Since the Reform and Opening up* I, p.260.

3 ibid, 268.

The phrase of "reform and opening-up" appeared in the section of the 13th National Congress report concerning the basic line of building socialism with Chinese characteristics in the primary stage of socialism. It was then put forward as one of the two basic points of this basic line and mentioned many times in the report. From then on, the phrase of "reform and opening-up" was recognized officially as a political term. The report said, "the general policy of reform and opening-up is a new development of the party's line since the Third Plenary Session of the 11th Central Committee". Since then, this term was widely used.

It always takes some time before any correct theory or policy is established, and there is no exception to the policy of "reform and opening-up". The Third Plenary Session of the 11th Central Committee did open a new era of the reform and opening up, but its theory and policy was still then in the making, which can also be seen from the evolution of the wording of "reform and opening-up". It did take some time before the "reform and opening-up" became the dominant discourse in our social, economic and political life as well as the guiding line for the people.

2. The reform and opening-up will be established as the long-term national policy in the new phase.

After the completion of socialist transformation, Mao Zedong wrote an article entitled *On the Correct Handling of Contradictions Among the People* in 1957, in which he said "socialist relations of production fitting the development of productive forces have been established, but they still have many drawbacks which do not fit the development of productive forces. So, here is the paradox: relations of production are both in conformity with and contradictory to productive forces. And the same is true with the relations between the superstructure and the economic base… In future, we must still strive to solve these contradictions in the new circumstances."

Here, "to solve contradictions" is equivalent to "reform" in a sense. As we all know, the first Decision on Economic Restructuring was adopted in the Third Plenary Session of the 12th Central Committee of the CPC since the reform and opening-up. The resolution defined economic restructuring in this way, "our economic restructuring aims to reform a series of interconnected links or aspects of both relations of production and superstructure that do not fit the development of productive forces under socialism."[1] This definition is distilled from the aforementioned remarks made by Mao Zedong in 1956.

In fact, the task of building socialism goes hand in hand with that of reform.

But we must admit that in the second half of the 60 years, China has indeed achieved many remarkable achievements after the policy of reform and opening-up was prioritized as the long-term national policy, and included as one of the two supporting basic points in the guideline of building socialism with Chinese characteristics. The 17th National Congress of the CPC pointed out that the policy of "reform and opening-up" is "the most distinct feature in the new era" since the Third Plenary Session of the 11th Central Committee.[2] The reform and opening-up, as a new great revolution, should be guided by "the Four Cardinal Principles", so that our country would head in the right direction and on the right track.

Why did I say that the reform is always heading in the right direction? Because the reform, in general, is meant to have the relations of production and the superstructure adjusted constantly to the development of productive forces so that the productive forces could be further developed. As a matter of fact, Mao Zedong has long since advocated such reform, as I had mentioned earlier. So, the reform would remain the everlasting theme and as a norm all through the historical period from the stage of socialism to that of communism.

Besides, the reform, as the national policy in a particular period of time, also aims to bring about changes to a particular system, mode or pattern. For example, a highly centralized planned economy needs to be changed into a socialist market economy; the economic structure in which we just had an exclusive public sector needs to be diversified by allowing many types of ownership to develop side by

1 *Collection of Selected Major Documents Over the Three Decades Since the Reform and Opening up* Ⅰ, p.347.

2 *Collection of Selected Major Documents Over the Three Decades Since the Reform and Opening up* Ⅱ, p.1716.

side; if viewed in a larger picture, China is to be built into a basically modernized nation, etc. Once these temporary targets were finished, the goals for the reform as the national policy in a particular period of time need to be reset, and thereby its relations of production and the superstructure should be adapted to the development of productive forces so that the productive forces would be further developed. It is a endless process, in which adjustment needs to be constantly made. And this is the way the reform is supposed to be.

We can say that the current task of reform proposed by the party serves as a national policy in the current phase. According to Deng Xiaoping, we should uphold the basic guideline, including the task of reform and opening-up, for at least a century, that is to say, from the mid 20th Century, when socialism was established, to the mid 21st Century, by which the task of socialist modernization will have been basically achieved. By the mid of the 21st Century, when we will have realized modernization, the reform and opening-up would not be the national policy any longer, but instead it would be replaced by other policies so that the economic base and superstructure must, by then, be adjusted to the development of the productive forces. However, before the task is completed, we must persist with the general policy of reform and opening-up! No wavering! [1]

3. keeping track of the reform in different fields

The promise that we should never waver in the policy of the reform and opening-up within a rather long period is made on general terms. However, as the reform and opening-up involves numerous tasks and various fields, it is unlikely to keep all reforms in the same pace. For example, some reforms might go very well and are almost completed, which, therefore, just need some finishing touches; as for some reforms, things might be more complicated or they might get started rather late. Therefore, these reforms need to be carried on till the final moment of victory.

1 Collection of Selected Major Documents Over the Three Decades Since the Reform and Opening up I, p.633.

Take the transition from a traditional, highly centralized planned economy to a socialist market economy as an example. In the circulation of all commodities, over 90% products are regulated by the market forces. It was estimated several years ago that around 70% of china's economy had been then marketized. In this sense, we can say that the socialist market economy has been initially established in China. Does it mean that the transition from the highly centralized planned economy to the socialist market economy has been completed? It turned out that market economy was still not developed enough in a few fields; besides, in quite many fields, the economy was even over-marketized. We surely need attend to these matters, but they are already not the mainstream problems in the period of transition from traditional planned economy to market economy any more. In the spirit of the 17th National Congress of the CPC, we should increase the guiding and regulatory role of state macroeconomic planning.[1] As Deng Xiaoping ever put it, "planning and market forces are both means of controlling economic activities", the regulatory roles of both means should be brought into full play. In this sense, the term of "marketization reform" without any modifiers is inappropriate.

Take the reform of ownership structure as another example, which aims to change the previous economic structure in which we just had an exclusive public sector into the one in which many kinds of ownership are to develop side by side. Compared with the time when the PRC was newly founded, the non-public sector of the economy has grown by leaps and bounds. Besides, the rise in the proportion of the private sector and the decline in that of the public sector has already begun to affect the mainstay status of public ownership. The reform of ownership structure has now been basically completed, and the new task would be to consolidate and improve the basic economic system in the primary stage of socialism, especially to consolidate the mainstay status of public ownership and guide the non-public sector to develop in the right direction.

---

1 *Collection of Selected Major Documents Over the Three Decades Since the Reform and Opening up* II, p.1726.

Take the reform of distribution system as the third example. The reform aiming to abandon the principle of indiscriminate egalitarianism and to widen income gap moderately by giving priority to efficiency has long since succeeded. The task of "encouraging some people to get rich first" was even over-fulfilled, which Deng Xiaoping had anticipated to be completed at the turn of the 21st century. According to Deng Xiaoping, we should strive to achieve common prosperity after some people and some regions got rich.[1] However, the second task was then postponed due to some reasons, including both objective and subjective ones. Now, it seems to be the time that we should step up efforts to solve this problem and set the right path for the reform of distribution system so that Deng Xiaoping's warning that distribution inequality would result in polarization and that problems would become a full-blown crisis at some point would not come true.[2]

Take the rural reform as the fourth example. The rural reform aiming to replace the People's Commune system with the household-responsibility system has long since succeeded, too. Especially a dual level management system, in which household management took precedence over collective management, has also been practically promoted. This is "the first leap" of the rural reform proposed by Deng Xiaoping, thanks to which, the rural area has witnessed tremendous economic growth over the three decades. Now it's time to attach more importance to the collective management, that is to say, we need develop a new rural collective economy, which constitutes "the second leap" of the rural reform. This is the only way to make the rural reform keep to the socialist direction. After the realization of the first leap, we should consider carefully how to achieve the second one.[3]

1 *Collection of Selected Major Documents Over the Three Decades Since the Reform and Opening up* I, p.635.

2 see *Chronology of Deng Xiaoping's Career* (1975-1997) II, Beijing: Central Party Literature Press, 2004, p.1364.

3 About the "two leaps" proposed by Deng Xiaoping, please refer to *Chronology of Deng Xiaoping's Career(1975-1997)* II , Beijing: Central Party Literature Press, 2004, pp.1310-1311, 1349-1350.

Transition from the New Democracy to Socialism with Chinese characteristics

How has China undergone these sixty years since the founding of the PRC? In the first half, China has achieved the transition from new democracy to socialism. Since we carried out the reform and opening-up, China has witnessed a new transition from the socialism initially established since the founding of the PRC to the "socialism with Chinese characteristics".

1. A transition from new democracy to socialism

According to Mao Zedong's theory of new democracy, a new democratic country should be established after the victory of the new democratic revolution and the whole country should be devoted to building a new democratic society within a rather long period. When conditions permit, the new democratic society would change to a socialist society.

Besides, this theory also includes the conception that "two revolutionary phases must be joined with each other", which means that there shouldn't be another phase between the new democratic revolution and socialist revolution. It can be interpreted in this way: once the new democratic revolution is ended, socialist revolution should start immediately.

As a matter of fact, it took three years for China's economy to recover from the ravages of war after the nationwide victory of the new democratic revolution. After the completion of land reform, the party came up with the general line for a transition to socialism since the founding of the PRC, due to class differentiation in rural areas and the worsening of contradictions between the bourgeoisie and the working class in cities. Having basically completed the socialist transformation in 1956, China officially embarked on the journey of building socialism. This is "the most profound and the greatest social reform in China's history, as well as the very foundation for any progress and development in the future". [1]

---

1 *Collection of Selected Major Documents Over the Three Decades Since the Reform and Opening up* I, p.185

After the basic completion of socialist transformation, we continued to build socialism and succeeded in making remarkable achievements during tortuous explorations from 1957 to 1958. However, at the same time, we also made some mistakes: some historical stage was skipped due to a rush for quick results both in the relations of production and productive forces. For example, we used to value the economic structure with an exclusive public sector, pursue an excessively centralized planned economy, and neglect the necessity of non-public sectors and market economy at a time when the productive forces were not developed enough. In other words, we didn't realize that we were still in the primary stage of socialism at that time.

2. The primary stage of socialism and socialism with Chinese characteristics

Mao Zedong ever talked about the primary stage of socialism in some articles such as "Reading Notes on the Soviet Text *'political* economy'" etc. He said that socialism is divided into two stages, underdeveloped socialism and developed socialism. "It seems to me that it will take China, with a large population and a weak economy, at least a century to surpass the most developed capitalist countries in terms of productive forces; otherwise, it will not be accomplished."[1] The concept of "primary stage of socialism" officially appeared for the first time in *The Resolution Clarifying Certain Questions in the History of the Party Since the Foundation of the People's Republic of China* adopted in the Sixth Plenary Session of the 11th Central Committee. The resolution says, "Our socialist system was still in the primary stage."[2] This idea actually grew out of Mao Zedong thought I mentioned above.

Since then, Deng Xiaoping continued to integrate basic tenets of Marxism with China's concrete practice just like what Mao Zedong ever did and came up with the policy of building socialism with Chinese characteristics according to

1 *Collected Works of Mao Zedong*, vol. 8, Beijing: People's Publishing House, 1999, p.116, 302.

2 *Collection of Selected Major Documents Over the Three Decades Since the Reform and Opening up* I, p.212.

our national conditions. It was in the 12th National Congress of the CPC in 1982 that he firstly announced such a policy and called upon the people to push our great cause of building socialism further forward into a new stage.[1] And then, the political report of the 13th National Congress of the CPC systematically elaborated on the meaning of "the primary stage of socialism" and "the basic line of establishing socialism with Chinese characteristics". The basic line is as follows: we should make economic development as the central task and uphold the Four Cardinal Principles and the reform and opening-up, incorporating all these aspects into the practice of building socialism with Chinese characteristics.[2]

In 1997, the 15th National Congress of the CPC further expounded on the features of the primary stage of socialism and the basic line of socialism with Chinese characteristics, and came up as well with the basic goals and policies of building socialism with Chinese characteristics in terms of economy, politics and culture. Besides, the report also made it very clear that the economic system in which public ownership is the mainstay and other kinds of ownership develop side by side constitutes the basic economic system in the primary stage of socialism of China and that to establish a socialist economy with Chinese characteristics means to develop a market economy in socialist conditions.[3] So far, the framework and meaning of the primary stage of socialism and socialism with Chinese characteristics have been very clear.

Despite the fact that socialist road with Chinese characteristics has already been clarified and further elaborated in a series of party documents and that many remarkable achievements along this road have been made, several years later, some people still believed that the issue as to what is socialism and how to build socialism hadn't been solved. "Socialism" was given various definitions or labels,

---

1 *Collection of Selected Major Documents Over the Three Decades Since the Reform and Opening up* I, p.260.

2 ibid, p.477

3 *Collection of Selected Major Documents Over the Three Decades Since the Reform and Opening up* II, p. 899.

such as “democratic socialism”, “people’s socialism”, “constitutional socialism”, and “market socialism” etc. And what is more, these so-called “socialism” are trying desperately to integrate into socialism with Chinese characteristics. For example, some people claimed, “What we have been practicing these years is exactly democratic socialism”, “socialism with Chinese characteristics is exactly people’s socialism”. However, these so-called “socialisms” disregarded the Four Cardinal Principles and the basic economic system in which public ownership is the mainstay, and thus are totally incompatible with socialism with Chinese characteristics. Our party has gone so far as to allow these so-called “-isms” to talk so freely in the media! Our party is too lenient!

3. Does it mean to revert to new democracy by practicing socialism with Chinese characteristics?

Recently, some people said that “socialism with Chinese characteristics” means “to revert to new democracy”. Someone wrote in the article, “new democracy was successfully practiced in China before our party seized power in 1949. However, it was afterwards abandoned and China rushed to build socialism, which turned out to be a fiasco. Luckily, these errors were corrected due to resumption of new democracy, and remarkable achievements have thus been made.” “This is a rough sketch of the 60 years’ history of the PRC,” he added.[1] This author had no idea that new democracy was just a transitional phase leading up to socialism; he denied all the achievements that our party has made in building socialism in the first half of the 60 years, elevating the significance of the second half so as to give credit to the “resumption of new democracy”. Actually, this article is full of flaws, which I would not name but one. He said, “the concept of ‘socialism with Chinese characteristics’ was originated from the theory of ‘the primary stage of socialism’, but the latter is the resumption and further development of new democracy.”[2] We should keep cautious and avoid being misled by such specious argument.

1 See: *Yanhuang Chunqiu* (*China Through the Ages*), 2009, No.4.

2 *ibid.*

We have to admit that the Sixth Plenary Session of the 11th Central Committee came up with the concept of "the primary stage of socialism" mainly for the purpose of correcting our past mistakes of having skipped some historical stage due to a rush for quick results in socialist revolution and the period of building socialism. For example, in terms of ownership structure, large public-owned people's communes and a unitary public sector were believed to be the best forms of socialism.

By acknowledging that we we are still in the "primary stage of socialism" since the "reform and opening-up", we meant to correct things that did not conform to the development of the productive forces. The core or basis of the theory concerning the primary stage of socialism lies in the basic economic system in which public ownership is the mainstay and many kinds of ownership develop side by side. Tolerance of private capital and its development is part and parcel of the theory. In this sense, the "primary stage of socialism" is indeed similar to "new democratic society".

The "Common Program" formulated in the Second Plenary Session of the 7th Central Committee in 1949 and the programs formulated before the founding of the Republic of China all stipulated that five types of ownership including the private sector would develop side by side in the new democratic society after the victory of revolution; Besides, it was also pointed out that in a fairly long period of time, we should make the best of urban and rural capitalism to benefit the development of the productive forces. Given the circumstances, socialist transformation was then an unstoppable trend. However, it unexpectedly wiped out all forms of private capital in the late 1950s due to some mistakes, and they didn't recover until the loosening of the policy in the early 1980s. Now they have become part of the economy under socialism with Chinese characteristics again, which can be justified and conditioned by the theory of the primary stage of socialism. In some sense, such change is indeed an indication of retrogression because we did sort of use some policies quite similar to those in new democratic societies, especially in terms of private capital. However, we shouldn't regard such necessary retrogression needed by the reform as the resumption of new democracy, because the reform is in essence the self-improvement of socialist system. This reform is based on the socialist system well established in the first half of the six decades, rather than an overthrow of such socialist system or a retrogression to the "new democracy" envisaged in the very beginning of the new China.

4. Treatment of the non-public sector: two periods, two policies

Even in terms of treatment of private capital and non-public sector, the policy in the new era is also different from that in the period of new democracy. In the "period of new democracy", the policy of "using, restricting and reforming" private capital, i.e., "regulating private capital", was made in accordance with the spirit of the Second Plenary Session of the 7th Central Committee and the "Common Program". On the one hand, the development of private capital was encouraged and supported so as to benefit the national economy and the people's livelihood; on the other hand, all the undertakings comprising the lifeline of the economy and vital to the national economy and the people's livelihood were still dominated by the state. At the same time, private capital was also encouraged to cooperate with state capital to form state capitalism. All these efforts were made to develop the productive forces and prepare a transition to socialism. That period has witnessed a gradual decrease in the share of private capital and that of non-public sector in the national economy and a gradual increase in the proportion of the public sector accordingly. This is a natural tendency of new democratic economy.

However, in the new era, the economic policy in dealing with the non-public sector is strikingly different from that in the period of new democracy. It was summarized as "to encourage, support and guide" the non-public sector, phrases like "restricting" or "regulating" private capital having been excluded. According to No. 3 [2005] document of the State Council, private capital is allowed to enter major industries or key fields having a vital bearing on the lifeline of the national economy such as monopoly industries. Besides, private capital wasn't required to be integrated into state capitalism; rather, SOEs were even encouraged to carry out demutualization and privatization as alternatives. All in all, China is far more lenient with the non-public sector in the new era than the period of new democracy, or even has turned the previous policy upside down.

The era of reform and opening up saw a sharp increase in both the total volume of private capital and its proportion in national economy, in sharp contrast with the period of new democracy when the proportion of private sector kept falling. Moreover, the proportion still keeps increasing, so much so that many people have begun to worry about the mainstay status of public ownership. There are many causes of such trend, for example, the non-public sector started almost from zero in the beginning of the reform, classes are not the same as they used to be, etc. Besides, such increase is also the result of some policies, strategies or tactics. Here, I would not like to explain them in details.

To sum up, there is no denying that polices in these two periods are different. But in the current period, it should also be noted that the very premise, i.e., the basic economic system of socialism in which public ownership is the mainstay, must be maintained and that socialism as the general direction can never be abandoned, either. As far as the policy of "encouraging, supporting and guiding" the development of the non-public sector is concerned, the party and government could use their discretion to decide in which direction or in what ways the non-public sector should be "guided". It is in our party's interest to make due adjustments to policies in accordance with the changing national conditions to promote the healthy development of the non-public sector and to keep public ownership, in the meanwhile, as the mainstay of the economy. Therefore, the saying that socialism with Chinese characteristics in the primary stage is the resumption of new democracy is lame and ill-founded.

5. The model of socialism with Chinese characteristics against global economic crisis

With the increase of China's national strength and its integration into global economy, the model of socialism with Chinese characteristics has been recognized by the world and triggered heated discussions as well. Among various interpretations of the Chinese model, I believe personally that the core of socialism with Chinese characteristics lies in the co-existence of capitalist and socialist elements of socialism while upholding socialism.

This is also the key to understanding why China has withstood this global economic crisis. Why didn't the former Soviet Union, the first socialist country, and the PRC before the reform and opening-up get involved in the world capitalist economic crisis? At that time, the Soviet Union and China hadn't had any capitalist elements yet, so that they didn't fall victim to the capitalist cyclical economic crisis.

But why has China got involved this time and met with some unprecedented difficulties? Aside from China being a deeply externally-oriented economy, the major reason is the explosive growth of capitalist elements within China with the deepening of marketization and privatization, which has thus made China relatively vulnerable to the economic law of capitalism. But why was China able to withstand the global economic crisis and outshine others in handling the crisis? Why has China won applause from some capitalist countries? The key is that China has the capacity of concentrating national resources on accomplishing great things and regulating economic activities through planning intrinsic to the socialist system. I ever analyzed this in another article, so I would not repeat it here.

However, some people misinterpreted socialism with Chinese characteristics as a capitalist model, or even labelled it "capitalism under the leadership of the communist party", which I believe is totally groundless. China has been adhering to the model of socialism with Chinese characteristics and especially socialist elements within this model, so that it could withstand the global economic crisis and handle it fairly well. Therefore, we must adhere to socialism with Chinese characteristics, keep public ownership as the mainstay, and continue to develop many kinds of ownership side by side and carry out the market-oriented reform under the guidance of state macroeconomic planning; we must adhere to the principle of distribution according to work and attach more importance to social equity; we must fight against privatization, marketization, liberalization and polarization peculiar to capitalism with the weapons of basic socialist principles and confine the influence of capitalist countries and the capitalist law of market economy to a small area. Only in this way can we avoid falling victim to the capitalist cyclical economic crisis and thus preserve Chinese characteristics!

(This article was published in *Social Sciences in China*, 2009, No.5)

On Several Issues Concerning Socialist Political Economics

1. The class character and scientific soundness of socialist political economics

Marxist political economics is usually known as a proletarian science, standing for the interests of the proletariat and thus having a very distinct class character, which is not wrong. It is also often said that Marxism is meant to stand for the fundamental interests of the masses permanently, which is generally not wrong, either. However, we need to be aware that the masses are divided into different classes, and it also applies to the primary stage of socialism. In the current phase, the masses include not only the overwhelming majority of workers and farmers, but a minority of the exploiting class.

In principle, Marxism and the Communist Party cannot stand for the interests of the exploiting class, but in certain historical conditions, such as the period of democratic revolution and the primary stage of socialism, we should care for and defend the legitimate interests of some people among the exploiting class (including the national bourgeoisie and owners of legal private enterprises), having them united to work for socialist revolution or the great cause of building socialism. However, we must avoid supporting the exploiting class unconditionally, unswervingly, and without any restrictions; we must avoid benefiting them at the expense of the interests of the working class, which has already led to the widening of the gap between the rich and the poor and the trend of polarization. This is utterly incongruous with the position of Marxism and the purpose of the Communist Party. Therefore, we must always maintain such position in socialist political economics and bear it in mind anytime and anywhere.

Marxist political economics is called a science because it brings to light the objective laws of economic and social development, combining the use of historical methods with logical methods as basic analytic approaches, such as dialectical materialism and historical materialism. We used to adopt the normative approach in studying socialist economy. Scholars tended to focus on "what socialist economy should be" and tried to infer from given premises logically. As far as the study of socialist economic reform is concerned, scholars also need study "what the economy in the primary stage of socialism should be", but the overriding thing is to figure out "what the economy in the primary stage of socialism actually is". That is to say, we need adopt a realistic approach to analyze and explain facts and their inner links and then try to bring to light the objective laws. Otherwise, we would not know the problems perfectly well so that it would be impossible for us to find out any plausible solutions to them.

We have to admit that empirical analyses have proven to be more capable of arousing students' curiosity and passion for study than lectures about pure theories or principles in political economics classes. Why are some western bourgeois textbooks so popular and attractive to students in socialist countries? But why has Marxist political economics been marginalized or even mocked by students in class teaching? I think that it might have something to do with the flaws in its research approaches and the way of narration, which therefore should be improved in textbooks so that Marxism could be publicized more effectively. For example, quantitative analysis and case studies etc. can help students learn economic theories better.

2. Contradictions in the primary stage of socialism

According to the party's document, the principal contradiction in Chinese society in the primary stage of socialism is the one between the ever-growing material and cultural needs of the people and the low level of production, which dates back to the Eighth National Congress of the CPC in 1956. At that time, socialist transformation was just completed and the campaign of building socialism just began. Therefore, it was then officially announced that the contradiction between the ever-growing material and cultural needs of the people and the low level of production should be the principal contradiction in the period of building socialism. Since the Third Plenary Session of the 11th Central Committee of the CPC, it was reestablished as the principal contradiction. After the concept of primary stage of socialism was later introduced, it became "the principal contradiction in the primary stage of socialism". In view of the failure of social production to meet the ever-growing material and cultural needs of the people, it is urgent that we should step up efforts in economic development. Therefore, it is very necessary to clarify the principal contradiction in the primary stage of socialism in order to justify in theory the shift of focus of the whole party's work in the Third Plenary Session of the 11th Central Committee.

However, there do exist "insufficient domestic demand" and "overcapacity" in some cases, i.e., domestic production capacity exceeding domestic demand, which conflicts with the definition of current principal contradiction. Political economics can explain this.

Do the ever-growing "needs" of the people refer to the physiological and psychological needs or purchasing needs? If the answer is the former, i.e., subjective desire, social production will always lag behind desires, and thus human and social progress will be constantly made. If the answer is the latter, i.e., purchasing needs, the relations between social production and consumption demand would be up to social system. In the capitalist system, the relations between social production and effective demand are inhibited by the basic contradiction of capitalist economy, that is to say, people's effective demand is always lagging behind the ongoing expansion of social production, which often results in overproduction and the outbreak of cyclical economic crises. In the socialist system, due to mainstay status of public ownership and distribution according to work, along with regulation and overall equilibrium through planning, problems like insufficient effective demand and overproduction do not usually occur.

For example, in the past when planned economy was practiced, indiscriminate egalitarianism and soft budget constraint led to shortage economy, in which there was often too much effective demand and insufficient supply. This is one of the flaws of traditional planned economy. In no circumstances would insufficient effective demand and overproduction occur in the socialist society, as it is totally incongruous with the nature and purpose of socialism. However, socialism in its primary stage is not socialism in a complete sense. Aside from socialist economic sectors, capitalist economic sectors such as private and foreign-owned enterprises are also allowed to exist and develop in the primary stage of socialism. Therefore, laws of capitalist economy would also exert some influence on the socialist economy in the primary stage, resulting in overproduction and insufficient domestic demand in some cases.

Therefore, in order to explain clearly why China has outperformed capitalist countries in fighting against this world capitalist cyclical economic crisis, we also need use the same approach for clarification, which I ever analyzed in the article entitled "China's Successful Crisis Management in Face of the Current Global Economic Crisis and the Model of Socialism with Chinese Characteristics" published in *Qiushi (Seeking Truth)*.

The principal contradiction in the primary stage of socialism has determined that the focus of our party' work should be shifted to economic development since the Third Plenary Session of the 11th Central Committee, which is very correct. So, what will we do? To put it simply, we need to complete two major tasks, one is to make a bigger cake, i.e., GDP, that is, to build a strong economy; the other one is to divide this cake, i.e., GDP, more equitably to make the fruits of development shared by all. In general, we surely need pay equal attention to both of them. However, given the circumstances in the primary stage of socialism, one should be given precedence over the other, that is to say, we need make a bigger cake at first and then try to divide it more equitably. But in due time we should pay attention to both or even attach more importance to the equitable division of the cake, otherwise we couldn't make an even larger one any more. Political economics should highlight that it is already the "due" time now.

According to Deng Xiaoping, by the end of the 20th Century when China is moderately prosperous, we would put the problem of income inequity on the table and try to solve it."[1] That is to say, since the turning of the 21st century, we should pay attention to the equitable division of the cake while we are trying to make a bigger one, and even prioritize the former in our economic work. Especially now when the tendency towards polarization is much worse than that in 2000, we need attach even more importance to the equitable division of the cake and consider it as the most central task while continuing to enlarge the cake.

Now China has ranked as the second largest economy, with its economic aggregate even larger than that of Japan, but at the same time, our per capita GDP is still less than one tenth of that of Japan. Given such circumstances, we still need work hard to bake a bigger cake though not viewed as the most central task. However, we should be more dedicated to dividing the cake equitably, that is to say, we should attach more importance to social equity. This is what all the people are concerned about and it also conforms to the essence and purpose of socialism. Deng Xiaoping ever said that distribution inequality is a big "headache", and that it was even more difficult to handle than economic development.[2] In other words, to divide a cake equitably is even harder to achieve than to bake a bigger cake, so the whole party should prioritize this tricky issue and strive to find out practical solutions.

Even though the contradiction between classes is not the principal one in the primary stage of socialism, we have to admit that there are still classes and thus contradictions between them and class struggle. And what is more, these contradictions would probably be aggravated in certain conditions. At present, a lot of people deliberately did not mention class, contradictions between classes

---

1 *Chronology of Deng Xiaoping's Career(1975-1997)* II, Beijing: Central Party Literature Press, 2004, p.1343.

2 *Chronology of Deng Xiaoping's Career(1975-1997)* II, Beijing: Central Party Literature Press, 2004, p.1364.

and class struggle, preaching covertly the disappearance of class and the end of class struggle, which is not right.

Actually the contradiction between classes and class struggle would still exist "within a certain scope". At first, very obviously, they exist in political thoughts and ideology, which Mao Zedong has long since pointed out. Besides, they also exist in the economic filed. Not only private enterprises have seen the contradiction between labor and capital, exploitation of the working people and recurrent disputes between employers and employees, but in some transformed state owned enterprises, antagonism between senior executives and common employees can also be sensed since the proletariat became hire labor again.

If political economics evades the duality of the new bourgeoisie in China, that is to say, if it just depicts them as "builders of socialism" without mentioning the other role of "exploiters" and even refuses to call them "new bourgeoisie", political economics cannot be called a science at all. Rather, it is incumbent on the science of Marxist political economics to analyze objectively class, class contradiction, and class struggle in the primary stage of socialism. It is absolutely right that our society needs harmony. The principal contradiction in the socialist society needn't be solved through violent class struggle like what the capitalist society did, because our principal contradiction is non-antagonistic; rather, it would be overcome by the socialist system in the process of its self-improvement.

However, on such pretext, some people began to play down class, class contradiction and class struggle and to preach in disguised forms the disappearance of class and the end of class struggle, which would just end up covering up and appeasing the endless class struggle waged audaciously by some people against the working class, and thus throwing the communist party that stands for the interests of the working class into an unfavorable situation in face of the class struggle. Didn't it happen this way? I hope not.

3. Essential characteristics of the socialist system

The essence of socialism refers to the most fundamental characteristics of the socialist system which set it apart from the feudalistic system and capitalist system. From the perspective of the relations of production, this definition is right; but it cannot explain why Deng Xiaoping also defined the essence of socialism from the perspective of productive forces in his South China Tour talks in 1992.[1] According to Deng Xiaoping, the essence of socialism involves two aspects: productive forces and the relations of production. In terms of the relations of production, the essence of socialism is "elimination of exploitation and polarization and the ultimate achievement of prosperity for all", which did set it apart from other social systems such as capitalist system. In terms of the productive forces, the essence of socialism is "liberation and development of the productive forces", which is however not the essential characteristic of the socialist system, because all societies need to liberate and develop the productive forces when the social system is newly established. In the *Manifesto of the Communist Party*, Karl Marx and Friedrich Engels ever described the great achievements of capitalist system in the development of the productive forces in its early phase, "The bourgeoisie, whose rule hasn't reached one hundred years yet, has however created more massive and more colossal productive forces than what all preceding generations together have."

Deng Xiaoping included "liberation and development of the productive forces" in the essence of socialism, mainly because at that time China's productive forces were lagging far behind the capitalist countries; and what is more, the "Gang of Four" were then chanting the absurd slogan that "it is better to be poor under socialism than to be rich under capitalism", which has severely hindered the development of the productive forces. Given such circumstances, Deng Xiaoping just wanted to remind the people that it is very urgent that China develop productive forces to lift it from poverty and backwardness, which was of critical importance at that time. However, if socialist revolution were to be achieved in the capitalist countries with highly developed productive forces, "liberation and development of the productive forces" wouldn't be included in the essence of

1 *Chronology of Deng Xiaoping's Career (1975-1997)* II, p.1343.

socialism; rather, it would just be "elimination of exploitation and polarization and the ultimate achievement of prosperity for all".

The "essence" of socialism was also mentioned by Deng Xiaoping in another occasion. During his talk with Jiang Zemin, Yang Shangkun, and Li Peng, then leading members of the CPC Central Committee, on December 24th 1990, Deng Xiaoping said, "The greatest superiority of socialism is that it enables all the people to prosper, and common prosperity is the essence of socialism."[1] In the South China Tour Talks, he ever said that the essence of socialism is partly "elimination of exploitation and polarization". He meant the same thing in these two talks, that is, they both refer to the relations of production rather than the productive forces.

Deng Xiaoping did not say too much about the "essence" of socialism. He just mentioned twice, which I have already listed. Rather, he often talked about the "nature", "principle", "the two fundamental principles", "the most important principle", or "the two extremely important aspects" of socialism.[2] To sum up, they are "public ownership as the mainstay and common prosperity without polarization". He mentioned these two aspects repeatedly, which totally correspond to the essence of socialism in terms of the relations of production he mentioned in the South China Tour talks in 1992.

The reason why Deng Xiaoping has repeatedly emphasized the essence, nature and principle of socialism from the perspective of the relations of production is that the relations of production instead of the productive forces is the essential characteristic of each social system that sets one apart from another. Marxist political economics is targeted at the relations of production linked with the productive forces and the superstructure, aiming to improve the relations of production and the superstructure so as to promote the development of the productive forces. Therefore, while studying and elaborating on the essence of

1 *Chronology of Deng Xiaoping's Career (1975-1997)* II, p.1324.
2 *Chronology of Deng Xiaoping's Career (1975-1997)* II, P.1033, 1069, 1078, 1075, 1091.

socialism, we should devote more time and energy to the study of the relations of production, that is, we should emphasize that the essential characteristic of socialism is elimination of exploitation and polarization, and that its fundamental principle is public ownership as the mainstay and the realization of prosperity for all.

In fact, many textbooks have already given a very detailed analysis of the nature of socialism from the perspective of the productive forces, which is very much needed. But they all overlooked the relations of production. Why is it so common? Probably because we are still in the primary stage of socialism, in which exploitation still cannot be eliminated completely and the tendency of polarization has occurred inevitably. Some relations of production, though not socialist ones, should still be allowed to exist and develop, so long as they conform to and promote the development of the productive forces in the primary stage of socialism. This is why capitalist elements (including exploitation) are tolerated in the primary stage of socialism.

Therefore, in order to develop the productive forces, we have to tolerate the existence of exploitation and the tendency of polarization resulting from it and even try to evade such topic, which however does not correspond to the essence of socialism. Due to the contradiction between the essence of socialism and our practice in the primary stage of socialism, these textbooks have to focus more on the productive forces rather than the relations of production. Notwithstanding this, the core of Deng Xiaoping's socialist theory still lies in the relations of production. If not so, why did Deng Xiaoping say that our reform would end up with failure if our policies lead to polarization?[1] Here, the premise of such hypothesis refers to the relations of production. "Failure" here means that socialist relations of production, rather than productive forces, would fail if the premise comes true. And even if it comes true, the productive forces would still probably flourish within a short period of time.

1 *Collected Works of Deng Xiaoping*, Vol. 3, p.111.

So, how should we solve the contradiction between the essence of socialism and our practice in the primary stage of socialism? We can count on political economics.

In accordance with the spirit of Deng Xiaoping's talks in many occasions, political economics should shift its focus of analysis in terms of the essence of socialism back to the relations of production and try to analyze less the productive forces, which Deng Xiaoping just mentioned once by the way in his South China Tour talks. However, it should be noted that development of the productive forces is very crucial not only to a poor, backward China striving to establish socialism, but also to material preparation for the future establishment of communism. Deng Xiaoping also elaborated on this aspect before. [1]

In view of this, political economics should open a new category by setting the development of the productive forces as "the fundamental task of socialism" just like what Deng Xiaoping ever said. As for the theory concerning the essence of socialism, it should be all about the relations of production.

Having found out that the essence of socialism is the essential characteristic of socialism distinct from capitalism, namely, "elimination of exploitation and polarization and the ultimate achievement of prosperity for all", we should move further forward and strive to overcome the contradiction between the essence of socialism and our practice in the primary stage of socialism. The essence of socialism applies to the whole historical period of socialism, including the primary stage. The primary stage of socialism should not only be dominated by socialist elements such as public ownership and distribution according to work, but also has to tolerate the existence of capitalist elements such as private ownership and distribution according to capital. As a result, private ownership and the law of capital accumulation did exert some influence and thus result in inevitably exploitation and the tendency of polarization.

As far as the essence of socialism is concerned, socialism would tolerate

1 *Collected Works of Deng Xiaoping*, Vol.3, pp.137, 199, 157, 225, 227.

no capitalist elements, but at least in the primary stage it cannot be fulfilled. Therefore, some capital elements have to be tolerated for the sake of the development of the productive forces. But as required by the essence of socialism, too much exploitation or a too serious trend of polarization would not be allowed even in the primary stage of socialism. As a result, these capitalist elements need to be regulated and restricted properly.

A careful perusal of the Constitution of the PRC would reveal the fact that it has long since been prescribed in this fundamental law. It stipulates to the effect that socialist public ownership is the mainstay in the basic economic system and distribution according to work plays a dominant role in the distribution system. By these stipulations, the Constitution aims to prevent capitalist elements such as the private sector and distribution according to capital from expanding too dramatically to the extent that the mainstay status of public ownership and the dominant role of distribution according to work would be affected and thus the socialist nature of the society would be changed by privatization and polarization.

Therefore, only by unswervingly upholding the mainstay status of public ownership and distribution according to work prescribed in the constitution could the essence of socialism be gradually realized in a real sense. Otherwise, Deng Xiaoping's warning would come true, and this is what we must guard against.

4. Socialist market economy also has planning

According to Marxism, the national economy should achieve balanced, proportionate development in communal production. Here, "balanced, proportionate development" is not equivalent to traditional planned economy regulated by administrative mandatory planning. Since the reform, we have managed to overcome limitations of traditional planned economy and establish a socialist market economy in conformity with the national conditions in the primary stage of socialism. At the same time, we mustn't discard the economic law of balanced, proportionate development under public ownership, which is especially true for political economics.

Based on Deng Xiaoping's creative idea that "planning and market forces, as both means of regulating economic activities, can be used" in his South China Tour talks, the 14th National Congress of the CPC (1992) proposed to establish a socialist market economy as the target of our reform. Not long before that, Jiang Zemin, then General Secretary of the Central Committee of the CPC listed three versions of reform target in a speech in the Party School of the Central Committee of the CPC, namely, to establish a socialist planned market economy, to establish a socialist commodity economy characterized by the combination between planning and market, and to establish a socialist market economy. The three options are all available, with no one being superior to another.

However, Jiang Zemin decided on the third version, excluding the modifier "planned" literally. He said, "A planned commodity economy is equivalent to a planned market economy. Socialist economy had planning since its establishment, and everybody knows it perfectly well. Therefore, one should not infer from the missing of the word "planned" that planning would be aborted." [1]

The exclusion of the modifier "planned" from the wording of reform target at that time and Jiang Zemin's oral clarification before the congress that it does not mean to abandon socialist planning were mainly due to the reason that traditional planned economy was then very deep-rooted in people's mind and that the concept of market economy hasn't been that penetrating yet. Therefore, in order to improve the image of market in people's mind and encourage people to accept the concept of market economy, the Central Committee elected to omit the word "planned" and still preserve the important modifier "socialist" before "market economy". Just as Jiang Zemin ever put it, "socialism has already had planning since its establishment"! In this way, the spirit of reform target is very complete. I firmly believed then that the Central Committee has made a very right choice by putting so much effort into this. However, nowadays few people could understand it this way.

1 *Collection of Selected Major Documents Over the Three Decades Since the Reform and Opening up* I, Beijing: Central Party Literature Press,2008, p.647.

Market economy has now been practiced in China for almost two decades, but planning seemed to have faded away. In the past, traditional planned economy was overvalued due to historical reasons. However, things are different now. Some people who used to have blind faith in planning have now begun to worship market blindly, going from one extreme to the other. They hyped up the minor change of the Chinese wording of the 11th Five-Year Plan, i.e., from the 11th Five-Year "jihua" (plan) to the 11th Five-Year "guihua" (program), raving that we have managed to get away from planned economy. I do not oppose such change of word, because they would make no real difference at all. However, it seems to them that only "guihua" (program) is capable of providing guidance and being strategic and flexible. As a matter of fact, "jihua" (plan) also includes mandatory planning, guidance planning, strategic planning and predictive planning.

The market economy we aim to establish is the market economy subject to macroeconomic regulation, just like what the 14th National Congress of the CPC proposed. Over these years, China has been trying to improve macroeconomic regulation and thus has made a lot of progress. Especially since the 14th National Congress, we have succeeded in putting inflation and deflation under control in the short run successively. However, the guiding role of state planning in both short- and long-term macroeconomic regulation has drastically declined. Plans involve mostly compilation of polices but seldom include any tasks with accountability or binding quotas; local plans are divorced from central ones, with the latter being unable to control the former's severe "GDP Complex" (i.e., blind pursuit of GDP growth); a huge mismatch exists between plans and real work. All these facts have affected the effectiveness of macroeconomic management, resulting in many imbalances in social and economic development.

It suggests that planning has already been weakened in our economic work and marginalized ideologically. Therefore, it is incumbent on the textbooks on political economics to reemphasize that socialist market economy also has planning. Under the circumstances, the 17th National Congress restated, "We will give play to the guiding role of national development plans, programs and industrial policies in macroeconomic regulation."[1] We should not only carry through this guideline in practice, but also reemphasize the role of planning while publicizing the theory of socialist market economy and resume the general spirit of the 14th National Congress in terms of reform target. This is what the textbooks on political economics should do in the first place.

A sound macroeconomic regulation system is something that socialist market economy must have, which is surely very correct. However, when Hungarian economist Junos kornai suggested that China should establish a market economy subject to macroeconomic regulation in Bashan Cruise meeting in 1985, French economist Albert O. Hirschman echoed that France was also using the very model. Therefore, market economy subject to macroeconomic regulation is also practiced in capitalist states, not exclusive to socialist countries at all. But what sets socialist market economy subject to macroeconomic regulation from the capitalist market economy in which macroeconomic regulation is also used? Aside from its basic economic system, planning, or guidance from state planning, is another distinctive feature of socialist market economy.

In quite a few market economies, such as Japan, South Korea and France, organizations like "Economic Planning Agency" were ever set up to make predictive plans occasionally. In most market economies such as USA and UK, they only use fiscal and monetary policies instead of planning as a means to regulate economy. However, in contrast, it is very necessary and probable for China, as a great socialist power with public ownership as the mainstay of the economy, to use planning as a means of macroeconomic regulation to guide balanced, proportionate development of the national economy, which constitutes the superiority of socialist market economy.

There are several means of macroeconomic regulation, among which planning, fiscal policies and monetary policies are the most important. The 14th National

1 *Collection of Selected Major Documents Over the Three Decades Since the Reform and Opening up* II, Beijing: Central Party Literature Press, 2008, p.1726.

Congress report specifically pointed out, "State planning is an important means of macroeconomic planning,"[1] without highlighting the importance of fiscal and monetary policies. It is not because they are not important at all, but instead, they are under the guidance of state macroeconomic planning. Besides, the guidance of state planning for macroeconomic regulation was also emphasized in the 17th National Congress report. To sum up, macroeconomic regulation is inseparable from state planning, with the latter as the backbone of the former. Market economy subject to macroeconomic regulation can also be called a market economy subject to state macroeconomic regulation by planning, which is the very meaning of socialist planned market economy as well as the distinctive characteristic that sets itself apart from the capitalist market economy with macroeconomic regulation.

The guidance of state planning in macroeconomic regulation is not equivalent to the "traditional planned economy". In theory, we have explained clearly why socialist market economy should have planning; in practice, the 17th National Congress of the CPC has reemphasized the guidance of state planning for macroeconomic regulation. Does it mean "a retrogression to the traditional planned economy", just like what some people accused of? I don't think so. As a matter of fact, it is a combination between planning and market on a higher level.

The reasons are as follows. First, the current state planning is not inclusive, but instead it only attends to the macroeconomic activities, whereas the micro-economic activities are assigned to the market. Second, market is the current basic means of regulating resource allocation, whilst planning is the necessary means to remedy the defects of the market. Third, the current plans do not mainly refer to administrative orders any more, but include guiding, strategic and predictive plans instead. And at the same time, these plans must serve as a guide and commit entities to complete tasks and to take responsibilities when necessary. That is to say, these plans also need contain some mandatory tasks rather than be shelved

1 *Collection of Selected Major Documents Over the Three Decades Since the Reform and Opening up* I, *Beijing: Central Party Literature Press,* 2008, p.660.

after they are made.

The 12th "Five-Year Plan (2011-2015)" is the first medium-to-long term plan that we have ever formulated and implemented since the 17th National Congress, which has profound implications for the transformation of our economic development patterns and solutions to problems in social relations. We need to implement the policies of the 17th National Congress and the Fifth Plenary Session of the 17th Central Committee practically. During the "12th Five-Year Plan" period, we need to improve state planning and macroeconomic regulation as much as possible so as to bring their guiding roles into full play in the national economic development; we need to transform our economic development patterns and maintain a moderate economic growth; we need to promote the development of both the public sector and the private sector while consolidating the socialist basic economic system; we need to reverse the trend of polarization while attaching more importance to social equity.

In order to achieve all these, we mustn't rely exclusively on market economy, but also resort to state macroeconomic regulation by planning as well. A noteworthy thing here is that macroeconomic regulation by planning must be controlled by the Central Committee and local plans must be subject to central plans. I approve of some people' suggestion that local governments should stop making any inclusive national development plans driven by and centered on GDP growth; rather, they should make local plans for their own economic and social development in proportion to local financial resources and transfer payments granted by the central government, and reinforce local governments' roles in market supervision, social management and public service.

Besides, we should also preserve the government's function of regulating resource allocation, especially when it comes to major structural adjustment and major capital construction etc. Even capitalist countries have never forsworn the use of the so-called "socialist policies" such as nationalization, not to mention socialist countries! So, we shouldn't make market dictate the economy, but combine it with planning instead.

5. On the basic socialist economic system

Another fundamental difference between socialist market economy and the capitalist one is the basic economic system. The former is founded on the basic economic system in the primary stage of socialism, in which public ownership is the mainstay and other kinds of ownership develop side by side, whereas the latter is grounded on the basic economic system dominated by private ownership. The basic economic system is the prerequisite for socialist market economy.

The Fifth Plenary Session of the 17th Central Committee reiterated that we should "uphold and improve the socialist basic economic system". Therefore, we must avoid both privatization and a system that just has a unitary public sector , which is one of the "four important distinctions" proposed in the Fourth Plenary Session of the 17th Central Committee of the CPC. Currently, we need to find out which trend is more serious, "privatization" or "a system that just has a unitary public sector". The latter is the result of a certain mentality in the era when people used to believe that large public-owned people's communes and a unitary public sector are the best forms of socialism, but now very few people are thinking in that way except some radical "leftists". Nevertheless, a lot of evidence shows that the ill trend of privatization does exist and pose a serious threat. Marxist political economics cannot afford to ignore this. If these two ill trends were dealt with the same amount of punishment indiscriminately, it is nothing different from cutting slack the more serious trend of privatization.

It is right that Marxism did not judge the nature of ownership only by the proportion of ownership; but according to Marxism, complete disregard for the proportion of ownership is not recommended, either. If the proportion of public ownership in national economy keeps declining to almost zero, is it still socialism? Recently even Commissioner of the NBS (National Bureau of statistics of PRC) also kept saying that the proportion of the public sector (esp. the state sector) is declining whereas that of the private sector rising.

In the macro-level, there was no such a trend of "guo jin min tui" (the state advances whereas the private sector retreats) in China's economy just like what rightist elites claimed; In the micro-level, it is mostly "guo tui min jin" (the state retreats whilst the private sector advances). That is to say, in most cases, the public sector retreats whilst the private sector advances. However, "guo jin min tui" only occurs in rare cases for the sake of resource allocation, which also makes sense. So, on the whole, the share of the public sector is declining whereas that of the private sector rising, or "Guo tui min jin".

But what is the lowest bound? As far as I remembered, Jiang Zemin ever said that there should be a limit to the reduction in the proportion of the public sector, that is, public ownership must remain the mainstay of the economy. But quite a few people have begun to doubt it. One of the ways to convince them is to provide them with statistics, which is the duty of Marxist political economics so as to increase people's confidence in the basic economic system in the primary stage of socialism.

As the basic economic system dictates, public ownership should be the mainstay of the economy and the state sector play a leading role. Therefore, the state needs to control the lifeline of the national economy and the state sector's control, influence and competitiveness must be enhanced. In capitalist societies, the state sector mainly provides services that private enterprises won't do, only serving as a supplement to the private sector to make up for the deficiency of market mechanism. However, in socialist societies, the state sector, indispensable to sustained, sound and coordinated economic development, is established for the sake of consolidating and improving the socialist system. Therefore, the state sector should cover these major industries and key fields concerning the lifeline of the national economy, such as energy, transportation, communications, finance, infrastructure and pillar industries, and have "absolute control" or "fairly strong control" over them; enterprises should be wholly or partially owned by the state, with the state holding an absolutely or relatively controlling number of shares. All these are prescribed and emphasized by the documents of Central Committee. The state sector must maintain control on these fields or industries so that the national economy could be regulated by state planning and thus develop in a more sustained, sound and coordinated way.

Besides, the state sector is obligated to ensure social equity and justice as well. As for competitive fields and industries crucial to social equity and justice, we should also regard them as "major" fields or "key" industries and strive to do a good job, though they do not matter too much to economic regulation by the government. Therefore, in order to stabilize employment, create more jobs, ensure social welfare, provide public services, increase transfer payments and guarantee social equity through redistribution, we need not only maintain the state sector's control on the major fields concerning the lifeline of the national economy characterized by natural monopoly, but bring its role into play in the competitive fields.

Why can't SOEs enter the competitive fields? Why should all the profits be gained exclusively by private enterprises? The Central Committee has always been insisting that state-owned capital move in and out of the competitive fields based on rational choices so as to bring their competitiveness into full play, rather than withdraw completely from these competitive fields, just like what neo-liberalist elites and its followers "inside the system" *(ti zhi nei)* kept preaching! Of course, to encourage fair competition, these competitive fields should be open to all. All these things should be made crystal clear in the textbooks on political economics.

Advocates of privatization requires the state sector to withdraw not only completely from competitive fields, but also from major fields and key industries concerning the lifeline of the national economy. They often labelled the state sector as "monopoly enterprises or industries" due to its control on these industries or its sharp edge over its rivals. They often levelled random criticism at SOEs, condemning that they colluded with the government to exercise monopoly. Besides, they even reduced all state-owned capital to "bureaucratic monopoly capital".

Some people proposed that one way to reform monopoly industries is to create favorable conditions for private enterprises' entry into these profitable industries, which is exactly what advocates of privatization have been desiring for. However, what really matters is not whether these industries concerning the lifeline of the national economy and vital to the national security are monopolized or not, but instead who controls them. More capable of standing for strategic interests of the state and social public interests, public enterprises are in general in a better position than private ones to run these special sectors and industries.

Defects of administrative monopoly should be eradicated. Specific solutions are nothing different from those employed in the reform of common SOEs, such as separation of government administration from both enterprise management and state assets, corporatization, establishment of modern corporate structure, reform of income distribution system, improvement of legal and supervision systems, etc. In terms of income distribution, the current reform of SOEs is mainly focused on the recommitment of SOEs to turn in profits to the state treasury, the readjustment of senior executive's high pay (some of them have exorbitant pays), and the prevention of SOE interests from being departmentalized or privatized since the "marketization reform". Besides, we should further improve the Staff and Workers Representatives Congress (SWRC) system to make it truly represent the interests of the working people. If employees were allowed to supervise during SOE reorganization in a real sense, tragedies like Tonghua (Jilin province, China) Iron and Steel Group riot would have probably be avoided.

The private sector is also part of the basic economic system in the primary stage of socialism, and therefore we should expound on the positive role that the non-public sector including the private sector has played in promoting the development of the productive forces in China. However, the private sector also has duality: it not only benefits the development of productive forces, but involves exploitation. Notwithstanding this, the façade of exploitation is still tolerated in the primary stage of socialism, but the development of the private sector should be restricted. As its exploiting and profit-seeking nature has resulted in a series of bad consequences such as disputes between employers and employees, polarization, etc., Marxist political economics has to highlight and study it.

Due to the duality of both the private sector and owners of private enterprises, we should not only guide them to run the business legally and healthily, but also impose restrictions on their unhealthy and illegal operations as well as their range of business. For example, they should never be allowed to control key industries concerning the lifeline of the national economy or monopoly industries. As these industries have always been producing high profits and are vital to the interests of both our country and the public, they must be controlled by the public sector rather than serve as milk cows for the private sector. Even Sun Yat-Sen (1866-1925), the great forerunner of China's democratic revolution, also called on his men to restrict capital!

6. On Income distribution

Production determines distribution; ownership relations determine distribution relations; only if the means of production is owned by the society, distribution according to work would become the dominant principle. All these constitute the tenets of Marxist political economics. Marxism introduces a pair of concepts, namely, "labor income" and "non-labor income", corresponding to another pair of concepts, i.e., the "income distributed according to work" and the "income distributed according to factors of production", which is of great significance. However, the two ways of division are overlapping to some extent. "Factors of production" include capital, knowledge, technology, information, managerial expertise and land etc. However, Marxist political economics considers technology and management as "complex labor", and therefore the income accrued by them can also be viewed as "labor income" or "complex labor income". Besides, knowledge, information, and patents etc., as transferable capitalized property rights, also fall into the category of capital, and therefore the income accrued by these factors of production should also be considered as capital income. The same is true with rents. Therefore, it can be said that personal income includes labor income and non-labor income, because the income distributed according to factors of production is in essence capital income.

Such clarification has significant implications for our study of income inequality. As a result, we found out immediately that the core issue of primary distribution is the relations between labor and capital, i.e., V. M. In the primary distribution of national income, the income is highly related to factors of production, especially non-labor factors. As the gap in non-labor factors of production keeps expanding and capital income keeps increasing, primary distribution will surely lead to the widening of income gap and distribution inequality.

People made a long list of reasons for the widening of the gap between the rich and the poor, such as the expansion of urban-rural disparity, regional imbalances, industry monopoly, corruption, uneven supply of public goods, and inadequate redistribution etc., to name but a few. All these reasons make sense, but neither of them is the most fundamental one. The rooted cause of inequitable distribution has been ignored.

As a matter of fact, primary distribution is to be held accountable for inequitable distribution, and V/M, i.e., the relationship between labor income and capital income, is the core factor that determines the former. Therefore, it is also related to production relations and property relations. Property ownership tends to affect income gap the most. Even Paul Anthony Samuelson[1], an American bourgeois economist, had to acknowledge that wealth affects income gap the most, whereas individual capabilities do not make any big difference. He said that property ownership is the number one factor determining the income gap, with individual capabilities, education, training, opportunities and health coming next to it one by one.

It is a very scientific argument. But such point will be even clearer if we explain it with Marxist political economics. According to Marxism, production determines distribution; the mode of production that of distribution; and the relations of production distribution relations. Therefore, the capitalist mode of production determines distribution according to factors of production (mainly capital) as its

1 Samuelson, Paul A.: *Economics: An Introductory Analysis,* 1948.

major mode of distribution; whereas the socialist mode of production distribution according to work. Marxist political economics has always been insisting on this. Due to the tolerance of some capitalist elements in the primary stage of socialism, distribution according to capital or non-labor factors is also a mode of distribution, which however must be subordinate to distribution according to labor, with the latter being the dominant mode of distribution. It is decided by the socialist ownership structure in which public ownership is the mainstay.

The above are orthodox views of political economics, but empirical political economics concluded, "distribution according to production factors has already replaced distribution according to work as the dominant mode of distribution for the national economy."[1] I analyzed in another article, "We can infer from the general law of capitalist market economy and the real development of our market economy that capital income, with the relative expansion of private property rights, would relatively increase in proportion to labor income, resulting in a widening of income gap. This explains why absolute wealth goes hand in hand with relative poverty."[2] Aside from the above-mentioned important reasons, the widening of the income gap in China is also closely linked with the change of ownership structure, the decline in the proportion of public sector, the rise in that of private sector, privatization and excessive marketization, which is already an indisputable fact.

Since we have already found out the causes for the widening of income gap, it would not be hard to formulate policies and measures. Since the beginning of this year, the phrase of "adjusting income distribution" has been used in official documents unprecedentedly; government leaders have talked about plans for the reform of distribution system with great determination many times.

When it comes to adjusting income distribution relations and narrowing the

1 Wu Li, Wen Rui, "My Perspective on Changes in Distribution of Income Since 1992", *China Business Times*, May 26th, 2006.

2 Liu Guoguang, "Reflections on Several Issues Concerning the Relations between Distribution and Ownership", *HongQi Wengao (Red Flag Manuscript)*, 2007, No. 24.

gap between the rich and the poor, people tend to check the system of distribution first, especially means of redistribution such as taxation and transfer payment so as to enhance social security and public welfare, and improve the livelihood of low-income people. These measures are absolutely necessary and we've already begun to take them. However, all these measures are still far from enough, we still need further step up efforts to implement them, such as to adjust the personal income tax threshold and progressive tax and to levy property tax, inheritance tax, and luxury consumption tax. Our government should use these new tax revenues to increase spending on social security and public welfare and to improve the low-income people's life.

As a matter of fact, it is impossible to reverse the widening of the gap between the rich and the poor by just focusing on distribution and redistribution. Besides, we also need check our ownership structure and property relations. That is to say, we need consolidate the basic economic system in the primary stage of socialism, strengthen the mainstay status of public ownership, develop different economic sectors side by side, and weaken the trend of privatization. Only in this way can we possibly prevent the income gap from further widening, guard against any worsening of the polarization trend and finally achieve common prosperity.

Just as Deng Xiaoping ever noted, "so long as public ownership remains the mainstay of the economy, polarization will be avoided". "If basic means of production is owned by the state or the collective, i.e., public-owned, a new bourgeoisie would not emerge," he added. Such inference is so profound that textbooks on political economics cannot afford to abandon it. It pointed out that in the primary stage of socialism, private property rights and distribution according to non-labor factors (mainly capital) would be both tolerated only if public ownership is the mainstay of the economy and distribution according to work constitutes the major mode of distribution.

Policies allowing private capital to penetrate into profitable industries and fields (including major industries and key fields concerning the lifeline of the national economy; even Sun Yat-Sen, the pioneer of China's democratic revolution, also called on his men to restrain private capital from entering these fields), and strongly encouraging to increase "property income"(which will cause the rich to become even richer; whereas most workers and peasants will just gain some petty profits from their meager property) can only end up with a even wider gap in both income and wealth. In the circumstances, changes must be made. So long as public ownership is the mainstay of the economy and distribution according to work constitutes the dominant mode of distribution, the gap between the rich and the poor would never reach the limit, i.e., polarization. Just to the opposite, it would be well controlled within proper bounds and common prosperity would be eventfully achieved. Otherwise, polarization and social split will inevitably happen.

(This article was published in *China Review of Political Economy*, 2010, No.4.)

This book is the result of a co-publication agreement between China Social Sciences Press (China) and Paths International Ltd (UK)

This book is published with financial support from Innovation Project of Chinese Academy of Social Sciences (CASS)

Title: On the Theory of Socialist Market Economy
Author: Liu Guoguang
Translated by Sun Weiwei
ISBN: 978-1-84464-604-3
Ebook ISBN: 978-1-84464-605-0

Paths International Ltd
www.pathsinternational.com
Published in the United Kingdom

Printed in the USA
CPSIA information can be obtained
at www.ICGtesting.com
LVHW020832040823
753971LV00003B/7

9 781844 646043